# LESSONS OF STRUGGLE

# LESSONS *of* STRUGGLE

## *South African Internal Opposition, 1960–1990*

ANTHONY W. MARX

*New York Oxford*
OXFORD UNIVERSITY PRESS
1992

Oxford University Press

Oxford New York Toronto
Delhi Bombay Calcutta Madras Karachi
Petaling Jaya Singapore Hong Kong Tokyo
Nairobi Dar es Salaam Cape Town
Melbourne Auckland

and associated companies in
Berlin Ibadan



Published by Oxford University Press, Inc.,
200 Madison Avenue, New York, New York 10016



Library of Congress Cataloging-in-Publication Data
Marx, Anthony W.
Lessons of struggle : South African internal opposition,
1960–1990 / Anthony W. Marx.
p. cm. Includes bibliographical references and index.
ISBN 0-19-506815-7; ISBN 978-0-19-507348-5
1. Anti-apartheid movements—South Africa—History.
2. South Africa—History—Soweto Uprising, 1976.
3. Blacks—South Africa—Politics and government.
4. Trade-unions, Black—South Africa—Political activity. I. Title.
DT1757.M38 1991
968.06'27—dc20 90-26546

Portions of this book appeared in altered form in:
"Race, Nation, and Class Based Ideologies in Recent Opposition in South Africa," *Comparative Politics* 23 (April 1991), and "South African Black Trade Unions as an Emerging Working-Class Movement," *Journal of Modern African Studies* 27 (September 1989), and appear by permission of the City University of New York.



3 4 5 6 7 8 9

Printed in the United States of America
on acid-free paper

*To my parents*

# PREFACE

For me, as for many in my generation, entering college in the wake of the 1976 Soweto uprising, the South African struggle was an early focus for our political education. Our antiapartheid activism at the time was no doubt naive in some respects, but it expressed our moral outrage at a distant form of injustice that somehow resonated. Later, South Africa remained a living illustration of the issues that I had studied and pondered. Perhaps it gave me some connection with the experience of discrimination that so disrupted the lives of my grandparents and parents as Jews in Nazi Germany. Or perhaps I was drawn by vague comparisons with race relations in New York City, where I had grown up amidst neighborhoods demarcated by an informal urban apartheid. But for whatever reason, I wanted to know more.

In 1984 I had my first opportunity to see South Africa. I spent much of that year helping plan and establish what was to become Khanya College, a university preparation program for politically active black students. It was exciting work during a time of burgeoning activism under the banners of the newly formed United Democratic Front and the National Forum. I found myself in the midst of many ideological debates about how educators, black elites, and whites could contribute to the struggle for a new South Africa. I even inadvertently contributed to such debates by accepting an invitation to attend the National Forum meeting of that year, where Black Consciousness adherents objected to the presence of whites, no matter how sympathetic. But adherents of nonracialism disagreed. Abstract debates about how best to confront oppression suddenly took on a more concrete dimension.

After such experiences, I wanted to understand the differences of ideology and strategy within the opposition—in terms of both why they had developed and what differences they had made. In 1986, during the height of renewed repression, I was back in South Africa for a shorter trip to begin research for this study. In 1988 I returned there for much of the year to conduct more than two hundred interviews and to find as many other sources of primary information as I could. After a year of writing in the United States, I went back yet again for further interviews and material and to share my manuscript with South Africans who could give me criticism and further guidance. Throughout this process, I found invaluable the initial contacts I had made when helping set up Khanya College. Many doors were opened to me that might not otherwise have been, though it was never easy to conduct research in the midst of apartheid and a national state of emergency.

Anger was part of what kept me going. I was continually confronted by the harsh realities of life in South Africa. The house where I lived illegally with blacks in a white-designated area was raided by police. My housemates and I had to take separate buses into town. When going into Soweto or other townships, I learned to avoid police roadblocks or to talk my way through them. Meetings that I attended were occasionally disrupted by riot police. Activists I had come to know and respect were killed. When I stayed with friends in squatter camps, I caught glimpses of life without electricity or plumbing. Visas were denied to me several times. Of course, my hardships were nothing compared with those suffered constantly by most South Africans. I could always escape to the luxury of the white suburbs or, even further, to home. In white South Africa, I became acutely aware of how much privilege and wealth were taken for granted. The clearest symbol of this numbing effect of wealth was, for me, to be found in the office of the head of the University of the Witwatersrand, the largest white "liberal" university in the land. There is kept a solid gold statue of a springbok calf, donated by the mining houses to celebrate the university's seventy-fifth jubilee. Few there ever seemed greatly disturbed by the cravenness of this image, molded from gold dug by low-paid black miners. Even away from South Africa, I was haunted by these memories, as I am still.

But more important than the anger was the inspiration I drew from so many South Africans who emerged from repression more committed to their struggle and to having an outsider understand them. I never felt unwelcome in the squatter camps or in Soweto, where Albertina Sisulu once explained that as long as I did not come in with a gun, people would assume that I must be a friend. For me, the Sisulu family came to symbolize this openness. The first time in 1988 I met "Ma" Sisulu, the copresident of the UDF, her husband had been in jail for twenty-five years. One of her sons was in exile and another in prison. Yet when I arrived early one morning, she talked to me without a trace of bitterness. In 1989 Walter Sisulu welcomed me into his home on the first morning after his release and on numerous other visits, inviting me to join his reunions with activists from competing opposition groups who had been with him on Robben Island.

My visits with the Sisulus were among many moments in which I was struck by the openness of South Africans reaching out not only to a foreign student but also to one another, respectfully, across ideological differences. Every time I went to visit "Terror" Lekota and others from various opposition tendencies, on trial for treason during 1988 in the same courtroom where Nelson Mandela had been sent to Robben Island, they were always willing to pass notes surreptitiously from the dock answering my questions. Kgotso Chikane, an eighteen-year-old I helped to hide from the police while he tried to continue organizing his fellow students in Soweto during 1988, was similarly patient with me. Beyers Naude, an Afrikaner clergyman who had been ostracized by his relatives, renounced by his church, and banned by the state because of his opposition to apartheid, spoke of his experiences with grief rather than hate. On separate occasions, Smangaliso Mkhatshwa and Saths Cooper both took time to talk with me, and even to joke, immediately following their release from detention. Perhaps this patience and openness has slowed the process of change in South Africa, but it also helps explain why greater bloodshed has been avoided. This lack of rancor continues to inspire me.

One need not have had such personal experiences to be inspired by the South Africans. The principles that have emerged from the crucible of struggle against apartheid have set a world standard. In the midst of one of the cruelest forms of institutional racism ever devised, most South Africans have remained committed to the formation of a nonracial society, in which races are not merely accommodated but cease to be divisive. In the midst of tyranny, South Africans have struggled to be as democratic as possible in their own organizations. And in the midst of severe economic exploitation, they have looked forward to a more just distribution of wealth. Of course, these ideals remain far from fully developed or realized in South Africa, but they continue to inspire people there and around the world. The joyous reception given in the United States to Nelson Mandela in June 1990 attested not only to his charisma but also to the broad appeal of these principles that he symbolizes. In part, I hope that this study will help explain how such ideals have formed from the experiences and debates within the South African opposition.

I cannot claim that this book will satisfy all readers. This is a study of South Africa's internal opposition movements focusing on the years between the banning of the ANC and the PAC in 1960 and the lifting of that ban in 1990. The central issue is the internal dynamics that have shaped the opposition, particularly its shifting ideology and strategy. To account for these shifts, we must examine changes in economic conditions, state policy, international influences, and other factors, but our consideration of these is guided by the central focus. A more complete analysis of the state, movements dependent on the state, exile activities, women's issues, or ethnicity, for instance, can be found elsewhere, as can more detailed narrative accounts of specific incidents such as the Soweto uprising. In particular, I have described Chief Buthelezi's Inkatha movement more as a client of the state in conflict with the opposition than as a part of that opposition on which I have focused. This analysis has been reaffirmed by the revelations of July 1991 that Inkatha rallies and unions received direct state funding and that police colluded in Inkatha-initiated violence. Additionally, much of the material for this study is drawn from interviews and material collected largely in the Transvaal, the center of most national political and labor activity, and the site of the greatest concentration of people and industry in the country. Readers looking for a more detailed account of developments specific to the Natal or Cape regions or the rural areas are forewarned to look elsewhere.

There are, no doubt, further limitations implicit in the methodology of this book. I have been guided by a variety of different "ways of knowing" developed in the fields of political science, history, sociology, anthropology, and economics. In part, I depend on primary documents, statistical reports, and secondary literature. But I rely most heavily on the reports of people directly involved in the opposition, whose views are colored by their own interests, loyalties, and retrospective interpretations. I have tried to assess these views by comparing them with historical records and by asking various actors to comment on the views and recollections of others. The results remain subjective. Not all participants were available for interviews, and some interviews were conducted under less than optimal conditions. I often had no choice but to arrange meetings clandestinely with people hiding from the authorities or to conform to activists' busy schedules by postponing or breaking up interviews into shorter segments.

Mindful of these limitations, this book tries to meet three aims. First, I have set out to tell the story of recent South African opposition, relying as much as possible on the multiple voices of those involved. Second, I have attempted to distill from these stories overall patterns according to which the opposition has responded to different pressures in formulating their ideology and strategy, and the degree to which these formulations have shaped political action. It is my hope that such patterns will help us prepare for future events, for instance, as my analysis of the rising influence of the union movement anticipated the ANC's recent engagement in union-style negotiations with the state and the election in June 1991 of unionist Cyril Ramaphosa as secretary general of the ANC. Of course, more finely detailed or confident predictions remain impossible given historical variation.

Finally, I have attempted to connect the South African experience to the larger theoretical issues of how ideas and material structures interact in the process of social change. This analysis should suggest how the South African struggle compares with other instances of popular opposition, particularly in cases in which such opposition has shifted its target among various elements of overlapping racial discrimination, political domination, and economic exploitation. Of course, no single longitudinal study can suggest patterns or theories that can be directly applied elsewhere, and for now I must leave it to experts on other countries to determine how my findings might be applied elsewhere.

If one overall conclusion arises from this study, it is that history is born of the subjective interpretations of specific experiences. That is not to say that people are free to act as they wish, for material constraints do impinge. But people respond to such constraints and try to learn from them. This learning process is not linear or abstractly rational, but it is evident. I do not believe that history always progresses toward its most positive possible outcome, but people do try to learn from past experiences and failures how to become more effective at achieving their goals. If we believe this about ourselves, then we must believe it of others. Without this belief, the educational enterprise—and thus the point of writing this book—would itself become meaningless.

In South Africa, the development of the struggle for liberation has generated a diversity of views and approaches. We need not pick one ideological or strategic approach to opposition as preferable; all have contributed to an ongoing process. To understand the South African struggle, we must learn to see conflict even among the oppressed as part of a political dialogue. This is of particular importance now, as a newly conceived South African nation finally nears its birth, in a process inevitably full of pain, risk and hope. What Francis Wilson has described as a necessary recognition of the birth pangs of conflict should not diffuse our commitment to the overall goals of liberation; rather, it should inform that commitment and help avoid factionalism and disillusionment. This is the central lesson of the South African struggle, and it is the lesson of all struggles. It is the lesson of Matthew 10, quoted not only as an epigraph here and by various South African clergy over the years, but also by Lenin at the start of this century. And it is a lesson of perseverance, as evoked by an old Afrikaner expression, "You cannot squeeze a peach ripe."

*New York*
*August 1991*

A. W. M.

# ACKNOWLEDGMENTS

There are many whom I wish to thank for their teaching, support, advice, and friendship during the years of my studies and writing, including Brian Fay, Colin Campbell, and the late Louis Mink, at Wesleyan University; Robert Lane, Robert Dahl, Gary Bayer, and Jerry Stevens, at Yale College; and Richard and Gail Ullman, Atul Kohli, Kay Warren, Jane Menken, and Jeff Herbst, at Princeton University. I am particularly indebted to Sheldon and Lucy Hackney and to Susan Watkins, at the University of Pennsylvania, who have been unstinting in their offers of principled advice, warm encouragement, and repeated hospitality. As a graduate student at Princeton, I benefited greatly from the incisive guidance and unflagging support of my adviser, Henry Bienen, and from the wisdom and nurturing of Jennifer Hoschschild. Without them this study would not have been possible. I am also particularly mindful of my brief studies with Albert O. Hirschman, Theda Skocpol, and Perry Anderson, which were pivotal in my intellectual development.

Financial support was generously provided by Princeton's Center for International Studies, Department of Politics, Culture and Conflict seminar, Council for Regional Studies, and the President's Fund. The John D. and Catherine T. MacArthur Foundation provided the crucial funding for my research, with additional funding for related projects from the Ford and the Rockefeller foundations. I am also grateful for advice and opportunities to present my work, from the Program in African Studies, the Woodrow Wilson School of Public and International Affairs and Department of Politics at Princeton; the Committee for Research on Political and Social Organization at Harvard; the Southern African Research Program at Yale; the Center for the Studies of Social Change of the New School for Social Research; the Institute for International Studies of the University of California at Berkeley; the University of Southern California; Bryn Mawr College; Tufts University; Colgate University; and my new institutional home, the Department of Political Science at Columbia University.

My experience in South Africa was encouraged and richly informed by William Carmichael, who was generous enough to see the possibilities in my work before anyone else did. The South African Committee for Higher Education (SACHED) Trust often gave me a base from which to operate in South Africa, and I am particularly grateful to its director and the current education director of the ANC, John Samuel, for his insightful guidance, friendship, and trust. To Neville Alexander, who first suggested the topic of this study and who has continued to provide invaluable counsel, I am deeply indebted. Mark Orkin, of the Community Agency for Social Enquiry, and Jenny Glennie, of SACHED, offered crucial logistical support, essential guidance, and loving friendship—a debt I cannot hope to repay.

Of course, all of the informants mentioned (and those not mentioned) in this study have my continued gratitude. In addition, I wish to thank Myra and Clive Harrison, Francis and Lindy Wilson, Neil and Yvonne Myburgh, and the Kentridge family for their hospitality and encouragement. I drew considerable inspiration from Kgotso Chikane, the students at Khanya College, and all of the other young people I met in South Africa who have learned so well the lessons of struggle. It was with them in mind also that I was motivated to learn, and it is for them that I have written.

Writing this book would have been much more difficult, if not impossible, if not for the time, material, suggestions, and selfless assistance provided by Tom Karis and Gail Gerhart. In addition to those already mentioned, I wish to thank the many who have read, listened to, and provided material, contacts, and helpful comments on my work in progress, including Charles and Louise Tilly, Leonard Thompson, Robert Price, Robert Rotberg, William Foltz, Mark Kesselman, Mark Quarterman, Andrew Pugh, Eddie Zwane, Marge Brown, Eddie Webster, Smangaliso Mkhatshwa, Joe Seremane, Tom Lodge, Vusi Khanyile, Salim Vally, Buti Tlhagale, Ben Carton, Steve Mufson, Kalyn Culler, and Helene Perold. I am also grateful to Mildred Kalmus of Princeton's Department of Politics and to those who have helped see this project through to publication, particularly Valerie Aubry and Paul Schlotthauer at Oxford University Press, and David Todd for his valiant efforts to straighten out my prose.

I would also like to thank my family and other friends who have supported and fortified me through too many years of writing: my late grandmother and uncle, Debby and Chip, Eric and Nina, Andrew Pugh and Kristen Mertz, Paul Rice, Claire Shea, Josh Ginsberg, Irma Elo, Susan Brown, and all the folks who came and went at "Shambles" in Johannesburg, especially Rachel and Tony. Loving thanks also to Karen Barkey, who lived through the final birth pangs with me.

Finally, I owe greatest thanks to my mother and father, without whose love and encouragement this project would never have come to completion. All I can give them in return is my love, and this book.

# CONTENTS

# ABBREVIATIONS

ANC African National Congress
founded 1912, inclusive opposition, prohibited 1960–1990
*leaders*: Nelson Mandela, Walter Sisulu, Oliver Tambo

AWB Afrikaner Weerstandsbeweging (Afrikaner Resistance Movement)
founded 1973 by Eugene TerreBlanche

AZACTU Azanian Confederation of Trade Unions
BC-oriented unions, joined with CUSA to form NACTU

AZAPO Azanian People's Organization
founded 1977–1978, heir to BC after 1977 bannings
*leaders*: Saths Cooper, Lybon Mabasa,
Ishmael Mkhabela (Curtis Nkondo—first president)

BAWU Black Allied Workers' Union
founded in 1972 as a BC trade union
*leader*: Drake Koka

BC Black Consciousness
movement founded by Steve Biko
includes SASO, BCP, BPC, BAWU (banned in 1977), and AZAPO

BCP Black Community Programmes
founded 1973 as BC service organization
*leaders*: Ben Khoapa, Peter Jones

BPC Black Peoples Convention
founded 1971 as political affiliate of SASO in BC
*leader*: Ken Rachidi

CAL Cape Action League
founded 1983, in Trotskyist–Unity Movement tradition, helped found National Forum
*leader*: Neville Alexander

CCAWUSA Commercial, Catering and Allied Workers Union of South Africa (later SACCAWU)
founded by Emma Mashinini, divided during late 1980s
*leaders*: Anti-Charterists Vivian Mtwa, Kaiser Thibedi, Graham van Wyck, Jeremy Daphne,
*charterists*: Herbert Mkhize, Papi Kaganare

CNETU Council of Non-European Trade Unions
federation in the 1940s

Committee of Ten later the Soweto Civic Association
*leaders*: Dr. Motlana, treasurer—Nat Ramokgopa

COSAS Congress of South African Students
leading Charterist organization for secondary school students

COSATU Congress of South African Trade Unions
founded 1985 as largest union federation, Charterist-aligned.
*leaders*: Jay Naidoo, Elijah Barayi, Cyril Ramaphosa, Alec Erwin, Chris Dlamini, Khetsi Lehoko

CUSA Council of Unions of South Africa
founded 1970 with BC and Africanist tendencies, joined NACTU
*leaders*: Phiroshaw Camay, James Mndaweni, Pandelani Nefolovhodwe

FOSATU Federation of South African Trade Unions
founded 1979 as largest, nonracial nonaligned federation, joined COSATU
*leaders*: Joe Foster, Chris Dlamini, Alec Erwin

FRELIMO Front for the Liberation of Mozambique
first ruling party of independent Mozambique

GAWU General and Allied Workers' Union
founded 1980 out of BAWU, independent
*leader*: Samson Ndou

ICU Industrial and Commercial Workers' Union
founded 1919
*leader*: Clements Kadalie

INKATHA Inkatha yeNkululeko yeSizwe
founded 1975
*leader*: Chief Gatsha Buthelezi

MK Umkhonto we Sizwe
armed wing of ANC, translated as "spear of the nation"
*leaders*: Chris Hani, Joe Modise (formerly Joe Slovo)

NACTU National Council of Trade Unions
founded 1986 as second largest federation, Africanist
*leaders*: James Mndaweni (formerly Phiroshaw Camay, Pandelani Nefolovhodwe)

NECC National Education Crisis Committee
founded 1984 to negotiate end to school boycotts
*leaders*: Rev. Molefe Tsele, Eric Molobi, Vusi Khanyile

NF National Forum
founded 1983 as coalition of AZAPO and others, BC and socialist
*leaders*: Saths Cooper, Neville Alexander

NP National Party
ruling party of South Africa since 1948
*leaders*: H. F. Verwoerd, B. J. Vorster, P. W. Botha, F. W. de Klerk

NUM National Union of Mineworkers
founded 1982 in CUSA, largest COSATU affiliate until 1991
*leaders*: Cyril Ramaphosa, James Motlatsi, Marcel Golding, Kgelema Mothlahte

NUMSA National Union of Metalworkers of South Africa
second largest COSATU affiliate, in FOSATU tradition
*leader*: Moses Mayekiso

NUSAS National Union of South African Students
white liberal university student federation

NUWCC National Unemployed Workers Coordinating Committee
founded by COSATU

PAC Pan Africanist Congress
founded 1959 as breakaway from ANC, prohibited 1960–1990
*leaders*: Robert Sobukwe, Zeph Mothopeng

PEBCO Port Elizabeth Black Civic Organization

Poqo PAC armed internal wing in 1960s, translated as "we alone"

SAAWU South African Allied Workers Union
founded in early 1980s out of BAWU, independent

SABC South African Broadcasting Company
state television and radio

SACC South African Council of Churches
major association of Protestant churches other than the Dutch Reformed Church
*leaders*: Archbishop Desmond Tutu, Frank Chikane, Beyers Naude, Manas Buthelezi, J. Seremane, Saki Macozoma

SACP South African Communist Party
allied with ANC
*leader*: Joe Slovo (Chris Hani in 1991)

SACTU South African Congress of Trade Unions
ANC-affiliated labor organization in 1950s absorbed into COSATU in 1990

SASM South African Student Movement
Soweto high school organization during 1976 uprising
*leader*: T. Mashinini

SASO South African Student Organization
founded 1969 by Steven Biko, first BC organization
*leaders*: Biko, Diliza Mji

SASO 9 Nine SASO and BPC leaders tried in 1974 and imprisoned, including Saths Cooper, "Terror" Lekota

UDF United Democratic Front
founded 1983, Charterist
*leaders*: Albertina Sisulu, Archie Gumede, "Terror" Lekota, Popo Molefe, Allan Boesak, Smangaliso Mkhatshwa, Ismail Mohamed, Aubrey Mokoena, Cassim Saloojee, Azhar Cachalia, Vincent Mogane

WOSA Workers Organization for Socialist Action
founded 1990
*leader*: Neville Alexander

# LESSONS OF STRUGGLE

Behold, I send you out as sheep in the midst of wolves;
So, be wise as serpents and innocent as doves. . . .
So, have no fear of them;
for nothing is covered that will not be revealed,
or hidden that will not be known.
What I tell you in the dark, utter in the light;
and what you hear whispered, proclaim upon the housetops.
Do not fear those who kill the body but cannot kill the soul;
rather fear him who can destroy both soul and body in hell. . . .
Do not think that I have come to bring peace on earth;
I have not come to bring peace, but a sword.

Matthew 10:16–34

# 1

# *Introduction: The Vicissitudes of Struggle*

The full unfolding of South Africa's modern tragedy and promise began with the discovery by George Harrison on a winter day in June 1886. Having wandered around much of the Transvaal looking for a place to stake a claim, Harrison literally stumbled on what every prospector has always dreamed of. There, on the surface, was gold. Harrison had found a unique geological formation, a vein of gold-encrusted rock and other minerals more than a foot wide, running along the crest of a reef and penetrating the ground at a 22-degree angle. For more than one hundred years since, miners have plumbed this vein deeper and deeper into the earth, not yet exhausting its riches and producing over half a trillion dollars in gold, silver, and uranium.[1] Unfortunately for him, Harrison did not realize the scope of his find and within a few years had sold off his claim.

The site of Harrison's discovery is now marked by a small fenced enclosure next to Main Reef Road, which connects Johannesburg to Soweto. Every working day, the road is clogged with traffic bringing black workers to and from the most modern city on the continent, known in the vernacular as "eGoli," or the place of gold. The regular black commuters drive past the site, too rushed ever to pull over for a visit. Those whites who live and work in the city or its plush suburbs to the North rarely venture out in the direction of Soweto. The occasional worker from a nearby warehouse enters the enclosure to seek a spot for a lunchtime nap rather than to see where gold was discovered. For most South Africans, there seems little to celebrate in this place where Johannesburg and much of the country's modern economy were born.

Had South Africa not been blessed with one of the world's greatest deposits of natural resources, it still would have had a history distinct from that of the rest of the continent. Cape Town, at the tip of the continent, was an obvious spot for the Dutch to establish an outstation to serve their trade route between India and Europe. These burghers initially grew fresh produce to help passing sailors avoid scurvy. They later traded with and gradually dispossessed the local pastoralists, the Khoikhoi, and eventually more fully exterminated the local San hunters. From this first settlement in the seventeenth century, the white population grew and moved inland, attracted by fertile land and freedom from colonial authority. These white settlers engaged in various further wars of dispossession, defeating scattered resistance from the African population during the eighteenth and ninteenth centuries.[2] During this period, the settlers learned to make alliances with some tribes, paving the way for further white advances by encouraging divisions within the indigenous population.

The discovery in the Transvaal of diamonds in 1867 and of gold nineteen years later fueled an explosion of economic development and immigration that further distinguished the development of South Africa from that of the rest of the continent: The rush for gold left South Africa with by far the largest and richest settler population in Africa. This natural wealth also heightened the interest of the British Empire, whose forces had taken control of the Cape Colony in 1806 and conquered Zululand in 1879 after the initial defeat of an entire regiment at Isandhlawana. With the forced submission of the indigenous population, British efforts to win control over all of South Africa culminated in a surprisingly costly defeat of the Dutch descendants in the Boer Wars. After the turn of the century, an uneasy peace was finally developed, leaving the British with significant economic power, the Afrikaner-based National party in formal control of the state after 1948, and the indigenous Africans as the victims of "apartheid" discrimination. Throughout this century, white South Africans have continued to sell much of the world's diamonds and gold, sharing a small portion of the profits with their workers and the rest of the black populace. The result has been one of the fastest transitions to industrial development and First-World consumption, at least for whites, and one of the highest-recorded indices of economic disparity, indicating the outcome for blacks.[3]

The white South Africans have oppressed the native black Africans over the last three centuries through a historical combination of racial discrimination, national domination, and economic exploitation. The distinction, relationship, and priority among these social, political, and economic aspects of oppression have been the subject of considerable debate.[4] Marxist analysts, for example, argue that racially discriminatory apartheid laws serve the interests of continued economic exploitation.[5] Liberal analysts and business leaders dispute this, contending that since World War II apartheid has become an impediment to the continued development of skilled labor, domestic consumption, and foreign investment, all of which serve the interests of both capitalists and workers.[6] This incessant debate rests on mutually exclusive assumptions about the nature of South African oppression, that is, whether it is primarily economic or racial. Although such aspects of oppression can be distinguished analytically, historically they have overlapped. Only by rejecting an exclusive focus on racial, national, or economic aspects of oppression can we see how business's recent antiapartheid stance fits the interests of both the state and the economy in resisting any more radical change that would undermine their continued power. A full understanding of oppression rests on an inclusive analysis of South Africa as "a capitalist social formation, but one without the features of a bourgeois-democratic state precisely because forms of labor coercion, buttressed by race and national oppression, are essential to the process of accumulation and the politics of race rule."[7]

Much as analysts of oppression often focus on one of its overlapping aspects at a time, so opposition analysts and activists shift their examination from race to nation to class and the interaction among them. For example, the Black Consciousness movement, which was established in the 1970s, concentrated largely on ending black acceptance of their own racial inferiority and excluded whites from the struggle for liberation. The African National Congress–aligned United Democratic Front of the 1980s envisioned a more inclusive South African nationhood, attempting to unify supporters of all classes and of all races, including whites. More radical socialists and unionists have promoted an opposition movement led by the black working class to challenge apartheid and the economic order of capitalism with which it has been associated. Because oppression in South Africa applies to racial discrimination, national domination, and class exploitation alike, each of these has been a viable target. Different interpretations of the fundamental nature of domination are reflected in the definitions, constituency, and strategies of its opponents, with each movement formed to defeat a particular aspect of multifaceted oppression.

Even though racial discrimination, national domination, and economic exploitation often reinforce one another, they have been interpreted as separate "ideal types" used to describe South African social relations. According to the same logic, opposition movements have challenged each aspect of oppression along such analytically distinct, though empirically connected, racial, national, or economic class lines. Opposition groups often concentrate on one of these aspects of social relations at a time while describing the other aspects as secondary. For instance, South Africans who challenge racial discrimination argue that their success will be the first step toward ending national domination or class exploitation, which they view as outgrowths of discrimination. Movements targeting national domination assume that their success will also bring an end to discrimination and exploitation, and movements concerned with class assume that economic justice will undermine discrimination and domination. Each of these approaches has been tried in South Africa.

The terms of and discourse through which each opposition movement might interpret its oppression and define its options in specific contexts are not issues of merely abstract concern. Rather, the focus of a particular movement determines its potential constituency, distinguishing "us" from "them." For example, Black Consciousness and related opposition groups concentrating on race attempt to unify those who suffer from discrimination, including the African majority, mixed-race coloreds, and Indians. These officially distinct groups all were referred to by the Black Consciousness movement as blacks. This usage has been widely adopted since the 1970s, as it is in this study. Appeals for national unity fulfill the "nonracial" criteria of the African National Congress (ANC) and its allies, including sympathetic whites and excluding only those who support continued minority domination. Movements based on class identity appeal to an economically defined constituency, including most of South Africa's poor or, more exclusively, its black industrial workers.

However these categories of potential constituents are defined, the central concept of a movement also reflects its goals and strategies. Opposition based on race is aimed primarily at ending discrimination, a goal that the Black Consciousness movement had sought to achieve by countering blacks' psychological dependence and acceptance of projected images of their own natural inferiority. A concentration on nation implies a more active resistance to domination, for which the ANC-aligned United Democratic Front had mobilized protests across class and racial lines. Class-based movements have targeted exploitation, challenged by the labor unions through strikes and related activities. An ideological focus on race, nation, or class identity thus not only defines antagonistic relations but also implies the opposition's goals and elective affinity for certain strategies. These practical consequences of opposition ideology have not escaped the attention of the South African state, for it has often tried to direct the opposition's ideology and strategy into areas where it feels less vulnerable, much as states and other institutions elsewhere try to do.[8]

The countrywide opposition in South Africa has also rejected certain forms of identity that might otherwise have gained wider currency. The most obvious of these is ethnicity, an idea that remains influential in South Africa, not least because of the state's efforts to offset the homogenizing influence of urbanization by reinforcing tribalism in order to divide its potential opponents. Black groups have formed according to ethnicity, the most prominent of which is Chief M. G. Buthelezi's Zulu-based Inkatha movement, which has engaged in a vicious campaign to become a major contender in the political process of change. But at the same time such groups effectively define themselves as subnational by appealing only to a minority of the population. According to John Brewer: "Inkatha remains a peripheral organization to the extent it is isolated from the radical black organizations, and has little support among the militant and politicized urban black population."[9] These limitations, together with the organization's reliance on support from the state-supported Kwa–Zulu homeland government and police, from international business, and allegedly from white conservative vigilantes, distinguish this movement from those seeking a national opposition constituency. Inkatha is instead best understood as a financially dependent ally more than an opponent of the state. The major opposition movements also do not tend to define themselves according to religion or gender, although they have given some attention to gender discrimination as a significant problem among both blacks and whites. Though ethnicity, gender, and religion remain fundamental aspects of South African society, these issues have not become central defining concerns of those countrywide opposition movements that I have set out to analyze.

This book seeks to clarify the implications of ideology for recent South African opposition constituencies, goals, and strategies and also to place into historical context what might otherwise appear as rather sterile analytical distinctions. Recent South African opposition demonstrates the effects of divergent ideologies and also variations of strategy associated with a concentration on race, nation, or class identity. However, such distinctions are also often compromised in practice. For example, the United Democratic Front's central concept of a unified South African nation did not preclude its organizing protest groups according to race or strikes by sympathetic workers. The diversity and competition among different opposition groups also have led to cross-fertilization, reflecting individuals' multiple loyalties and shifts from one group to another. Indeed, these opposition groups have been populated by many of the same individuals at different times.

## Ideological Conceptions of Recent Opposition

While examining how the opponents of the minority South African regime have interpreted various concepts of identity, we must remember that such concepts are subjective mental constructs. Race, nation, and class are situational categories, used by activists and commentators to interpret how social relations are ordered and can be changed. These categories encapsulate ideology as it is lived through. They are more than ideas; they are a way of experiencing historical situations in which one or another or a series of identities suit people's interests and are purposefully adopted by elites.[10] The subjectivity of such constructs and categories does not imply that they do not matter, as they do influence the social relations to which they are applied. Rather, the fact that different consequences flow from the use of different ideological concepts of identity helps explain why these concepts are so vigorously contested.

The inherently subjective nature of social categories has undermined the state's attempts at imposing ascriptive divisions. South African opposition movements have redefined state-enforced categories of static racial, national, and class identity. The popular modifications of such official categories and the rejection of the policies and laws they justified demonstrate that such concepts are not fixed and can be contested. Categories of social relations operate only to the extent that people act in accordance with them. Max Weber made this point by arguing that all identities require some transparency, communication, and a minimal size to be consequential. Karl Marx contended similarly that a class defined objectively in itself by the identity of its members' "interests" or "economic conditions of existence" exists and acts for itself to the degree that common interests are perceived and organized.[11] Opponents of the regime have learned, perhaps in part from the regime itself, how such subjective categories can be manipulated, the importance of challenging the ideology of authority, and the power of asserting alternative conceptions of social relations.

The applicability of different categories of social relations can be contested, not only because of their subjective meaning, but also because of the complex nature of social relations. Even as they are most broadly defined, racial discrimination, national domination, and class exploitation often overlap, as they clearly do in South Africa. To the extent that actors assign priority to only one aspect of oppression, the superimposition of other categories generates debate. But the superimposition of various forms of oppression can also unite. In an extreme example, if racially, nationally, and economically defined groups include exactly the same individuals, they will be more likely to unite around a coherent sense of their common social position.[12] Such a complete superimposition of different social categories rarely if ever exists, however.

Although South Africa is a relatively extreme example of the superimposition of discrimination, domination, and exploitation, these components of oppression do not completely overlap in their impact, nor do activists consider their distinction insignificant. Differences of status within the community of oppressed South Africans have increased over at least the last two generations. Economic development, shaped in part through state intervention, has enriched some and impoverished others. Reforms have awarded various political rights to urban and rural dwellers, homeland citizens, officially designated Indians, and coloreds. This diversity of status has intensified the debate within the opposition of whether race, nation, or class is the most pertinent aspect of oppression. And the state has encouraged such debate, in the hope of further dividing its potential opponents.

The opposition groups' interpretations of and responses to continually changing state policy, economic conditions, and international influences determine their ideologies and strategies. Because these movements are distinguished by their strategies, implied or justified by their ideology, groups competing for members and seeking to consolidate their efforts often emphasize the exclusive salience of their particular view. Indeed, opposition ideologues have often understated the connection among various facets of oppression, even though experience has often refuted such dogmatism. For example, I shall discuss the efforts of some opposition groups to present race as the principal determinant of class or to place national unity above class differences, and I shall consider how these efforts have been confronted by differing expressions of class interests.

My analysis will concentrate on the three distinct but connected opposition movements that since 1969 have sought a countrywide following and have built on the efforts of the African National Congress, Pan Africanist Congress, and other earlier opposition groups. Hence the Black Consciousness movement reached the peak of its popular following and influence in the 1970s; the United Democratic Front then emerged in the mid-1980s; and the black trade unions have grown throughout these years. Each is based—in real and not just analytic terms—on an ideology focusing on race, nation, and class, respectively. The implications of such focuses are suggested by how each of these groups defines itself, its goals, and its strategies as consistent with its central ideology.

The Black Consciousness (BC) movement, a uniquely South African form of opposition conceived around race and popularly associated with the leadership of Steve Biko, was established in the late 1960s. Black Consciousness had its roots in the intellectual and relatively privileged black universities and among the clergy, and concentrated on changing individual self-image rather than organizing blacks for action. Whites were excluded from the movement in order to encourage black self-reliance. Although BC eventually did have tremendous emotional appeal beyond its intellectual roots, its ideology retained an emphasis on changing self-image and ideas about power rather than on directly attacking the physical manifestations of power. Even after other groups began to confront the state in physical terms, the BC adherents continued to maintain that "ideas and men are stronger than weapons."[13]

The Black Consciousness concept of race was in large part based on the South African state's racist policies of distinguishing groups according to physical characteristics, policies that were used to justify minority domination and institutional discrimination. The architects of apartheid understood that the power of racism stems from the false belief that socially created and enforced inferiority is innate. If those branded as inferior can be made to believe this, then escape will seem impossible and resistance to domination futile.[14] Racist apartheid policies are designed to instill in their victims an acceptance of themselves, in Orlando Patterson's terms, as being "natally alienated," or deprived at birth from all the rights of being human.[15] No social construct could be more spiritually deadening.

To challenge the South African state's racial structure, Black Consciousness embraced a conception of race that directly contradicted official policy. Both to gain a wider following and to assert its new definition of race, BC defined coloreds and Indians, together with Africans, all as blacks who suffer from various forms of discrimination, thereby defying the state's divisive use of physical differences among these groups. The BC movement used this new inclusive concept of black unity to demonstrate that volitional or behavioral characteristics and political aspirations do not correspond to physical distinctions, which anyway differ too much to be neatly sorted into objective categories. Blood ties were not so much ignored as they were denied primacy in social relations. Rejecting the scientific fact of race, the movement nonetheless recognized that racism exists in South African society.[16] Consistent with more general situational theories of race, Black Consciousness held that race relations were determined by social history, while acknowledging that relations among nations or classes were distinguished from race relations in which differences in skin color are used as a justification for discrimination.[17]

The BC movement understood, according to Neville Alexander, that race "as only a social practice, can be transformed" and set out to disabuse blacks of their psychological acceptance of inferiority. By pointing out the "bitter truth" of blacks' submissiveness, in part by ending their reliance on sympathetic whites, BC endeavored to act as a sort of Socratic sting, provoking blacks to regain their capacity to think and act for themselves. Believing that "the most potent weapon in the hands of the oppressor is the mind of the oppressed," the movement was seen as a way of freeing the minds of blacks, no longer available for their own oppression.[18] As such, in the words of Bishop Manas Buthelezi of Soweto, "Black Consciousness was a spiritual movement, not an organization, aimed at spreading a certain self understanding."[19] However, the movement's aim to change blacks' ideas about themselves, as preparatory to altering material relations, required a basic level of organization. For instance, the South African Students Organization, the first Black Consciousness group, was founded by Steve Biko as a means of encouraging "the liberation of the black man first from psychological oppression by himself through induced inferiority complex, and second from physical oppression."[20]

The Black Consciousness's goal of ending black South Africans' acceptance of their own inferiority could be achieved if blacks ceased to believe that race was the cause of their oppression. Discrimination would remain but would be revealed as based on political and economic relations, which BC did not directly address. This emphasis on changing consciousness was the movement's immediate aim, with physical challenges to domination effectively postponed to a subsequent phase of opposition.

Underlying the Black Consciousness goal was the assumption that social order is ideologically malleable rather than institutionally brittle. The BC ideology presumed that the ideas that blacks held about themselves could be changed before addressing the material oppression that shapes those ideas. Adherents of the movement occasionally even slipped into the millenarian belief that a change of self-concept alone could alter material relations; "a sense of pride and awareness . . . is all that we need in South Africa for a meaningful change to the status quo."[21] Such idealism is reminiscent of that of the nineteenth-century English followers of Robert Owen, who believed that "in the messianistic dawn of their movement the mere consciousness of their mission was supposed to make [their] aspirations . . . irresistible."[22] Although most adherents of Black Consciousness did not endorse such extreme idealism, they did believe that changing blacks' ideas would suffice at least to revive, if not maintain, their opposition.

Black Consciousness's aim of reshaping blacks' self-image is not unusual; a whole range of modern social movements have been described as similarly "identity oriented."[23] Such movements typically view changing one's self-perception as a means of empowerment, believing that such a change can be effective without a more concrete concern for resources, organization, and the social environment. The assumption underlying this approach is that society is "fluid," made up of a consensus of values, reinforced through culture and civil institutions that can be altered through a significant change in these values.[24] Antonio Gramsci described the strategy that this belief implies as analogous to a military "war of position": New values claim the trenches of civil society, which protect the established order, as distinguished from a frontal assault on the state by force.[25]

All of this discussion of BC's definition would remain of only theoretical interest to the actors and to us if it were not for the real, albeit limited, implications of the movements' ideology for its strategy and political action. The direction and strengths of the movement consistently reflected BC's basic intentions, despite adjustments and efforts that were made with time to overcome implicit limitations. A primary focus on race justified the BC movement's relative disregard for class and coercive domination, indicated by its purposeful avoidance of strikes and physical confrontation. The movement's strategic reliance on changing consciousness showed in its preference for spreading ideas through discussion, publicity, and example, rather than for organized protest or mass organization. BC leaders considered their ideas powerful enough to attract followers, without any offer of material incentives. And when mass protest did erupt, as in Soweto in 1976, the movement embraced it as an expression of a new set of aggressive values, with little concern for organization.

The United Democratic Front (UDF) was the umbrella organization for what became in the 1980s the most popular internal opposition movement in South Africa. The Front grew out of local civic and professional groups with specific grievances, seeking to use organizational cohesion and resources to press for concrete gains. Collective action replaced the amelioration of self-image as the main goal of opposition; that is, the movement was defined by strategy more than ideology. To attract all possible allies the UDF remained as vague in its specific policies as the African National Congress (ANC) had in the 1950s. Unlike BC, the Front's affiliates included white members, as had the ANC since 1969. Indeed, the Front eventually adopted the ANC's own purposely rhetorical Freedom Charter (see Appendix A) as a summary of its own local and national demands. In keeping with this "Charterist" tradition, the UDF eschewed absolute ideological coherence in favor of the most inclusive possible unity, to be forged into a nonracial South African nation, dedicated to isolating and confronting minority domination.

As with the BC movement's concept of race, the UDF defined its concept of a nonracial nation partly in response to South Africa's traditional national divisions. Conceived by its adherents in response to British colonialism, and the particularly harsh treatment by the British of Afrikaner prisoners during the Boer Wars, Afrikaner nationalism projected an insular ethnic community tied by blood, church, and land. Afrikaners justified their domination of the black majority with the claim that such domination was needed to protect their very existence, cultural heritage, and language.[26] They imputed African national ties according to tribal heritage, language, and, more recently, state-created homelands, and they labeled the Indians and coloreds as distinct "national groups." All such ties were regarded as static, in accordance with an ascriptive definition of a nation as "an historically evolved, stable community arising on the basis of a common language, territory, economic life and psychological make-up," this conception having been enunciated by, among others, Joseph Stalin.[27]

In order to unify all South Africans opposed to apartheid, the UDF embraced a definition of nation that directly contradicted the divisive assumptions of Afrikaner nationalism and tribalism. Reaching out beyond BC's inclusion of Africans, coloreds, and Indians as blacks, the Front envisioned a "national liberation struggle" which included all of the nation's peoples, white and black, opposed to continued minority domination. The only criterion for inclusion in its alternative concept of nation was opposition to apartheid and "voluntary adherence" to the broad principles of nonracial democracy.[28] Identification with the nation was separate from all imposed ties, much as Black Consciousness had redefined race in situational terms. The UDF leadership, however, pushed this tendency toward more inclusive opposition to its most extreme possibility. The Front preferred to err on the side of inclusion and tried to avoid alienating potential white supporters by referring to its enemy as an impersonal "system" of oppression rather than as the more "visible enemies."[29] The Front also rejected ties based on ethnic nationalism, reinforced by the state, as well as Africanist conceptions of "orthodox" nationalism that included only indigenous peoples with a historical claim to the land.[30] Consistent with more general situational theories of nationalism, such as that formulated by Benedict Anderson, the UDF conceived of the South African nation as a self-defined "imagined community," united by the experience of "simultaneous existence," shared ideas, and a sense of historical destiny.[31] In a sense, this concept of a nation was a catchall form of identity, claiming to represent common interests, rather than the interests of more exclusive identities.

Both the BC's concept of race and the UDF's concept of nation were defined by situation, and both were malleable mental constructs that refuted the state's definitions. The important differences in how these movements conceived of themselves according to race and nation reflected in part their differing responses to ascriptive definitions. The minority regime regarded race as existing in biological differences of skin color that predated society and its exclusive national identity as embedded in culture and social history. This regime had achieved national domination through physical coercion, reinforced by inculcating submission to discrimination. In response, Black Consciousness used racial assertiveness to dispute the psychological image of physical inferiority, whereas the UDF and the ANC used nationhood as a strategic metaphor for a more inclusive community, created by the experience of physical domination and active resistance to it. Much as French revolutionaries rejected traditional associations of their nation with the rights and offices of the monarchy, the UDF envisioned a South African nation distinct from the minority regime's imposed sovereignty and based instead on the people.

The UDF opposed the physical aspects of national domination and, accordingly, was concerned less with changing individual consciousness or identity than with mobilizing material resources and followers across perceived racial divisions. Its central tenet was nonracialism, compromised by the practical necessity of activating distinct groups in the legally segregated residential areas in order to bring them under the Front's unifying umbrella.[32] This compromise was consistent with the United Democratic Front's priority of broad mobilization over conceptual purity. To achieve the widest adherence and to avoid antagonizing any potential sources of funds needed to organize mass action, it was in the UDF's interest to remain vague enough to appeal to a variety of groups. Black Consciousness had contested ideologically those racial divisions justified by the authorities as innate. In contrast, the UDF and the ANC had contested physically those national divisions officially justified as historical and cultural.

The UDF's strategy of mobilization intentionally built on BC's effort to transform individual self-image so as to achieve psychic liberation. Assuming that the earlier goal of ending black submissiveness had been largely achieved, at least among a core urban constituency, the Charterist UDF felt confident of a receptive populace, ready to join active protests that would gain material benefits and thereby would attract even broader participation. Without the preconditions that BC had already achieved, a movement of national mobilization would not have been possible. And without continued material results from protest, the Front's national coalition could falter.

The UDF's aim of attracting and channeling resources to organize people is not unusual: such "resource mobilization" is a recognized paradigm of social movements.[33] Movements of this type typically seek material advancement through a redirection of material resources rather than through the psychological empowerment sought by "identity-oriented" movements, such as BC. Such an approach assumes that the social order is brittle, based on static material interests that are defended more by institutional coercion than by consensus. It expects a "linear" cumulative progression rather than a more fluid change through the transformation of values.[34] It assumes that Gramsci's more active, frontal "war of manoeuvre" must be waged to make concrete gains.[35] The UDF sought material resources for such change, in part, through broad alliances. The Front, however, viewed a continued BC emphasis on change through altered self-image and values not only as counterproductive—as it might offend potential allies—but also as ill conceived; the Front's leadership tended to believe that values flow from material relations more than they determine them.

How the UDF defined itself was critical to its strategy and action, as discussed more fully in Chapters 4 and 5. Its focus on a unified South African nation justified its loose organizational inclusiveness, its avoidance of potentially divisive economic policies, and its encouragement of confrontation through carefully orchestrated protest. The Front used the material concessions gained in such protests, and the direct services funded by donations, as incentives for mass participation and adherence. The highly organized protests launched under the Front's banner, including massive rent, labor and consumer boycotts, reflect the UDF's concentration on national mobilization, as contrasted with the more fitful outbursts associated with Black Consciousness. The Front did not always strictly observe its ideology, however, nor did ideology always determine the UDF's strategies and outcomes. But the UDF's focus on building a unified nation helped drive its considerable accomplishments and set its self-imposed limitations.

Throughout the period during which BC and the UDF were seen as the most popular internal opposition movements in South Africa, industry steadily grew, and the increasing number of urban black workers formed their own unions. With the effective banning of the UDF and many of its major affiliates in February 1988, these groups' public activities were curbed, though some church-based supporters did remain active. Union activities were less severely restricted. As a result, the already well established union movement emerged publicly as the leading form of popular organization and expression. Adherents of Black Consciousness, the UDF, and other political groups whose membership overlapped with the unions have nurtured and gained some control over parts of the union movement, and others have fought to keep the labor movement distinct if not fully independent. As the unions have been pushed toward greater political engagement, they have been guided by an increasingly prominent focus on class-based ideology, mixed with ideologies emphasizing racial assertion and national mobilization.

Industrial development and the growth of manufacturing in post–World War II South Africa created a large, skilled black work force on which the state and capital became more and more dependent. In 1979 the state legalized the formation of unions by these workers in the hope of expediting labor negotiations and with the expectation that improved economic status would mollify the workers and turn them into an apolitical labor aristocracy. The state also assumed that the threat of replacement by the unemployed and the underemployed would further instill submission and foster antagonism among the various black economic groups. Most important, the destitute lower strata would remain too preoccupied with their mere survival to engage in significant political activity.

Although the trade unions and other opposition groups based on class identity have defined their constituency according to economic status, subjective factors have also been important. By law and function, trade unions organize workers according to economic position, workplace, and industry. But the unions have also heeded the political and racial constraints on their members' opportunities, the consciousness of which further demarcates the black working class in South Africa and distinguishes their experience from that of unionists in more homogeneous and democratic countries. The unions understand Karl Marx's dictum that a class existing objectively "in itself" can become a coherent and effective social force only to the extent that it perceives itself and acts self-consciously "for itself." In South Africa, the circumstances that created an industrial proletariat have also naturally heightened such class consciousness.[36] Deprivation and class conflict have further revealed what Max Weber described as "the connections between the causes and the consequences of the class situation."[37]

These objective and subjective pressures and influences on South Africa's unions have contributed to their defining themselves as a class movement, which is one reason that these unions have identified their core constituency as different from those of movements based on race or nation. Economic position has set a minimum for inclusion that is consistent with basic union structure, as contrasted with, for example, the UDF's openness to all voluntary adherents. At the same time, a worker who does not share the unions' conscious aspirations will not choose or be encouraged to join, nor would such a worker be considered an ally, regardless of economic position. Accordingly, the unions exclude those black middle-class managers and professionals welcomed by Black Consciousness and the UDF, regardless of their racial or national awareness or of whether they have been coerced to work. Although many unions have remained formally open to white membership, for most white workers, loyalty to continued minority privilege has obscured the shared objective economic interests that might otherwise have led them to join predominantly black unions. Indeed, the inclusion of white intellectuals and officials in the unions has been the subject of some controversy, fanned by political sensibilities brought to the unions by their members' participation in Black Consciousness, or other groups. In part to minimize such controversies and to avoid the difficulties associated with the UDF's disparate coalition, therefore, most unionists have emphasized their cohesion and ability to represent the black working class as a whole, based explicitly on shared economic interests.

The unions' focus on class has been reflected in their goals and strategies. Economic position and interest in improved wages and working conditions have provided the basis for union organizing; gains from collective bargaining boosted union membership that had grown above one million by 1987. Work stoppages, typical of class movements, have been the primary collective action by which unions have pressed their economic agenda.[38]

Just as the unions have not defined themselves only in objective economic terms, they have also incorporated subjective class consciousness in their goals and strategies. They have related short-term economic concerns to broader issues of exploitation, democratic rights, economic transformation, and cooperation with those outside their formal ranks, including the unemployed. Educational programs and internal debates have explored and deepened the rank and file's understanding of these ties. The cost of this development has been occasional disagreements over how closely the unions can ally with movements based on race or nation without compromising the unionists' interest in material advancement and economic redistribution. Governance structures that are formally more democratic than those of Black Consciousness or the United Democratic Front have further raised the workers' consciousness. The unions have sought to develop the consciousness of their members in order both to strengthen their collective identity—the relatively exclusive focus of BC—and to reinforce their organizational cohesion, which the more diverse UDF coalition had tried to achieve. The unions concentrated less exclusively on reshaping identity than had the BC movement because they could build on the popular assertiveness that had already been achieved. They also shared the neo-Marxist assumption that the working-class experience did not necessarily include the psychological damage associated with race discrimination.[39]

This brief discussion shows that the unions' conception of themselves does not fall exclusively into either the BC movement's or the UDF's categories of social movements. The unions have been both "identity oriented" and "resource mobilizing" and, by combining these two approaches, have tried to incorporate both of the other movements' strengths. The unions have largely understood that if they fail to combine mobilization for action with development of class consciousness, they will remain shortsighted and narrow. In regard to British Romantics who focused on working-class consciousness and radicals who alternatively focused on active mobilization, E. P. Thompson concluded that "in the failiure of the two traditions to come to a point of junction, something was lost."[40] South African unions have tried to avoid such a failure, seeking to create a comprehensive class consciousness built on the continuous development of both identity and mobilization.

The unions' concept of class has also been reflected in their activities. Their use of work stoppages, their efforts to structure governance based on shop-floor democracy, to foster unity among the workers and the unemployed, and to assess alliances according to working-class socialist interests all are direct consequences of this preoccupation with class mobilization and identity. Shortcomings in what the unions have achieved are also a result of their self-imposed ideological limitations, particularly because their original focus on the workers' immediate economic demands initially impeded their development into a broader movement. Although the unions continue to suffer from the faults of oligarchy, economism, and division, their later activities have also shown their commitment to a more complete, class-conscious organization. And their activities certainly contributed to the pressure on the state to move toward negotiations with the ANC and others in 1990.

This brief overview of recent South African opposition indicates how these different ideologies have figured in political actors' definitions and priorities among race, nation, or class. Each ideology has led to specific constituents, goals, and strategies, with significant consequences for each. Thus, varying conceptions of identity expressed in the idioms of mass movements have affected political action, and such consequences can be explained only with reference to those movements' subjective ideas. As I shall discuss in the next section of this chapter, material conditions, such as economic changes and state policy, also constrain the opposition and influence its focus. But despite its mixed sources, the resulting ideology then influences how material social conditions are interpreted and challenged. This reciprocal relationship between opposition ideology and dominant social conditions demonstrates that any structural analysis that fails to consider the internal dynamics and conceptions of opposition movements will remain incomplete.

## The Interplay of Structure and Ideas

Underlying each of the approaches of recent opposition movements in South Africa are distinct assumptions about whether the established social order is based on persuasion, institutional coercion, or their interaction and about whether to challenge that order primarily by posing alternative ideas, mobilizing protests, or both. Such differences correspond to the theoretical and historical debates over why regimes collapse and why their opponents succeed or fail at gaining power. This debate, fundamentally concerned with the causal relation between ideas and material structures, also applies to the formation of opposition movements; it demonstrates the effects of ideas and material forces on a movement's ideology and strategy.

Karl Marx presented the classic argument that social relations, and even ideas about those relations, are determined by the material economic structure.[41] According to this analysis, political regimes are shaped by the relations of production they defend; they are abruptly rather than incrementally altered, in accordance with a linear economic transition. Such revolutionary change and indeed all of "life is not determined by consciousness, but consciousness by life."[42] The ideas and historical actions of political actors are determined by economic class interests; therefore the ideas of individuals are largely inconsequential as independent forces. The idealism of Hegel was thus turned on its head by Marx.

Because he accorded subjective consciousness little importance in social relations, Marx was not greatly concerned with the adoption of different ideologies, other than to describe them as subordinate or epiphenomenal expressions of class interest. Marx also ridiculed the power of ideas—such as the Black Consciousness movement's assumption that oppression was maintained by the blacks' acceptance of their own natural inferiority—as analogous to reasoning "that men were drowned in water only because they were possessed with the idea of gravity."[43] Marx also criticized efforts similar to those of the United Democratic Front to create a cross-class national alliance to challenge minority domination, held distinct from economic transformation, as underemphasizing the economic basis of social relations. Marx and many of his followers denigrated all such movements conceived around race or nation as expressions of "false consciousness." But had he "devoted more attention" to how various popular movements could contribute to structural transformation, Marx might have been less disdainful of the subjective sources of "political changes."[44]

More recent scholarship has suggested that structural economic faults have led to social revolutions only when regimes are weakened by military overextension and are too closely tied to entrenched economic interests to be able to meet challenges flexibly.

Based on her analysis of the French, Russian, and Chinese revolutions, Theda Skocpol argues that states weakened in this way do fall but that otherwise they do not.[45] Although her examination of the state reveals an important intermediate factor in the processes that Marx described, Skocpol remains fundamentally structuralist in assuming that a regime's viability rests on its relative independence from economic interests. She assumes that autonomous states use their flexibility effectively to avoid revolutionary change, ignoring the possibility that errors of judgment or political intransigence can also undermine state rule. The South African regime, for instance, has been weakened by the unintended consequences of its own policies and been more constrained by entrenched political interests than by the control of capital.

Skocpol's study of only cases in which revolutions have succeeded allows her to assume that an opposition is able to take advantage of a state's weaknesses. She mentions only in passing, in her analysis of the Russian and Chinese examples, such revolutionaries as Lenin and Mao and the ideology and debates within their opposition movements. As a result, Skocpol cannot fully account for the possibility of an economic and military crisis that leaves a weakened but not an effectively challenged state limping along, as happened to Russia in 1905.[46] Her structural analysis also never considers seriously that an effective opposition can help create a crisis for a regime, as has been the case in South Africa. Skocpol's seminal analysis of the state is essential to assessing the strength of a regime, which Marx's class analysis does not fully provide, but Skocpol's approach remains too one-sided to explain the various possible outcomes of conflicts between a regime and its opponents. The failure of a regime is necessary for social revolution, but it is not a sufficient cause unless there is an effective opposition. The disregard of this point seems endemic to any overly structural approach.

Whereas those who emphasize the role of structures in social change refer to Marx's classic analysis, those who advocate a more idealistic approach follow the classic works of Max Weber. According to Weber, "Ideas become effective forces in history. . . . Countless historical circumstances . . . cannot be reduced to any economic law."[47] For instance, Marx implied that capitalism had given rise to protestantism, but Weber argued just the reverse. To do so,

Weber had to base his explanation of human behavior on subjective values and inspirations rather than rationalized materialism, on desires for community rather than isolated selfishness.

For those in Weber's tradition, the collapse of perceived legitimacy determines and indicates an impending change in regime. Societies are held together by values rather than interests, and any disjunction between such values and the society often leads to coercive rule until a new set of values and corresponding regime emerge.[48] De Tocqueville, for instance, argued that the French Revolution was precipitated by a shift of values among influential intellectuals, which turned them against the ancien régime, and by reforms that created "the most perilous moment for a bad government" in revealing the regime's own uncertainty about its values.[49] This historical analysis emphasizes ideas and rests on the assumption that people are not exclusively motivated by material interests; it does not prove that values evolve independently of material conditions or alone can cause political action or change.

Ideas do motivate people, but an exaggerated emphasis on them distorts any proposed explication of social change. Ideas about legitimacy, for instance, cannot explain when and why a regime ceases to meet popular expectations. Nor, as Charles Tilly's work suggests, does a loss of legitimacy determine the process by which grievances are transformed into collective action. The Russian Bolsheviks and Mensheviks debated this as much as the South Africans have.[50] In the case of France, values shifted partially in response to physical conditions, and reforms were rejected most strenuously after the material expectations they had raised remained unmet. In addition, the ideas propounded by the Montagnards and Girondin do not fully explain why people supported one or another of these revolutionary parties nor why the Jacobin club gained temporary power when others did not. Indeed, all the intellectuals in France could have switched allegiance to the revolution, but they all surely would have been returned to subjugation had not the people united in 1792 to defend the republic at Valmy.[51] Unfortunately, theories stressing ideas enable the intellectuals who write history also to exaggerate the influence of their ideas while disregarding the pertinent structural considerations.

Revolutionaries who are also theorists often perceive both the structural and the intentional aspects of a weak regime and a strong opposition. Lenin, for instance, contended that economic hardship could, but would not necessarily, make radicals of the masses and that reforms could either mollify them or encourage them to reject incremental change.[52] Lenin devoted himself to organizing a revolutionary party, centralized but not "detached from the masses," that would provide a guiding "line" for mass perceptions of material conditions and would use all opportunities to organize resistance.[53] In this way, Lenin tried to "reconcile his Marxist determinism with his voluntaristic system of vanguardism," believing that "to say that ideologists cannot divert from its path the movement created by the interaction of environment and elements, is to ignore the elementary truth that consciousness participates in this interaction and creation."[54] For all their differences, Lenin and Trotsky were able to cooperate after 1917, in large part because they agreed on the need to combine attention to structure with conscious intervention.

Another theorist and practitioner of revolutions, Antonio Gramsci, also understood revolutionary struggle as both a contest among ideas, in a "war of position," and a material conflict in a "war of manoeuvre." Gramsci implied that when a strong economy enables domination by persuasion, the opposition must engage in a war of position against such persuasion to gain control of civil society. When the economy is weak and the state relies on force, counterforce must be applied in a war of maneuver. Economic structure influences the relative emphasis that both the state and its opponents place on persuasion or coercion, but Gramsci also believed that "the degree of homogeneity, self-awareness and organization attained by various social classes" affects the outcome of their conflict.[55] Gramsci thus agreed with Lenin's avoidance of an exclusive emphasis on either the structural or volitional. Gramsci evoked the vivid image of the centaur, the mythical half-man and half-horse, to suggest that rulers must fuse the human use of ideas with the animal drive to meet material needs.[56] Lenin's and Gramsci's work suggests that in order to conquer the state, revolutionaries must also learn this lesson of the centaur.

Lenin's and Gramsci's advocacy of combining the two approaches for practical effect may also be found in a more complete reading of the same theories used to support the classic distinction between the primacy of structure and that of ideas. Marx understood that vulgar materialism "forgets that circumstances are changed by men and that it is essential to educate the educator himself" to develop a conscious will to act.[57] Weber similarly referred to the "interdependent influences between the material basis, the forms of social and political organization and the ideas current," concluding that "it is, of course, not my aim to substitute for a one-sided materialistic an equally one-sided spiritualistic causal interpretation of culture and of history. Each is equally possible, but each, if it does not serve as the preparation, but as the conclusion of an investigation, accomplishes equally little in the interest of historical truth."[58] Marx stressed the material and Weber the spiritual, but both understood that social relations evolve through a continuing interplay of action organized to meet needs, and values developed by education to guide such action. Aware that material experiences and new ideas inform each other in the progress toward revolutionary change, Lenin concluded that each step in that dialectical process "teaches not only the leaders, but the masses as well. . . . [Both] education and organization . . . are, of course, necessary."[59]

Theoreticians may praise one another for demonstrating the explanatory power of either structure or ideas alone, but the two intersect so constantly in reality that they force political actors to face them both. And because social order depends on dominant ideas and material structures, coercive and persuasive levers of oppression also expose, ironically, the vulnerabilities of its own sources and the trenches to be won. Revolution requires that revolutionaries be prepared to challenge both ideas and structures, if not simultaneously then in complex alternating approaches. Active resistance to repression often requires prior inspiration; the regime's failure to meet material needs often erodes submission to dominant ideas, thus clearing the way for such inspiration. An opposition must organize and inspire its followers to magnify crises and attack "the points of least resistance" in the regime's will and capacity to maintain its rule.[60] Neither analysis nor participation in an opposition can rest solely on ideas or pragmatic motivation that ignores "the interplay of material and ideal interests."[61] A single case study cannot definitively analyze how structure and ideas interact, but it can illustrate the weaknesses of both an economic determinism that ignores agency and a cultural determinism that ignores physical obstacles.

Crises of legitimacy and of unmet material interests have significantly weakened the minority South African regime. That the South African state has nonetheless been able to maintain its power suggests that its capacity or its will to rule has not been weakened enough, that no opposition of sufficient capacity or will has yet challenged it, or both. All of these conditions of regime weakness and opposition vitality must hold in order for a revolutionary outcome of the South African conflict to be possible. Even a less dramatic outcome will depend on the relative strengths in the ideas and structures of oppressor and oppressed.

Recent transitions in opposition ideology in South Africa, with different tendencies vying for shifting popular allegiances, reveal some recognition among activists that their forces have not become strong enough. Individuals in the opposition have shifted from a primary focus on BC's efforts to shape identity, to the UDF Charterists' more active protest, to the unions' efforts to combine these strengths. Opposition movements have refined abstract ideas against the harsh realities of experience, and failure has been a powerful teacher. The lessons of struggle have led each movement to complement the others' omissions, though this process has been far from linear. But despite repeated missteps, the opposition's struggle has taught it the need to combine efforts to reshape ideas and organization, in order not just to disrupt temporarily but also to challenge effectively and thereby replace the established order.[62]

The need to combine a focus on ideas and structures has been evident not only in the South African opposition's internal ideological development but also in those external influences that have led to that development. The opposition functions both as subject and object; it challenges and is shaped by material conditions and values. Opposition ideology and strategy, as well as associated political action and popular allegiance, have been conditioned by changing structural economic conditions, state reforms and repression, international acts, imported ideas, leadership debates, and efforts to learn from mistakes. For instance, economic growth and abated repression have promoted a popular preoccupation with material gains, whereas recession and repression have aggravated mass militancy, although the form of both reformist and militant collective action has been shaped by the prevalent ideology and strategy. The opposition's subjective ideas have thus interacted with the structural space in which the regime's opponents must operate. These pressures and influences also cause shifts in the state's policies and activities, including strategic responses to opposition challenges. For instance, recession and mass militancy appear to have repeatedly coincided with the state's greater reliance on repression, though this pattern has more recently been broken by increasing international pressure on the state to reform.

Our theoretical discussion to this point has confirmed the need for us to consider how ideas and structures have operated both in the shifting focus of the opposition and in the broader settings through which they have developed. As Lynn Hunt suggests in her study of the French at the end of the eighteenth century: "The revolution in politics was an explosive interaction between ideas and reality, between intention and circumstance, between collective practices and social context."[63] The ideology of South African opposition, encapsulated in different central conceptions of race, nation, and class and implying different strategies, provide a "unity or coherence in the revolutionary experience" that helps organize analysis.[64] In my exploration of how South Africa's opposition has evolved and shaped its society, opposition ideology will be the nexus for my analysis of this historical interplay of structure and ideas.

## Looking Ahead

In this book I shall describe variations and shifts of the opposition's ideology and strategy, among both its leaders and the rank and file, during the years since the banning of the ANC in 1960. I shall examine changes of approach and of political action in the context of historical social conditions and ideas, and I shall test arguments concerning the possible causes against the sequence of events. This longitudinal comparison has led me to see certain patterns of influences on opposition movements and shifts in allegiances, and also patterns through which opposition ideologies and strategies have affected political change. These patterns appear to be both cyclical, as the state and opposition respond to each other, and linear, as social conditions evolve. The following chapters attempt to explain these patterns; my emphasis on certain aspects of what has occurred during the past thirty years of opposition stems from my analytical interest in how and why it has occurred. In the final chapter, I shall gather up the threads to see how the opposition's ideology and strategy have responded to and determined changes in the economy, state action, ideas, resources, or some combination of these and other factors. By considering how oppressor and oppressed have learned from and acted on these changes, I hope to deepen our understanding of change in the past and possibly in the future.

I shall concentrate on the rise and decline of BC's influence and popularity between the late 1960s and 1979, the subsequent reemergence of adherence to the principles of the Freedom Charter as enunciated by the United Democratic Front, and the simultaneous increase of political involvement by the union movement, brought to a head by the state's repression of the UDF in 1988. Just as particular events may signal key points of transition, so allegiances and engagements among opposition groups have consistently overlapped, which makes it impossible to divide the development of the recent opposition into neatly sequential periods. In addition, because black South Africans have no voting rights and incomplete rights of association, it is difficult to discern shifts in popular allegiance. Opinion surveys can provide only rough indications of comparative allegiance, as their results may be flawed owing to the techniques used, repression, and the risk that the responses may reflect organizational influence more than true individual conviction. The stated views of opposition elites often reveal their own subjective perceptions more than popular attitudes. Indeed, fine ideological distinctions are likely to matter more and to be used to exaggeration by "those who state the case for a faction . . . and address the upper and medium layers of the movement rather than the rank-and-file."[65] However, organizational membership and action, publicity, resources, international attention, and even the language commonly used all provide indications of popular ideological and organizational allegiances, against which other measures can be compared.

I believe that my focus on these movements is fully justified, there being no logical reason that historical processes cannot be analyzed by examining pressures from below rather than authority exerted from above. Indeed, a study of either oppression or resistance must consider the other side, because a regime's fate rests not only on its own capacity and will but also on those of its challengers. History abounds with examples of weak states that survive because no unified or effective opposition is able to confront them and take power. Because the outcome is less dramatic, they tend to attract less attention than successful revolutions do. Hannah Arendt argued that at least in the case of the Russian Revolution, if not more generally, state power was not wrested away but simply picked up once the existing state had lost its ability to rule. Arendt is surely correct in asserting that the failure of a regime is a prerequisite to revolutionary change, but she does not adequately demonstrate that had there been no opposition ready to pick it up and defend it, the state's power might simply have been recaptured by the Romanovs or their allies. Because an effective challenge to a regime is an equal precondition for revolutionary change, basing our analysis on the South African opposition will help indicate how much progress has occurred toward meeting this precondition.

The effectiveness of the opposition forces influences whether change will be revolutionary or incremental, and it helps show the policies of the regime that may emerge from such a change. In the Russian example, knowledge of the Bolshevik and Menshivik tendencies would have helped clarify the policies that either would pursue once in power. The South African opposition deserves to be considered just as seriously. Although my book certainly cannot predict the outcome of the current conflict in South Africa, it can illuminate some of the recent causes and outcomes of the different movements' ideologies and strategies, and it can outline the future paths that each intends to follow after winning state power. Of course, the future leaders of South Africa, whether they come from the African National Congress, other groups, or some coalition, will, like all leaders, face constraints. How they react to such difficulties will matter greatly, and we can get a good sense of how these processes might unfold by exploring the intentions and limitations that the leading opposition tendencies have experienced thus far.

It is useful to understand the recent changes in the South African opposition for their own sake, but there also are practical benefits from doing so. That is, finding general patterns in past responses of opposition movements to various social conditions, such as economic change or state repression, might help us see how those movements are likely to respond in the future. Presumably, state officials engage in just this sort of calculation, and opposition leaders undoubtedly do the same. Such efforts at prediction can only be inexact: Structural pressures and state policies vary, have unforeseen consequences, are interpreted differently, and evoke divergent responses, exhibiting unrepeatable historical developments. How the interaction of structure and ideas is interpreted by any actor depends on his or her previous experiences; such interpretations and subsequent action are "path dependent." My analysis will therefore enrich our understanding of these past patterns of particular political activities and also demonstrate the danger of imposing such past patterns on possible future developments.

# 2

# *Racial Assertiveness and Black Unrest: The Black Consciousness Movement Through 1976*

Many of the ideas and strategies that opposition groups in South Africa have embraced since 1969 developed with reference to earlier experiences, carrying the lessons of struggle forward over generations. For example, differences over whether challenges to the state should center on resisting national domination or racial discrimination have been regularly debated ever since the emergence of formal minority rule and apartheid, if not longer. Such debates are not resolved as much as they reverberate and evolve over time, as seen in a selective review of the history of opposition leading up to the formation of the Black Consciousness movement.

## The Parents' Movements

The modern history of organized, countrywide opposition in South Africa began twenty-five years after George Harrison's discovery of gold on the Reef in 1886, once the effects of that discovery had taken hold. The ensuing fight between the British and Afrikaners for control of the country and its wealth was formally resolved with the Act of Union in 1910. In 1911, a bill was tabled in the British-controlled parliament to prohibit African landownership outside set "reserves" and to regulate African employment. The roots of legal apartheid thus took hold more than a generation before the Afrikaners' National party formally came to power. Leaders of the African community responded in 1912 to this increasing exclusion from political dispensation by forming what became the African National Congress (ANC).

The ANC was founded by a coalition of the "small emerging professional African middle class . . . with the conservative rural chieftaincy," seeking to protest the discriminatory political order in South Africa.[1] As an organization composed of African elites, the ANC was begun as an expression of the conservative impulse to protect the traditional rights of the chiefs and the gains by which a small number of African professionals had distanced themselves from the rural African poor. These elites did not seek to overthrow the government but to use formal legal protests to pressure the government to "come to its senses." The rationale for this strategy was never openly expressed but simply accepted as a proper response to political exclusion.

Ideological coherence among the divergent initial constituencies of the ANC probably was not possible and, in any case, was not as highly valued as was organizational unity. In its early years as a protest group, the ANC could function and remain unified by concentrating on specific tasks, such as the organization of annual conferences, and on protests against the deterioration of basic rights formerly guaranteed in the liberal Cape Colony constitution of the mid-nineteenth century. There was little pressure exerted in the ANC to address the potentially divisive question of what alternative form of governance its membership would prefer to the current order. Groups with more radical intentions and strategies, such as the Industrial and Commercial Workers Union and other early forms of worker organization discussed more fully in Chapter 6, remained outside the ANC.[2] The Congress retained its focus on organizational tasks based on opposition to the minority regime, as enunciated in the ANC's 1919 constitution. With the formation of the Congress Alliance in the 1950s, the ANC aligned itself with representatives from all of South Africa's officially designated "national" groups (whites, Africans, coloreds, and Indians). Any policies that would alienate potential allies and divide constituent groups according to their disparate racial identities or class interests were avoided. These tendencies to be inclusive and to emphasize organizational unity over ideological cohesion have remained hallmarks of the Congress's nationalist tradition.

The ANC's elitism and moderation diminished, however, as experience demonstrated the authorities' intransigence. Respectful protests resulted in no significant gains through the 1930s, when the ANC's continued insistence on avoiding direct confrontation led to a significant loss of popular support for the Congress.[3] The organization's conservative approach waned only grudgingly. The influence of the traditional chiefs declined accordingly, signaled by the disbanding in 1943 of their separate "Upper House" in the ANC. Meanwhile, the relatively radical influence of the South African Communist party grew, cemented by an informal alliance forged in the late 1940s and early 1950s.[4] The party itself had been founded in 1921, initially to organize white workers, and began to shift toward black workers only in the mid-1920s. Faced with a reality in which race played a more prominent role than it did in the writings of Karl Marx, the Communist party joined the ANC's cross-class alliance in calling for black democratic rule as a distinct but necessary first step toward a workers' state. The party's continued support for the ANC, together with the government's repression of the Communists, gradually increased the party's influence within the ANC, to the dismay of an emerging Africanist faction among the ANC's younger members.

The ANC's more conservative tradition had eroded even more by the 1940s, with the coming of age of a new generation of more confrontational young leaders. In 1943 the ANC Youth League was formed under the influence of Anton Lembede, an early Africanist who rejected Communism and instead advocated a more militant ideology aimed at overcoming "the psychological inhibitions produced by racial oppression."[5] The Youth League's influence grew quickly, shifting from Lambede's concern for ideology to a greater concern with mass organization than that advocated either by Lembede or by the president of the ANC at the time, A. B. Xuma. Under the leadership of Walter Sisulu, an organizer with Africanist sympathies who had been elected secretary-general in 1949, the Youth League successfully pushed for the ANC's adoption of a program of action in the same year. With this program, the ANC dramatically shifted to a strategy of mass mobilization that has since remained one of its hallmarks.

In 1952, the Youth League launched a defiance campaign led by a "volunteer in chief," Nelson Mandela. The civil disobedience that occurred as part of this campaign, as well as major school boycotts in 1955 and an antipass campaign in 1959, all gained the ANC new adherents, particularly among the youth who were then feeling the additional brunt of a series of economic downturns.[6] For the first time, the Congress gained a significant mass base of support. By the mid-1950s, Sisulu, Mandela, and other Youth Leaguers had abandoned their early Africanist sympathies and moved into leadership positions in the ANC itself. In 1953 they formulated the "M plan," a new organizational structure attributed to Mandela that advocated the division of the Congress into clandestine "cells" in the eventuality of more severe repression. The implementation of this structure was interrupted in 1955 by bannings and by the "treason trial," originally involving 156 defendants, 30 of whom remained on trial for over four years until their acquittal.

In the face of both criticism from early Africanists and legal attacks from the state, the ANC and its allies decided to consolidate their position with a gathering of all their constituents. A wide spectrum of South Africans attended the "Congress of the People," held in Kliptown outside Johannesburg on June 25 and 26, 1955, at which the Freedom Charter (see Appendix A) was presented as a unified set of demands. Africanists and radical socialists have questioned the democratic nature of these proceedings, noting the lack of debate and the prominent role played by middle-class whites. In any event, the Charter was adopted by acclamation of the Congress.[7] Regardless of any imperfections in the process, adoption of the Charter remains a salient "foundation myth" for Charterist adherents to the ANC tradition, as indicated by comments made at a local branch meeting of unionists in June 1988: "The Freedom Charter came about with the direct participation of the people. It is rare that people were directly involved in the drawing up of such a document. Ours may be the only country where it was not just drawn up by leaders."[8]

The Congress of the People and the resulting Charter impressively demonstrated the wide-ranging appeal and organization of the ANC and its allies, as well as their willingness to compromise or remain vague on commitments so as to attract as broad a national opposition as possible. The Charter's clause of equal rights for all national groups, adopted unanimously as a rebuke to apartheid, implicitly accepts the premise of the existence of ascribed national differences and protects minority rights, as an inducement for white support. In calling for the nationalization of the mines, banks, and monopoly industry, the Charter was the Congress's "first attempt to link the process of political emancipation to the transformation of the economic system," but this plank was not interpreted as an explicit demand for socialism.[9] The Communist party itself argued that consideration of such a radical economic transformation should be postponed to a later but distinct stage, after national political rights had been won. In the following year Mandela described the Charter as "by no means a blueprint for a socialist state but a programme for the unification of various classes and groupings," all of whom would benefit from breaking the monopolies.[10] These remarks underscore the Charter's original intention, to chart a middle course on economic issues, in order to antagonize as few potential allies as possible.

Intended to gain support, the adoption of the Charter also helped increase impatience among some who had earlier joined the Youth League. Africanists, in particular, objected to the Charter's description of the land as belonging "to all who live in it" and its demand that the land should be divided "amongst those who work it." Instead, they felt that the indigenous people had a birthright to all of the land, including that worked by whites, and that in its attempts to appease other groups in the inclusive Congress Alliance the Charter had sold that birthright for a few pieces of political silver. This group—led by Robert Sobukwe and including a constituency somewhat "better educated" than that of the ANC—broke away from the ANC in 1959 to form the Pan Africanist Congress (PAC).[11] They rejected compromises to gain allies in favor of an opposition effectively open only to the Africans and thereby excluding whites, Indians, and coloreds, with only few exceptions. Formally open to all who claimed allegiance to Africa, the PAC insisted on an indigenous leadership who could press to regain the birthright of landownership. But with its exclusively African leadership and relatively radical policies, the PAC attracted only African members and was thus tied to a thinly camouflaged ascriptive definition of race merged with national aspirations.[12] Extreme in its claim to the land and in its attitude toward whites, the PAC was anti-Communist in its economic policies, favoring an indigenous "communalism." In this sense, the PAC shared aspects of the ANC's approach, according to which "our immediate task . . . is not socialism, but national liberation."[13]

Although it agreed with the ANC's at least temporary unwillingness to advocate socialism, the PAC was clearly less accommodating in the means it sanctioned for challenging national domination. The PAC's strategic focus was on mobilizing a spontaneous revolt similar to that advocated in China by Mao Zedong rather than relying on the state to respond to protests. As described by Tom Lodge, "The PAC leadership was convinced that Africanism made articulate a deeply rooted ethnonationalist popular consciousness. A political appeal founded on such sentiment would immediately attract massive support."[14] The PAC did indeed enjoy a meteoric rise of popularity, reinforcing its tendency to disregard formal organization in favor of using ideology to appeal to mass consciousness. This reliance on ideology was later inherited by the Black Consciousness movement, although BC was somewhat more concerned with organization, more patient, and less inclined toward a romantic vision of mass insurrection.[15] BC also shared the PAC's focus on racial identity and exclusion of whites, though in a revised version, rejecting the ANC's national inclusiveness of all groups in the struggle for liberation.

Following the ANC's lead, one of the PAC's first public actions was to call for a campaign against the passes that Africans were required to carry. This campaign gained widespread support, leading to a rally in Sharpeville on March 21, 1960, at which sixty-nine unarmed men, women, and children were shot and killed by police. The international outcry against this use of force was soon drowned out by the imposed silence of Pretoria's swift banning of both the ANC and the PAC. The renaissance of open and organized internal opposition was over with a volley of gunshot and the stroke of a pen. But in closing the curtain on openly organized resistance, the state only pushed the opposition into more clandestine uses of violence as the sole form of action remaining open to it.

With the bannings, the focus of opposition activity shifted to the urban sabotage organized by the ANC through 1964 and to the externally based guerrilla operations of the ANC and the PAC after that. Both the ANC and the PAC suffered from their unexpectedly sudden move to exile, before contacts, future arrangements, and internal underground structures had been fully established. The ANC therefore had to build up its international contacts and the organizational structures begun by Nelson Mandela to form its armed wing, Umkonto we Sizwe (MK, or "Spear of the Nation"), as a regimented guerrilla unit. By giving its army the same name that had earlier been used to refer to education as means of recapturing what had been lost in the battlefield, the ANC clearly signaled its shift from what Gramsci called a war of position to a war of maneuver.[16] Incursions into Rhodesia (now Zimbabwe) in 1967, which resulted in significant casualties for MK, were hailed by the ANC as an inspiring "baptism by fire" but were equally vigorously ridiculed by the PAC.[17]

From exile the PAC formed its own internal armed wing, Poqo ("We Stand Alone"), and the Azanian Peoples' Liberation Army. Despite some early successes, their lack of structure, programs, or resources gained these units a reputation for being "anarchistic" and ineffective.[18] It is not surprising that the differences in armed strategy between these insurrectionist units and the more regimented MK correspond to the PAC's generally greater emphasis on spontaneity or mass consciousness and to the ANC's generally greater emphasis on organization. The relative lack of success of the PAC's armed wing cannot be completely explained by this difference of approach, however, as the PAC was subsequently weakened by the irregularity of its support from the People's Republic of China, a series of leadership disputes, and problems of corruption. Of the eight original PAC leaders who went into exile, six had been expelled by 1976, whereas Oliver Tambo remained president of the ANC throughout its thirty years in exile.[19]

Once the leadership was out of the country or in jail, popular opposition in South Africa was effectively halted by unprecedented police force and the disrupting effects of millions being "endorsed out" of urban areas or subject to "forced removals" to separate homelands. The result was almost a decade of pervasive fear and imposed silence. With little active internal resistance, international attention turned away from South Africa, and few resources flowed to those exile groups that might have supported their efforts. Underneath the surface of enforced tranquillity, however, reevaluation and discussions of the possibilities for future opposition began, particularly among black students in the segregated universities.[20] But the results of that rethinking did not become public until the end of the 1960s, a decade notable elsewhere for the popular mobilization relatively absent in South Africa.

When opposition did reemerge in the late 1960s, it was, of course, influenced by the debates and lingering allegiances from this earlier era. For instance, Steve Biko later reflected on his previous experience and identified the Black Consciousness movement he led with those earlier critics of the ANC who "were questioning a number of things, among which was the go slow attitude adopted by leadership, and the ease with which the leadership accepted coalitions with organizations other than those run by blacks."[21] Referring back to and building on such earlier debates, the founders of Black Consciousness established a movement that attempted to synthesize aspects of the ANC and PAC, by being, for instance, less open to the broad alliances and vague rhetoric of the ANC and less rigid and exclusive than the PAC had been. Only by learning from the lessons of their parents and predecessors could the next generation hope to build on earlier strengths and compensate for evident weaknesses in their attempts to pick up the struggle where it had left off.

## The Emergence of Black Consciousness

Repression and economic hardship, as manifestations of continued domination and exploitation, have long provoked opposition in South Africa. The failure of earlier efforts, through the 1960s, to eliminate these aspects of oppression encouraged the need for the opposition forces to reconsider how they could more effectively challenge the established order. The need to adjust the opposition ideology and strategy was apparent but could not be easily done during the greater repression and hardship of the 1960s, when simply ensuring survival took precedence. Only in the calm after the storm, when some degree of security had been regained, could new approaches to opposition be weighed and implemented. In South Africa, economic growth and the winding down of state repression in the late 1960s provided conditions conducive to this process of evaluation and realignment, analogous in some respects to the years after 1905 that the Russian revolutionaries used for debate and consolidation.

The repression and imposed quiescence of the early 1960s had marked the beginning in South Africa of a period of unprecedented economic growth that blossomed later in the decade. Foreign investment, attracted by the apparent calm, almost doubled during this decade, while the concentration of assets and market share held by a few oligopolies and public corporations also increased markedly.[22] Real growth rose between 7 and 13 percent annually, sustained largely through greater investment in industry and manufacturing, which since World War II had replaced mining as the largest sector of the economy. African employment in industries other than mining increased from 3 million in 1960 to 4.7 million in 1970.[23] This investment and growth helped pay for the consolidation of apartheid and the state's repression in the 1960s, with subsequent prosperity gradually reducing the impetus for popular militancy and making it possible for the state to complement legal restrictions and repression with economic constraints on behavior. Many of those who had gained employment during this period were loathe to sacrifice their material gains for political struggles that had thus far had little success. The state was eager to encourage such reasoning.

As much as economic growth culminating in the early 1970s served the interests of the state, however, it also undermined the strict enforcement of apartheid. Rapid industrialization required more skilled workers than could be found among whites, and so this gap was increasingly filled by blacks. From 1969 to 1977 alone, the number of skilled jobs grew by more than a third, and the portion of those jobs filled by Africans increased from 9.3 to 23.2 percent.[24] As a result, more blacks were brought together in the workplace, where they were later able to organize unions to press for material gains beyond those already achieved, as discussed in Chapter 6. Of more immediate consequence, large numbers of blacks were drawn out of the rural areas by the better prospects of employment near the cities and towns, furthering the process of rapid urbanization dating back at least to the 1940s.[25] This urban migration brought together Africans from various regions, countering the state's simultaneous efforts to enforce tribal divisions and to push the Africans into the rural homelands.[26] Opposition activities had long been centered in the burgeoning black townships, where the rapidly growing population of urbanized youth provided an important constituency for the Black Consciousness movement, which emerged in the 1970s.

Perhaps the most politically significant immediate consequence of the structural changes culminating in the 1960s was the dramatic increase in segregated black education required to provide a larger skilled work force: Preuniversity black enrollment increased from 1 million in 1955 to over 2.5 million in 1969, while the black university population increased from a meager 515 in 1961 to almost 3,000 by 1972.[27] But during this period, the percentage of the GDP spent on black education actually declined, creating massive overcrowding in the schools; only a high rate of failure kept the upper school grades from being swamped.[28] Meanwhile, state policies of purposely inferior "Bantu education" continued, giving students an additional and immediate experience of racial discrimination.[29] The overcrowded schools and growing universities created abundant opportunities for students to meet informally, with the discrimination they suffered providing a topic for discussions that helped mold direct experience into political consciousness.[30] Ironically, just as the Afrikaners had learned from their own experience that "a nation is born by having its youth impregnated at school in the . . . ultimate destiny of its people," so the black South Africans' school experience helped form their own political sensibility.[31]

Black South African students, particularly those who succeeded in climbing up the steep pyramid of obstacles in the township schools to the university level, were distinguished from other urbanized blacks as members, or potential members, of the middle class. In the early 1970s, these students were often perceived by other blacks as an elite, likely to end up with high-paying jobs or in government service, including the year of teaching in state schools that was often required in return for a university "bursary." As a result, "the community was hostile to [and suspicious of] university students."[32] This social distance, reinforced by the physical isolation of the black university campuses, further encouraged the formation of separate student organizations. Although the students in these organizations did not hold themselves entirely aloof from their home communities, they did tend to think of their education as preparing them for future leadership roles. Once the Black

Consciousness movement had assumed a more definite shape, its student members were described by one analyst as claiming proudly the role of "officers, not rank and file. To train, not to be trained. Such were the dreams of this small, relatively privileged group."[33]

Set apart by their relative privilege, the students tended to become absorbed with ideas, struggling to set their imaginations free from the harsh material realities of their world and to explore avenues of escape. On occasion, even elements of the formal curriculum, such as history lessons on the French Revolution, inspired new ways of thinking, despite official efforts to control how such subjects were presented in the classroom.[34] But this excitement and this ingestion of new ideas were more importantly directed to literature outside the bounds of the curriculum and permissible readings, with an array of well-thumbed, banned material passed around on campuses and in townships.[35] As one unionist, who was then a student, recalled the effect of these books: "In the early seventies our political ideas were still in the formative stage; at the stage where you cannot be sure if one's ideas are not plagiarized from the book read the night before."[36]

Prominent among the illicit literature shared by students were the writings of Amilcar Cabral and Frantz Fanon, whose work was influential in the formative stages of Black Consciousness. Both Cabral and Fanon rejected classical Marxism's lack of interest in the significance of race or in groups other than the urban proletariat, and both also emphasized the need to use the culture of the oppressed to build self-confidence and to challenge the enslavement to colonial ideology.[37] Interpretations based on Fanon's call for a positive racial identity to overcome the psychological damage of discrimination became a centerpiece of BC.[38] Cabral's related discussion of the connection between racism and colonialism was evidently more influential than was his concern for organizing resistance in a vanguard party, an approach not pursued by the BC movement.[39]

Black Consciousness was influenced not only by African thinkers but also by the Black Power movement, a volatile expression of racial assertiveness that had begun in the mid-1960s in the United States. The ideology of Black Power was widely discussed, although that movement's party structure and use of material services to meet community needs was less well known, reflecting the informal way in which South Africans learned about their American counterpart. For instance, Bishop Manas Buthelezi of Soweto recalls first learning about Black Power while he was a student at Drew University in 1965, where he heard Stokely Carmichael speak, and telling others about it on his return home in 1968. Fatima Meer describes how Black Power permeated South Africa through books, the media, and movies, all benefiting from the "high projection of U.S. culture," as compared with the dearth of information about ideas from other African countries.[40] Perhaps the way in which Black Power was most influential in South Africa was through the adoption of its derivative Black Theology by popular religious figures, including Bishop Desmond Tutu, Dr. Allan Boesak, and others in the South African Council of Churches and in the African Independent churches. Advocates of Black Theology, inspired particularly by the writings of James Cone, emphasized spiritual rather than material oppression, and also healing. Black Consciousness adopted the same nonmaterial emphasis, albeit in a more secular guise, concluding that "it is a sin to allow oneself to be oppressed."[41]

Although Black Power was influential, Black Consciousness was not considered a carbon copy of this American movement. Expressions of racial assertiveness in South Africa long predated the rise of Black Power, with Lembede and others in the ANC Youth League and later the PAC having earlier been influenced by Marcus Garvey, Ethiopianism, and various Pan-African thinkers. In addition, South Africans were aware that differences in their situation and that of black Americans made the wholesale importation of Black Power inappropriate. For instance, black South Africans did not enjoy any of the civil rights formally protected in the United States, which ensured some tolerance of the open expression of Black Power in the United States. There was no such formal protection in South Africa, where assertions of Black Power implied a legitimate claim to govern over the white minority.

Imported ideas, including aspects of Fanon, Cabral, Black Power, and Black Theology, were incorporated into BC, but the applicability of a form of racial assertiveness was not imposed from the outside, by either intellectuals or the clergy. More significantly, everyday experiences reinforced the idea that oppression was linked to race. The South Africans who formed BC understood their situation in terms of the racial distinctions of apartheid, the most obvious manifestation of their oppression. As unionist Alec Erwin pointed out, "Discrimination against students is overtly racial, as compared to the work place where discrimination relates more directly to capitalism."[42] The poor and overcrowded conditions of schools were the result of the educational authorities' overtly racial policies. Indeed, apartheid in its various forms was pervasive, creating a sense of commonality based on the "everyday experience" of discrimination that was far stronger than an "abstract political bond."[43] It is not surprising, then, that when Biko and other students began to analyze oppression and formulate a response to it, their focus on the need to overcome racial discrimination came directly out of their own experiences.

Outside ideas were not needed to frame the problem of racism, but they did contribute to the realization that this aspect of oppression could be turned around to the advantage of the oppressed. Indeed, this was the fundamental insight common to Fanon, Cabral, and Black Power. Revitalizing the internal opposition required an awakening of group solidarity, for which "the strong foundation" of racial identity had been used by the state to distinguish those it had "disinherited and dispossessed."[44] Vincent Mogane, a young Black Consciousness activist at the time, remembered how this group identity was used to rekindle people's spirit of resistance:

> By 1968, people were beginning to reorganize themselves. BC was rallying the people for unification, using color to appeal to people to unite around their problems. We appealed to the consciousness of a people . . . and the people became aware of themselves as human beings. We thought that from that confidence they would then be a force to challenge national atrocities. BC was a way to rally the people.[45]

The key symbolic transition to a positive group identity based on race came in 1970 with the rejection of the negative label *nonwhite* in favor of *black*. According to Aubrey Mokoena, another Black Consciousness activist at the time, even "Biko had used non-white to avoid the image of being racist. . . . [We] pushed him at a meeting in 1970 to use black."[46] Biko himself later described this transition as the embracing of a derogatory reference by whites in order to "elevate it to a position where we can look upon ourselves positively."[47] The point was for blacks to define themselves as a group, rather than to accept a negative self-conception defined in terms of what they were not and referring only to their exclusion from the privileges of being white.

The adoption of the term *black* did not imply acceptance of any assumptions about the innate characteristics attributed to race. As we saw in Chapter 1, the inclusion by BC of coloreds and Indians as fellow blacks, despite differences in the groups' legal rights, directly contradicted the state's efforts to divide these officially designated racial groups as distinct. Although BC adherents did on occasion slip into using a biological definition as shorthand, activists carefully defined "being black" as the condition of being excluded from power based on state-imposed categories of race. Racial discrimination was understood and challenged by BC as a product of social relations and consciousness rather than innate fact. Because officially ascribed differences formed the basis for that discrimination according to which BC defined blacks, this distinction was confusing and did not eliminate the occasional popularized reference to racial justifications for excluding whites.[48] But the BC elite understood that by focusing on social practice rather than physical appearance, entrenched discrimination would be revealed as malleable, though for some this remained an odd fine point of ideology.

Although it may not have fully permeated all corners of the movement, BC's formal rejection of the official definitions of race did permit a more varied, or situational, concept of collective identity based on race. According to Ken Rachidi, president of the BC movement's Black People's Convention (BPC) from 1974 until its banning in 1977, "BC adherents believed that the time had not yet come for joining hands with whites—the time would not be ripe for that until after liberation."[49] The situation of oppression tactically required racial unity and exclusivity as a basis for opposition, but this tactical necessity did not imply any fixed racial division after liberation.[50] The coincidence of race and oppression was the focus of Black Consciousness, but that coincidence would be broken with the end of apartheid, when race would cease to be a salient distinction. By using race as a means for reviving opposition but rejecting official differences, the BC movement was fulfilling its "cruel responsibility of going to the very gate of racism in order to destroy racism—to the gate, not further."[51]

BC's conception of race implied a set of strategies similar to those of the PAC and inconsistent with the ANC's nonracial tradition of compromising in order to attract allies from across the color line. According to Bishop Manas Buthelezi, a leading proponent then and now of Black Theology, "BC had said we need to concentrate on our identity first, to assert that South Africa belongs to [us]. Whites can stay, but only on our terms."[52] To assert their self-determination, blacks were warned against the ANC's traditional alliances with white liberals who continued to benefit from apartheid despite their self-proclaimed rejection of it.[53] But this position did not constitute reverse racism, BC adherents argued, because it was merely a response to their situation rather than an assumption of white inferiority and because there was no possibility of powerless blacks' being able to "subjugate" whites.[54]

A racially exclusive form of opposition was described by Black Consciousness, as it had been earlier by Lembede, as essential to the psychological liberation of black South Africans. Only through self-assertion without the help or leadership of whites could blacks prove to themselves that they were ready for liberation. Only then could they take power, rather than waiting for fulfillment of the false hope that whites could somehow be persuaded to give their power away.[55] Indeed, BC implied that power could be gained through black self-assertion. This approach was designed to engage "the idealism of studenthood" prevalent in those black schools and universities that provided the movement with its core constituency.[56]

The BC ideology, with its emphasis on altering self-awareness, was based on an idealistic conception of how a movement can affect social change. BC advocated that blacks' ideas about themselves could and must be changed before the material circumstances of oppression shaping those ideas could be addressed. Even more boldly, many BC adherents believed that a change of self-concept was not just a prior condition but was also by itself able to change material relations. Ideas were considered sufficient means for reinvigorating and maintaining opposition, with even the more mundane tasks of "community action" described in terms of "spreading consciousness" rather than more concrete forms of organization.[57] A greater weight placed on using material incentives and resources as a basis for mobilization was seen by many in BC as opening up the possibility of being mollified with compromises and reforms.[58] Instead, the goal of changing blacks' self-image was seen as both the means and the end of liberation. This concentration on ideas, described alternatively as consistent with "African tradition" or as "extreme naivety,"[59] remained fundamental to BC, thereby weakening interest in any prior planning for when the state would again fall back on the use of force that it largely held in reserve throughout the early 1970s.

BC was avowedly nonconfrontational toward whites and nonviolent in its effort to construct an alternative set of values rather than a more material "counterforce" to domination.[60] Indeed, the movement so assiduously avoided violence that the judge who found nine BC leaders guilty of organizing protests staged in 1974 made special note that BC had proved itself to be neither revolutionary nor violent.[61] But the movement had to walk a narrow line on this issue, for as Saths Cooper, one of the nine found guilty, explained, "None of our official documents talked of non-violence since we did not want to appear to be against the activities of the exiles."[62] Despite such careful handling of the issue, the movement's nonviolence later contributed to disenchantment, particularly among those BC adherents who preferred more open support for the ANC's armed struggle. But the initial avoidance of violence was a useful tactic, aimed at both minimizing state repression of the movement in its early stages and broadening the appeal of BC's message among a populace that remained fearful of the repression that it had seen unleashed in the 1960s.

It was not only tactical considerations, however, that motivated the Black Consciousness movement's nonviolence and avoidance of confrontation. Rather, the use of force was—perhaps more importantly—inconsistent with the movement's basic ideological consideration. For BC, the use of force to undermine the regime's will or capacity to rule was simply unnecessary, according to its assumption that "the limits of tyrants are prescribed by the endurance of those whom they oppress."[63] For the same reason, it was considered both unlikely and unnecessary to try to persuade whites to abandon their power. Instead, whites' power would be lost as soon as blacks asserted their unwillingness to abide by it, regardless of the intentions of those in power, or the balance of material forces controlled by the state and its opponents. The only consistent justification for using violence would have been Fanon's suggestion that active aggression undermines the psychology of submission, an argument that BC initially ignored.

The emphasis on change through ideas reflects BC's disregard not only of Fanon's view on violence but also of the tradition of Marxist thought. According to Frank Chikane—who as a student had been an early advocate of BC—the absence of class analysis was due in part to the fact that "we never saw books on Marx at the universities."[64] Biko and others who were familiar with Marx rejected class analysis as a foreign ideology that white liberals sought to impose along with their own inclusion in the struggle.[65] In addition to the lack of information and tactical concerns, class analysis was also perceived as inconsistent with the movement's central ideological focus on race. BC adherents acknowledged that in South Africa, both blacks and the working class referred to largely the same population, but as students the BC adherents considered racial discrimination to be more pervasive, damaging, and salient than economic exploitation was. Accordingly, BC was more concerned with the psychological damage associated with race than with the more material issues implied by a focus on class, and feared that class analysis would detract from its message of racial assertiveness.

Instead of advocating a socialist outcome of class conflict, BC adopted an economic policy calling for "communalism," defined as an "economic system which is based on the principle of sharing [and] lays emphasis on community ownership."[66] Consistent with its central focus, BC was primarily concerned with using this economic policy to project a positive image of the precolonial black community and, by implication, the possibility that blacks could regain their self-reliance. But the economic implications of such a policy were never worked out. As we shall see in the next chapter, Black Consciousness later incorporated a more explicit class analysis, which those who remained loyal to the movement described as having been implied—albeit in a tactically camouflaged form—by communalism. Others who abandoned BC, ostensibly because of its initial lack of class analysis, argued instead that "communalism did not fit the material conditions" of a developing industrial base and that this policy revealed the contradictions of BC.[67] That these alternative interpretations did not emerge more explicitly in the first years of the BC movement underscores the importance at the time of BC's greater emphasis on race and the general lack of interest in class issues.

The movement's initial lack of any confrontational, violent, or anticapitalist rhetoric ultimately proved divisive, but in the short run it served the movement's purposes. Its avoidance of such radical rhetoric distinguished BC from its exiled predecessors and also lulled the state into a policy of benign neglect. The authorities' lack of concern about BC at first may have been reinforced by the racist assumption that a movement without whites could never pose a serious threat to the state and that the exclusion of whites would further divide the opposition.[68] Former BC supporter Fanyana Mazibuko contends, however, that the state was not just neglectful but was actually supportive of the emergence of BC "as consistent with its own separate development policies" and as an expression of a less confrontational, aspiring black middle class.[69] Among the rapidly radicalizing students, the resulting absence of early state attacks on BC created suspicions, though these were overcome as the students became more familiar with the movement and as the state also became more familiar with and aggressive toward BC.[70] In the meantime, the state's early inaction had given BC the space it needed to develop.[71]

In retrospect, it is clear that the government's initial lack of concern about the Black Consciousness movement was clearly shortsighted or misinformed. In part, the state's inaction was based on its materialist assumption that the relative strength of the state and the opposition depended solely on the balance of organized force and resources that each commanded and with which BC was not mainly preoccupied. The state apparently ignored the possibility or potential significance of its being challenged on a more abstract level or that the dissemination of ideas could, in itself, contribute to a revitalization of its opponents. By not taking BC more seriously, the state misconstrued the movement's exclusion of whites from the preliberation struggle as consistent with official projections of racial differences and with state efforts to divide potential opponents. Instead, BC's inclusion of coloreds and Indians undermined the idea of ascribed differences and served only to unify important opposition constituencies. The state's continued concern about domestic loyalty to the exiled ANC diverted attention from these internal developments, which were pursued independently of the ANC.

A brief comparison of Black Consciousness with the exile movements may help place BC in the context of its predecessors and also help explain the state's initial passivity. BC's emphasis on black unity, on cultural activity and ideological assertiveness over organization and alliances, was reminiscent of the positions taken by Lembede in the ANC Youth League and by the PAC, in contrast with the traditional nonracialism and alliances of the ANC as a whole. These similarities suggest a connection to the PAC, which was reinforced by the well-publicized conviction of Kaya Biko, Steve's elder brother, for being a member of the PAC's Poqo. All of this helps explain why some Charterists regarded BC as an outgrowth of the PAC. However, the BC movement was conscientious in its efforts to project itself as "nonaligned" to either the ANC or the PAC in order to avoid division in its own ranks, which included many with ANC sympathies or family connections.[72] In addition, BC's nonalignment was designed to avoid what was perceived as the mistake made by earlier student organizations in the 1960s, such as the ANC's explicit alignment with the African Students' Association and the PAC's alignment with the African Students' Union of South Africa, which had divided students and provoked state repression.[73]

Superficial similarities with the PAC were defused not only by BC's tactical distance and more diverse sympathies but also by more fundamental differences of ideology. The PAC's central focus on an ascribed Africanist identification with the land and on its resistance to "settler colonialism" was different from BC's target of a new form of racial identity aimed at subverting discrimination. Indeed, BC's focus on reshaping ideas was criticized by the PAC's founder, Robert Sobukwe, as an elitist concern.[74] The implications of this difference in focus were elucidated by PAC-aligned union leader James Mndaweni: "We say that if whites accept that the land belongs to the African people and accept being under the control of the black majority, they are with us. BC says that whites can never be with us until after liberation. The PAC says whites can be accepted before liberation, as sympathizers working in their own community," though in practice few if any whites were accepted by the PAC.[75] In addition, BC's inclusion of all blacks who suffered from discrimination promoted unity with those coloreds and Indians embraced by the ANC but effectively excluded from the PAC as not indigenous.[76] In this respect, BC sought a middle ground between the exclusiveness of the PAC and the inclusiveness of the ANC.[77]

BC emerged out of a student constituency buoyed in its numbers and expectations by prosperity. As students, this group was inclined to be attracted to ideas and to be concerned mainly with the discrimination it suffered. BC formulated and embraced an ideology that stressed the importance of changing values, self-image, and psychology to undermine the idea of ascribed inferiority, as compared with a more concrete form of active confrontation aimed directly at altering material relations. The goal was mental liberation as a necessary and possibly sufficient precondition for physical liberation. This ideology was crystallized in the need to reshape racial identity by using that identity to revitalize mass opposition, building on the lessons of previous movements. Having formulated its ideology first, the BC movement then set out to put it into practice, using a variety of mechanisms to spread a message of racial assertiveness that could challenge the established order through its very affirmation.

## The Development of the BC Movement

During the early 1970s the black universities, swelling together with the economy, were the center for enthusiasm about new economic opportunities and the rising power of an emerging black elite's ideas to engender change. Not only did the increase in black university enrollment help spread the ideas that coalesced into the BC movement, but the black universities also provided an institutional setting for the establishment of the first BC organization.

Already in the late 1960s, black students found themselves concentrated in segregated universities without their own formal structure of representation. The liberal National Union of South African Students (NUSAS) had tried to organize and represent black students without losing its primarily white constituency and at the same time seeking to avoid the direct state attacks of previous years. According to Fanyana Mazibuko, a prominent Soweto teacher and

BC adherent at the time, "The white students seemed reluctant to really challenge the system . . . which we saw as a fear of their losing the advantages they had."[78]

Throughout the 1960s, as black enrollment in the segregated universities increased, so did the blacks' frustration with white-led student representation. The turning point came at the 1967 NUSAS conference in Grahamstown at which the black students were forced to stay in the segregated township while the white delegates were comfortably housed on the campus of Rhodes University. From that point on, plans for a separate black student organization grew quickly, receiving a surprising degree of support from the white leaders of NUSAS, who acknowledged the constraints of apartheid in their efforts to represent blacks as equals.[79] Indeed, until his death Steve Biko remained quietly friendly with a few of his former NUSAS colleagues, thereby testifying to his personal rejection of any ascriptive or reverse racism.

Discussion of a new black student organization reached a crescendo at the 1968 national meetings of NUSAS and the Student and University Christian movements. The latter, ostensibly religious, groups had been allowed to organize on black campuses, providing an opportunity for future BC adherents to meet.[80] Out of these discussions emerged an agreement to form the South African Students Organization (SASO), formally launched in 1969 as a separate black student group, with Steve Biko as its president.[81] By 1970, SASO had issued its Policy Manifesto, which declared:

> SASO is a Black student organization working for the liberation of the Black man first from psychological oppression by themselves through induced inferiority complex and secondly from physical oppression accruing out of living in white racist society. . . .
>
> SASO upholds the concept of Black Consciousness and the drive towards Black awareness as the most logical and significant means of ridding ourselves of the shackles that bind us to perpetual servitude.[82]

From its very start SASO saw itself as a vehicle for a set of values and assumed that upholding the concepts of Black Consciousness was "the most logical and significant means" of ending oppression.[83] Psychological liberation was both prior to and the most important means of achieving physical liberation; indeed, a more idealistic conception of social change is difficult to imagine.

SASO's idealism evidently appealed to its student audience, for the organization grew quickly in its first years. A subtle rise in rhetorical militancy and a broadening of concerns over the years also helped gain new adherents. By 1972, a less idealistic conception was just beginning to emerge, as implied in the view that "people more frequently act their way into a new way of thinking than [think] their way into a new way of acting."[84] According to Dr. Mamphela Ramphele, then a BC adherent, the pressures to move beyond student concerns was constant: "The foundation was initially laid in the student ranks but we became increasingly caught up in larger issues—theology, community development—we moved increasingly into the political sphere. We tried to lay the foundation for effective political action so that people could feel aggrieved and be energized by it."[85] As a result of such rising militancy, the authorities' initial lack of concern about BC was replaced with open hostility. As early as 1971, BC leaders were being banned from public speaking or meetings; by 1973 a BC leader had been jailed on a political charge; and by 1975 SASO was banned as an organization on all black university campuses. Although the movement did suffer from the various restrictions on many of its older leaders, such repression gave BC a boost of legitimacy in the eyes of many black youth, further swelling its ranks. By 1976, SASO's newsletter had between four thousand and six thousand subscribers, suggesting that its supporters had grown to at least that number.[86]

An event signaling the start of a trend away from a purely cultural or idealistic approach occurred at the University of the North's (Turfloop) graduation ceremony of 1972, when a speech was given by O. R. Tiro, a leader of the campus's SASO chapter. To his student audience—accompanied by startled parents and government officials who had assumed that the graduating students aspired to join the growing black middle class—Tiro asserted: "The price of freedom is blood, toil and tears. . . . History has taught us that a group in power has never voluntarily relinquished its position. It has always been forced to do so."[87] The state's response to this less idealistic and more confrontational view was swift and dramatic. Expelled from the university after his speech, Tiro was killed in 1974 in Botswana by a parcel bomb. His final posthumous contribution to the struggle was the opportunity that his funeral in Botswana provided for BC leaders to meet with exiled representatives of the ANC. At that meeting, a "division of labor between internal and external . . . and a mutual agreement not to obstruct each other" was informally agreed upon.[88]

With the graduation of a portion of its members each year, by 1972 SASO realized the need for an affiliated organization of BC adherents who had left school or had never been students. The BC movement could no longer restrict itself to its core constituency of the increasing but still relatively small population of black university students. The Black People's Convention (BPC) was thus founded in July of that year as a "political movement" with a set of aims more action oriented than those adopted by its parent body. SASO's "first" aim of psychological liberation was accordingly subtly demoted by BPC, with its stated goal "to unite and solidify the black people of South Africa with a view to mobilizing the masses toward their struggle for liberation and emancipation, both from psychological and physical liberation."[89]

The growth of the Black People's Convention, to more than forty branches and over three thousand members by the end of its first year, was even more spectacular than that of SASO.[90] Encouraged by its popularity, the BPC leadership called for protests in May 1972 and by 1973 had organized "pro-FRELIMO" rallies in support of Mozambican independence. When the coup in Portugal in April 1974 brought within reach a transition of power in Mozambique, BPC joined SASO in calling for victory celebrations, which were then halted by a month-long government ban. Twelve top officials from the two groups were charged, and nine were convicted for organizing these protests, robbing SASO and the newer BPC of essential leadership just when they most needed it. As a result, the movement had to fall back on unprepared leaders, unable or unwilling to shore up the organizational structure. Excitement had overreached caution.

The loss of the top BPC leadership in 1974 was a great problem because the remaining leaders were unable to resolve the divisions that were then emerging in BPC. In part, such divisions were inevitable in an organization that had purposely drawn in both newly politicized students and more seasoned advocates of the previous movements who were less willing to abide by BC's formal policy of nonalignment. Many of these signs of underlying tensions SASO had been able to avoid, but the BPC was unable to do so.

Even the standard BPC membership card was inscribed with a potential contradiction, declaring both "I shall always believe in the equality of all men" and "I shall at all times owe my undivided loyalty to my Black community."

Within a year after the arrest of its top leadership, the tensions in BPC became even more evident. At the December 1975 annual conference of BPC, ANC loyalists openly challenged its economic policy of communalism, and some of the older activists in BPC criticized student concerns about discrimination, arguing that the black working class, rather than the students, should form "the vanguard of the struggle."[91] At this meeting was the first open call for socialism. SASO struggled to contain these divisions within BPC, though the damage of disunity severely curtailed the further development of BPC.[92] By 1976, however, these divisions had exploded into a major ideological conflict, with broad implications for the BC movement as a whole, as discussed in the next chapter.

In 1972, before these divisions had become so obvious, BPC had cooperated with SASO in forming the Black Community Programmes (BCP) as an additional effort to spread BC beyond its original student base. The BCP was designed to provide small-scale services and, through these vehicles, to spread the message of BC to the less privileged who were desperate for solutions to their material problems. This activity was seen by BC leaders as consistent with their central focus on black self-image, with the services provided by BCP not intended to solve problems on a grand scale but, rather, to serve as pilot projects that would convince blacks that they could solve their problems on their own, without the aid of whites. As Ben Khoapa, the executive director of BCP for its first four years, observed, "Our focus was education, not to solve problems. The programs were purely demonstrative, illustrative. The major [criterion of success] was to what degree . . . it contribute[d] to self-awareness. . . . Our focus never changed—to conscientize people on self-help toward self-sufficiency."[93]

The establishment of the Black Community Programmes was an implicit acknowledgment by the movement's leadership of the limits of the BC ideology. Despite all their efforts to describe BCP as merely an illustration of BC ideas, the move beyond organizing with ideas alone implied that BC's central *raison d'être* of achieving change by altering values was insufficient. The provision of services was supposedly incidental to the confidence gained by having those services provided by blacks. Yet the very need to provide services to reach a broader community suggests a partial recognition that not everyone would be convinced or motivated by ideas alone to join an opposition group. The movement's "endless philosophizing" had to be complemented by action.[94] BC's internal focus on change through ideas had conflicted with the practical necessity of using material services to gain adherents and to convince them of BC's message.

For the same reason that BCP was recognized as necessary, it was also highly controversial within the movement. That is, there was considerable concern among BC leaders that the provision of services would be so successful in meeting immediate needs that the idea of psychological or any other form of liberation would be eclipsed. According to Lybon Mabasa, then a student adherent of BC, "SASO did not want to see suffering decline or repression become acceptable."[95] Even the ANC voiced its concern that BCP would detract from enthusiasm for resistance to white domination, implying some agreement with BC that the opposition then required an assertion of ideals more than it did concrete advances.[96] As odd as such comments seem in retrospect, they reveal an awareness that the Black Community Programmes' provision of material services was inconsistent with its ideological focus on shaping values. That such services were recognized by BC as necessary in order to spread its message and to attract a wider base of support suggested that the material motivations for political action could not be ignored, as BC had assumed. Although the movement was not ready to confront or resolve this fundamental issue, by continuing the BCP it was attempting to harness material services to its more idealistic aims.

Not only did BCP raise doubts about BC ideology, but it was also more consistent with an ANC tradition of using resources to build organization than with BC's basic focus on identity formation. Whereas other BC programs aimed at simply spreading ideas could operate with little external support, the BCP's provision of services required extensive funding not available in the black community itself. BCP therefore relied on raising funds from church organizations, such as the South African Council of Churches and its affiliated Christian Institute, and even from white business people, including supermarket mogul Raymond Ackerman and the giant Anglo-American Corporation.[97] As it did later for the UDF, such fund-raising implied some practical compromises and the avoidance of more radical rhetoric that might antagonize donors, for, as Ben Khoapa admitted, "We simply did not want to jeopardize what we had. We had gotten big and gave the impression of being careful."[98] In terms of ideology, this financial reliance contradicted BC's rhetorical assertion of black self-reliance and its dismissal of white support, as well as nascent calls for socialism.

Despite inconsistencies with its broader ideology and strategy, the BC movement could not practically afford to distance itself from the BCP, the one program that was able to attract substantial resources. Principled purity gave way to practical necessity. After the unrest in 1976, donations to BCP increased dramatically, with an annual budget of over R500,000 and assets worth more than R1 million by 1978.[99] By then, BCP had become "an obvious channel for money" to many of the affiliated BC groups, enabling them to purchase cars and to provide support for banned BC leaders.[100] BCP's ability to help bankroll the rest of the movement in this way spread the taint of practical compromise and muted many of the BCP's former critics and later beneficiaries. At the same time, the availability of funds did enable the BCP to support a variety of projects that helped spread BC's message, even if these projects could not make a significant impact on the material conditions of life for the majority of impoverished South Africans.

The Black Community Programmes were not the only BC affiliate that implicitly raised questions about the movement's ideological focus on changing values. Prompted by its rhetorical commitment to a working-class vanguard, in 1972 the BPC launched the Black Allied Workers Union (BAWU) in order to bring workers into the BC fold.[101] Students in SASO responded to this initiative with some skepticism that uneducated workers would be receptive to the abstract ideas of Black Consciousness, nor did they appreciate BAWU's explicit focus on class over race and its anticapitalist implications.[102] Indeed, they regarded the workers' organization as inconsistent with the BC movement's rejection of class analysis and with specific efforts to attract black entrepreneurs into BC and to encourage black self-reliance in business through "Buy Black" campaigns.[103] But SASO also understood that the workers represented a large potential constituency for BC and on those grounds was willing to accommodate BAWU, and it even made its own half-hearted attempt to form a Black Workers Project.[104]

Much as the Black Community Projects had set out to provide pilot projects rather than direct services, BAWU's efforts to organize workers remained more symbolic than substantive. Whereas class analysis implied organizing workers to confront their employers and the state, BAWU was avowedly nonconfrontational and became directly involved in only one of the hundreds of strikes held between 1972 and 1976.[105] Wage demands, generally the unions' basic "bread and butter" issue, were largely ignored. Instead, BAWU concentrated on trying "to get rid of mental inferiority with an emphasis on seminars . . . and education on rights," which was more consistent with the BC movement's focus.[106] The difficulty was not that workers did not understand this approach, as some in SASO had feared, but, rather, that BAWU failed to help workers address their more urgent material interests.[107] As a result of this ideologically inspired constraint, as well as its lack of experience in organizing workers, BAWU never succeeded in gaining more than one thousand dues-paying members.[108]

The extent to which the Black Consciousness movement's failure to organize workers can be attributed to its own ideological limitations becomes clearer in the context of the major wildcat strikes staged in Durban in 1973. Prompted by media reports of the need to increase the absurdly low wages paid by the highly concentrated textile industry in the area and by a speech by Zulu King Goodwill, the strike started in a single factory. Police repression and media coverage further inflamed the workers, causing the strike to spread in only a few weeks to thirty thousand workers. But in these events, the BC movement was most remarkable for its absence. The strikers were evidently more influenced by Zulu leaders who acknowledged the workers' material aspirations than by BC abstractions.[109] An assessment at the time concluded that BC "organizationally is undoubtedly still middle class and . . . inactive in Durban" but that the concept of BC "was one element in the increasing black political consciousness that preceded the strikes."[110] In retrospect, BC adherents have claimed more direct responsibility for the Durban strikes, pointing out that Durban was the headquarters for SASO and BAWU, but there remains little evidence for such claims other than the banning of Biko and seven others less than a month later.[111] By arguing that the strike "happened because of its own circumstances, but these were translated in a way by BC, which put out the ideas," BC adherent Peter Jones implicitly admitted that material conditions were conducive to worker organization and that BC intentionally remained abstract and distant in its involvement with the striking workers.[112]

This review of the major organizational components of the BC movement reveals how the basic conceptual themes of Black Consciousness were played out in practical terms. The emphasis on values and education to achieve a positive racial identity hit a responsive chord among university students, who formed the core of a new generation of activists in South Africa. Their target of ending acceptance of ascribed black inferiority played an essential role in reviving the spirit of resistance in the country and in unifying and reducing the fear within the black community. The movement's activities in the 1970s attest to its success in questioning the psychology of submission and in creating a receptive base of support on which all subsequent efforts at opposition could build. Even though another movement, with a different ideological and strategic focus, might have had equal success, there were no other opposition tendencies as active in South Africa to revive black resistance in the wake of a decade of repression.

For all of its success, formal Black Consciousness activities were also restricted by the self-imposed limits inherent in its ideological focus on racial assertiveness. In fact, the movement's emphasis on such ideational concerns and suspicion of more practical efforts helps explain BC's shortcomings in providing community services for material benefits and the limited appeal of BC unions to workers concerned with wages and benefits. For those constituencies less swayed by ideas, BC limited itself by its extreme emphasis on idealistic forms of exhortation, as indicated by the movement's reliance on its core constituency of students.[113] As Smangaliso Mkhatshwa, a BC adherent at the time, pointed out, the movement "only reached the educated and sophisticated segment of the population. . . . Black people demanded more praxis than theoria."[114]

As much as its ideology proved important to the BC movement's strengths and weaknesses, opposition activities in the early to mid-1970s cannot be explained by reference only to BC's intentions. The movement's concentration on ideas about race was not just the outcome of abstract considerations but also reflected the lack of resources and popular will necessary for a more direct and physical form of confrontation. BC's activities helped redress these deficiencies for the efforts at opposition that followed. Nor should the BC movement's relative lack of concern for more material forms of organization lead us to overlook the unprecedented, albeit small, organizational structures that BC instituted to help spread its message of racial assertiveness. The movement did hold regular meetings, keep extensive records, publish regular newsletters, recruit new members and leaders, and enforce a degree of procedural formality, despite the state's expanding efforts to disrupt such processes. These achievements were substantial, though such material advances might have gone even further had the BC movement focused more on this realm of activity rather than targeting so exclusively a change in the realm of ideas.

Had BC been more willing to compromise some of its self-proclaimed purity and theoretical cohesion and had it become more involved in material issues, it might have continued to grow and organize beyond its initially elitist constituency. It might also have been more successful at addressing the concerns of some of its internal critics, who wanted a greater provision of services and use of class analysis to help build the movement's membership among those adults and workers who were primarily concerned with their material conditions. But by 1975, BC's wavering over revisions of its relatively exclusive focus on ideas was already beginning to be overrun by changes in material conditions.

## Anger and Explosion

Although Black Consciousness concentrated on shaping ideas, those ideas alone cannot explain the allegiance or the behavior of those who acted under its banner. During the early 1970s, the development of the Black Consciousness movement had been coterminous with an expansion of the South African economy and the number of black university students and professionals. The BC movement made only halfhearted efforts to reach beyond its elite audience, but the movement's reputation grew among less privileged blacks, albeit less as a result of organized BC activities than because of the popularity it enjoyed as the only active internal group. When a wider array of the oppressed were roused by changing material conditions to join the opposition, the mood and language of Black Consciousness proved to be more pervasive than the breadth of formal BC affiliation had suggested. At least among urban youth, the days of bowing and scraping were long gone, with the positive self-identity consistent with BC expressed as an angry desire to tear down rather than to build up.

By the mid-1970s, more than fifteen years of South African economic boom had begun to bust, changing the conditions in which BC had developed. Most significantly, the South African economy had begun to suffer from the structural constraints posed by apartheid, with its requirements of duplicated administration, additional military and police expenditures, restrictions on the growth of domestic markets and skilled labor among blacks, and inefficient investment to offset the oil and arms embargoes. These burdens were exacerbated at the end of 1974 by the recession triggered in the West by the oil shocks of 1973. Unemployment doubled in the year before the 1976 uprising. In the manufacturing sector, in which an average of 2,850 new jobs had been filled by Africans each month throughout 1974, fewer than half as many new jobs were created in the subsequent eighteen months.[115]

The effect of this economic downturn on the black population was dramatic, and as usual, the poor suffered the most in the downswing. In 1975, the officially measured "cost of living" for a family of five in Soweto increased by 10 to 12 percent. The price of corn meal and cooking oil, diet staples on which the African poor spend a disproportionately large share of their income, jumped by 18 percent in April 1976 alone. At the same time that prices were rising, the prospects for employment among the growing number of black school dropouts were plummeting. Unemployment among blacks was estimated to be increasing by three thousand each month in 1975, and by considerably higher levels in the first months of 1976.[116]

The political consequences of these changes in economic conditions have been heavily debated. The rise in black wages slowed only after the uprising of June 1976, leading John Kane-Berman to question how directly the declining economic conditions had affected the political unrest. But as Brooks and Brickhill maintained, even if economic distress were not the precise cause of the final explosion, the general worsening of economic conditions certainly was a significant factor contributing to popular unrest.[117] A poll of Africans in six urban areas showed that the number who felt "worse off" in 1975, compared with 1973, had grown from 18 to 41 percent, and those feeling "better off" had fallen from 42 to 20 percent. In 1973 one third of those polled had predicted improvement in race relations, but by 1975, 84 percent saw no such improvement as likely.[118] The undercurrents for the first wave of revolt in over fifteen years were strengthening.

The economic downturn in South Africa in the mid-1970s was experienced not only through a direct impact on employment or the cost of living but also indirectly as a decline in general living conditions. Many more people had been attracted to the cities by the economic growth of previous years than could have been absorbed even if the growth had continued, and those who arrived after the recession were increasingly unable to find jobs or amenities, by then scarce. The African population in the ten largest urban centers doubled from 1971 to 1975, but the housing stock grew by only 15 percent in the same period. By 1975, each house in Soweto had an average of seventeen inhabitants, and the vast majority of these houses had no toilet, running water, or attached ceilings.[119] Those who could find no room in these houses built their own adjacent shacks, thereby ending the concept of backyards and privacy. Much of the resulting tension was vented at first on fellow township dwellers, with violent crime in Soweto increasing by 100 percent between June 1974 and June 1975.[120]

The urban population explosion had a particularly strong impact on the township youth. African secondary school enrollment across the country had increased by 160 percent in the five years after 1970, reaching 318,568 in 1975, with much of this student population concentrated in the severely overcrowded urban schools.[121] In the year before the uprising, half of Soweto's population was under twenty-five years old, and there were over sixteen thousand families for every high school, as compared with thirteen hundred families per high school in white Johannesburg. At Morris Isaacson High School, which was a center of the later uprising, there were more than seventy students in each classroom.[122] Squeezed into the schools and with increasingly bleak prospects for employment, the students grew angry, both at the whites they saw as oppressors and at their own parents for not challenging that oppression for fifteen years.[123]

Added to the tinder of urban growth, economic dislocation, and youth anger was the growing insecurity posed by the government's ongoing attempts to counteract black urbanization. From 1960 to 1970, over 327,000 urban families had been forcibly removed by the state to the rural homelands, and by 1972 another 171,000 families were scheduled for removal in the next few years.[124] By 1978 a staggering total of 3 million people had been forced into the homelands. Urban dwellers knew that their removal to the rural areas from which many had recently fled meant both extreme economic deprivation and the likely breakup of their families.[125] Even those who escaped actual removal were not free from the harassment associated with controls on urbanization, with one out of four adult Africans having been arrested at least once by the mid-1970s for violations of "influx control."[126] As a result of these regulations, "no average black man [could] ever at any moment be absolutely sure that he is not breaking a law," further undermining respect for white laws that seemed to imply that in South Africa it was illegal simply to be black.[127] As a result, for blacks who had come to the urban areas, any economic gain won or hoped for was under the real threat of being lost at the whim of the apartheid authorities. This threat significantly inflamed an already deprived black urban populace.

All of these pressures combined to form a large population of urbanized blacks whose entry into the middle class had been frustrated and whose future prospects looked dim. A small but significant number had been successful, with the proportion of Africans designated as middle class by one estimate having grown from 8.66 percent in 1969 to 12.82 percent ten years later.[128] But their children or those who had come to the cities too late to have prospered before 1975 increasingly saw themselves as locked out of the middle class, and they thus became even more bitter and militant. By 1976, a poll in Durban found 26 percent of fifteen- to twenty-year-olds openly advocated violence to end apartheid, despite the risks of state reprisal. As an indication of the widening generational divide, only 10 percent of forty-one- to forty-five-year-olds agreed with the need to resort to violence.[129]

By late 1975 and early 1976 several other factors were added to the level of anger and militancy already developing in the townships. Both the South African Defence Forces' setbacks in Angola and the victory of FRELIMO in Mozambique contributed to a sense among more educated blacks of the South African regime's vulnerability.[130] According to BC leader Ben Khoapa, "We thought, if [FRELIMO] can do it, so can we; it just needs another push. There was a high level of optimism."[131] In addition, the economic recession generated a degree of indecisiveness on the part of the state, no longer able to meet the needs of business and those of black and white workers all at once.[132] Whites, who had benefited disproportionately from economic growth through wage increases at a higher rate than those given to blacks, were particularly unwilling to accept a reduction in those benefits and, of course, could use their votes to ensure that the state protected their interests during the recession.[133] Meanwhile, the black unions had been increasingly harassed in the years following the Durban strike in 1973. All of these pressures—building on the recession and overcrowding in the townships and the schools—prompted Bishop Desmond Tutu to write to Prime Minister B. J. Vorster only five weeks before the uprising: "I have a growing nightmarish fear that unless something drastic is done very soon then bloodshed and violence are going to happen in South Africa almost inevitably. A people can take only so much and no more. . . . A people made desperate by despair and injustice and oppression will use desperate means."[134]

Consistent with BC's emphasis on values and racial assertiveness, grievances were formulated at the time in terms of discrimination in educational policy or the inspiration of FRELIMO's victory, rather than being based on the more material terms of the economic downturn. It is a tribute to the pervasiveness of the BC frame of reference that even in the wake of the most significant economic recession in more than fifteen years, the popular consciousness remained fixed on racial rather than economic issues. But as much as the BC ideology was reflected in how people interpreted their situation, the worsening material conditions heightened the mass anger expressed in the readily available terms of Black Consciousness. The idea of racial assertiveness and the experience of material deprivation came together in a combustible combination, with the flames of BC ideology spread by the fuel of apartheid and exploitation that had built up with seeming disregard for the risk of fire.

As much as the widespread anger of the mid-1970s was expressed in the language of BC, that language was also reinterpreted in the process. The fine points of BC ideology remained the domain of the intellectual elite while the masses embraced the movement's rhetoric in its spontaneous and emotionally appealing guise, as a form of angry self-assertion. As Ben Khoapa explained, "By 1975, the youth had grown up in BC in a conceptual sense but without leadership. After the 1974 Pro-FRELIMO arrests, even the second tier of BC leadership was taken. The youngsters were then very angry and began to formulate their own description of what BC was."[135] The ideology of BC was boiled down by these angry youngsters to an emotional core identified by the students as Black Consciousness, even though it only vaguely resembled the set of complex ideas that had been elaborated by the movement's leaders. The leaders' subtle description of whites as historical oppressors who could be included in a postliberation South Africa was largely drowned out by the denunciations of whites as ascriptively distinct enemies who would remain "dogs until they died."[136] A student living in Tembisa recalled how "in 1976, Soweto students . . . used emotional images, describing the clenched fist salute as crushing the white of our palms. They said white coffee is weaker than black."[137] For the youth in the township, such emotionalism was itself Black Consciousness, as it articulated their pent-up anger in the only idiom of opposition then widely used in the country.

Rather than distancing themselves from the youths' emotional interpretation of BC ideology, the movement's leaders embraced these expressions of anger as an indication of their success in inspiring blacks to assert themselves more openly. Biko's contention that BC had "much more following than it has got members in the country" was effectively verified by the widespread adoption of BC rhetoric, which had become familiar from years of informal discussion and publicity.[138] That youth were proclaiming their Black Consciousness without formal affiliation with the movement and with little training in the fine points of BC ideology was perfectly consistent with the movement's own focus more on spreading ideas than on formal organization. The implication that

BC was an "effective conscientizing agent, but not an effective mobilizer" did not trouble the movement's leaders, who had always argued that mobilization would be a natural outcome of the dissemination of their ideas.[139] Instead, they applauded the transition of BC from "being an intellectual exercise for SASO, to a program of action for the youth of 1976."[140] The movement's leaders were pleased that their message had been heard and, as described by one Soweto worker looking back on this period, that "everyone [had come to] understand that being black doesn't mean we are inferior."[141]

Although the spreading use of BC rhetoric did not arise out of a corresponding breadth of formal organization, the limited structures of the BC movement did provide the only effective forms of organization then available to the township youth. But rather than working through one of the major BC affiliates, these youth began to coordinate their efforts through the South African Student Movement (SASM), a small BC affiliate concentrated in three Soweto high schools and in the eastern Cape. SASM's initial militancy was evident in its rejection of some of the BC procedures, such as the careful keeping of minutes, which the youth believed was inappropriate to a covert opposition. Early in 1976, this small group became involved in resisting the new policy of having mathematics taught in Afrikaans, which they saw as an effort to reinforce inferiority among blacks, many of whom were ill prepared and unwilling to use this "language of the oppressor." That this issue became the spark for a major uprising is further evidence of the influence of BC, which had inspired resistance to just such efforts by the state to impose debilitating foreign ideas and culture on the black students. On June 8, 1976, two policemen attempting to arrest the secretary of SASM at his school were beaten off by students. On June 13, the students met to plan demonstrations, calling themselves the Soweto Students Representative Council. A first protest was set for June 16, and in perhaps the single most impressive organizational feat associated with BC, they gave the demonstrators at twelve assembly points exact departure times to ensure that all the groups would converge in secrecy.[142] There was no theoretical debate. The plan worked.

The Soweto students did receive some organizational support from the better-established and well-funded BC organizations, particularly after the June 16 march had elicited a violent reaction from the police. As BC leader Peter Jones tells it:

> In 1975 we had a secret program to protest the independence of the Transkei [homeland]. . . . We wanted a massive demonstration and were getting ready. We were stockpiling A4 [copy] paper.
>
> By 1976 the economy was really deteriorating. We knew every township was a bomb waiting for a light.
>
> The June 16th demo caught us off guard. It was led by SASM, which the police saw as the most impatient and least intimidated [of our groups]. It wasn't part of our plan but the BC structures rose to the occasion. No other structures existed.[143]

It is ironic and revealing of BC's limited capacity for mass mobilization that its one planned demonstration, against Transkein independence, was overrun by the actions of one of its own affiliates. It is also telling of BC's priorities that in preparation for a mass action, it stockpiled paper for leaflets rather than establishing clear lines of internal authority. That is, even as it was moving beyond its elitist roots, BC's intellectual origins remained evident. Having long engaged in a battle of ideas, the movement suddenly found itself engaged in open conflict with the state.

The absence of a more coherent organizational involvement by BC in the events of June 1976 has enabled other groups, most prominently the ANC, to claim that they had clandestinely filled this gap. According to an aging Alexandria resident, Martin Ramokjadi, the ANC's chief internal organizer at the time, "We came off of Robben Island from 1974 through 1977 and we worked with the youth. We organized the uprising. We were strong underground and didn't want anyone to know. . . . We would just call in two youths at a time and teach them and they would spread out. It was like pouring petrol on fire."[144] This claim that the ANC "organized the uprising" exaggerates the influence of a few ANC cadres, who were not always aware at the time of one another's identities or activities. Had the ANC been stronger inside the country at the time, it surely would have employed the services of younger cadres who had closer links to students in the townships.[145] Instead, the ANC reemerged as an active internal force only after many of the youths active in the uprising had fled the country in the wake of the repression and had joined the ANC. Students at the time certainly followed the news about the ANC, met in small groups with older ANC cadres, and in a few instances were actually members of the exiled organization.[146] But most of the activists in 1976 had no contact with the ANC or believed the exiled group then to be effectively "extinct internally," and certainly Black Consciousness ideals were more popular than was the ideal of nonracialism associated with the ANC.[147] Ironically, the ANC itself implicitly acknowledged its own lack of direct influence at the time by its later attempts to describe the BC movement as one of its subsidiaries.[148] Claims of greater direct ANC involvement in the uprising, endorsed by various analysts, are largely based on a strong dose of retrospective wishful thinking or a pro-ANC bias, just as claims of more direct organizational responsibility by BC also have little grounding.[149]

Adherents of both BC and the ANC have a substantial interest in claiming responsibility for the events of June 16 and the unrest that followed, for these were the most dramatic instances of mass political resistance in South Africa in fifteen years. The original aim of the protest against the imposition of Afrikaans as a medium of instruction was quickly eclipsed by the unexpectedly harsh response of the police to that protest and by the popular reaction to the police brutality. Not only were at least twenty-five students killed when their march was met with an armed response, but workers returning home at the end of the day also were attacked by police without provocation. And unlike the enforced submission that followed the killing of sixty-nine persons in Sharpeville in 1960, the casualties of June 16, 1976, were only the start of a violent conflict, exacerbated by discontent over material conditions and assertiveness encouraged by BC rhetoric, which could not be quieted so easily. Within twenty-four hours, anger over the police brutality had sparked protests in townships across the Transvaal and beyond.[150] Six days after the initial uprising, one hundred thirty people were officially listed as having been killed.[151]

The events in Soweto on June 16, 1976, elicited an immediate and spontaneous response in other townships, but shortly thereafter considerable disagreement over further actions divided the broader black community, which had largely been taken by surprise by the rapid turn of events. Once school was disrupted by the protests, student groups lost their primary locus for organization, which suddenly had to be orchestrated more clandestinely. In some cases it took months before the urban areas outside Johannesburg received from participants a direct report of events in Soweto. The physical isolation of black university students on their campuses further hindered their efforts to reach out to other constituencies. And the BC movement's failure to consolidate support through its community projects or among workers provided no effective channels for orchestrating activities outside the schools and universities. Unilateral student efforts to call a protest "stayaway" by Soweto workers in early August went largely unheeded. During a second more widely observed "stayaway" later in August, migrant Zulu workers at Mzimhlope Hostel, angered at the disruption of their work and allegedly encouraged by the police, attacked the protestors. Seventy were killed.[152]

Continued police repression, anger, and grief did unite the black community, despite the initial difficulties and the lack of a more effective organization. The Black Parents Association was formed under the chairmanship of Bishop Manas Buthelezi to coordinate the response to the uprising and to act as an advocate for the students. By mid-October, hundreds of teachers in Soweto had resigned in protest, expressing their support for the students. Taxi drivers and undertakers volunteered their services. Stayaway calls were given increasing support after students learned to discuss them in advance with workers rather than try to force their adherence at the last moment. Even the migrant workers living in the hostels cooperated, though in later years these same hostels had become bastions of Inkatha conservatism. By September, protest and strike activities were being coordinated between Johannesburg and Cape Town. As described by Peter Jones, "The Coloureds in Cape Town responded after Soweto in what was the first time we had that sort of community response here in the Cape."[153] Before they were quelled by continued repression, protests had been staged in townships throughout South Africa, and a quarter-million students had boycotted classes, leaving one thousand dead and twenty-one thousand prosecuted for related offenses by September 1977.[154] In retrospect, the shootings by police had provided "a very useful weapon in merging the young and old," with the resulting unrest having proved that countrywide unity was possible.[155]

The one major exception to the unity achieved after the start of the 1976 uprising was the relative quiet among the mass of the less educated, older poor people living in the rural areas. There were incidents in such areas, but nothing like the urban areas where overcrowding and unmet expectations of material advancement had created conditions that helped spread anger and protest.[156] The lack of rural protests suggests that the message of BC had not spread fully beyond the urban centers and universities. It is also possible that rural people were confused by the "parroting of BC" by homeland leaders seeking to present themselves as advocates of change while enforcing continued submission.[157]

There can be no doubt that the 1976 uprising indicated the spread throughout the urban areas of the ideas and sentiments associated with BC, even if the uprising was not formally organized by the movement. Like the ANC Youth League before it, BC set out to end black submissiveness rather than to challenge the established power directly. Soweto 1976 demonstrated that BC's aim had by then been achieved to a greater extent than ever before, at a time when the ANC and no other opposition group could credibly claim to have been equally influential in the country. ANC partisans have remained quick to dismiss BC as "concerned only with intellectual ideas, incapable of moving the minds of people on the ground or of affecting the masses."[158] But such views were eloquently rebutted by Steve Biko in his response to a request for evidence of support for BC: "In one word—Soweto. The boldness, dedication, sense of purpose, and clarity of analysis of the situation—all of these are a direct result of BC ideas among the young. This is not quantifiably analyzable, for the power of a movement lies in the fact that it can indeed change the habits of people. This change is not the result of force but of dedication, of moral persuasion."[159]

Biko's assessment of Soweto as an indication of BC's influence rings true, although it also demonstrates that the movement continued to concentrate on the power of its ideas, even after the state had used force to crush those ideas and the protests they encouraged. Others looking to the movement for material assistance were less sanguine about BC's continued emphasis on ideas; for instance, one group in Cape Town suggested that "the people were waiting for us to direct the course of events. . . . Our policy was to stay put, watch, [and] analyze."[160] Evidently the movement's focus on ideas was too ingrained to adjust—or even to see the need to adjust—to new circumstances requiring a more active and less abstract response.

As much as BC's idea of racial assertiveness was a significant component of the events of 1976, ideas alone cannot account for the massive unrest and anger expressed by many more than had been formally affiliated with the movement. It was only when the economy pinched that BC's message was taken up more broadly and submissiveness faded. According to Peter Jones, "Once BC expressed the people's concerns, these were linked to the material conditions from which they came."[161] The framework of BC ideology was filled out and given substance only when the rising anger and mobilization of a people were aroused not just by inspiring words but also by the experience of worsening deprivation and state force. Ideas had proven consequential for both the earlier formal activities of the BC movement and the less carefully orchestrated unrest they inspired. But it was only when those ideas were combined with specific material conditions that the message of BC was widely embraced. A new generation of activists had taken up the struggle, though still unarmed in the face of the state's unleashed force. The early days of polite petitions to the government were clearly long gone.

The 1976 uprising indicates the influence of the Black Consciousness movement, but this uprising did not set off a revolution, in part because of the weaknesses of the movement itself. Unrest was the result of both ideas and material conditions, but within the movement the focus remained on ideas. If the movement had developed a more extensive organizational network, perhaps the momentum of unrest could have been maintained for longer, as it was in the mid-1980s despite vigorous state repression. Of course, such a counterfactual possibility cannot be proved. We do know that the BC movement was not well suited to move from inspiring an end of psychological submission to orchestrating a physical struggle for liberation, having long eschewed the forms of organization necessary for the latter. Other than scattered student groups, no local organizations had been established that could maintain discipline and oppositional momentum once state repression was heightened. Links with the workers had not been solidified by BC, and the workers themselves were not yet organized enough or otherwise ready to confront the state. Nor did the BC movement, particularly as it was expressed by the youth, present a concrete program for a transfer of power. In the words of the ANC cadre most active at the time in trying to channel the anger of the youth, "Hatred is powerful for mobilization but in the longer run it doesn't work. It leads no where."[162] As a partial result of these shortcomings, the uprising that began in anger in 1976 had been largely exhausted by 1977.

The failure of the 1976 uprising to precipitate a transfer of power cannot be attributed to the weaknesses of the BC movement by itself, as it also reflects the strength of the state's ability to hold onto power. Neither the loss of popular submission nor the defeats in neighboring countries had undermined the basic military might of South Africa's police and defense forces, with the latter held in reserve through much of the uprising. The state's repressive forces made the most of the movement's vulnerabilities, disrupting the dissemination of ideas or efforts to expand the movement's organizational capacity, by banning seminal writings and jailing or killing BC leaders. Although liberation "was no longer blocked by the mental and psychological enslavement of the masses; it was blocked by the open repressiveness of the white state," which the BC movement had never directly challenged or sought to weaken.[163]

Much as the 1976 uprising reflected the important impact of the BC movement, it was also a watershed of opposition politics and the beginning of a decline in the mass influence of the BC movement. Economic distress and repression ended any false hopes that racial assertiveness, no matter how extreme, could undermine the continued oppression. As at Sharpeville and in its aftermath, the state revealed the coercive apparatus that lay beneath its efforts at cooptation. But once the state had revealed its iron fist, the need for an active opposition to counter the state became all the more apparent. BC, with its emphasis on changing values and its ambivalence toward more material concerns or forms of organization, was simply not suited to this new task. Its ideas did not provide sufficient cover once the bullets started flying. For the Black Consciousness movement, the greatest signal of its success was also a signal of its limits. A new form of opposition would have to emerge—building on the achievements and avoiding the weaknesses that had become apparent—for the South African struggle to develop further.

# 3

## *After the Uprising: Division and Realignment, 1977–1979*

Black Consciousness emerged out of the undercurrents of resistance severely repressed in the 1960s, founded by a new generation of student activists as a movement to reinvigorate popular internal opposition. BC challenged the negative self-image of blacks imposed by apartheid, substituting an assertively positive racial identity aimed at inspiring, if not fully organizing, unity among all blacks opposed to white rule. When the costs of apartheid and recession in the mid-1970s brought to an abrupt halt more than fifteen years of South African economic growth, this popular resentment deepened and spread, as expressed in the only terms then current in the townships, Black Consciousness. The Soweto uprising of 1976, sparked by the rejection of state educational policies implying black inferiority, reflected the ideals and strategy of BC with which blacks had come to identify. Just as BC had emphasized the reawakening of a positive identity over organizing for material benefits, the 1976 uprising was an emotional assertion of anger more than an organized protest for any specific gain.

The anger of 1976 was soon replaced by grief and dismay as the state moved in to crush the revolt. In the wake of the strongest show of state force in more than a decade, BC leaders and their followers began a process of reconsideration. All agreed that BC's goal of redefining racial identity had been largely achieved, with the prevalence of a more positive self-image evident in the assertive popular militancy in the urban areas. Many came to believe that a continued focus on reshaping identity would not by itself constitute a sufficient response to violent repression. Some of the BC adherents still at liberty revived fairly quickly the BC movement in a new organizational form, as the Azanian Peoples Organization (AZAPO), arguing that the need to move beyond racial assertiveness could be incorporated in the tradition of Black Consciousness. Others pursued ideas and strategies that had begun to be debated within BC before the uprising, setting them apart from the BC movement and moving them closer to the tradition of the exiled African National Congress.

Ideological debate that had begun earlier within BC on the use of racial versus class identity as the central focus of opposition had been pushed aside by the events of 1976. But this debate resumed with greater intensity as soon as the 1976 uprising was exhausted and the immediate issues of survival gave way to longer-term strategic considerations. Those who would soon consolidate their position as Charterists argued that BC's focus on race was no longer appropriate and tentatively proposed the use of class in its place. With their adoption of Marxist terminology, this group hoped to win the support of a populace further radicalized by state repression, overcoming BC's failure at organizing beyond student ranks during the early 1970s. Although their use of class analysis helped discredit an exclusive emphasis on race and justify a move toward more concern with action, their Marxism proved to be largely rhetorical. The new movement was neither led by the working class nor mainly concerned with economic exploitation. Instead, it was led by many of the same students and young activists who had been involved with BC, turning their energies from asserting their racial identity to fighting repression and domination. Their class rhetoric loosened the grip of an exclusive focus on racial identity, allowing the movement to be broadened to an inclusive South African nation, united in its opposition to apartheid. This concept of a united South African nation, based more on a strategic assessment of how to mobilize broader resistance than on an idealistic goal of reshaping ideas, became the goal of the opposition in the 1980s. The impact of this transition, however, became apparent only after a realignment of loyalties had been consolidated.

## Debates and Transitions Within Black Consciousness

By 1975 the BC movement had extended its influence beyond its elite core of student members. As the only major opposition group then active in South Africa, BC had succeeded in shaping the language, debates, and ideas of urbanized blacks throughout the country. Although the movement was unable to translate this influence into broad organizational membership, this shortcoming did not greatly curtail the dispersion of Black Consciousness ideas and was consistent with the movement's own idealistic approach. Popular assertions of a positive racial identity and psychological resistance to continued oppression indicated that the message of Black Consciousness had been heard beyond the movement's formal ranks and that an idealistic approach to opposition had borne fruit. When the students and later their parents took to the streets in 1976, Black Consciousness provided the basic rhetoric and a minimal organizational network. Associated in this way with the most significant episode of mass resistance in over a decade, the popular appeal of BC was unchallenged. Yet the first cracks of division and criticism within the movement had already begun to show.

In part, the ideological tensions that had been present in BC before the 1976 uprising reflected differences in the experience and interests of the movement's student and older members. These constituencies had much in common, particularly as compared with the workers and others outside the movement's formal ranks, but this relative homogeneity did not erase their remaining differences, which were reinforced by organizational structures. The movement's continually changing student membership was concentrated in the South African Students Organization (SASO), whereas a relatively stable group of older adherents were concentrated in the Black Peoples Convention (BPC), which had been formed precisely for the purpose of expanding beyond student ranks. The students in SASO "were by their very nature more adventurous, analytic, more interested in reading, open-minded and less arrested in their thinking, if only because there are constantly new faces."[1] Those in BPC were "more mature, established, in touch with funders and had more at stake, in some cases having jobs in the BCP."[2]

Aubrey Mokoena, formerly of SASO and later an official of the UDF, suggested that the disagreement between the leaders of these two major BC constituent groups in 1975 was an early indication of how the movement would split after 1976: "Leaders of the UDF now were in SASO then, and leaders of AZAPO now were from the BPC."[3] Mokoena's analysis is contradicted, however, by the many former SASO members who remained BC adherents when they became leaders of AZAPO, and by BPC members who later abandoned BC doctrine to join the UDF, suggesting that political loyalties in the 1980s were the result of more complex interactions of experience and influence. But even if such subsequent loyalties cannot be attributed to earlier organizational affiliations among students and nonstudents, the debates in BC in 1975 did prefigure those differences that later divided the movement.

Early disagreements in BC were raised most publicly, if not for the first time, by Diliza Mji, president of SASO in 1975. Mji's father, president of the Transvaal ANC Youth League in the 1950s, had himself created considerable controversy as an early advocate of class analysis, establishing a family tradition of sorts maintained by his son.[4] In retrospect, some BC stalwarts have argued that the younger Mji's family allegiance to the ANC was well known and that he had simply waited until he was in a powerful position and BC had grown in prominence to try either to divide BC or to move it toward the ANC by urging the use of class analysis, much as his father had done. Diliza Mji counters that his interest in issues of class was not preordained but instead was the result of his own readings at the time in the Marxist/Leninist tradition, popular discussion of FRELIMO's nonracial position in Mozambique, and observation of the 1973 strikes in his hometown of Durban, which had raised "certain questions we could not answer" within a BC framework.[5] Only in 1975 was Mji prepared to go public with his concerns.

Mji launched a rhetorical attack on BC's exclusive focus on race at SASO's eighth General Student Council, held in Mafeking in early 1976, before the uprising. In his presidential address to this meeting, Mji pressed for

> the need . . . to look at our struggle not only in terms of color interests but also in terms of class. . . . Apartheid as an exploitative system is part of a bigger whole, capitalism.
>
> Having taken into account the socio-economic factors affecting any person involved in a struggle for change, then it is logical to

> expect that group action is more effective than individual actions. Group action means organization of the people having common values and aspirations. We are aware that times have changed, therefore having a greater need to be more organized than before.[6]

Mji went on to describe black homeland leaders as "counterrevolutionaries" and to warn against basing an opposition movement on the leadership of his elite audience of black students who "will not want to change the system because of your own class interests."[7] With these remarks, Mji directly contradicted BC's basic assumption of unity among all blacks as victims of oppression. He contended instead that blacks had diverse interests and that the opposition should embrace those with common values of resistance, a view later embraced by the UDF. That this critique came from the president of SASO—the first BC organization and the central organ of the movement's core student constituency—made it all the more startling. Mji proposed the use of class as a new conceptual and practical base for opposition, not because the economic status of the movement's constituents had changed, but in order to reduce the preoccupation with shaping racial identity and to encourage active mass organization.

Mji's proposal for grafting class analysis onto BC ideology was met with a muted response, suggesting some receptivity to the idea. Although Biko himself had ridiculed class analysis back in 1971, five years later his primary concern about adopting class analysis was apparently more strategic than ideological. Mji reports that after his speech, "Steve asked to see us. He expressed his disquiet, arguing that 'we are not ready' to confront the anti-communist sentiment and that 'Durban is red.' But we just wanted to add another tool of analysis. Race criteria [are] not enough."[8] Despite these reservations, the experience of the Durban strikes in 1973 had convinced Biko and other leaders of the movement that Black Consciousness should incorporate aspects of class analysis and work more closely with the newly formed unions. But the banning orders imposed on Biko and other BC leaders prevented them from entering into an open debate through which a coherent ideology based on both race and class could be formulated. Without such a discussion, Biko was concerned that simply adopting class rhetoric would confuse many followers and invite greater state repression, for which the movement was not prepared. As explained by Pandelani Nefolovhodwe, Mji's predecessor as president of SASO and later a leading BC unionist, "BC debated how explicit to be about class and decided not to confront the system at that stage, until after the masses were more fully conscientized in a struggle. You don't jump just to appear Marxist since if you jump too early you won't have everyone with you."[9] Only after the 1976 uprising were a greater number of BC adherents convinced that the masses were prepared for the "jump" to incorporation of class analysis.

Whether and how to incorporate class analysis and worker organization into the movement were the most prominent but not the only issues debated in BC in the years leading up to 1976. BC's exclusion of whites from the preliberation struggle and its emphasis on black unity were also being questioned. The movement's leaders were confronted by the reality of homeland officials and other black state functionaries whose alliance with the oppressive authorities could not be ignored. Although these collaborators were dismissed by BC theorists as "nonwhites" rather than blacks, this distinction could not hide the contradiction with popular conceptions of black solidarity associated with skin color. Nor could exclusive black solidarity be easily reconciled with the small number of whites who, like the clergyman Beyers Naude, had worked quietly behind the scenes to support the BC movement and remained true to their convictions despite their increasing victimization by the state. BC leaders, more than the rank and file, worked closely with these white supporters, and it was on the leadership that these examples of white solidarity made their earliest impression. These contradictions with the assumptions of exclusive black unity became all the more evident during the 1976 unrest, when even the white student union from which SASO had seceded launched protests and was attacked by the state. By then the seriousness of such involvement could not be denied, for white activists had become "more daring, to compensate for the fact that they felt BC was not their home."[10]

It was not until the 1976 unrest had subsided and the BC leadership had regained control of their movement from the activist youth in the townships that the implications of this white involvement could be fully discussed. Even then, some BC leaders continued to advocate excluding whites from the preliberation struggle, maintaining that whites are not "genuine South Africans."[11] But by 1977, Biko himself openly advocated greater cooperation with supportive organizations of whites, confessing that "my worst fears are that working on the present analysis, conflict can only be on a generalized basis between black and white. We don't have sufficient groups who can form coalitions with blacks—that is groups of whites—at the present moment. The more such groups will come up, the better to minimize the conflict."[12] With this statement, Biko apparently moved toward the idea of closer cooperation between white and black groups, with which not all of his colleagues agreed but which would later be embraced by those who joined the UDF.

As much as ideological debate contributed to the reconsideration of basic BC precepts, it was the strategic necessities of responding to state repression that finally impelled a change of focus of the sort hinted at by Biko in 1977. During the bloody year that followed the first unrest in Soweto, it had become clear that active confrontation had begun. On strategic and tactical terms all could agree that the police violence against demonstrators required a more physical response. Shortly before his death in 1977, Biko himself acknowledged that "any recurrence of disturbance of that nature can only result in more careful planning and better calculation, thereby achieving the desired results to a greater extent than this spontaneous situation we had last year."[13] This greater concern with organized confrontation was overshadowing the movement's earlier goals of reshaping values and inspiring racial assertiveness, which were not by themselves sufficient to counter repression. The strategic necessities of the moment also buttressed arguments for working with supportive whites, both to further isolate the regime and to gain greater access to the resources needed for organizing more active resistance. To move beyond their initially idealistic approach to more active confrontation, BC adherents would have to abandon many of their earlier precepts, including their racial exclusivity and their emphasis on spontaneity over formal organization.

The debates within BC in the years immediately preceding and following the 1976 uprising foreshadow the significant ideological realignments that would soon emerge. As we shall see in subsequent chapters, early debates about class analysis did not immediately lead to an opposition movement based primarily on class issues, for workers as such were at this point neither sufficiently organized nor able to take a leading position in pursuing their economic and political interests. In retrospect, the debates in the 1970s over class were more important for the questions they raised about BC's focus on race and continued exclusion of whites. Class analysis may have appealed to students' appreciation of theory and consistency, but the practical impact of discussions of class was to begin a move toward a more inclusive and active approach. What emerged was a movement that was less concerned with class theory than with nationhood defined by a united opposition to apartheid. Appeals to exclusive racial identity that had proved effective for inspiring resistance were not abandoned by those BC adherents who went on to found AZAPO, despite their agreement with the need for a more activist strategy. Nor were appeals to race quickly abandoned by critics within BC who sought to merge such appeals with the recognition that "black awareness is only a part of national consciousness."[14]

The simultaneous development of ideological debate and strategic consensus at this time seems curious at first, but the pressures for division and unity came from different sources. Ideological debate developed within Black Consciousness as groups with different constituencies and individuals with different historical ties looked to both new ideas and new supporters. This debate centered on the incorporation of class analysis and white supporters. A consensus on the need for a more activist and less idealistic strategy, on the other hand, apparently was based more on an objective assessment of the need to respond to the state repression that the opposition was confronting. While ideological debate grew within, strategy was shaped by the threat from without and ultimately forced many activists to abandon BC's idealistic approach and to embrace the concept of national unity as a strategic necessity. An ideological transition from a primary concern with values to a greater focus on mobilizing physical resistance was taking shape within the opposition, driven by the external pressures of state repression as these were assessed and interpreted. But this transition was not consolidated until after Steve Biko's death in late 1977, the subsequent banning of BC organizations, and the formation of AZAPO during the following year by those who remained BC stalwarts.

That the ideological debates that began again in BC after the 1976 uprising did not immediately divide the movement suggests that the strategic necessity for a unified response to state repression outweighed the more abstract considerations. Indeed, during this period of intensified debate, there was little open discussion by even the most strident internal critics of the possibility of breaking away from Black Consciousness to form a new and distinct movement. Instead, debates were contained in Black Consciousness structures and concerned how the movement's ideology and strategy should be adjusted to fit the new circumstances. Few if any activists were willing to undermine the unity that had been achieved under the BC banner. State repression reinforced practical commitments to maintaining that unity. For example, the state's two-year prosecution and conviction in December 1976 of two former SASO presidents, two former BPC general secretaries, and five other officers of both groups unintentionally demonstrated to both these groups that their commonalities were more relevant than were any disagreements between them. Having begun before any acts of violence had been associated with BC, this trial was clearly an attempt to squash the ideas of BC, and as such it reinforced the need to defend those ideas that still unified the movement.

The need for maintaining strategic unity despite the growing ideological differences was acknowledged not only by activists within the BC movement but also by those with a primary loyalty to the competing exile groups. Particularly during the 1976 uprising, internal advocates of the ANC and the PAC had made every effort to cooperate with each other on pragmatic grounds, setting a precedent for continued unity. As a result, student leaders were able to seek advice openly from Winnie Mandela, wife of the ANC's most prominent prisoner, and from Robert Sobukwe and Zeph Mothopeng, the current and future presidents of the PAC. These and other leaders of the ANC and PAC gave priority to their common interest in resisting state repression, purposely submerging their differences with acknowledgments of each other's contributions.[15] The BC movement's continued popularity in South Africa and refusal to openly align itself with either the ANC or the PAC enabled the movement to encourage such cooperation and unity. The ANC and the PAC had a direct interest in following BC's lead in this regard, as both hoped to win support among the movement's internal following, which according to a 1978 poll included more than half of all South Africans.[16] Smaller independent groups, such as the Unity Movement discussed in the next chapter, were also pressed to cooperate. The BC movement itself had a direct interest in retaining its independence and the cooperation of the ANC, PAC, and others, in order to avoid association with the shortcomings of these groups or division of its following according to their other nascent loyalties.

The post-1976 consensus on the strategic need for cooperation gave the BC movement a unique opportunity to draw up a more formal agreement of unity among all opposition tendencies. Such an agreement would both strengthen the opposition as a whole and solidify the BC movement's position as the central unifying force in the country. Steve Biko welcomed this opportunity, admitting in 1977 that he "would like to see groups like ANC, PAC and Black Consciousness movement deciding to form one liberation group. It is only, I think, when black people are so dedicated and so united in their cause that we can effect the greatest results."[17] Although many agreed that conditions were ripe for unity, at that time only Biko had the prestige and following to persuade more recalcitrant leaders of the existing organizations to reconcile their differences and compromise their autonomy. Biko seized this opportunity for unity by engaging in direct negotiations with other opposition leaders, thereby ignoring the banning order that had been imposed on him. This effort finally cost Biko his life, as explained in 1988 by Peter Jones, Biko's close friend and last traveling companion:

> Unity talks had been initiated by Steve and were over four years old by the time of his death. We had established relations with senior people in every organization. . . . We knew everyone had a problem. The organizations had gone to exile as a forced process, not of their choice, before they had developed infrastructures. There were regular arrests [and convictions], creating resentment even among cadres. We knew there was a big bone of contention with the exile organizations assuming they could take the political initiative even though they were out of the country.
>
> [The exile organizations] saw over time that we were not a danger to them, so [we] decided to start a debate over unity. . . . We knew we would have to have an historical excuse for excluding anyone [from

> the unity, so] all had to be invited. The ANC was agreeable, if reluctant, with even the [ANC] fat cats in London going along. . . . They knew they had to cooperate with us to ensure an internal base. . . . We said the ANC could continue, since it was best at what it does, if they would be willing to accept a new name. . . . By mid 1977, all the internal leadership were part of a program of minimum consensus, . . . based on the assumption that differences were not so fundamental as to be not postponable. It was clear [unity] was in all of our long-term interests. We hadn't debated yet the merging of leadership structures or finances.
>
> We came to Cape Town [to tie up some loose ends.] . . . We were uneasy and ended up leaving hurriedly. Steve wanted to meet Neville Alexander. . . . Neville is like all Unity Movement people. They always speak well but have no people behind them. They had this fear for their integrity we never had. Neville kept Steve waiting in his garden for three hours and refused to see him. We decided to drive back late that night.[18]

This description suggests that Biko's efforts at building a basis for unity had met with considerable success, no doubt because, as Jones observed, "we had the aces and could determine what the grounds for unity were" but also because some of the difficult details had not yet been discussed.[19] What Biko could not control were the debates within BC, which Jones minimizes. Indeed, Biko's and Jones's risky drive to Cape Town, out of Biko's banning area, was undertaken in part to enable them to meet with the BC groups there that had been hampered by divisive debates over the class analysis proposed by Mji and related issues. Biko also could not control the peculiarities of some smaller groups, including that led by Neville Alexander, considered to "be the brain behind some of the divisions."[20] Alexander's own version of the events, including Biko's last night at liberty, largely confirms that of Jones:

> By mid 1976 the idea of a minimum consensus for unity had spread, under Biko's influence. Winnie Mandela and Robert Sobukwe were deeply involved in the process. Everyone had agreed on the BPC as the center for a united front, including the exiles, and that Biko and I [Alexander] would go to speak to the exiles. . . .
>
> By September 1976, however, it was clear that there were two tendencies in BC, with Biko appearing to be more willing to negotiate and Mji being more radical. Biko was really in between the factions and both now claim him, but we did not know that then.

> Our group was afraid of taking sides, and of consorting with Biko who had been consorting with [U.S.] Senator Clark. We asked Biko not to come down, but he came, both to see us and to settle the BPC rift in the Western Cape. I had not been mandated to see him and could not get such a mandate in time. Obviously, I could not know what would happen to him after he left my house, but I could not see him under those circumstances. We must be disciplined.[21]

What happened after Biko left Cape Town is part of the lore of the South African opposition. It is well known that Biko and Jones, driving back late that night toward Kingwilliamstown, were stopped at a roadblock and arrested. What is not widely known is that they were carrying what Jones describes as the only copy of the one-page "minimum consensus" they had negotiated, which Jones managed to hide in his shorts. The paper was not found during two body searches. After an initial interrogation, Jones and Biko were placed together, for the last time, in a cell. Jones discreetly retrieved the document, quietly ripped it in half, and "we ate it, half for me, half for Steve."[22] Jones never saw his best friend alive again after that last supper. Biko was brutally assaulted in detention and died on September 12, 1977. With Biko's death, the focal point and opportunity for formal unity negotiated by the opposition leadership were lost. Tragically, the South African opposition paid the price of this loss with over ten years of disunity and occasionally bloody internecine conflict over the issues that Biko had been unable to resolve.

On October 19, 1977, five weeks after Biko's death, the government moved in and banned seventeen leading Black Consciousness and affiliated organizations, abandoning its earlier restriction of only individuals associated with these groups. The timing of this move by the state is revealing. Had the state felt more threatened by the dissemination of BC ideas or held the BC movement directly responsible for the 1976 uprising, it is reasonable to assume that it would have banned the BC organizations earlier. Instead, the state was apparently more concerned by the BC movement's efforts to unite formally with the exile groups, which the state still considered its greatest enemies. The state may also have feared that Biko's death would cause the BC movement to abandon its policy of nonviolence, if only for self-defense. As after Sharpeville in 1960, the state acted to break up the opposition, based on its anticipation of an organized response to its own brutality. But in removing the opportunity for greater cooperation with the exiled groups or for more violent confrontation, the state did not and could not preclude the further development of other forms of nonviolent internal opposition.

The 1977 bannings marked the culmination of a period of violent repression and the disruption of the leading internal opposition. Black Consciousness organizations were disbanded, and many of their leaders were imprisoned, thereby ending the immediate possibility of organized action and the strategic necessity of unifying to support such action. The stage for internal opposition having in effect been wiped clean by the state, the "political stage was again open for reoccupation and competition reemerged."[23] Such competition put stress on the cracks forming in the former BC ranks. As discussed in the next section of this chapter, the critics of BC who had remained in the movement, previously their only available base, were now free to discuss and organize alternative approaches and groups that more accurately reflected their class rhetoric and inclusion of whites. Others who remained loyal to Black Consciousness were also free to regroup, to distance themselves from BC's critics, and to adjust their approach to include aspects of class analysis in a BC framework. Thus, the state's disruption of established BC structures allowed for a realignment and division of the movement that earlier had been prevented by those structures. According to Popo Molefe, a BC activist who abandoned the BC framework in this period:

> When in 1977 the government banned all BC organizations, the debate started as to whether to form another BC organization and the wisdom of doing so. Two major camps emerged . . . [both of which] acknowledged the necessity and the imperative of addressing the issues of race and class simultaneously. . . . One advocated the formation of an organization in the tradition of the BC . . . [contending] that race was a class determinant. . . . The other one advocating a non-racial organization. . . . Over and above these polemical debates, there was the most concrete question of strategy and morality that presented itself.[24]

Even before the dust had settled from the bannings, those who wanted to retain the basic framework of Black Consciousness—

incorporating class analysis as a subordinate expression of racial identity—set out to organize themselves under a new structure. They had agreed on this arrangement in their detention cells and publicly announced it a week after the bannings, although another round of detentions just as quickly postponed its implementation for another year. Finally, in April 1978, this group formally established itself as the Azanian Peoples Organization (AZAPO), committed to continuing overt and nonviolent internal opposition under the banner of Black Consciousness. The term *Azania*, originally adopted in exile by the PAC, was heralded as a new name for the country as part of an effort to "create an alternative cultural identity," even though it had also come to signal allegiance to BC or Africanism.[25]

AZAPO stated its aims both to maintain BC ideology and to alter traditional BC strategy in response to the recent repression, thereby indicating a hybrid approach to continued opposition. The AZAPO constitution proclaimed "an irreversible process of self-understanding and self-assertiveness . . . that relatively translates itself into an active opposition to government policies." In this seminal document, AZAPO committed itself "to conscientize, politicize and mobilize Black workers through the philosophy of BC in order to strive for their legitimate rights." This formulation clearly included a greater concern with active mobilization than had the original BC focus on using ideas to inspire racial assertiveness. Even these BC stalwarts recognized that their earlier and more idealistic approach had been limited and that a state that shot schoolchildren and killed Biko had to be confronted not only by ideas but also by more material means guided by those ideas. In this sense, those who continued to follow the BC line had been influenced by their critics and by the strategic impetus to respond to state repression. Their continued adherence to BC ideology, on the other hand, indicates that such convictions are self-determined and not necessarily or fully malleable according to external pressures. Circumstances had changed, but those in AZAPO did not fully abandon the ideas through which they interpreted that change.

AZAPO's rhetorical incorporation of class analysis revealed an unresolved tension between the revision of earlier BC precepts and an insistence on preserving the framework of an ideology based on racial identity. AZAPO was eager to retain the loyalty of an increasingly radical constituency and to broaden its appeal to workers organized in the trade unions, by openly embracing the Marxist terminology that had been dismissed by the early BC movement. AZAPO dropped the economic policy of communalism and later replaced it with a commitment to socialism, which a 1978 poll suggested a plurality of South Africans were already prepared to accept.[26] But in order to make class analysis consistent with Black Consciousness, the subordinate class position of blacks had to be described as the result of "determinant" racial discrimination. In this way, AZAPO acknowledged the superimposition of race and class in South Africa while maintaining an emphasis on racial identity as the basis of social relations. Blacks were described as "a race of workers," thereby collapsing the class category of workers into the racial category of blacks. Whites, including the white working class, were still excluded from the movement's preliberation struggle as beneficiaries of continued oppression. According to Ishmael Mkhabela, one of the founders of AZAPO, this hybrid position constituted

> an adaption of the broad principles of BC. We were engaged in a process of criticism and what emerged was an eclectic position, adapting various analyses to the unique South African situation. We married race and class, describing how industrialization heightened class division and how the history of South Africa could be characterized by racial conflict. . . . Some saw our use of class as undermining the emphasis on race, but we did not.[27]

The founders of AZAPO saw that these ideological revisions also would require that its strategies be reformed. The BC movement's traditional focus on reshaping ideas had largely achieved its goal of revitalizing popular resistance, and so it could now be amended to include a greater concern for mobilizing resistance against state repression. According to Mkhabela, AZAPO recognized that "the means may not be fully psychological for liberation."[28] Official AZAPO policy was formulated around the belief that "the development of a meaningful self-image is dependent on the complete restructuring of society," which could be achieved only through a broader organization of mass action.[29] This materialist view of social structure determining self-image could not be more opposed to the initial conception that the idea of Black Consciousness would itself alter the social structure. AZAPO claimed to have embraced this conception of material causation and corresponding strategy that was very different from the idealistic BC tradition, without abandoning BC's fundamental ideological focus on racial identity.

The founders of AZAPO apparently believed that they could both revise and remain committed to the basic precepts of BC, although their continued emphasis on racial identity undermined their rhetorical intention to act in accordance with a more material conception of social processes. Whites had originally been excluded from the movement in order to bolster black self-confidence, but even after the myth of black submissiveness had been shattered by the 1976 uprising, AZAPO refused to admit white members. They contended that the idea of racial "dignity" and "pride" was still necessary to motivate resistance, ignoring the contradiction between this view and the more materialist arguments just cited.[30] Apparently a core of AZAPO leaders "felt the stage for a change had not yet been reached [and that to change] would have been a betrayal of their ideals."[31] Many of AZAPO's critics interpreted the retained focus on the ideals of racial identity as indicating that AZAPO's call for moving beyond a purely psychological approach to liberation, toward more concrete forms of confrontation, was purely rhetorical. These suspicions were confirmed by the extent to which AZAPO remained absorbed by ideological positioning, with little or no effort given to organizing concrete forms of confrontation. AZAPO thus remained true to the idealistic tradition of Black Consciousness, despite its protestations to the contrary.

AZAPO's limitations can be directly attributed to its ideological insistence on concentrating on reshaping those ideas about racial identity that lay at the heart of the BC movement. Those who departed from the BC tradition had been a part of the earlier BC movement and had backgrounds similar to those who remained in AZAPO. They soon became engaged in more concrete forms of organizing, under the same conditions in which AZAPO failed to implement its call for such action. What distinguished AZAPO's core constituents was their clinging to the central BC emphasis on racial identity, with its concomitant stress on the psychological elements of opposition. Their ideology continued to determine AZAPO's priorities, whereas others responded more directly to the strategic necessity for action, formulating an alternative ideology to fit the requirements of the moment.

The extent to which AZAPO's ideological intransigence outweighed its rhetorical commitments to pursuing a less idealistic and more active approach became clear only later. But there were enough early indications of this outcome to raise the suspicions of more strategically minded activists. These critics dismissed AZAPO's policies as a thinly camouflaged recapitulation of Black Consciousness, in which rhetorical references to class were subordinated to a focus on race.[32] The speed with which AZAPO had been formed after the bannings of the original BC organizations, and the continued exclusion of whites, suggested that there had been little serious reevaluation of ideology or strategy. Thus, although its leaders saw themselves as having amended the BC strategy to fit new challenges, AZAPO was already being attacked for its inflexibility and stagnation.

The founders of AZAPO acted quickly to try to diffuse this criticism and to win popular support for their new organization. With seemingly little regard for caution or consistency, they elected as their first president Curtis Nkondo, a former Soweto high school principal whose articulate support for the students in 1976 had attracted considerable notoriety. His vehement rhetoric had incorporated significant aspects of Black Consciousness, prevalent at the time, though he had remained outside the movement's more youthful organizations. Nkondo was a generation older than the other leaders of AZAPO and had been more closely associated with the ANC before its banning in 1960 than with the subsequent BC movement, indicating that he could help repair the rift opening between BC stalwarts and their nonracial critics. Removed from the debates in Black Consciousness, Nkondo had remained sympathetic to BC for its earlier success at inspiring and unifying popular resistance, and he was presumably flattered to be asked to help reconstitute the movement under the AZAPO banner. Nkondo himself explained, in retrospect, the basis on which he was persuaded to accept the presidency and the reasons that he then became disillusioned with AZAPO in its early days:

> I think they asked me largely because of my influence with the youth and my popularity with the parents of my students. They thought I would make it easier for AZAPO to grow quickly. My wife encouraged me to do it, in order to help change their BC attitudes. I thought AZAPO was intended to be a stop gap. It could never be a revolutionary organization. I realized I was in the wrong camp.

> I couldn't understand how BC could address itself to the workers since it would exclude whites who were not but should have been involved in the struggle. . . . I worried about AZAPO's approach to revolution without workers; you can't be interested only in black workers since white workers are also exploited. We need a broader program of organization than . . . BC. How do you fight apartheid when your organization contains it? I was suspended after one and a half months.[33]

During his brief tenure at the head of AZAPO, Nkondo tried to bridge the growing gap between the BC and its critics in order to reinforce the unity within the opposition. Contrary to his more recent remarks just quoted, Nkondo advocated the exclusion of whites and emphasized the importance of education over direct confrontation. At the same time, he insisted on a "shift from this idea that race is the main issue."[34] Nkondo pushed for a more serious class analysis, with his description of race "as an instrument of economic exploitation" directly contradicting AZAPO's formulation of class subordination as an outcome of racial discrimination.[35] The younger AZAPO leaders were dismayed by this renunciation of BC's central focus on race, and less radical and older activists who had become involved with AZAPO, such as Dr. Nthato Motlana, rejected Nkondo's advocacy of class conflict.[36] These ideological divisions could not be covered over for the sake of unity, and Nkondo's presidency quickly became untenable. To contain the damage of antagonizing Nkondo's followers, his suspension was justified by attacks on his lack of accountability to the organization and his purported violation of AZAPO's policy of rejecting all forms of negotiation; Nkondo had solicited assistance from Helen Suzman, a white liberal member of parliament, in gaining the release of his detained brother.[37]

Just as his popularity had made Nkondo's appointment attractive, it also made his suspension costly. Vincent Mogane, who also left AZAPO after helping found it, reported that "the expulsion of Curtis created real problems. We felt it was unjust since the principles he was accused of violating seemed vague."[38] In his short tenure, Nkondo succeeded in encouraging the formation of two popular student groups aligned with AZAPO, the Congress of South African Students (COSAS), for those in secondary school, and the Azanian Students Organization (AZASO), for those at the universities, thereby fulfilling the expectations that had originally justified his appointment. But these gains in organizing students were severely threatened, if not completely lost, by Nkondo's suspension. The president of AZASO was Nkondo's son, Reavell, who decried the accusations against his father. Within two years, both AZASO and COSAS abandoned AZAPO, thus isolating the BC camp from the major components of its student constituency.

The Nkondo episode, intended to unify support for AZAPO, ended by widening the rift in the opposition and antagonizing both activists willing to work within AZAPO to revise BC ideology and critics who did not think BC could or would be revised. These divisions were exacerbated by personal relations, with individual loyalties and family relations pulling followers to take sides on Nkondo's suspension and on the debates over class analysis and white inclusion. Material conditions had compelled an ideological and strategic reevaluation, but responses to this situation were determined by individual convictions and loyalties. The core of the AZAPO leadership refused to compromise on the fundamentals of BC ideology, but others, motivated more by strategic concerns, became increasingly disillusioned. As these varying responses and allegiances became more apparent, the BC stalwarts in AZAPO became less tolerant of their critics and more interested in asserting their views and taking control of the organization, thereby isolating themselves further from pressures for a more fundamental revision of earlier BC ideology. As a result, activists who had joined AZAPO and others who had remained on the sidelines were forced to accept an apparently stagnant form of Black Consciousness or to formulate an alternative to it. Many apparently agreed with Vincent Mogane that the "lines were now being drawn. . . . For BC to stay as it was would mean it would not survive," as the outlines of an alternative approach, based on achieving national unity rather than racial assertiveness, were already beginning to take shape.[39]

## Realignment Outside the Black Consciousness Framework

The 1976 uprising and the repression that followed created a new set of circumstances to which the South African opposition was compelled to respond. The initial impetus, giving rise to AZAPO, remained in the BC framework of racial identity, with its ideology adjusted only rhetorically on the edges to accommodate a subordinated version of class analysis. But this effort quickly became a sideshow, which was dismissed by many activists as more of the same. As this disillusionment and division congealed, a growing number of activists began to discuss how better to meet the challenges of heightened repression, to avoid the failures of previous efforts, and to build on the renewed spirit of self-confidence in the townships. Many concluded that the post-1976 era required a more complete reformulation of opposition ideology and strategy than did those who remained in AZAPO. Just as the shortcomings of AZAPO's approach became increasingly evident in later years, its concrete alternative took shape only in the early 1980s.

Both of these developments are discussed in the next chapter. In the remainder of this chapter we shall consider the variety of influences and experiences that contributed to the formulation of an alternative to BC. These included a resurgence of the ANC's internal activities and prestige, and discussions among activists in prison and among the population as a whole.

The realignment of popular allegiances and ideas concerning continued internal opposition, moving beyond the BC framework of AZAPO, gained considerable momentum outside South Africa. A large number of students who had participated in the 1976 uprising fled the country, both to escape arrest and to prepare themselves for armed attacks against a state that they had seen respond to protest with violence. In the two years following the uprising, secondary school registration in Soweto dropped by almost 60 percent, with over twenty thousand pupils having disappeared from the rolls. According to some approximations, by 1978 two hundred fifty students were fleeing the country each month, with the number dropping to forty or fifty per month throughout the following year.[40] Many of these students had considered themselves to be part of the BC movement, then the only active form of internal opposition with which they could identify. But most had not participated in formal BC structures and had only a superficial loyalty to that movement and fragmentary knowledge of the history of the opposition. According to Vincent Mogane, "Many students who left were still young and unclear; not yet fully panel beaten."[41] If they knew anything about the exile groups to which they would have to turn for support outside the country, it was probably only to view both the ANC and PAC as "not only irrelevant, but wasteful."[42] Once outside the country, however, these students had to join one of these exile groups if they were to survive, let alone obtain the training and arms that many sought.

For most of the new exiles, joining the ANC was the only viable option. The PAC was then hopelessly disorganized and ill prepared to absorb the influx of youth. By 1979, one exasperated PAC official reported that even "the continued existence of the [PAC] as a functional entity must be considered in jeopardy."[43] In contrast, the ANC had maintained a disciplined leadership and quietly pursued international contacts and resources, enabling it to organize shelter, food, and training for the new young exiles who flocked into its camps. Eager to enhance their internal reputation, the ANC publicly claimed that the BC exiles turned to the ANC as a tribute to the ANC's "revolutionary prestige."[44] Instead, the flow of exiles to the ANC is a notable example of how material resources, rather than ideas or prestige, have determined opposition allegiances, among both the young exiles themselves and those who remained at home. Resources drew the militant youth to the ANC, increasing the exiled group's capacity to launch guerrilla operations inside South Africa that would fulfill popular eagerness for a counterattack on the state's repression. According to one analyst's approximations, the total ANC population in exile grew from one thousand in 1975 to nine thousand in 1980, with the average age of those ANC cadres caught inside South Africa dropping from thirty-five in 1975 to twenty-eight only a year later.[45] After more than a decade of relative dormancy, the ANC was able to challenge the Black Consciousness movement's popularity as the only internally active form of opposition.

The ANC's reputation was reinvigorated in South Africa by the "armed propaganda" of increased MK attacks made possible by the availability of fresh new recruits. Between October 1976 and March 1978, 112 attacks were staged, with an average of one small bomb exploded each week for the five months after November 1977.[46] These attacks were aimed not so much to gain military victories as to shake the confidence of the regime and to bolster both internal resistance and the ANC's reputation. According to Joe Slovo, who then was serving as both chairman of the Communist party and chief of staff of Umkhonto we Sizwe:

> It is during this . . . period that the ANC was accepted as never before as the only serious opponent of the racist regime. . . . This has happened not because people have suddenly come to understand what we are and the correctness of our policies. It has happened because people have seen what we have done in action. . . . It is this revolutionary practice and not just revolutionary theory which has won for us this unchallenged place.[47]

The young MK cadres who carried out the attacks inside South Africa had been quickly trained, were too few and ill equipped to confront directly or hope to defeat the state's modern defense forces, and many were either killed or captured. None of these limitations dampened the impact of their efforts on the black populace, however, who were gratified by any evidence of proactive resistance to oppression. Resurgence of the ANC's armed struggle during a period when internal activists were still debating new approaches among themselves turned popular attention to the exile group as a force for liberation that had survived despite the state's ban on its internal activities. The ANC's persistence was a source of pride, with which a growing number of South Africans came to identify themselves. Much as the ideas of Black Consciousness had inspired greater assertiveness, the physical attacks launched by the ANC renewed confidence that the state could not crush all of the opposition.

Not only did the ANC build its internal prestige by absorbing the exiled youth and staging attacks, but its also carefully positioned itself to broaden its ideological appeal. In the wake of the state's repression after the 1976 uprising, the ANC had tried to capitalize on the growing popular disillusionment by criticizing the BC movement's continued idealism, its "confusion" over economic issues, and its inability to organize large-scale resistance.[48] After the BC organizations had been banned, the ANC moved to take advantage of the more fluid situation in the country, appealing for the allegiance of former BC adherents by softening its criticism and even embracing BC as "part of the genuine forces of the revolution."[49] As described by Peter Jones, "The ANC had wanted to be the only organization and they had vilified [BC]. When Biko died, they tried to own him."[50] At the same time that the ANC adjusted its response to BC, it also continued to disseminate its basic policies, consistently calling on the people to move beyond idealism to action and to grow beyond antiwhite anger toward a more inclusive nationalism. Seeking to maximize its appeal to the broadest possible section of the populace, small disaffected elements desiring a greater focus on Africanism and a Marxist worker's tendency were expelled from the ANC in the late 1970s.[51]

To encourage further an internal resurgence of its popularity, in the late 1970s the ANC began a campaign to draw attention to itself through appeals to symbolic loyalties that had been largely overshadowed by Black Consciousness. Throughout the 1960s and 1970s, the ANC's seminal document, the Freedom Charter, had been allowed to drift into obscurity. By the early 1980s, the ban on this document was largely ignored, as copies of its began to circulate in the townships. Similarly, the government could not prevent the renewed interest in and admiration for Nelson Mandela and the other ANC leaders who by 1978 had been imprisoned for over fourteen years. Held on Robben Island, visible off the shores of Cape Town, these prisoners provided a powerful symbol of the ANC's long commitment to the struggle, unsullied by association with any of the shortcomings of internal or exile opposition in the intervening years. Supporters claimed that the salience of such symbols represented concrete allegiance to the banned ANC, which harsh penalties prevented from being more openly expressed. In a situation in which people were reconsidering their loyalties, even the suggestion of a resurgence of support for the ANC or interest in its symbols would become self-fulling prophecies.[52]

All of this suggests that the post-1976 realignment of political allegiances away from the Black Consciousness was significantly influenced by the activities and ideas of the ANC in exile. The resources commanded by the ANC enabled it to absorb those youths who fled the country and to send them back to stage armed attacks, which in turn enhanced the ANC's internal prestige. At the same time, the ANC carefully manipulated and disseminated its ideas and symbols to attract even more support away from BC. Neither the ANC's material resources and activities nor its ideology and symbolic allegiances, therefore, can fully account for the ANC's success during this period of realignment, for both were significant.

Although many were inspired by the actions and symbols associated with the ANC, the widespread realignment of loyalties during this period was not only the result of these external influences. Many former BC adherents who were cut off from these influences because of prolonged detentions were also similarly drawn away from their BC allegiances. To explain this largely independent but parallel development, we must consider the experiences of those activists who found themselves imprisoned as part of the crackdown on BC activities in 1977. During the nine months that followed the bannings of the major BC groups, up to eighty of the most senior BC leaders were imprisoned together in Modderbee Prison, east of Johannesburg. There the remaining elite of the BC movement was held together as an isolated group, with the younger "stone throwers" held in local prisons and the veteran ANC and PAC prisoners held on Robben Island.

After more than a year of scattered efforts to maintain the 1976 uprising and of hiding from the police bent on crushing any resistance, the BC leadership was forcibly reunited in Modderbee Prison, with each cell holding more than twenty prisoners. There they were free from distractions, from immediate concerns for their own or their movement's survival, and from responsibility for their younger militant followers. This situation presented a unique opportunity for reevaluating and discussing ideas and strategy. According to Tom Manthata, one of those imprisoned at the time, the arguments of the previous two years were reexamined, with some asserting that there was "no need for a BPC economic policy since the ANC had one and others arguing that we needed a separate policy for just that reason."[53] The question of whether to continue with overt BC organization was also debated, and perhaps it was Curtis Nkondo's recommendation in favor of continuation that led to his being asked to head AZAPO upon his release. Manthata contends that most of the arguments at Modderbee were "more personal than ideological."[54] But even if confinement bred tension, it also certainly encouraged reconsideration. Everyone who was at Modderbee came to look on that time as a formative experience. Almost all agreed that state repression required a less idealistic and more activist response and that class analysis should be given more serious consideration. Few who were there remained in BC for long.

The other locus for concentrated discussion among the leadership during this period was Robben Island, the main prison for those who had been convicted of a crime rather than just detained.

There the BC leaders were isolated from the influence of the ANC in exile, but they instead found themselves in direct contact with the ANC's most influential leadership, including Nelson Mandela, Walter Sisulu, and Govan Mbeki. With the influx of young prisoners around 1976, the island came to be known as a "university," whose released inmates were considered "graduates." One such graduate, Saki Macozoma, describes his experience on the island in some detail:

> Before we all arrived, the ANC and PAC folks on the Island did not take BC seriously. Once we all arrived, the ANC became particularly alarmed. All of us from the 1976 group were put in a separate section, sealed off ideologically, where we could teach each other BC. The catch word was the need for us to be "grounded." The SASO [leadership who were imprisoned for their role in the pro-FRELIMO rallies] had to tell us about the policy and decisions. We tried to write it down and to discuss it. Those most involved were caught after four months and put in solitary. After that, new leadership emerged. Six new prisoners then arrived from Maritzburg, including some who had been on the Island before [and were staunch ANC supporters]. They turned the tide once people had become saturated with BC.
>
> BC militancy on Robben Island had a political cost since people didn't want to fight every day. By the time we were out of solitary, everything was up in the air. "Terror" [Lekota] had become isolated, having corresponded with the old leaders who had influenced his ideas. A significant exodus began to the ANC. We said they had been seduced by the idea of MK. They said we need a way to implement liberation, not just ideas. [The question of] white involvement was always secondary. [The ANC had the advantage of providing what for us were] new ideas, with lots of romantic appeal. . . .
>
> We came to see that the problem of BC was that it couldn't be extended to the struggle beyond initial conscientization. It had failed to address the class issue and had come more from literature than experience. People were drifting and finding new allies. It was mere coincidence that we were reading and discussing [Marx] while the workers outside were experiencing class more directly. We had no access to outside information, [so we had no idea what they were up to.] Our debates were purely theoretical, without any empirical movement. . . .
>
> There was a crisis for BC when it turned out that [BC leader] Strini Moodley's brother, who had been tried and acquitted as a member of the BC Movement, had fallen in love at his trial with a

> court stenographer, the daughter of a judge. [He was] now an organizer for the BC office in London. We asked what BC said about that. We said they had to either expel him or accept him with his white wife. To expel him would be like adding our own Immorality Act. This raised ideology to the fore and BC was put in a tough position. We said this is what we have been saying for two years . . . that BC ideas crumble outside of South Africa, where the definition of "black" as oppressed doesn't necessarily exist. We used [Moodley] to illustrate our argument. Things got very hot then.
>
> Eventually there were two separate BC groups on the Island. We said that the SASO constitution discouraged contact with whites but did not rule it out. We said class issues are important, that Marxism has an influence and is not just dusty old books. We said that all strands have been influenced by Marxism and by the new left. We argued about Marcuse, Trotsky, Mao, Stalin, all of them. BC just couldn't deal with it. We didn't want to join another organization since that would create confusion and limit our influence. [In the end] we were left with ideological ambiguity. We related to both the ANC and the PAC, at least until I was released in 1982. . . . Like any political realignment, [ours was] a combination of conscious views and personal relations.[55]

Ideological realignment among the younger prisoners on Robben Island was the result of their readings and discussions, the influence of ANC's elder statesmen and enthusiasm over reports of increased MK attacks, and the relative disarray within the BC and PAC camps. The ANC adherents on the island, hardened in their views by years of imprisonment, effectively launched an ideological offensive to win new recruits. The experience of Sisulu and others from the ANC, who themselves had abandoned their youthful Africanist sympathies in the 1950s, enabled these older leaders to be particularly persuasive in encouraging the BC youth to make a similar transformation.[56]

These efforts by the ANC leaders placed the BC and Africanist stalwarts in the disadvantageous position of having to defend policies that had more recently proved insufficient to maintain popular resistance in the face of heightened repression. Simply by virtue of their more recent imprisonment, many of the younger BC leaders were susceptible to doubts about their own approach, and before they left the island many had been converted into internal allies of the ANC. For example, of the thirty-one prisoners who arrived in

1976 from Port Elizabeth, only five remained in BC, one joined the PAC, and the remaining twenty-five all joined the ANC's Charterist camp, which later became the United Democratic Front.[57] That such a dramatic transfer of allegiances did not involve more open conflict among these groups can be attributed to the mutual respect among these prisoners, united by their common opposition to the regime despite their own ideological differences.[58] But the overriding effect of imprisonment on Robben Island, as at Modderbee, was to achieve a resurgence of support for the ANC and a rededication to continued opposition among the generation of activist leaders who had earlier launched the BC movement. Their realignment was a direct consequence of imprisonment, intended by the state to dislocate its opponents through punishment.

It is possible that some activists, both inside prison and at liberty, were predisposed toward a realignment of opposition allegiances as an opportunity to advance themselves beyond the level of leadership they had achieved within BC. Indeed, many of the junior BC activists who joined the transition toward Charterism did become more influential in the UDF, and some of the more senior BC activists retained their leadership positions by remaining in AZAPO. However, it would be unreasonable to attribute such alignments completely to opportunism, for none of these activists could have been sure at the time of their future prospects in either camp. Those who abandoned BC before the UDF had become the powerful force it did, took some risk in rejecting AZAPO, in which they might very well have become more influential and which was then the only internal organization in existence other than the more narrowly based Zulu movement, Inkatha. These activists may have been motivated to turn away from BC in part because of self-interest, but assessments of personal prospects in AZAPO could not be disentangled from assessments of the prospects of AZAPO as a whole. As suggested by Cassim Saloojee, future treasurer of the UDF, "If BC [in its new form, AZAPO] had had real roots in the community, leaders would not have changed."[59] Leaving BC because of exasperation with AZAPO appeared opportunistic only in retrospect and was more likely motivated at the time by more substantive concerns.

For many former BC activists, their ideological realignment during this period can be attributed to an array of personal experiences and deliberations that cannot be summarized as easily as the result of imprisonment, operations by the exiled ANC, or jockeying for leadership positions. For instance, Joe Seremane of the South African Council of Churches regarded his turn away from BC as the result of his own unique experiences: "My views on whites were changed by small things. When I was tortured, the blacks were much harder than the white police. My sister married a Dutchman and I have seen many whites sacrifice and blacks who have sold out."[60] Zwelakhe Sisulu, son of the imprisoned ANC secretary general, saw his transition from being a leader of the BC-oriented media workers' union to becoming a leading figure in the UDF as the consequence of his own private deliberations. He concluded that BC was no longer necessary, as "the process of conscientization is now done" at least in the urban areas, and because current circumstances require "cooperation with whites—all must be included in the nation."[61] Albertina Sisulu, who, as copresident of the UDF, came to be hailed as a "mother of the nation," describes this transition by her own son as due less to such analytic considerations and more to personal influences:

> I had to educate Zwelakhe back from BC. He had been influenced by his journalist friends. I had to sit him down at the kitchen table and teach him about history and about his family. [I explained that] not every white is responsible for repression, but just a few. Whites were born here and have a right to be here; many have no other place to go. . . . I sent him home with some books on Marx and when he came back, he said, Mom, you were right.[62]

Subjective experience, including the unpredictable influence of a mother on her son, was only one of several factors that apparently contributed to the post-1976 realignment away from Black Consciousness. We have already noted the impact of renewed ANC activity, ideology, and symbolism, as well as discussions in prison and the possibility of some jockeying for future leadership positions. It is difficult to generalize about how these influences and experiences caused a realignment before we have examined how the new ideological and strategic approach fared in the early 1980s. But by looking at the broad trends that emerge from early anecdotal evidence, we should be able to detect some overall patterns that can help explain why the turn away from BC occurred during this period and how this process led to a shift away from the BC approach. In doing so, we shall concentrate on how material conditions and subjective interpretations of those conditions interacted and contributed to the transition that was developing within the opposition.

Tensions suggesting the emergence of a realignment away from BC were evident even before the 1976 uprising, though they were clearly exacerbated by differences over how to react to the repression used to crush that uprising. The debates over class analysis and inclusion of whites that had surfaced in Black Consciousness before the movement was forced to respond to renewed state repression is indicative of the important role of ideas in such a realignment. The movement's ability to remain unified as a strategic necessity during the uprising shows that many did put aside ideological differences in the face of a crisis. Once the violence abated, the differences became more apparent, as a growing number of BC adherents concluded that the state repression required a more active response than BC's idealistic approach dictated. The material conditions of oppression thus brought the ideological differences to the fore. Those who turned their backs on Black Consciousness were emboldened by the spontaneity and scale of the uprising to envision a more active and inclusive form of struggle, with their earlier idealism transformed by repression into a more confrontational approach. But material conditions alone were not the only reason, as those who instead renamed themselves as AZAPO were faced with the same reality but interpreted the implications differently, arguing that opposition was still possible in the BC framework.

A major factor in the rethinking of many former BC adherents was a growing sense of disillusionment with the idealistic precepts of the movement with which they had been associated. Unionist Khetsi Lehoko, for example, recalls a growing sense that BC was "all talk and no action . . . unable to answer day to day problems in the community and workplace. It couldn't be translated into practice and we needed a theory that presented a program for action."[63] BC's emphasis on shaping ideas and values over mobilizing action had been designed to create an exclusive racial assertiveness, which, having inspired a popular uprising, came increasingly under fire as no longer being an appropriate goal. In addition, the ongoing support of sympathetic whites made many uncomfortable with the internal contradiction of an antiapartheid movement that reflected aspects of apartheid's own racial divisions and exclusion, much as such white support had deeply influenced Mandela, Sisulu, and others a generation earlier.[64] Again, these realities were equally evident to those who remained in AZAPO, who disagreed with including whites in the struggle and felt that a more active approach could be incorporated in BC. But many others did not share this interpretation, did not perceive AZAPO as significantly different from earlier BC structures, and preferred to devise a more distinct approach that would progress beyond BC ideology. This alternative view was further propounded by older township residents, who were encouraged by the 1976 uprising to speak more openly of the disobedience campaigns and other forms of mass resistance that had been organized in the 1940s and 1950s.

Disillusionment with BC was largely generated internally, in response to the movement's shortcomings and experiences, but it was also urged by the ANC in exile. Armed attacks by ANC guerrillas, made possible by new recruits and available resources, increased the exile group's prestige among a populace eager for any active response to state repression. The ANC intentionally separated itself from BC's idealistic approach with these attacks and, after 1969, by arguing that "physical liberation will create the basis enabling us to . . . propagate ideas."[65] In the years following, the ANC continued its armed struggle from exile, calling on the internal opposition to stress organization and alliances that would allow for direct confrontation with state power. The receptivity to this approach among a people eager to resist repression and activists chafing under the confinement of prison is indicated by the sharp swing in popular support from BC to the ANC, as shown in surveys conducted at the time. Both the ideas and the actions of the ANC were ingredients in this transfer of allegiances.

Although a concrete alternative to BC strategy and ideology did not fully develop until the early 1980s, the outlines of a new approach were being created already in the late 1970s. Many felt that BC had been an appropriate response to the situation in the early and mid-1970s but that after 1976 it was necessary to build on what had been achieved in terms of spontaneity and black unity and to move on to a more actively organized form of opposition. As summarized by a leader of a student group associated with the UDF:

> BC was important. The people needed a psychological reawakening, but not as an end in itself. Then we needed a political strategy. BC was necessary for the previous generation due to the opposition having been crushed, . . . but for the generation growing up [in the eighties], at a time of mass resistance, the people already felt confident. . . . BC was a foundation, a launching pad.[66]

The new strategy was conceived as both building on the previous achievements of BC and rejecting BC's idealism, elitism, and racial exclusion. The movement's exclusion of whites became a lightning rod for more general criticism and reconsideration. As later explained by the UDF's Popo Molefe:

> We saw [BC's] strategic approach as parochial and hemming the expansion of the anti-apartheid movement. At another level, the approach became morally indefensible in the sense that if we had condemned the racism of whites, we could not posit what is immediately perceived as the reverse of that same racism as an alternative. We had to posit a kind of alternative capable of uniting the largest section of South Africans committed to a peaceful and just future—an alternative that could lay a foundation for racial reconciliation.[67]

The alternative to BC's attempt to remold ideas about race—which emerged more fully in the late 1980s and is considered in the next chapter—was a vision of a united South African nation actively opposing continued minority domination. With this new approach, strategic unity replaced an ideologically driven concern for psychological transformation as the primary goal of the opposition, analogous to a reversal of the process by which Africanists in the late 1950s abandoned the ANC's diverse coalition to form the PAC.

As the earlier insistence on spreading ideas before action lost popularity, it was replaced by an overriding urge to act first and let theory emerge as the struggle developed. BC's goal of inspiring mass political consciousness had been effective, as most dramatically indicated by the uprising itself and as further suggested by survey reports of frequent political discussions and increased reading of newspapers.[68] Many assumed that mass assertiveness could henceforth be taken for granted and that the "organization by itself would play an important role in continuing to conscientize."[69] Not everyone agreed with this conclusion, noting in particular the continued isolation of the rural areas. For instance, Saths Cooper of AZAPO argued that the explicit "task of conscientization will only cease at the rendezvous with victory."[70] Despite such disagreement on the need to continue developing a popular will, even AZAPO agreed that after 1976 it had become possible and also necessary to take a less elitist and more confrontational approach. AZAPO's acknowledgment of the need for a more active opposition indicates a broad consensus that popular values rejecting black inferiority or submission had been sufficiently consolidated to provide an urban base for a more concerted physical fight for power. In the early 1980s, AZAPO's continued adherence to Black Consciousness diluted its attempts to implement such a strategy of confrontation, further impelling a realignment away from the BC camp.

As much as the widespread disillusionment with BC reflected a diminished focus on psychological liberation, those who abandoned BC did not dismiss all concern for ideas but instead conceived of ideas as less independently determined. Rather than trying to address self-image as directly as BC had, a new position was forming that "it is through action that the people acquire true psychological emancipation."[71] The central philosophical precept of the opposition was shifting from idealism—that ideas will and should determine behavior—to a form of materialism—that behavior and interests will shape ideas. Accordingly, action could not be postponed until even higher levels of self-confidence and clarity had been achieved, as only through action could consciousness develop further. Psychological liberation required physical liberation, and many sought to redirect the opposition to achieve the latter. Changing values would no longer take center stage, replaced by a primary concern for changing material and social relations. The three years immediately following the Soweto uprising were a period of debate, reconsideration, and realignment among the leading activists of the South African opposition. They were not years of action, in which ideological positions were translated into strategy. The state's repression after the uprising both encouraged reconsideration and discouraged activity. But by late 1979 the quiet maneuverings had started to solidify around a move away from the reflective mode of BC toward a more active mode promoted by the ANC and the people's rising impatience. Conditions were about to change that would lead to mass activity. That activity, as we shall see, gave substance to this emerging shift of allegiances, forcing a refinement of the new ideological position as it was confronted by strategic choices. The new Charterist ideology guided the form that mass mobilization then took.

# 4

# *Toward a National Front, 1980–1983*

In the years immediately following the 1976 uprising and its suppression, a growing number of South African activists had begun to move away from the racial focus and idealism of Black Consciousness toward a more active strategy of opposition and an inclusive national ideology. By late 1979, the economy showed signs of recovering from the recession of the mid-1970s. More significantly, mass militancy and state repression abated, allowing activists to begin to pursue the pragmatic approach they had been discussing. They set out to form local organizations of civil society to press for material gains and later for further political reforms. By 1983, mass participation, rekindled in the 1970s, had been channeled away from outbursts of anger and into more structured forms of mass organization following a national agenda consistent with that originally set forth in the ANC's Freedom Charter. A broad alliance of these Charterist groups, loosely coordinated by the United Democratic Front, managed to ride the wave of mass activism to the forefront of opposition. Those that retained a less pragmatic focus on shaping ideas and racial or class identity, such as AZAPO and others that came together to constitute a National Forum, found themselves caught in the undertow of a decline in mass support.

As the Charterist movement consolidated and moved from ideological realignment to action, its concern with developing an effective strategy began to force subtle changes in its ideology. The rhetorical use of class waned, as it both scared off potential supporters and did not accurately describe a movement that was more active in communities than factories and led more by professional activists than by workers. In its place, the Charterists used the unifying concept of a national opposition to define the goal of antiapartheid organizations that included members of various classes and races. They declared victory in the psychological struggle against the acceptance of racial inferiority and postponed the class struggle for economic justice until after the national struggle for democratic political rights, which was reminiscent of the ANC campaigns of the 1940s.

## Economic Recovery, Reform, and the Local Response

By 1979, the economic downswing that had presaged the 1976 uprising had begun to turn around, and the severe repression that had inflamed and eventually quelled the unrest eased. Activists were released from prison determined to try a more practical form of opposition, as had been discussed in group cells and with the imprisoned veterans of earlier campaigns of active resistance. A mass movement grew to take advantage of the strategic opportunities implied more by structural change than as a direct response to the ideological debates of activist elites. The Charterists used the opening of political space and available economic resources to encourage pervasive localized mobilization.

From 1979 through 1981, the South African economy enjoyed a brief period of renewed growth, counteracting the four years of recession that had severely curtailed the prospects of recently urbanized blacks. The annual gross domestic product rose by an average of 4.5 percent between 1979 and 1981, with increases in revenues from mining, up from R4.1 billion in 1977 to R12.7 billion in 1980, and manufacturing, up from R6.9 billion in 1977 to R15.6 billion in 1981.[1] This economic recovery was notable, though it remained below the 8 percent annual growth rate necessary to create jobs for all of the quarter-million blacks who were leaving school each year.[2] For those who already had jobs, a relative improvement in living conditions became possible; for instance, the number of cars legally registered to black owners increased by a third between 1977 and 1982, although even in 1982 less than 9 percent of all cars in the country were registered to the black majority.[3] Whites no doubt benefited disproportionately from the economic recovery, but the benefits of regained growth did "trickle down" to black South Africans. The state was also a direct beneficiary of economic growth, with state revenues rising to over R2 billion in the first six months of 1980, a 225 percent addition over the same period in the previous year.[4]

To be sustained, the economic recovery required both a skilled labor force and a sufficient market, as both state officials and business leaders well understood. To provide skilled labor that would later have the spending power to add to domestic consumption, African enrollment in universities was raised from 12,800 in 1978 by an average of 3,684 each year up to 1984, as compared with an average addition of 917 students between 1975 and 1977.[5] State expenditures for this expansion of educational opportunities were funded out of the larger revenues resulting from the overall economic growth. The pattern of the early 1970s was, in many ways, being repeated. Economic growth both required and enabled the expansion of educational and economic opportunity for blacks eager to take advantage of their improved prospects.

The impact of this brief expansion of economic activity on the black population should not be overstated, for the economic constraints posed by apartheid and the limits on black advancement remained in place. But the recovery was evidently sufficient to encourage the government to try to restore public confidence by moving away from a reliance on force and by instituting a variety of material reforms. The Botha regime set out, at least in the view of its opponents, to use "reform to buy off certain sectors of the population by granting limited political and economic concessions, while still ensuring that ultimate power rests with itself."[6] In 1979, government commissions recommended improvements in education, legalization of black unions and the relaxation of certain "influx" restrictions on the development of the black urban population. Most of these reforms simply legalized existing practice. The unions had grown without legal protection after the 1973 strikes in Durban had led employers to encourage the formation of worker organizations with which they could negotiate in order to avoid wildcat strikes. The proportion of blacks living in urban areas had risen steadily from the official levels of 33.1 percent in 1970 to 37.9 percent in 1980, largely overwhelming the control systems long before these were modestly amended.[7] In 1984, the state also opened up central urban business districts to black-owned businesses, though few such firms could pay the downtown overhead. These reforms were heralded by the state, in part to please foreign businesses and Western governments seeking justification for continued investment and for resisting sanctions.

The state's publicity regarding its reform program was not intended only for a foreign audience. It was part of a "total strategy," devised in response to the 1976 uprising and subsequent ANC attacks and designed to placate blacks through political and economic reforms while crushing internal and external resistance. The state used both persuasion and coercion to ensure domestic stability, much as opponents of the regime tried both to inspire and mobilize resistance. Government planners hoped that the discipline created by economic opportunity could replace legal constraints, at least those on the urban black elite. To expedite that process and to act as a go-between with the government, local councils of pro-government blacks were established. Starting in 1978, monthly rentals of some township housing were replaced in some areas by ninety-nine-year leases. The guarantee of secure housing in return for continued lease payments was designed to discourage strike activity or other forms of resistance that would lead to missed payments and the loss of housing. The higher public expenditure on schools and housing, supplemented by private efforts coordinated by the corporate sector's newly formed Urban Foundation, were similarly intended to foster an interest in stability among urban blacks. Impoverished rural and migrant Africans, whom the state regarded as more submissive and less needing to be mollified, continued to be consigned to the homelands. Just in case these measures failed, the state also reinforced its coercive strength, with the defense force budget conservatively estimated to have risen from R44 million in 1960 to R47 billion in 1985–86, or approximately 14 percent of total public appropriations.[8]

State reforms funded through increased revenue encouraged a new goal of opposition activity, distinct from that of the early 1970s on reshaping mass psychology through the dissemination of BC ideology. The brief economic recovery implied that resources were now available to fund further material reforms and to improve the living conditions in the townships. The people were eager to organize to press for such gains. Activists who had become disillusioned with the idealism of BC were quick to see the opportunity that this situation presented for putting into practice their more active form of opposition. Unlike the earlier Black Community Programmes, this local mobilization would not be aimed at spreading an elite's ideas but, rather, at actually satisfying the grass roots' "bread and butter" demands. The BC movement as a whole had dismissed this approach as necessitating some form of compromising negotiations and as inconsistent with their idealistic agenda. Many activists now disagreed, however, sharing Lenin's pragmatic belief that "the struggle for reforms is but a means of marshalling the forces" for more fundamental change.[9] According to Popo Molefe, the future national secretary of the UDF, local mobilization in the late 1970s and early 1980s meant the emergence

> of first-level grassroots organizations which have the ability to address that which is essential, real and vital to them. And on the basis of that [we can] teach them the skills of organization and democracy, to give them the confidence that through their united mass action they can intervene and change their lives on no matter how small a scale. . . . Of vital importance, is the ability of the activists to identify burning issues and then to go on mobilizing the people around these issues.[10]

The issues that first galvanized the communities were wide ranging but consistently focused on local concerns and involvement. Rent increases in Lamontville led people there to form a civic association to present their grievances. And a similar housing crisis led to the creation of the Port Elizabeth Black Civic Organization (PEBCO), a group led by a Ford Motor Company worker, which gained additional prominence during a strike against Ford in the same year. In Katlehong, near Johannesburg, a community organization was formed to combat efforts by the state to evict squatters and to press for the installation of electricity, plumbing, and other basic necessities. The organization of squatters in Crossroads, near Cape Town, was started spontaneously by women to defend their homes.[11] Even the Soweto Committee of Ten, founded by members of national political organizations based in South Africa's largest township, set out to be more "involved in grassroots and less in national politics."[12] In 1979, this committee had helped form the

Soweto Civic Association aimed at addressing material issues, which had quickly attracted a large membership. According to Nat Ramokgopa, the association's treasurer:

> It all started when a bus and coal truck collided in Diepkloopf [a section of Soweto]. We started forming a group to pay for the funerals. People saw what Diepkloopf had founded and decided the rest can do the same. We started to address our problems, like electricity, water, sewage, roads, street lights, fencing, transport, etc. . . .
>
> In 1982 Popo Molefe [joined] the Committee of Ten . . . and it started talking more about local issues. Previously they were too busy with international contacts. By 1982 [the Civic] had 15 branches operating with executives elected under the auspices of the Committee of Ten, but with people from the area. In 1983 it started mushrooming to 26 areas, [mostly] because the executive then had a proper programme of action. People read about it in newspapers and pamphlets.[13]

The basic strategy common to all these civic organizations was to mobilize communities around concrete grievances or demands and to protest peacefully for redress until agreements could be negotiated. In applying this strategy, the civic associations became "local political centers [functioning] as the heart and engine of a united front."[14] In part, the tactical means used were simply those that the people had at hand as workers and consumers and that they had employed in a more limited form under the leadership of the ANC in the 1940s and 1950s. Over the next few years, local civic organizations orchestrated the withdrawal of black labor and purchases, in the form of rent boycotts, consumer boycotts against white retailers, and mass "stayaways" from work. As we shall see in the next chapter, these strategies were effective at winning concessions, at least through 1985. The main target of these protests was private businesses and local governments, which the central state government largely left on their own to decide how to respond. As long as local popular, government, and business groups were willing to negotiate solutions, there was little need for central state involvement.

In many of their activities, civic associations were greatly strengthened by their allegiance with the growing number of local and national student and youth organizations. These organizations reflected the "precocity and immaturity" of South Africa's urban youth, open to ideas but insistent on action, forged by the common experience of repression into a generational consciousness not unlike that linking a class or nation.[15] Led principally by the Congress of South African Students (COSAS), which had left BC in the wake of Curtis Nkondo's expulsion from AZAPO, these young people gradually came to understand and identify with the frustrated urban working class more than had the elite student core of BC. For these students,

> the key transition was the 1980 school boycott in Cape Town. The leaders said we must learn the lessons of 1976. Those lessons were [the failures of] black exclusivism, the failure to see the working class as vanguard, and [the reliance on] charismatic leadership. For example, the Committee of 81 [leading the 1980 boycotts] was a revolving membership, and they worked closely with trade unions, since the students were also the sons and daughters of workers.[16]

Building on this experience, students in COSAS and other youth organizations mobilized on a national scale, supported demands beyond those relevant only to education, cooperated with worker and civic structures, and even on occasion joined or helped form unions. Although these groups did not provide the overall leadership that the BC students in the 1970s had, their youthful militancy played a vital role in energizing the communities with which they were more directly associated.[17]

Other than supporting the activities of civics and unions, the only sanction that the youth organizations had at their own disposal were school boycotts, which they exercised with some caution. Critical of the lack of organization of the 1976 uprising, the new student and youth groups instead stressed disciplined strategic action. As early as the 1980 school boycotts in Cape Town, students called for "a new revolutionary strategy" that would build on the achievements of BC and in which workers, parents, and students would "stand united as one community." In the same statement, the Cape Town students declared that "we have achieved a high degree of political awareness and consciousness. . . . Students who have been conscientized now will enter into the factories and workplaces. . . . The end of unorganized mass protest has arrived."[18] These lessons were again evident when student boycotts began in Craddock in 1983, spreading to Pretoria and eventually throughout the country in 1984, as discussed in the next chapter. Only then did the state show its alarm at the students' growing radicalization.

Influenced in part by these student efforts, many of the community groups that formed in the late 1970s and early 1980s to agitate for local issues also shared a commitment to less elitist structures and to nonracialism. They often perceived themselves as alternative structures of democratic governance and required that their leaders be "mandated" and give "report-backs," as was required in many of the unions with which civic associations often shared members.[19] These local organizations also targeted services, which may help explain the spread of nonracialism, a concept and practice with which these groups came to be identified. According to former UDF treasurer Cassim Saloojee, "The local civic organizations which emerged had to reach out to all who could help, including white professionals with experience [and training no blacks had]. Now we don't need so many white professionals since the pattern has been set, . . . the commitment to non-racialism has stuck."[20] The growth of local organizations also helped maintain order in the townships, reinforcing the impression that direct confrontation could be avoided, at least for the time being.

This development of an active opposition, emphasizing inclusive and locally based mobilization, was consistent with the inclinations of a growing number of activists who had turned away from BC's focus on values and psychological self-image. These local groups and activists were converging on an ideological commitment to Charterism, stressing a nonracial and nationally unified struggle to attain those specific political and economic aspirations enshrined in the ANC's Freedom Charter. The rise of Charterism was encouraged by the prevailing social conditions, inlcuding the brief economic recovery and the more broadly consequential state reforms, which both promoted national unity and made the Charter's goals seem more attainable. Even AZAPO felt compelled by these new developments to assert once again its intention "to be more involved in the daily lives of the people."[21] Having concentrated on racial identity and revising ideas, AZAPO remained reluctant to implement its new policy of more active local involvement and thus failed to attract a broad following among a practically minded population. Those who had abandoned their BC ideology, on the other hand, embraced and gained strength from the new form of local activism. For these activists and local groups, the constraints of preordained ideology were pushed aside by the strategic opportunities for renewed activism focused on more material and less idealistic goals.

## Ideological Consolidation

By the early 1980s, material and political reforms encouraged the formation of many local constituent and service groups seeking further gains for blacks. The more that local government and private business were able to grant, the more that local organizations were fortified by their ability to take advantage of new opportunities and to use those benefits to attract more members. Encouraged perhaps by their ability to channel opposition activity in this less confrontational direction, Pretoria proposed the most comprehensive constitutional reformulation in two generations. This move signaled that the political status quo was subject to change, even though the specifics of the change proposed by the state were far from that sought by the populace. In doing so, the South African government pushed national political issues to the fore of the opposition's agenda, where they were grafted onto local issues in a highly explosive mixture. As Tocqueville had perceived in the French Revolution, the very suggestion of reforms heightened expectations of greater change than was intended by the state, setting loose a process of counterdemands that later proved difficult to contain.

In May 1982, after two years of study, Prime Minister P. W. Botha's government published its proposals for a more inclusive form of representation, intended to confirm its reformist image. The proposed constitution gave the officially defined colored and Indian communities the right to vote for their representatives in ethnically separated houses of parliament. Responding to BC's success in combining, as blacks, these groups together with the Africans, the state's proposals were in part designed to separate and win back these two population groups from their growing involvement in the popular opposition. The state attempted in this way to pursue on a grand scale its long-standing "divide and rule" strategies. The new constitution also centered political power in the hands of the new office of the "state president" and his handpicked "President's Council" to oversee all issues of general interest. This council was empowered to break any deadlocks between any of the lower houses. But the most popularly objectionable aspect of the constitutional proposals was the continued total exclusion of the majority of South Africans. Half the African majority were presumed to be citizens of the "independent homelands," and the urban half were presumed to be ill prepared to represent themselves. For these millions, the reforms offered only continued political exclusion and oppression.

Defended by the state as a demonstration of its commitment to reform, the new constitution was seen instead by most South Africans as proof of the government's commitment to continue apartheid. Few if any internal critics were won over. Most viewed the proposals as having thrown down the gauntlet on the issue of political dispensation, which the majority could pick up only through means other than the formal process of ratification, from which they were excluded.[22] The state had presented its practical proposals, encouraging an unintended but equally practical response. Much as the move to eliminate the African franchise in 1936 had led to the establishment of the All-African Convention to coordinate protest, the new constitutional proposals had a similar unifying and concentrating impact on opposition in the 1980s. But unlike 1936, this popular response did not quickly dissipate, coming as it did after almost fifty intervening years of heightening opposition.

Having proposed the new constitution and dedicated itself to gain support for it among the white, Indian, and colored communities, the state was obligated to spread information about the proposals and to encourage discussion, if not debate. State planners may have expected these discussions to lead to the acceptance of their proposals. But the discussions led elsewhere. As Professor Ismail Mohamed, later a vice-president of the UDF in the Transvaal, reported:

> The Tri-Cameral Parliament proposals were a blessing. They gave us the opportunity to politic since the state wanted a broader base. . . . All of us who were opposed to the Tri-Cameral parliament were

> united. . . . Some of us understood that those early [local] organizations couldn't confront the state and resolve social conflict, but that out of them would grow other bodies that could confront and resolve, in part by identifying people for a vanguard. . . . Already in 1981 at the Anti-Republic Day Commemoration we tried to make a national organization. The repression of BC still made us wary of producing another mass organization. The possibility to do so was created by the state's efforts to broaden political involvement.[23]

The most immediate response to the parliamentary reforms came from the Indian community, which had been given the right to vote on its new role as a minor partner in the apartheid regime. Opposition to the proposals galvanized the reemergence of the Natal and Transvaal Indian congresses, which had remained largely dormant since their involvement in the 1950s as major affiliates of the ANC-led Congress Alliance. In 1983, these groups played a vital role in the creation of the United Democratic Front and continued their resistance to the new constitution even after two-thirds of white voters endorsed its adoption in November 1983. Much as their involvement in the Congress Alliance had been criticized by Africanists who later broke away to form the PAC, the distinct role of the Indian groups in resisting their separate enfranchisement was condemned—as an attempt to "fight ethnicity with ethnic organizations"—by BC adherents who remained outside the UDF.[24] Even committed nonracialists voiced concern that the involvement of these Indian groups had to be offset by greater African participation.[25] But these concerns were not sufficient to prevent the consensus in 1983 among all opposition groups on the need to unite in resisting the new constitution and to prepare for the future.

Beginning early in 1983, an effort was made to draw together all of those interested in opposing the parliamentary proposals. One of the leaders of this effort was Saths Cooper, convicted in December 1976 as one of the "SASO 9," who had joined AZAPO upon his release from Robben Island the year before. One of the relatively small number to leave prison as a continuing adherent of BC, Cooper had been singled out for criticism by ardent Charterists for his lack of respect toward the leading ANC prisoners on the island. He was joined in the effort to create a unified opposition to the new constitution by Dr. Neville Alexander, who had been released from Robben Island in 1974 after having won the respect of many of the

ANC prisoners during his eleven-year term. Alexander had long professed nonracialism combined with a more strenuous advocacy of socialism and a rejection of cross-class alliances than was consistent with Charterism, carving out a position that was independent of both the BC and the ANC traditions.[26] Cooper, Alexander, and others formed the National Forum committee, representing a wide spectrum of the opposition and constituting a locus for the discussion and coordination of efforts and ideas. This committee did indeed have an impressively broad array of members, including inter alia four who later played a prominent role in the UDF, four from AZAPO, two unionists, and four "independents."[27]

The formation of such a diverse group testifies to the unifying force of common opposition to the new constitution, which at least temporarily eased the tensions between AZAPO and those who favored the ANC's Charterist approach. Since 1979 there had been a series of conflicts among these groups in which AZAPO had antagonized many of its critics, resulting in even more activists' leaving the BC camp. In 1980, AZAPO had refused to participate in a commemoration of the Freedom Charter or a Soweto service for recently killed ANC cadres, thereby undermining any claims of continued nonsectarianism and forcing ANC sympathizers to choose between conflicting loyalties.[28] In a 1981 AZAPO conference, a "tough battle" had begun over the continuing issues of class analysis, leading Eric Molobi and others to conclude that AZAPO would not revise its fundamentally BC ideology and so should be abandoned.[29] Fights over control of the annual Soweto commemoration of the 1976 uprising had broken out between AZAPO and the Charterists in 1981, 1982, and 1983. And all of these conflicts had further weakened AZAPO's popular support, making it all the more surprising that AZAPO could still play a major role in the 1983 unity efforts.

The cooperation between Cooper and Alexander in forming the National Forum was also remarkable given the differences between the groups these two leaders represented. Alexander was associated with the Cape Action League, a small group of Trotskyists with historical links to the Unity Movement tradition, known for their radical advocacy of class analysis, socialism, noncollaboration, and refusal to exclude whites purely on the basis of race.[30] AZAPO, of which Cooper was a leading member, had remained committed to excluding all whites from the preliberation struggle, rather than only those with direct links to the state or capital.[31] But within AZAPO, Cooper was a notable advocate of socialism and of informal cooperation with sympathetic whites. Cooper also had a tense personal relationship with some of AZAPO's African leaders, who later unsuccessfully attempted to block his 1985 election as the organization's first Indian president.[32] Apparently there were grounds for cooperation among these individuals and groups, however, particularly in regard to their common desire for socialism and rejection of alliances with those white capitalists who later supported the UDF. Indeed, their somewhat uneasy cooperation lasted longer than did their attempts to work with the Charterists in the National Forum.

The first meeting of the National Forum brought together representatives of AZAPO, followers of Neville Alexander, and a small number of Charterists, for what was described as the opening talks about a united opposition to the new constitution. At that meeting in June 1983, liberal and ethnically defined organizations, such as the Indian Congresses, were criticized, and a vote was taken on what became known as the "Azanian Manifesto" (see Appendix B). This document, described at first as a compromise between BC ideology and the Freedom Charter, had a more explicitly socialist orientation than did either of its predecessors and clearly distinguished the Forum from the more inclusive Charterist tendency with whom unity was then being discussed.

According to the Azanian Manifesto, South African oppression is best understood as a unique form of "racial capitalism" in which the development of apartheid policies and capitalist exploitation have been complementary. By connecting apartheid and capitalism in this way, the manifesto tried to end the division within the opposition between those who preferred a racial and those who wanted a class analysis, and to ensure that opposition groups used the issue of economic exploitation in their criticism of continued oppression. As Peter Jones observed, the movement could thus "successfully fuse the national and social questions," assuming that "national liberation could be achieved only conterminously with the abolition of capitalism in South Africa."[33] The manifesto was an attempt to stay within the formal confines of a BC emphasis on race and still, as Griffiths Zabala maintains, to "learn from 1976 and the criticism of us as elite" and to focus increasingly on the workers' struggle.[34] The manifesto regarded nonracialism as a goal that could be achieved only after a social revolution had dismantled racial capitalism. In the meantime, the manifesto advised a strategy of "antiracialism," in which racial identity would continue to be used to mobilize protest. Whites would therefore be excluded from the struggle. The end result envisioned was a unified nation, as contrasted by the Forum with the Freedom Charter's guarantee of "all [distinct] national groups and races" being encouraged to continue to "use their own language and to develop their own culture and customs."[35]

The National Forum's immediate concern with formulating such an explicit statement of ideology was indicative of the continuing primary concern for ideas rather than action among the BC adherents in AZAPO and among the Marxists in the Cape Action League. These groups were unwilling to tone down their socialist rhetoric as a practical means to avoid alienating less radical potential allies. The Forum defined itself in terms of ideology, spurning any strategic compromises conducive to the formation of an alliance of all those opposed to the new constitution. They welcomed only those committed to eliminating "racial capitalism." This did not mean that the Forum leadership believed that the mere dissemination of its radical ideas would be sufficient to challenge continued oppression. Even Lybon Mabasa of AZAPO confessed in a speech to the first Forum meeting that the BC movement in the 1970s had relied too heavily on the power of ideas alone, mistaking "ideology [as] . . . an end for itself."[36] But the practical requirements for a more active approach had apparently not been fully absorbed. The Forum did not develop to the point that it could attract a broad following or pose a real threat to the state, which saw little need to respond to merely rhetorical attacks.

By committing itself to a radical program, the Forum had cut itself off from the growing, locally based efforts at forcing negotiations, which many Forum adherents saw as a form of collaboration. They also cut themselves off from important allies and sources of funds necessary for organizing direct confrontation, which the Forum never succeeded in achieving. BC adherents implicitly blamed this failure on the highly intellectual nature of their new allies: "The Trotskyites [in CAL and the Unity Movement] have one difficulty—for all their thorough analysis they are not very thorough in praxis. They see a world class struggle and lose their focus on reality. They are part and parcel of the struggle, having not sold out, but BC must make sure it is not swept away from reality by them."[37] Neville Alexander became no less critical of AZAPO, describing his alliance with it as a matter of convenience akin to that between Stalin and Churchill.[38] But despite such mutual recriminations, neither AZAPO nor Alexander's followers were willing to sacrifice ideological consistency for strategic advantage. By contrast, the Charterists who came together to form the UDF avoided any explicit and detailed description of their ideology and thereby succeeded in forming a broad and active coalition.

With the manifesto's adoption, a clear divide was established, and the pretense of the Forum's acting as an initial convention of unity fell away. In just a few days, those groups with Charterist tendencies that had sent representatives to the Forum—including the Congress of South African Students and two unions—had disassociated themselves from it. And in just two weeks the exiled National Executive Committee of the ANC, influential among the internal Charterists, derided the National Forum as "those who, while posing as socialists . . . and defenders of Black pride, seek to divide the people and divert them from the pursuit of the goals enshrined in the Freedom Charter. Through their activities, these elements show hatred for the Charter and mass united action, no less virulent than that displayed by the Pretoria regime."[39] Once this division between the National Forum and the Charterists had become clear, the Charterists turned their attention to the strategic and ideological issues that distinguished them as a unified group capable of launching its own campaign against the state.

The National Forum was composed of existing political organizations based on an established ideological allegiance. By contrast, those local organizations that had emerged since 1979 were united more by their common efforts to agitate for immediate demands than by their ideological affinity. These groups were provoked by debates over the National Forum and its manifesto to form an alternative coalition and an ideological position consistent with the strategic necessities of local politics and active confrontation. They found that the twenty-five-year-old demands of the Freedom Charter unified many of their local demands under general categories and provided a framework for cooperation that justified cross-class alliances. The Charter's relatively pragmatic demands and the ANC's tactical flexibility corresponded to their own eagerness to seize the strategic opportunities created by economic recovery and state reform. This perception was encouraged by those activists who had rejected BC and embraced the ANC tradition and who attempted to unify the increasingly popular movement of local organizations under their national leadership.

The Charterists argued that they could unite disparate groups because they did not insist on adherence to a narrow set of beliefs. Instead, they claimed to represent all who opposed a common enemy, "correctly defined, not as white people, but as a system of white supremacy and national domination."[40] According to "Terror" Lekota, publicity secretary of the UDF and one of the "SASO 9" defendants—whose nickname purportedly refers to his soccer abilities—defining the source of oppression not in racial or personal terms but as

> the system, is not at all vague. It is very real and experience has brought this home to us. . . . Only those who are lazy and seek short-cuts to freedom argue that "the system" is too vague. It is very possible to explain the nature of our oppression by pointing out those groups and classes which constitute its pillars. But to [vilify] individuals, groups, etc. is dangerous since one can quite easily create a followership that will forever be in search of visible enemies.[41]

The Charterists' refusal to define themselves in reference to the specific groups that they opposed, such as whites or capitalists, necessitated the adoption of a more abstract concept by which they could identify themselves as defying the system of oppression. A nonracial form of national identity, as originally formulated by the ANC, suited their purposes. Not only did such a national identity avoid the exclusion of any race or class, but it also was elastic enough to accommodate the broadest possible array of groups and ideas. The strategic necessity for unity and for isolating supporters of the regime set the terms by which the nation would be defined. Economic integration had already created the potential for a single nation, largely undermining tribal divisions despite the efforts of the state to create homelands. Only the Inkatha movement among the Zulus had succeeded in maintaining such tribal loyalties.[42]

Political domination had generated widespread opposition that could now be united in a "national democratic struggle" as conceived by this emerging movement. All South Africans who shared a "voluntary adherence" to the ideals of a nonracial, democratic country were defined as part of the nation, with those who continued to defend minority rule denigrated "as foreigners on African soil."[43]

Adherents of BC within AZAPO criticized the reemergence of this fluid concept of national unity for being overly inclusive, although it was precisely for this reason that this unifying concept appealed to the Charterists. According to Lybon Mabasa of AZAPO, such a broad alliance was unprincipled, reflecting a lack of "commitment as to who is included and excluded. Radical and liberal groups, Church and secular groups work side by side as political partners. Even organizations such as the Black Sash [women's legal aid group], who have a close and cordial relationship with ruling class parties, exist within the UDF. . . . Unity is good, but not at all costs."[44] Much as the early Africanists in the 1940s had criticized the ANC as an "ideological omnibus,"[45] AZAPO leaders protested having to make accommodations to diverse groups for mere strategic advantage and abstracting the enemy to the point that everyone seemed to be a possible friend. In their view, ideological coherence was still more important than strategic advantage, despite the evident inability of ideological assertions by themselves to end minority rule and repression. On purely ideological grounds, they rejected alliances with any beneficiaries of domination, regardless of their color or liberalism, as "it is ridiculous to hate the stick that hits you but love the man who wields it."[46] The strategic advantage of embracing even those who had rejected their historical ties to oppression did not impress these BC stalwarts, though it did impress the more practically minded Charterists.

Consistent with their strategic priorities, the national identity that the Charterists envisioned was distinguished from the "orthodox" tradition of exclusive Africanist nationalism by its inclusive, nonracial character. The Charterists built on Black Consciousness's admission of Indians and coloreds and adopted the description of all these officially distinct groups and Africans as being black. But the Charterists went the next step of also incorporating whites in a nonracial, national struggle. This move brought significant strategic advantages, much as it had for the ANC's Congress Alliance in the 1950s, when the opposition had been less fully developed.[47] White compatriots could provide financial resources and their own insights about the state, could make it more difficult for the state to identify its potential enemies, and could even plant bombs where the presence of blacks would have aroused greater suspicion. White allies in the struggle also made it more likely that they and other whites would remain in South Africa after a transition of power, providing their skills, expertise, and capital accumulated under minority rule, just as many whites had done in postliberation Zimbabwe. Such early concerns about a postapartheid reconciliation between black and white South Africans had a pragmatic basis but were also defended in more idealistic terms. This convergence of pragmatism and idealism is exemplified in a statement by "Terror" Lekota, written surreptitiously while he was imprisoned on charges of treason:

> It is my genuine desire that when freedom day comes it should not find reconciliation too far to attain. Our freedom day and reconciliation should be very close to each other. . . . The more jarring and shattering the methods [of struggle], the deeper the alienation of our people and, consequently, the more difficult the process of healing the wounds and reconciling the people.
>
> Non-racialism as a method embodies the process of pulling black and whites together so that they jointly dismantle apartheid. In the process they already have a chance of learning to know each other. . . . And artificial suspicions, nurtured by years of apartheid myths and propaganda, are demolished. And when freedom comes it will not be the victory of blacks over whites but that of the people of South Africa over an evil system that has for so long set them up one against another. . . . We cannot wait for freedom day to teach white and black South Africans to love and live with each other. We must begin today, now, because if we cannot do it now we shall not be able to do it some other day.[48]

The Charterists argued that achieving both the immediate and the long-term advantages of white inclusion required that the liberation struggle itself be nonracial. They disagreed with the Black Consciousness precept that a struggle conceived around exclusive racial identity could achieve the desired end result of nonracialism, which the Charterists described as trying to "rectify a wrong with another wrong."[49] Both views were based on the assumption that racial identity was situational and could be molded to suit the purposes of the opposition, just as the state had projected racial distinctions as a basis for oppression. The Charterists and BC did not disagree on the basis of racial identity, but only on whether the end goal of nonracialism was to be achieved through nonracial means. Again, Lekota argued for a consistent nonracialism as necessary to achieve an ideal:

> In political struggle . . . the means must always be the same as the ends. . . . How else can one expect a racialistic movement to imbue our society with a non-racial character on the dawn of our freedom day? A political movement cannot bequeath to society a characteristic it does not itself possess. To expect it to do so is like asking a heathen to convert a person to Christianity. The principles of that religion are unknown to the heathen, let alone the practice.[50]

The same pragmatism that implied the necessity of nonracialism as a means of struggle also implied that the ideal of cross-race cooperation could be compromised to the extent required by social and logistical reality. The state's imposed racial distinctions were reflected in many facets of social life, raising suspicions and creating different needs among groups. The Charterists acknowledged that these realities could not be simply ignored and could be overcome only gradually.[51] In the meantime, local structures were developed according to segregated residential areas, by activists drawn from the same community. As was the case in the mass mobilization by the ANC in the 1950s, communal distinctions would have to be observed in practice, because organizers were most effective if, in the words of Albertina Sisulu, they "work where you know best."[52] Even black student organizations remained separate from the white-dominated structures abandoned with the formation of BC. As a result, nonracialism remained a relatively abstract concept to blacks organized separately from whites, although this did not mean that the black rank and file of the Charterist movement were unacquainted with the concept.[53] Whites in the Charterist coalition were present at many of the larger mass meetings and funerals, and their opposition groups and activities received wide publicity. Nonracialism was compromised out of strategic necessity in the day-to-day struggle, but this compromise did not vitiate the principle.

Reflecting their primary concern for ideological consistency, BC adherents and their socialist allies criticized the Charterists for departing from, in practice, their own principle of consistent nonracialism. They contended that the Charterists' nonracial rhetoric camouflaged a fundamentally divisive "multiracialism" that assumed that racial distinctions were preordained. In the view of BC adherents, organizing alliances or recognizing minority rights among distinct groups, rather than encouraging national unity, would reinforce divisions and make future reconciliation more difficult. These critics objected particularly to the Freedom Charter's guarantee of distinct "group rights" and to more recent statements from the ANC that described as "fact that people happen to be members of different races."[54] The Charterists justified such statements as recognition of the practical realities of organizing within South African society, which did not, however, diminish their commitment to nonracialism. Only because AZAPO remained relatively inactive in organizing black communities and continued to exclude whites could they avoid the difficulties of mobilizing across racial and ethnic divisions. AZAPO's and the National Forum's alternative policy of combating racism through a racially exclusive struggle, described as "antiracialism," was perhaps more consistently observed in practice but, according to the Charterists, nonetheless misguided. The position of ideological purity from which AZAPO criticized the ethnic divisions of the Charterist organization carried with it the price of dwindling support among a practically minded populace that did not share AZAPO's more abstract concern with ideological consistency.

Both opposition camps sought the high ground of denying the ultimate necessity of racial or national division, in order to prevent the state from using such tools for domination and to present the people a vision of life without such division. They disagreed on whether a racially exclusive or inclusive struggle could more effectively achieve this goal. Both movements saw how powerful these identities could be, especially as they were used to the state's advantage, and they tried to use the same forces for their opposite ends. BC rhetoric rejected the scientific existence of race but used racial identity to define itself and to justify opposition by all blacks. Charterists also rejected race but sought to organize all population groups into a national opposition to systematic domination. Although both were concerned with future reconciliation, both also were guided by the strategic assessment made by Allan Boesak before his move to Charterism, that "true reconciliation cannot take place without confrontation."[55] BC and Charterism both attempted to heighten conflict while continuing to look for its resolution, though they differed in defining the conflict along racial or national lines, with the former justified ideologically and the latter based on strategic considerations.

The Charterists' strategic effort to build a united national opposition implied not only a nonracial coalition but also cooperation across class divisions. White businessmen were encouraged to join or support the emerging Charterist movement, serving the interests of the opposition by further isolating the regime and attracting financial contributions from this wealthy constituency. It was expected that businesses would welcome this invitation to align themselves with the movement, as capital had already begun to voice its disapproval of the economic constraints posed by apartheid and its eagerness to establish friendly relations with the country's possible future leaders. This strategy proved effective, with major industrialists such as Tony Bloom of Premier Milling and Chris Ball of Barclays Bank later providing the UDF with much-needed resources. Middle-class black professionals were also encouraged to join the movement, thereby impeding the state's efforts to mollify this elite through reforms. Embittered by having achieved greater economic prosperity while being denied corresponding social status, access to residential areas reserved for whites, and basic political rights, many middle-class blacks did join the Charterists, providing additional skills and resources. Eventually the UDF included among its affiliates the National African Federated Chamber of Commerce, NAFCOC, and regional black trade associations.

To attract such middle- and upper-class allies, the Charterists intentionally avoided recommending an immediate transformation to socialism, which would have alienated these potential supporters by raising fears of radical change and seizures of private property. The ANC later reinforced such reassurances, denied being "a socialist party," and held cordial discussions with major corporate executives.[56] At the same time, radicals were reassured by the Charterists' commitment to consider socialism, after national liberation had been achieved, and by the ANC's denial that it was opposed to "class consciousness and class emancipation."[57] To appeal to such contradictory interests, the Charterists simply avoided a more complete discussion of economic alternatives, and the South African Communist party continued to advocate a "two-staged revolution," according to which issues of economic transformation were to be postponed until after national liberation had been achieved.[58]

This avoidance of immediate advocacy of socialism enabled the Charterists to appeal to diverse interests, and it also had the practical benefit of focusing their energies on achieving one goal at a time. As argued by former BC adherent and later ANC supporter Cyril Ramaphosa of the National Union of Mineworkers,

> what prevents [our dealing with] economic transformation [now] is our having to deal with the eradication of apartheid [first]. For that we need a massive mobilization different from the mobilization necessary for [full] liberation. First we need to use instruments, such as the Freedom Charter, to mobilize and to encourage people to continue struggling for immediate demands. Such a short term program gives people incentive. Later we can conscientize and educate people toward greater class consciousness.[59]

This argument appealed both to those activists who believed that it would be impossible to mount a campaign for socialism under the current conditions of oppression and to the rank and file, whose most direct concerns were short-term material issues and the end of the immediately evident restrictions of apartheid. Although many Charterist leaders agreed with the more radical groups "that apartheid and capitalism are linked," they also believed that the masses did not yet fully appreciate this link and were not prepared to confront both aspects of oppression at once.[60] Forcing a direct confrontation with both the state and private enterprise would not only alienate potential allies but would also impose the demands of the "abstract intellectualism" of political activists and theoreticians on the "concrete and living reality" of the popular antiapartheid struggle.[61] Instead, the Charterists argued that in the short term, "we need to phase our approach and not look for one big jump to socialism."[62] A new political and economic order could not emerge full blown out of the social equivalent of an astronomical "big bang" but would have to be worked toward and built in a series of concrete steps.

The socialists and BC adherents in the National Forum were highly critical of these arguments for a struggle that avoided any commitment to socialism until after democratic rights had been won. They contended that such an approach ignored the historical links between apartheid and capitalism, which made it impossible to defeat one without the other. In their view, if socialism were not placed on the immediate agenda, it would never be achieved. The result would instead be liberal capitalism, like that resulting from the French Revolution and, in their view, as it was apparently being reconstituted in Zimbabwe. The poor would gain political rights but remain poor.[63] They dismissed the arguments for postponing consideration of these issues as a sham perpetrated by middle-class elements in the Charterist movement who were opposed to socialism even as a distant goal. These criticisms reflected the ideological concerns of the National Forum affiliates, who seemed more interested in enunciating the goal of eradicating "racial capitalism" than in deciding on a strategy and putting it into action. The more practically minded Charterists countered that spreading the idea of socialism would not by itself bring that goal closer but would instead raise fears and invite state repression, with which those in the Forum were apparently less concerned.

In general, much of the Charterists' rhetoric was intended to allay the fears of those more conservative potential allies who might be repelled by calls for black assertiveness or socialism. At the same time, more radical interpretations were not denied. With this two-sided approach, the Charterists attempted to revive the ANC's traditional alliance of the working class and bourgeoisie, united by national mobilization against apartheid. The long-term results of mass mobilization, and ultimately of negotiations with the state, were purposely left vague and open. According to Steve Tshwete, a UDF activist in the eastern Cape and later an official of the ANC: "What happens after the implementation of the people's charter—whether there is a socialist democracy or not—will certainly depend on the strength of the working class itself in the class alliance that we call a people's democracy."[64] In the meantime, potential allies who might have been alienated by explicit calls for socialism were reassured that the Charterists "have never claimed to be led by the working class."[65] Class distinctions and preferences for socialism or capitalism were simply irrelevant to the Charterists' efforts to build an inclusive national opposition.

The arguments of both the Charterist and the National Forum adherents had their own internally consistent logic, emerging out of distinct priorities with widely differing implications. The Forum, united by its interest in ideology and advocacy of class conflict, was less concerned with the practicalities of active mobilization. Instead, it relied more on the inspiration of its radical ideas to remove the psychological barriers to popular resistance, much as the BC movement in the 1970s had relied on racial assertiveness to bring an end to black submission. The Charterists, mainly occupied with the practical necessities of mobilizing and uniting a national movement, were more willing to compromise and accommodate diverse alliances to achieve incremental change. For them, action replaced ideas as an overriding issue. Even the Charterists' central ideological concept of national identity was determined by and subordinated to strategic imperatives, much as the ANC's earlier Congress Alliance had been "primarily a tactical, not an ideological one."[66] Charterism was less jarring to whites in its call for an inclusive effort toward piecemeal change. But because it evoked a more active form of opposition, the Charterist movement would also prove to be a step toward "deeper polarization and conflict."[67]

While intellectuals and leaders sought to consolidate their positions through arguments about the fine points of ideology and strategy, the mass of South Africans were increasingly drawn to the Charterist camp by its practical appeal. By the early 1980s, abated state repression and the brief economic recovery had convinced a large portion of the populace of the need for a more active form of opposition, more robust against the possibility of future repression, and better able to press for available material benefits. AZAPO and its National Forum allies tried to use this opportunity to reinvigorate popular support for their ideals. Their abstract arguments failed to attract a significant following among a populace tired of rhetoric and eager to act. Disillusionment with the Forum helped focus popular attention on the alternative approach of a national democratic, nonracial, and cross-class opposition, better suited to take advantage of opportunities presented by prevalent conditions and buttressed by the rising popularity of the ANC. The emergent Charterist movement consolidated its support, unifying local organizations into a broad antiapartheid coalition that continued to gather momentum even after the initial impetus for coordinating opposition to the new constitution had faded from view.

## Building a National Opposition

As much as its ideology was elaborated in debates with the National Forum and AZAPO, the new Charterist movement remained characteristically more concerned with action than ideas and did not come forward with a clear statement of its own policy. Even the Freedom Charter, adopted by the ANC in 1956, was not formally embraced until years after the transition away from BC was clear. No new ideological manifesto was drawn up, as it was at the first and divisive National Forum meeting. Instead, the focus was almost purely organizational, and the strategic needs of the movement encouraged both a reluctance to be constrained by specific policies and a pragmatic openness to alliances across class and color lines. An "umbrella" front was established to coordinate local opposition activities, but not ideas. All those groups united in their rejection of apartheid were welcomed, regardless of their individual members' positions or ideology. Indeed, unity in opposition was the ideology, seen as defining and mobilizing the nation. The unity achieved by such a disregard of differences within the nation would be the strength of the new movement, although this disregard later proved to be also a weakness.

Brought together in response to the constitutional proposals of 1982, the opposition forces enjoyed opportunities to discuss openly their plans as part of the state-initiated referendum regarding political dispensation. In February 1983, the Reverend Allan Boesak used such an opportunity to propose a form of organizational coordination, linking all those united "in the politics of refusal," if they could not be united by more positive agreement.[68] This proposal echoed earlier efforts in 1981 to form a national organization of civic organizations, but only after another two years had enough local groups come to see their common purpose that a "United Democratic Front" became a real possibility.[69]

On August 20, 1983, in Mitchells Plain near Cape Town, with some of the overflowing and boisterous crowd literally hanging from the hall's rafters, the United Democratic Front was born. Delegates came from local organizations throughout the country, gathering in numbers never attempted by BC and thus testifying at the very start to the new movement's organizational capacity. Those who promoted the formation of a front described it as reminiscent of the Congress Alliance of the 1950s, "standing for unity in action, accepting the fact that all the organizations coming together have got differences . . . of class, differences of ideology, differences of intent, but all of them agree that they reject the reform proposals."[70] According to Cassim Saloojee, named as one of the two UDF national treasurers, all that was necessary for inclusion was a minimal commitment to "a unitary South Africa, non-racialism and democracy. . . . We began as a loose front, with the increasing need for ideological coherence emerging only later."[71] To maximize the Front's initial appeal, even its implicit association with the ANC and the Freedom Charter was at least formally denied, and affiliates of the National Forum were invited to join the UDF coalition.[72] Much as the BC movement in the early 1970s had presented itself as independent of both the ANC and the PAC, the UDF ostensibly presented itself as nonaligned and stated that it did not intend to "replace the accredited liberation movements of the people."[73]

Whereas the UDF avoided BC's greater insistence on ideological discussion and coherence, the Front's leadership acknowledged that they were building on the achievements of the BC movement in the 1970s. As Allan Boesak declared at the UDF's inauguration, his generation had not been "brainwashed" by "the tranquilizing drugs of apathy and fear" but had become after 1976 "the most politically conscious generation of young people determined to struggle for a better future."[74] That consciousness was BC's legacy to the UDF. Without it, the widespread local organization of the early 1980s would likely not have been possible. The dissemination of ideas had set the stage for action, which now moved beyond a primary focus on ideas.

Recognition of the debt owed to the efforts of the earlier BC movement may help explain the surprising degree of cooperation between the UDF and the National Forum in their first year. For instance, at the 1984 Soweto commemoration of the 1976 uprising—in past years an occasion for conflict—symbols of both the UDF's Charterist allies and the National Forum were evident. Chants hailed exiled ANC president Oliver Tambo, and model AK-47s emblazoned with ANC colors were waved in the same hall in which were hung banners proclaiming the Forum's slogan of "One Azania, One Nation." AZAPO and Charterist leaders cordially shared the platform. In September 1983, these leaders again cooperated to resist a clandestine effort to divide them, disclaiming the fake pamphlets according to which the UDF and National Forum had attacked each other.[75] The strategic imperative of unity was evidently more important to these leaders than were their differences, at least for the time being.

The cooperation between the UDF and National Forum was noteworthy, but it could not completely obscure UDF's strong partisanship toward Charterism. This bias was most clearly reflected in the policy of not excluding white groups or leaders and in the emphasis on strategic action over ideas, but it was also openly admitted in statements by individuals closely associated with the formation of the Front. For instance, in the month before the UDF's formal establishment, Curtis Nkondo, embittered after his removal from AZAPO, called for unity only among those who shared adherence to the Freedom Charter.[76] Even at the UDF launch itself, amidst protestations of neutrality between the Charter and BC, Indian leader George Sewpersadh proclaimed that "the ideas of the Freedom Charter will be pursued by the UDF."[77] Nelson Mandela's greetings from prison were read out at the launch, to the enthusiastically pro-ANC crowd. Evidently, the looseness of the initial coalition made it unlikely that the UDF's formal structures would overrule such expressions of allegiance to one ideological camp over another.

The UDF was structured so as to make it unlikely that statements of support for Charterism could be precluded, and enough of the UDF leadership and affiliated members shared this bias to make impossible any enforcement of neutrality. Much of the UDF's strategy, as we have already seen, was designed to antagonize as few potential allies as possible, but this intention was largely ignored by various pro-ANC speakers in their attitude toward those who remained loyal to BC. For instance, the veteran white activist and a symbolic "patron" of the UDF, Helen Joseph, labeled the UDF's inauguration as a "great gathering after a quarter century of silence."[78] This description must have startled the former BC adherents with whom she shared the platform at the UDF launch and surely alienated any BC loyalists who learned of it. One of the former BC adherents who had joined the UDF, Aubrey Mokoena, was less dismissive of the past significance of BC but was none the less disparaging of the National Forum as an attempt to fragment the opposition. According to Mokoena, "We cannot have a struggle within a struggle. Everybody is invited to come under the big umbrella of the UDF."[79] This view, though consistent with the UDF's official policy of remaining open to all opponents of apartheid, suggests a growing impatience with the only other significant opposition grouping and an insistence that only the UDF could be the locus of unity. The Front embraced its internal diversity; diversity outside the Front was rejected as divisive, although this did not immediately lead to conflict among the opposition groups.

Intolerance of BC stalwarts was indicative of the growing adherence to the internal Charterist movement, of which the UDF was itself a prominent expression, but it may also have been the result of the continuing resurgence of loyalty to the exiled ANC. In the years leading up to the formation of the UDF, the ANC had continued to stage guerrilla attacks, most prominently resulting in damage to one of South Africa's vital "oil from coal" conversion plants in June 1980, and a car bomb explosion outside military headquarters in downtown Pretoria in May 1983 that had left nineteen dead and over two hundred injured. In addition, the ANC attempted to associate itself with the growing FOSATU union federation, and in 1982 ANC flags were unfurled in the front of the funeral procession of unionist Neil Aggett, despite the objections of Aggett's own union.[80] By 1985, the ANC was even claiming to have organized historical events with which it actually had had little involvement, including the 1974 Pro-FRELIMO rallies that had led to the imprisonment of the "SASO 9."[81] All of these activities, and claims of responsibility for the activities of others, had further swelled the ANC's internal following. These activities also served to keep the state's security apparatus focused on the ANC, perhaps even more than it focused on internal developments, although concern at the time for the ANC reflected the state's preexisting fears more than any potentially viable threat posed by the ANC's attacks or internal operations.

Just as adherence to Charterism or the ANC and intolerance of BC remained an undercurrent at the formation of the UDF, so too were there hints of a growing adherence to the principles of socialism in the Front. For instance, unionist Samson Ndou addressed the UDF launch using rhetoric similar to that of the Azanian Manifesto in placing the working class's interests at the center of the Front's concerns. According to Ndou, "Responsibility for the defense of racial capitalism lies not with industrial capitalists but with their organized arm, the state. To defeat the apartheid state we need powerful mass based political organization capable of waging a political struggle on behalf of the oppressed and exploited."[82] Allan Boesak was similarly deferential to the interests and organization of the working class in his exaggerated description of the UDF as the "first overt political move by South Africa's potentially powerful black union movement."[83] Although the unions were not the leading organized force in the Front, and class analysis was not yet prevalent throughout the UDF, from the start socialists were attracted to the UDF because it appeared open to such direction. But for all its nascent tendencies toward class analysis, the UDF began as an alliance that included small traders and others whose early support might have been threatened by a more open commitment to socialism.

Together with the undercurrents of Charterism, loyalty to the ANC, anti-BC sentiments, and protosocialism, the UDF also managed to accommodate mass anger together with its more characteristic nonviolent stance. For instance, a UDF local meeting in 1984 included songs looking forward to the time when "we will shoot the Dutch people, shoot the white people."[84] But such advocacy of violence was largely kept in abeyance by the more widely accepted view put forward by the UDF copresident Archie Gumede, that "you must be aware that the system has many ways of provoking people into rash actions and that is one thing that all you must guard against."[85] Albertina Sisulu, another copresident, suggested that restraining mass militancy was part of the motivation for founding the Front: "The UDF formation was pushed by the leaders when the leaders saw the people getting out of hand. . . .

Leaders try to stop uprisings. It is the government that wants uprisings."[86] Such remarks indicated the strategic assessment of the UDF leadership that the 1976 uprising had been sufficient to inspire popular activity but that further spontaneous unrest would disrupt the process of organizational consolidation by inviting state repression. Instead, the UDF and its affiliates would increasingly promote highly organized forms of protest that would reinforce popular support for the movement without unnecessary violence.

The fact that the UDF could combine pro-ANC, anti-BC, and violent sentiments with its self-proclaimed ideological neutrality and avoidance of spontaneous unrest attests to the Front's inclusive nature. All of these views could be accommodated because all were voiced and no one position was formally adopted or enforced to the exclusion of the others. Ideological divisions were defused by the Charterists' fundamentally nonideological target of strategic unity. Indeed, unity itself had become the guiding ideology, justifying as broad a national opposition as possible, not as a tight political machine, but as an inclusive social movement.[87] The organizational framework of a front was perfectly suited to this goal, allowing for the coordination of groups with diverse and changing views. General principles were kept purposefully vague so as to make possible such a coalition.

Those who had formed the UDF's constituent organizations remained active mostly on the local level, with little direct formal control over the national leadership. This structure allowed the leadership to remain flexible enough to respond to its diverse constituents and changing circumstances. To the leadership also fell the responsibility of preserving unity by coordinating local activities and setting basic policies or demands. According to Gatsby Mazrui, the labor representative on the first Transvaal regional executive of the UDF,

> The grassroots, without education and politicization, don't put demands. The reality is that we are not at liberty to educate them. Unfortunately this means that intellectuals lead. The onus is on that level to take the initiative. It sounds undemocratic, but [our] situation is not a normal one. . . . Local organizations formed the UDF but at the leadership level those familiar with the complex nature of the issues get most involved.[88]

The UDF's free-floating national leaders came from diverse backgrounds. Reflecting the effects of enforced racial segregation and the lingering suspicion of some blacks toward whites, the National Executive Committee included no whites, though the regional executives did have a few white members. The Front's "patrons"—associated by name rather than by regular duties—included a more carefully representational mix of "celebrities."[89] Tom Lodge estimated that of the sixty-six elected UDF officials, fifteen were ANC "veterans" and six were BC "veterans"; eleven were middle-class professionals; seventeen were workers; only eight were women; and the majority were under forty years old. He concluded that taken as a whole, this group was "heavily middle class," though other analysts emphasize that "a high proportion" had working-class origins.[90] This is not to imply that a leader's family background or current professional status determines his or her class sympathies, which are more accurately assessed according to actions or policies regarding working-class demands and cross-class alliances. In this respect, many of the more influential UDF leaders consistently stressed the importance of cross-class unity, of promoting the "cult of charismatic leadership around Nelson Mandela," and of resisting anticapitalist rhetoric that might scare off middle-class allies.[91] Neville Alexander labeled these leaders as a clique of the "radical black middle class, who seized the opportunity of possible compromise . . . and are consciously against socialism."[92]

With its diverse leadership, coalition of groups, and purposeful vagueness on specifics of ideology, the cohesion of the UDF, like all popular fronts, depended more on organizational affiliation than on individual belief. The six hundred already-established groups that were originally affiliated with the UDF clearly did not owe their existence to the Front. They were based instead on local and constituent interests, in most cases with whites, Africans, Indians, and coloreds organized separately. As long as these groups retained their membership and found that the pursuit of their specific agendas was advanced by cooperation with the other affiliates and leadership of the Front, the UDF remained strong. Given the long history of enforced segregation, divisions within the opposition, and the inevitable diversity of views within a country as complex as South Africa, incorporating different constituencies loosely affiliated with a front was a logical basis for a movement. The UDF proponents argued that loyalty to grass-roots affiliates was bound to be stronger than individual allegiance to a monolithic organization and was the only base on which a united opposition could be built. The National Forum also reflected this compelling logic, although its two hundred to three hundred affiliates were united more by ideological agreement than by localized interests and represented a distinct and narrower array of views than did those in the UDF.

The different basis on which groups affiliated with the UDF and the National Forum reflected a fundamental disagreement over how social relations were established and could be challenged. The National Forum affiliates and the Forum itself shared the basic assumption of the BC movement, that social order was significantly reinforced by values and culture and that the consolidation of support for alternative ideas was essential to inspiring opposition. According to this view, a UDF-style coalition of groups that agreed to act together despite differences of ideology was flawed by its lack of ideological coherence. The Charterists countered that the social order and the ideas about that order were based more on material relations of political and economic power than on ideas. Opposition to the established social order had to be generated by appeals to the people's material interests and based more on a pragmatic mobilization of active protest than on ideology. Concern for ideas was subordinated to the balance of material forces, which the Charterists were determined to alter through mass action.

This difference of basic assumptions helps explain the National Forum's criticism and refusal to join the UDF. According to Peter Jones of AZAPO, the Charterists "who had lost out in the seventies grabbed their opportunity. They needed to get big as quickly as possible. They could only do so if they did not go through the process of organization building and if they depended on big splashes. As a result they don't have any cohesiveness and have great difficulty reaching a consensus."[93] To the Charterists, the rapid growth of the UDF was a sign of strength rather than weakness, as the goal was mass mobilization rather than consensus on the fine points of ideology. For them, cohesion in action was more important than cohesion around ideas, whereas for those more concerned about ideas, rapid gains in mass organization that ignored ideological cohesion were to be avoided.

Dismissing their National Forum critics as hopelessly intellectual and incapable of appealing to the masses, the Charterists continued to build organizational unity with little regard for ideological affinity. As an extreme indication of their priorities, the UDF even stooped to trying to compel affiliation by groups who did not share their basic outlook. According to lawyer Fikile Bam, "The UDF was not trying to win minds, just support, and were willing to use bullying and intimidation."[94] Godfrey Pitje, an Africanist-inclined veteran of the ANC Youth League describes how the Charterists "tried to get me to sign the Black Lawyers Association [which he chaired] on to the UDF. They came physically into my office. I refused to sign without consultation. At that stage ideology was not a factor [to the UDF]; they were just looking [to create] an umbrella organization."[95] In this case, the UDF failed to compel affiliation. Even sympathetic local groups expressed concern about the UDF's efforts to enforce unity or, later, to create its own affiliates where no indigenous groups existed.[96] Although such tactics were much more often the exception rather than the rule, their use signals the degree to which the UDF was willing to sacrifice ideological cohesion for unity.

For all of its successful efforts to unite a broad spectrum of opposition groups, the UDF remained notably unsuccessful in attracting affiliates from among the burgeoning black labor unions. At the outset, UDF copresident Archie Gumede had chastised those unions that "feel that they are powerful and can act on their own," and others spoke of the need to bring the unions into the UDF to ensure a working class perspective.[97] A few unions joined the UDF or were formed by it, but those unions in the two leading federations and most of the independent unions decided against affiliation, in at least one case objecting to the multiclass nature of the Front and to its lack of unionlike democratic structures by which leaders could be held accountable.[98] Some unionists were also concerned that affiliation with the Front would invite state repression before their unions had grown large enough to resist it. UDF officials tried to appear tolerant of this reluctance by the unions to affiliate, arguing that even the debate over affiliation was constructive in that it informed the workers.[99] These union debates indicate that the UDF's lack of ideological cohesion and its loose organizational structure were worrisome to these working-class organizations, rather than only to National Forum affiliates. This issue will be examined further in Chapter 6.

Although the UDF's organizational structure and strategic focus were incompatible with greater ideological coherence and alienated some of the more radical potential affiliates, they proved highly conducive to raising funds. The inclusion of whites also provided useful contacts. The emphasis on offering local benefits appealed to donors both because it made the use of their funds central to the movement and because it allowed for visible accomplishments for which donors could claim credit. Neither of these had been the case with BC. In addition, the lack of any strong ideological rhetoric meant that few statements were formally associated with the Front that could offend potential donors. By avoiding anticapitalist rhetoric, the UDF attracted an array of followers from the black middle class. Similarly, its nonracialism made the Front attractive to white donors, both inside and outside South Africa. Because the radical groups alienated by these same policies had considerably less access to funds, their refusal to affiliate did not result in a significant loss of financial support for the UDF. The overall effect of these alignments, according to the treasurer of the UDF in later years, Azhar Cachalia, was that "there will never be a problem of getting money; the only difficulty is administering it all."[100]

The UDF's pragmatic efforts to position itself to raise funds bore fruit on a scale unprecedented for the internal South African opposition. By 1987, the UDF itself had an annual budget of over R2 million, with over R200 million donated to Charterist organizations aligned with the Front.[101] The majority of these funds came from European donors, often personally solicited by Bishop Desmond Tutu, Dr. Allan Boesak, Beyers Naude, and other public figures. The UDF's informal connections with the ANC, which had cultivated close relations with many European governments and private agencies, were also invaluable for fund-raising. In 1987, the Swedish government alone donated over R40 million to internal Charterist organizations, including R225,000 to the Soweto Civic Association.[102] Funds from international donors were also given to the South African Council of Churches, which dispersed substantial amounts to Charterist groups, among others in the country.[103] In part, this inflow of funds was the result of the growing international concern about South Africa, from which the UDF benefited.

Just as the lower level of international funding to BC groups had increased dramatically after 1976 until they were banned, so Cassim Saloojee reported that the resources to the Charterists "doubled in the last three years" after the outbreak of unrest in 1984. Saloojee claimed that the source of such funds from the West "means nothing politically," although he added that the UDF affiliates refused funds from the Reagan administration.[104] The financial support for the UDF from foreign governments with which Pretoria was attempting to improve its own relations may have also given the Front an extra degree of protection from the state.

The UDF also received funds from inside South Africa, although in smaller amounts than those donated from abroad, and the sources of such funds suggest a significant benefit of the UDF's efforts to attract a broad array of internal allies. Wealthy white South Africans responded to the UDF's encouragement by forming a support group of "Friends of the UDF," led by Tony Bloom, chairman of a major service-industry conglomerate. This group raised a substantial but undisclosed amount of funds and, at least on one occasion, organized a reception at which leaders of the UDF and the business community congregated over drinks at the luxurious Carlton Hotel in Johannesburg. Another "friend" of the UDF, former Barclays Bank managing director Chris Ball, was investigated by the government for guaranteeing a R100,000 loan to pay for an "Unban the ANC" advertisement campaign organized by individuals in the UDF. For many unionists and radical purists, such cooperation with corporate employers and bankers was tantamount to consorting with the enemy. But for the UDF, it made good practical sense.

The successful solicitation of funds made possible the type of political activity for which the UDF had been formed, justifying the alienation of more radical groups and ideological purists who did not engage in the same level of activity. Mass mobilization, the provision of services, publicity, and the coordination of affiliates required resources and organization on a large scale. The Black Consciousness movement's focus on changing values and organizing a small elite of followers had not required the same level of funding, which in any case had not been available in the 1970s. Substantial funding was available in the 1980s, however, in part as a result of the UDF's alliances. These resources enabled the UDF to carry out its activities and attract a broad following. Even Africanist-inclined Godfrey Pitje was forced to admit that "the UDF surprised me the way it really snowballed. That was due to its being well supported financially, in part due to whites' participation and help in running organizations. They caught the present political fervor and capitalized on it."[105] Others who also remained outside the UDF, including various unionists, criticized the Front's reliance on funding, describing the resulting activities as "tinsel politics" aimed at buying media attention and popular support.[106] But there was no denying that this approach was highly effective.

Much of the money collected by the UDF and its affiliates was used for the publicity that became the envy and target of criticism of other opposition groups. Almost half a million posters, newsletters, and pamphlets were printed to announce the UDF launch. Two years later, a half-million copies of the Freedom Charter were printed and distributed, even though the UDF had not yet formally adopted the Charter. Throughout this period, a national newsletter with a circulation of twenty-five thousand was produced on a regular basis, as were a variety of posters, pamphlets, and T-shirts.[107] Newspaper advertisements announcing events, calling for the release of Nelson Mandela, and reproducing the Freedom Charter were purchased at considerable expense. Halls and public address systems were rented for mass meetings or official UDF concerts, with tickets for the latter available for purchase at Computicket in the major shopping malls. In part, the UDF and its allies spent much of their funds on these forms of publicity as a result of bitter experience with alternative strategies of mass mobilization. In 1984, the UDF had launched its "Million Signature Campaign," a highly publicized effort to build grassroots support and contacts through petition.[108] Door-to-door efforts to collect signatures did help spread information about the UDF, but the end result of less than half of the announced target of signatures was a source of some embarrassment. Afterward, publicity was more carefully controlled from above, so as to help build a popular base without setting a goal by which success could be accurately measured.

Once the initial expenditure on publicity had caught the public's attention, much of the subsequent publicity came free of charge. Details about mass rallies or concerts were often spread by word of mouth. Police actions against the UDF were given extensive media coverage, gaining further popular legitimacy and often larger audiences for subsequent events. Criticism of the UDF aired by the state-run television network also backfired to create additional interest and support. Even the state's formal prosecution of various UDF activists had similar results. The legal defense for these activsts was expensive, often requiring additional foreign donations to pay the lawyers' fees, but the regular coverage of political trials in the media was a boon to the UDF's popularity. Convictions in these cases raised popular anger, whereas acquittals raised popular confidence. Even when individuals suffered or were imprisoned, the UDF as a whole benefited. The culture of resistance was spread through the media, adding support for the UDF even beyond its formal organizational adherents. This process resembled the dissemination of BC ideas in the 1970s, although in the 1980s the rising popular interest was carefully channeled into mass mobilization, as seen in the next chapter.

The UDF's publicity campaigns, legal operations, and overall organization required a large staff of full-time activists. By 1987, there were roughly eighty full-time professionals paid by the UDF directly, in addition to the staffs of all the affiliated and service organizations. In comparison, Walter Sisulu had been the only paid ANC staff member during the Defiance Campaign in the early 1950s, and the BC movement had a significant but smaller staff only for the last two years before the major groups were banned in 1977.[109] Working closely with unpaid national officials of the Front, this large professional staff added to a perception of some critics of the UDF as being "top heavy" and less than fully democratic.[110] But the staff also enabled the UDF to function and grow on a national basis.

Beyond the centralized activities of the UDF and its staff, the other major activity on which funds were spent during this period was the establishment of local service groups. Many of these groups received their funding from foreign sources distributed through agencies closely aligned with the Charterist movement. The SACC continued to disburse undisclosed amounts of funds, both for projects and to support the families of detainees, most of whom had been associated with Charterist groups despite the church group's best efforts to remain nonpartisan. The Kagiso Trust distributed roughly R30 million annually of European Economic Community and other donated funds to local and national service initiatives. The Kagiso trustees included many of the most prominent leaders associated with Charterism, and the trust came to be widely viewed as a vehicle for the funding and coordination of the Charterist movement, although non-Charterist groups were also on occasion supported. The organizations that were established with this support were able to provide local communities with material assistance, legal advice, and other services. Their association with the Charterist movement helped consolidate allegiance to the UDF, building on the support gained through publicity. In addition, such services suited the state's own short-term interests in seeing popular demands met and larger confrontations avoided.

The provision of services was an essential complement to the UDF's other efforts to win popular allegiance. By providing concrete assistance to communities, the UDF demonstrated that beyond its rhetoric and publicity, it had both the will and the capacity to address people's material conditions. Indeed, the BC movement's failure to address such practical issues had led to popular disillusionment, whereas the UDF delivered and was rewarded with a massive following. The loyalty of that following was not only to local affiliates but also to the Front itself, by virtue of its national stature and also because the resources and services it provided made local victories possible. The UDF moved beyond inspiring resistance to supporting mobilization in material terms and to assisting people in solving their immediate problems themselves. The BC movement, however, had feared that such material assistance would mollify the people and so relied instead on the attraction of their ideas, but the UDF proved that broad popular support for an opposition could be won only by helping people. Indeed, for many South Africans, their allegiance to the UDF rested directly on that assistance, with ideological affinity coming only later. As described by the leader of the twenty-five thousand squatters who live in the shacks of Katlehong:

> In 1983 we were being harassed and chased from place to place. Dr. Asvat from AZAPO came and said we must not leave here. In March 1984 we demonstrated. We need houses, water, electricity. . . . After the demonstration AZAPO never came back. We phoned them when we were harassed again. Some other friends got me in touch with the

> UDF for help. . . . The UDF came and organized newspaper reporters [to cover the story, and put me in touch with the SACC].
>
> In May 1987, I went to the SACC to say I am starving; the children are dizzy from hunger. The SACC gave me some money for school funds and to help me reopen my shop. They also gave us R3000 for three trucks that were burnt. They paid for the graves and buses for three children killed in the truck fires. They gave money to another lady. They gave food and toys in December. They paid our lawyer. They pay [families of] detainees or if someone is killed they pay for funerals and child support. They give me food and clothes for others, and blankets.
>
> After that [the UDF] held meetings. . . . They explained the Freedom Charter. Now we have a civic and a youth organization. . . . People here understand about the UDF, particularly the youth. . . . People have copies of the Freedom Charter, given by the UDF. . . . If they didn't have money, that would be a big problem.[111]

With its financial resources, the UDF was able to gain considerable publicity and to offer various services, thereby encouraging the affiliation of many more local groups. The South African state's reforms in the years following the 1976 uprising had helped turn the opposition to local activity aimed at gaining a share for blacks of the material benefits locally available. The UDF capitalized on these developments, embracing hundreds of local affiliates and attracting considerable financial contributions. Though the impetus for local efforts came essentially "from below," the Front's national leadership was able to assist, coordinate, and claim these efforts for its own so successfully that it was credited with all that had been accomplished. As a squatter at Thokoza, near Johannesburg, explained: "The UDF has helped the people the most and has opened our minds and ideas to see oppression. We saw we were oppressed before, but UDF gave us the power to fight and to speak. We are all members of the UDF. . . . We have power as long as there is UDF. Even today our shacks are still standing, thanks to the UDF. That is why I trust them."[112]

The UDF could not have been so successful and could not have grown in popularity so quickly had the South African state acted decisively to crush the Front and its affiliates, for instance, by restricting publicity or the flow of resources. Instead, the state generally appeared to ignore the UDF. It could not block the open expression of resistance to the new constitution and maintain any semblance of these proposals as reforms, but the UDF in turn could not prevent the implementation of the new dispensation. The state did not perceive as a threat the greater ability of the local organizations to redress material grievances. Rather, it saw this development as deflecting popular concern from more contentious political issues and as reinforcing the state's international reformist image. In addition, economic growth made it possible for black demands to be met through private efforts. The state, in fact, ceded the space for local organizing to these affiliates, in part because the white electorate would probably have objected to further material aid from the state to the blacks and because the blacks themselves would have been suspicious of such aid. Much of the Charterist strategy was instead aimed at preserving this political space implicitly granted by the state, with alliances with whites, with business, and with foreign funders, all offering further protection, and with more militant rhetoric and official claims of allegiance to the ANC explicitly avoided. As a result, Pretoria evidently did not feel directly threatened by the UDF's initial growth, recognizing the need to allow some form of release for mass discontent.

The conditions in South Africa until late 1984 created a kind of dynamic equilibrium between the opposition and the state. The UDF was able to provide services and to claim local victories, which encouraged local pragmatism. As one Robben Island veteran explained: "We need concrete demands and victories to keep the people moving and the state at bay. . . . Concrete strategies constrain the masses—otherwise you lose your focus."[113] Allegiance to the Charterist movement grew with the provision of benefits, which also had the effect of initially localizing mass militancy. The state, preoccupied with its own reconstitution and concerned mainly with the potential threat of the exiled ANC, was content to let the black community sort out its own problems, with whatever help it could get. In a sense, much of the state's social welfare function for the majority of its people had been localized or privatized, to the apparent satisfaction of the state.

By 1984, the space left open for popular activity had been filled, and the vision of an inclusive national opposition movement had been largely achieved. The main goals of Black Consciousness had been declared as accomplished, and the ideology associated with racial identity was largely eclipsed. In its place, blacks and whites, rich and poor, were welcomed into a movement aimed not at changing the values or self-image associated with race but at more directly demanding a redress of material grievances and confronting apartheid. Consistent with these goals, intellectual discussion was replaced with an emphasis on pragmatism, national and local organization, and an ideological vagueness so as to foster unity. During a brief period of partially restored economic growth, available resources, and state reforms, this mode of opposition was tremendously effective and popular, without raising the fears of the state. The movement's very success, however, soon proved to be partly responsible for a change of conditions that broke the prevailing equilibrium, with growing popular demands asserted more aggressively as they went unmet and the state responded with force.

# 5

# *National Revolt, Repression, and Discord, 1984–1988*

Once the 1976 uprising had been quelled, both the South African state and its opponents embarked on complementary efforts at pragmatism. The idealism and emotionalism of Black Consciousness were gradually supplanted by an array of popular organizations established by local activists, seeking material benefits and specific accommodation. Eager to encourage this turn away from mass militancy, the state did not impede the development of these local organizations or their negotiations with local authorities and businesses, which granted concessions. The state also relaxed regulations controlling the legal growth of black trade unions and enacted a new, more inclusive constitution. In the space provided by these state reforms, national leaders formed the United Democratic Front, securing international donations to encourage and coordinate the local initiatives with which they were symbolically connected. Having well understood the situation at the time, the Charterists used the opportunity to build the opposition into a more organized and inclusive movement, seeking to unite all opponents of apartheid regardless of color, class, or specific ideology. Their efforts produced South Africa's most widespread and formidable internal opposition to date.

The opposition, which emerged in the early 1980s under the banner of the UDF, was shaped more by pragmatic efforts to build its strategic advantage than by ideology. In the 1970s, Black Consciousness had inspired a new generation of black students and had helped rekindle popular assertiveness, with organizational strategy secondary to the dissemination of the idea of a positive racial identity. Building on these earlier efforts and the emergence of less disruptive economic and political conditions, the focus of the opposition turned to the active pursuit of more concrete goals. Just as the ANC had attempted a generation earlier, these activists set out to unify the opponents and to isolate the regime, making compromises and alliances where required. Strategic necessity overwhelmed any interest in ideological coherence deeper than a minimum commitment to national identity based on nonracial unity in action. As long as popular organizations gained concessions, the driving force of national opposition succeeded in submerging any potential differences.

By late 1984, the conditions that had kept the South African state and its opposition in dynamic equilibrium had changed. South Africa slipped back into recession, suffering from the continued structural constraints of apartheid and the delayed impact of the West's decline in fortunes, thereby reducing the economy's ability and the state's willingness to provide further material concessions. Buoyed by the recent success and the encouragement of the still-exiled ANC, however, popular expectations and mobilization continued to build, exploding first as unrest in the Vaal triangle near Johannesburg in 1984 after the ratification by whites of the new constitution. Anxious to head off a crisis, the state moved to close the space it had opened and to discourage popular organization, declaring a state of emergency in which both local and national leaders were detained and mass meetings and other forms of publicity were curtailed. But the momentum of growing opposition activity could not be so easily contained and was instead emboldened by repression and anger into revolt. By 1987 the movement itself could not help but suffer from the dramatic change in the conditions that had created it, and the people blamed the movement for their disappointment over unmet expectations. Earlier strengths became vulnerabilities as the movement's purposeful avoidance of divisive issues left it open to conflict once the leaders were cut off from the local organizations and then further constrained by the effective banning of the UDF in February 1988. Like a giant tanker having lost its rudder and momentum, the movement began to drift with crosscurrents, running over smaller ships in its way, until it seemed close to breaching under its own weight and heavy seas.

## Organized Revolt and Repression

The period of economic growth after 1977 was neither as deeply felt nor as long lasting as had been the tremendous growth of the 1960s. The brief recovery began giving way to recession as early as 1982, a year after Western industrial economies had begun to falter, although most black South Africans were more noticeably affected a few years later.[1] Between 1981 and 1983, South Africa's GDP fell by almost 3 percent, or by almost 8 percent per capita, and the price of gold dropped from $850 per ounce in 1980 to under $300 by 1985.[2] The impact of this recession on the job prospects and living standards of South African blacks was severe. Official estimates suggested that 53 percent of the population in Soweto who had been employed in the past were, by 1984, without jobs.[3] In 1985, nationwide unemployment was reported to be rising by ten thousand every month, resulting in three million unemployed nationwide and 70 percent unemployed in 1986 among those under twenty-five years of age living in Port Elizabeth.[4] By 1987, between 54 and 68 percent of families living in Soweto had incomes below the "minimum living level" of R809 per month estimated to be necessary to support a family in the urban areas.[5] In the same year, the stock of housing units in Soweto was estimated to be 1.8 million below demand, with existing houses providing five square meters per person, as compared with fifty-seven square meters per person in white Johannesburg. Between 5.6 million and 7 million people throughout the country were estimated to be homeless or living in squatter camps.[6]

To make matters worse, stagflation began to push up prices sharply, particularly for those foods on which blacks spend between one third and two thirds of their incomes.[7] In March 1985, the average food bill was 21 percent higher than the previous year, with the price of corn, the staple of Africans' diet, having risen even more owing to a severe drought.[8] In the midst of these price increases, the government was forced by declining revenues to

*Steve Biko, founder of the Black Consciousness movement and first president of the South African Student Organization.* (The Star)

*Peter Jones, a close associate of Steve Biko in the Black Consciousness movement and later an official of AZAPO.* (The Star)

*Neville Alexander of the Cape Action League and later the Workers Organization for Socialist Action.* (*Anthony W. Marx*)

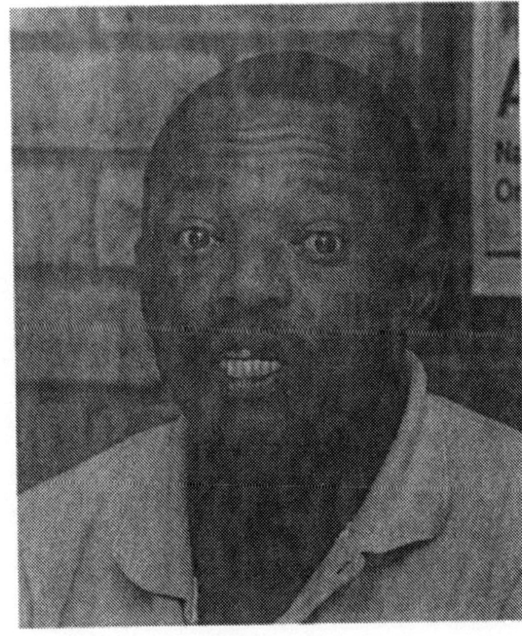

*'Terror" Lekota, publicity secretary of the UDF and, from 990, national convener of the ANC.* (*Afrapix*)

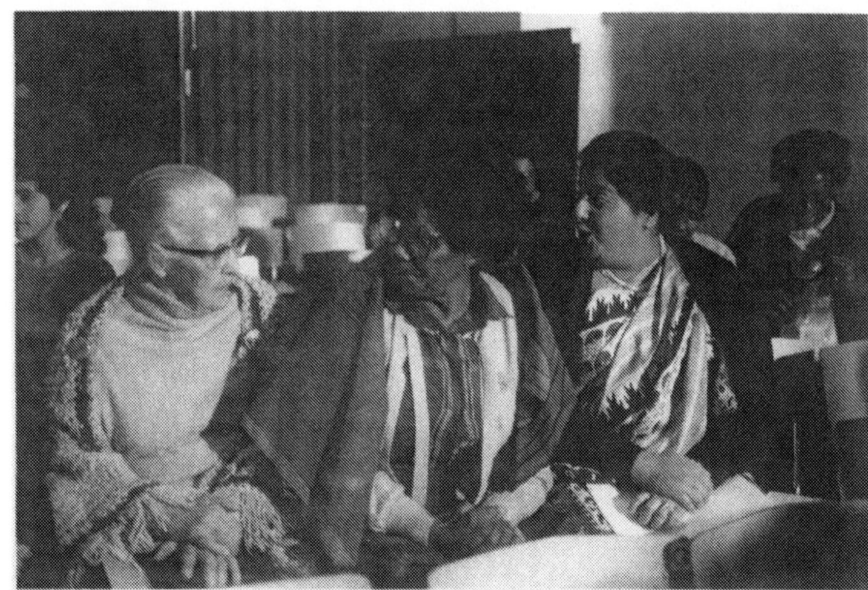

Above: *UDF patron Helen Joseph (left), UDF co-president Albertina Sisulu (center), and lawyer Priscilla Jana (right), at the Johannesburg Women's Day Commemoration, 1986.* (*Anthony W. Marx*) Below Left: *Elijah Barayi, president of the Congress of South African Trade Unions, COSATU.* (*Afrapix*) Below Right: *James Mndaweni, president of the National Council of Trade Unions, formed in 1985 out of a merger of the CUSA and AZACTU federations.* (*Afrapix*)

*Cyril Ramaphosa, general secretary of the National Union of Mineworkers, originally the largest affiliate of COSATU. (Afrapix)*

*Jay Naidoo, general secretary of the Congress of South African Trade Unions, COSATU. (Afrapix)*

Above: *Rival CCAWUSA unionists Herbert Mkhize, the pro-Charterist Vice President,* (*left*) *and Kaiser Thibedi, secretary of the anti-Charterist Johannesburg branch executive* (*right*), *during a rare light moment at a union meeting in 1988.* (*Anthony W. Marx*) Below: *COSATU unionists march from a meeting near Johannesburg in 1989.* (*Anthony W. Marx*)

*Former ANC general secretary Walter Sisulu on the morning of October 15, 1989, at the moment he first emerged from his Soweto home upon his release from twenty-seven years of imprisonment. (Anthony W. Marx)*

Below: *The ANC's Walter Sisulu meets privately at his home on October 16, 1989, the day after his release from prison, with PAC president Zeph Mothapeng. This is the only known photo of Sisulu and Mothapeng together after Sisulu's release and before Mothapeng's death one year later. (Anthony W. Marx)*

reduce expenditures, including its major subsidy on bread. A loaf of bread that had cost R.29 in 1984 thus cost R.54 in 1985, when the average African wage earner brought home approximately R14 per day.[9] The history of "bread riots" in the years before the French Revolution is suggestive of the potential for unrest implicit in these developments.[10]

Economic contraction also exacerbated the pressure on South Africa's government budgets and public services, already stretched by the expense of maintaining a huge security apparatus, homeland administrations, and multiple bureaucracies to serve segregated populations. The inefficiencies of apartheid are suggested by the estimate that in 1987, South Africa had one civil servant for every twenty-seven citizens, compared with one civil servant for every ninety-four thousand citizens in Britain.[11] The state faced considerable political constraints on trimming this bureaucracy, which constituted a sizable electoral block whose support for government policies had to be maintained by a 30 percent wage increase in 1984.[12] The government could not risk alienating white voters by cutting back on their employment and wages or increasing taxes to pay for services to blacks. The only expenditure on blacks on which this constituency could be depended to support was the continued enforcement of apartheid, including the mandatory migration that by 1984 had affected a total of 3.5 million blacks.[13]

Given the minority regime's inherent political resistance to reducing the number of white civil servants, the only way in which the state could halt the increase in its outflow during the economic decline of the mid-1980s was to allow services to blacks to be outpaced by the growth of their population. As in the previous decade, increases in African educational enrollment grew faster than outlays, again pushing black school enrollments to the bursting point. Per-student expenditure on education remained seven times greater for every white student than for every African. The result was a dramatic disparity in black and white examination scores and considerably less opportunity for advancement by black students. In 1984–1985, of the 55,778 white students who took the senior certificate examinations, 49 percent received marks high enough to qualify for university, as compared with 18 percent of the 34,213 Africans who took the exam.[14] State appropriations to township councils also were trimmed, limiting the ability of these local governance structures to win allegiance with improvements in infrastructure. These spending cuts hit hardest at the black community, however, which was unable to afford private schooling or to replace public services and had no vote by which to influence authorities to relieve their deprivation.

The impact of this economic downturn and of the government cutbacks was more profound than can be suggested by the magnitude of the relevant statistics. After the 1976 uprising, the inspirational ideas of Black Consciousness had been largely replaced by a more pragmatic concern for material advancement encouraged by economic recovery and even more so by state reforms. But with the onset of recession, not only were raised expectations left unmet, it also became difficult for most blacks to even maintain the low standard of living they had attained. As blacks' already meager lifestyle deteriorated, conservative impulses to resist falling any farther behind or to not lose what had been gained were expressed in a radicalization of political views, as they often have been in other countries in modern times.[15] By 1985, a nationwide poll of urban Africans estimated that 64 percent described themselves as angry; and 57 percent cited grievances related to economics, education, and welfare.[16] Based on such findings, Lawrence Schlemmer concluded in his 1984 study: "It is probably no accident that the disturbances of the late fifties and early sixties, of 1976 and 1977, and the current unrest, have occurred during periods of economic downturn, after phases of employment growth or real increases in black incomes."[17]

Anger over their worsening economic plight did not drive South Africans to a fitful but largely unorganized outburst similar to that in 1976. Instead, rather than looking first to relatively freewheeling protest against state policies, as the BC rhetoric had inspired, South Africans in the mid-1980s first looked for a means to express their grievances through the local civic and related organizations that had developed over recent years. A 1987 survey in Soweto found that more than one third of those polled had become members of community organizations and unions.[18] The focus of mass resistance had clearly shifted from ideas spontaneously expressed, to mobilization organized around material grievances. The strategic design of the Charterists was embraced and filled out by the people, demonstrating the influence of activist elites who had encouraged such a response.

The masses increased their participation in community organizations in order to address the local ramifications of economic decline. Their collective action was intended to add pressure for a redress of material grievances. For example, between 1977 and 1984, rents in the Vaal townships outside Johannesburg had risen 400 percent, bringing people to civic association meetings at which a rent boycott was discussed and initiated in 1984.[19] Such dramatic increases in rent—by which the township authorities sought to augment the reduced central state funding—became even more common throughout the country. Given the immediate benefit of saving on rent, boycotts and related protests spread quickly, requiring little enforcement. Occasional police attacks reinforced popular support for the boycotts. By acting collectively, the boycotters were reassured that evictions or attempts to place new residents in their homes would be jointly confronted and, if necessary, resisted. By 1986, up to fifty-four townships with over a half-million households were withholding their rent, with 95 percent of those polled in Soweto supporting the boycott even if not all participated in it.[20] Once begun, these boycotts became self-perpetuating, as the residents could not hope to pay the arrears that would have been added to the resumed rent payments. Although this largely unforeseen consequence reduced strategic flexibility, the rent boycotts succeeded in spreading protest and encouraging support for civic associations.

Also in 1984, civic associations began orchestrating the local equivalent of general strikes, thereby demonstrating the level of organization that had been achieved in the townships. The most notable of these early "stayaways" was that in the Transvaal in September and November 1984, when over a half-million workers and almost as many students stayed home to protest army "occupation" of the townships and to support the students' educational demands. Leading unionist Jay Naidoo of COSATU named this event as a "watershed in combining community, students and unions, with shop stewards and COSAS [the student organization] as key links."[21] Although there were occasionally tensions in this coalition—for instance, when a March 1985 stayaway in Port Elizabeth was unsuccessfully opposed by unionists who did not want their organizational work at the factories disrupted—alliances were generally strengthened by such "unity in action."[22] As with the

ANC's Defiance Campaign in 1952, such collective action attracted even larger numbers into the local Charterist organizations.[23]

Another major strategy of the local organizations, in this case channeling anger regarding price increases, was to boycott white retailers, first implemented in scenic Port Alfred, on the Indian Ocean coast. A civic organization had been originally formed in Port Alfred to run a day-care center and nursery school after residents had been encouraged by the success of local youth and workers' organizations. In June 1985, this local group staged a boycott of white stores, and within weeks the white businesses had agreed to end segregation in town council meetings and in stores and to lobby for the withdrawal of police from the township, the release of detainees, and the construction of a new school. Because all of these protest demands concerned local grievances, those businesses directly affected by the boycott were in a position to make concessions, limited only by their resources. Demands for a reduction in the rent increases and the expansion of public services to blacks were not met, because of the lack of sufficient funding.[24]

Publicity regarding the dramatic turn of events in Port Alfred helped spread the tactic of consumer boycotts, particularly in the eastern Cape. Activists found consumer boycotts an effective way to politicize and mobilize communities around popular resentment for those white retailers whose prices were then rising even more than usual in proportion to black incomes. Such activity had the advantage of being legal and difficult for the state to restrict, as purchases from particular vendors could not be enforced by the police. The boycotts were also useful for isolating the regime from some of its traditional supporters, with vulnerable white merchants being pressed to reduce prices and to present grievances to the state in order to win back their lost black clientele.[25] By targeting small merchants in particular, civic organizations in the 1980s improved on the model of the bus boycotts of the 1950s, in which the boycotted bus company had been too tightly controlled by the state to be able to respond or to act as an intermediary to the state.[26]

Like the boycotts of the 1950s, the success of consumer action in the 1980s depended on unity, reinforced by the inherently democratic nature of a boycott, which requires collective participation.[27] In instances in which the residents did not fully honor the boycott, militant "young lions" or "comrades" used coercion, checking bags at township entrances, but this faded as the boycotts matured and proved their effectiveness. By 1987, less than 9 percent of polled Sowetans complained of coercive enforcement of boycotts, suggesting wide popular support for such action.[28]

One of the alliances in the black community most directly strengthened by the consumer boycotts was that between the activists and the black middle-class merchants. The small white capitalists bore the brunt of the boycotts, whereas their township competitors reaped the benefits of a captive market. In some cases black merchants actively organized boycotts of white-owned stores while charging prices equal to or above those of the white merchants.[29] Roland White, an Eastern Cape UDF Executive member at the time, admitted that "the boycotts helped the black bourgeoisie, but they were eventually disciplined and did lower their prices."[30] That black merchants were often motivated by self-interest does not fully discount their involvement, which in fact helped unify the black community across class lines. Nor did their self-interested actions diminish the effectiveness of the boycotts at exerting pressure on white businesses.

The consumer boycotts, like the rent boycotts and the early stayaways, served to unify and broaden popular mobilization around local economic needs, and only later around more explicitly political demands. The initial nexus of these activities was the grass roots, reflecting the pragmatic concerns of a populace not principally concerned with ideology. By specifically targeting local businesses, which could not reasonably be expected to have considerable influence over the Pretoria regime, civic organizations and related groups signaled the local nature of their grievances. In later years, central state authorities claimed that the local protests in the mid-1980s were carefully planned by national leaders of the UDF and other groups, twenty-two of whom were accordingly prosecuted in the Delmas treason trial.[31] Although eleven of these leaders were eventually found guilty of lesser charges in 1988, the prosecution largely failed to prove that a conspiracy had existed, and the convictions were later overturned on appeal.

In rebutting the state's interpretation of local activism, national political leaders did not deny that such activism would eventually have broader implications. These leaders did not directly control local mobilization, but they did hope that "by winning, through struggle, short-term gains that improve aspects of daily living, i.e. real material concessions, [this experience would] demonstrate the benefits of collective action."[32] Only after 1984 were the tactics of local urban collective action applied to national political issues, much as the local boycotts of the 1940s set the stage for the ANC's countrywide Defiance Campaign in the 1950s.[33]

Much as the UDF supported but did not directly control local activism in the urban townships, the rural communities in the mid-1980s also engaged in collective action that was mainly determined by specific local conditions, though it was also supported by the UDF. Economic deprivation outside the urban areas was in many ways worse than that in the townships to which many blacks had migrated, and it was certainly sufficient to generate discontent. However, the isolation of the rural communities added to the difficulties of organization. According to a young activist from Lebowa, the potential for all forms of opposition activity was "better in a city where [the police] are afraid to do things in public. In the rural areas, it is so quiet and easy for the [police] to just pick you up and do whatever they want with you."[34] As a result, activism in the countryside was generally even more dependent on the leadership of students than it was in the urban townships. Students were able to organize at their schools, where the risk of attracting police attention was somewhat less, and they generally had more contact with their urban counterparts. Febe Potgeiter, a student member of the Western Cape UDF Executive, described the process of mobilization in her rural eastern Cape hometown: "Humansdorp had been quiet for twenty years. . . . We started organizing there in 1985 as an over-spill from the activity in Port Elizabeth. We campaigned over rent. . . . Contact among students led to youth organizations around the same time as the civic started to form. . . . There was no ideological education, just mobilization around immediate issues."[35]

Rural activism during the mid-1980s was guided by much the same pragmatism that was evident in the urban centers. Rural communities were also mobilized around local grievances, with ideology remaining a secondary concern. A 1985 survey of black political opinion found surprisingly little difference in urban and rural views.[36] In large part, this general coincidence of urban and rural priorities reflected the level of economic development that had been achieved in South Africa. This coincidence also reflected the degree to which popular ideas were spread by the mass media and by the incomplete but nevertheless significant outreach efforts of the UDF. Charterist professionals who traveled from urban centers to provide services in rural areas were often surprised by the extent to which local activism had spread on its own. As described by UDF-aligned lawyer Priscilla Jana: "The most profound observation for the post 1984 period is that awareness has reached the remotest village and rural area. We have been involved in unrest work in the tiniest villages. In one case it took us ten days to locate the area we were supposed to represent."[37]

The actual opposition activities undertaken in rural areas differed from those in townships. Boycotts and stayaways were difficult to organize because rural people were more economically vulnerable and often had few alternative sources of goods or services. In many instances, the rural activism was fundamentally conservative, provoked by state or local actions that threatened to hinder traditional life-styles, corresponding to the urban impulse to protect recent economic gains. For instance, the people of Driefontein in the northern Transvaal organized in 1983 to resist their proposed removal to make way for white farmers. This threat to a rural people's attachment to their land, an attachment on which the PAC had earlier built its rural support, elicited a response of petitions and protests. At one protest meeting, Saul Mkhize, the eldest grandson of the first settler, was killed by a policeman, deepening the people's resolve to protect his grave and those of their forefathers. With the help of lawyers and journalists—organized via the SACC and indirectly by the UDF—the removal was stalled. In the wake of this success, UDF-aligned activists made regular trips to Driefontein, spreading information about Charterism and gaining support for the movement. This process was repeated in numerous rural settings.

Rural activism was distinguished not only by issues of land tenure but also by the strategies employed to pursue such issues in isolated areas. Charterism as a whole encouraged a practical assessment of local strategic necessity, with the conditions of rural life justifying activities that would not have been equally appropriate in urban townships. In Lebowa, for example, local committees convinced two ANC veterans, the Mashile brothers, to represent their interests in the homeland parliament, even though corresponding apartheid structures were largely spurned in urban areas. According to the younger Mashile, he and his brother agreed to seek election to such a "dummy" parliament "not for our own sakes, but for the benefits for the people." Mashile claims that the ANC and the UDF supported their electoral campaigns and subsequent tenure as a means of "using the systems of apartheid to undermine it."[38] Chief Mabuza of the Kangwane homeland received similar ANC, UDF and popular support for his efforts to turn his homeland's government against Pretoria. In more radicalized urban areas, such attempts to work within the system were rejected as collaboration, but the UDF did not proscribe a more flexible approach in rural areas, where ideological purity was seen as a particularly unproductive constraint.

The ANC in exile embraced much of this activity as consistent with its own strategies, thereby seeking to encourage and to claim both urban and rural forms of local activism. In January 1985, Oliver Tambo issued a radio statement categorizing such protests as part of an overall effort to make apartheid unworkable and to "render South Africa ungovernable."[39] Shortly thereafter, Nelson Mandela was given his first opportunity in over twenty years to address the public in rejecting the state president's offer of a conditional release. In an unprecedented interview with a visiting British emissary and a statement read by his daughter at a UDF rally in February 1985, Mandela refused to renounce unilaterally the use of violence to gain his release, proclaiming that the people's "freedom and mine cannot be separated."[40] At the same time, the number of ANC guerrilla attacks in South Africa rose from 40 in 1984, to 136 in 1985, and to 228 in 1986.[41] Such statements and activities gave the impression of a close association between the ANC and the rise of local activism, although there remains little evidence to suggest that the ANC in exile did or could fully control internal protests. But the ANC did not have to exert such direct control to be able to benefit from the efforts of its internal allies, as indicated by the growing popular support for the exiled group during this period.[42]

The strategic role of the ANC's armed struggle at this time remained consistent with long-established policy and was responsive to immediate pressures. Armed attacks were not intended to defeat the Pretoria regime militarily, for the relatively open geographical terrain of the country and the vast superiority of the government's defense forces made it more difficult to wage a full-scale guerrilla war than to organize protests or strikes. The limitations of the ANC's own military intentions is indicated by the relatively small size of its armed forces within South Africa, never numbering more than approximately two thousand, as compared with the more than sixty thousand guerrillas active in less-populated Zimbabwe at the height its liberation struggle.[43] In addition, South Africa's destabilization of its neighbors succeeded in reducing the ANC's capacity to launch incursions from external bases. This difficulty was exacerbated by the 1984 Nkomati Accords, which led to the closing of the ANC's Mozambican installations in return for the unfulfilled promise of a cessation of Pretoria's direct attacks and support for Renamo hostilities against the FRELIMO government.[44] The ANC was also constrained by popular ambivalence toward the use of violence, with the more militant supporters and a large proportion of MK guerrillas recommending a greater use of force that might have alienated more conservative allies in the ANC and the UDF coalitions. These latter groups favored a greater reliance on protest and strikes against an economy that was much more dependent on black labor than had been the case in Zimbabwe.

To satisfy partially both its more and less militant constituencies, the ANC charted a middle path of limited military engagement that largely avoided civilian casualties but also served to weaken the belief among whites that the government could ensure their security. Increased guerrilla activity, though never posing a significant military threat to the regime, was able to "psychologically instill confidence by giving the people an army to be proud of."[45] But unlike the BC version of psychological liberation, the ANC attacks were intended not just to change values but also to inspire action against the regime. To achieve this result, the ANC projected its attacks as a form of "armed propaganda" and endorsed locally generated township protests, but at its Kabwe conference in 1985 the ANC also publicly encouraged a decentralized form of armed struggle reminiscent of the PAC's earlier call for mass insurrection.[46] The strategy from the 1960s of training a highly disciplined armed force was pushed aside by the practical necessity of action, with the training period of MK guerrillas reportedly reduced in some cases to a bare minimum of two weeks.[47] The ANC acknowledged that liberation could not be achieved by relying on carefully controlled incursions from surrounding states vulnerable to South African air and land attacks or to Pretoria-supported insurgents, such as Renamo in Mozambique or UNITA in Angola. Instead, the ANC proclaimed that "the people inside have recognized that victory will come as a result of their struggle, their own efforts; as a result of their reliance on themselves."[48] It was neither in the ANC's interests or in its capacity to restrain the rising mass militancy inside the country. Instead, the ANC implicitly encouraged all militants to identify themselves as part of MK, regardless of formal affiliation or training. Such militancy strengthened the ANC's position, even though internal protest largely developed independently of the ANC's direct efforts or control.

The coincidence of rising township activism, stepped-up guerrilla attacks, and calls by the ANC for a mass uprising put the South African government on the defensive. Eager to contain such threats, on July 21, 1985, a partial state of emergency was declared, giving the police and related security forces virtually unlimited powers in 36 of South Africa's 266 magisterial districts. Within eight months, more than eight thousand people were detained without charge, including over half of the UDF's national and local officials.[49] Mass meetings, advertisements, and even certain T-shirts were prohibited in the hope that cutting off the people from their leaders or symbols of resistance would curtail their activism. The state repression was coordinated by the State Security Council and its local committees, which developed into a "parallel government," taking over many of the routine powers of the Pretoria bureaucracies and the increasingly ineffective parliament.[50] Containing unrest became the state's highest priority. The period of government reforms, having had the unforeseen consequence of encouraging mass mobilization, was thus brought to a dramatic close.

The state's initial efforts at repression were based on the false premise that activism was instigated and directed by the Front's national leadership rather than by local impetus. This misdirected repression against those leaders succeeded only at heightening popular anger and at removing leaders who had worked to restrain and channel the unrest into more orderly protests. Almost immediately, more violence erupted. Limited repression having failed, on June

12, 1986—four days before the tenth anniversary of the 1976 uprising—a state of emergency was declared for the entire country. Mass militancy was met with further detentions and occasional bursts of police gunfire. Having learned from the failure of its security efforts in 1985, the state cast a finer and larger net of detentions to hold the UDF leadership and also to capture a larger number of activists. Within a year, twenty-six thousand people had been imprisoned without trial, 40 percent of whom were under eighteen years of age and 80 percent of whom were affiliated with the UDF.[51] This widespread detention had the immediate desired effect of dampening the popular unrest.[52] The eerie and tense calm imposed on the townships lasted only briefly, however, until those activists who had avoided detention by going into hiding resurfaced during the year to lead an even angrier following.

The state resorted to force not only because of its perception of conspiracy but also because economic dislocation had blunted its tools of redress and cooptation. The white electorate presumably was unwilling to absorb a larger share of cuts in its services in order to pay to mollify blacks with concessions. But neither the state nor the private sector could afford such measures during the deepening recession. The state therefore was pushed toward greater reliance on its military and police forces, for which continued funding was considered sacrosanct. As described in the UDF Secretarial Report of May 1987, "The regime . . . cannot mobilize consent. By becoming highly brutal, the regime had therefore been forced to retreat to its last trench," thereby revealing the raw physical power underneath its civil glove.[53] Had not the economic downturn provoked mass militancy and denied the state the funds for alternative methods of control, the state might have remained more committed to its reformist approach of trying to win popular support. In Gramsci's terms, the state was forced to abandon its war of position and to join its opponents in a more active war of maneuver, using force to try to turn back popular advances.

The state apparently could find no alternative to resorting to repression, despite the predictable repercussions of such a move. The state's earlier efforts to maintain control over the townships through civil and economic means had been designed, in part, to win international support and to allay fears among foreigners about the security of their investments in South Africa. But the failure of these efforts signaled a major crisis for the whites' continued domination. British Prime Minister Margaret Thatcher had been able to head off commonwealth sanctions against South Africa by promising that further reforms could be negotiated. Explorations of the prospects of such negotiations, headed by the Commonwealth Eminent Persons Group, were scuttled, however, by the state of emergency and subsequent attacks by South Africa on what the South African government claimed to be ANC bases in Zimbabwe, Botswana, and Zambia.[54] These events also set off a worldwide financial reappraisal as major banks refused to turn over loans to an increasingly unstable South Africa, deepening the economic crisis which had contributed to the use of repression in the first place.

The state was losing its room to maneuver, as the economy failed to provide the resources the authorities needed to function. In the four months after the first declaration of a state of emergency in June 1985, the number of United States loans outstanding to South Africa fell by an unprecedented $500 million. Total lending by U.S. banks, which had nearly tripled from 1979 to $5 billion in 1984, fell to $2.78 billion by June 1988.[55] Although these actions were taken more out of self-interest to protect capital than out of conviction, the impact of the withdrawal of capital on South Africa's balance sheets was more profound than had been any formal sanctions to date. The "total onslaught" long feared by Pretoria was being joined, albeit grudgingly, by unlikely foes of apartheid in the boardrooms of international banks and businesses.

Heightened unrest and diminished access to international capital did not prevent the state from being able to maintain control through force, for a state as modern and relatively wealthy as South Africa cannot be brought to its knees quickly. But this pressure did have significant consequences, including the exacerbation of emerging political divisions among whites, shaken by the failure of the state's more conventional mechanisms of persuasion. Charterists who had set out to isolate the minority regime from its domestic and international supporters were quick to claim these divisions as a consequence of their efforts. According to Rev. Allan Boesak, township activism had "achieved a division of white politics. . . . That is due to the campaign of ungovernability, not only to make black townships ungovernable but also white South Africa; to expose the inability of the government to govern."[56] This result, eroding the state's capacity and will to govern through repression, grew slowly over the next few years. In the meantime, the capacity and will of black South Africans to reject their continued domination grew more quickly.

The end of the government's reformist efforts to rule peacefully did not mean that its last trench of military force could easily be overcome, but it did instill a popular sense of the state's vulnerability, which emboldened the opposition. Township youth, caught up in anger and excitement, pushed the outer limits of mass protest in the expectation of an impending victory, unrestricted by the more circumspect leaders still in prison or hiding. Homemade catapults were used against police helicopters. ANC arms caches were used in direct gun battles with police, despite formal ANC policies against such confrontation, with the outnumbered armed blacks shielded by the unarmed youth. Armored police and army vehicles were attacked by hand and by stone.[57] These actions led to more defiance, overwhelming the people's fear of the police or the threat of other penalties. The spreading unrest added to economic dislocation in a cycle of mutual reinforcement. As local grievances were aggravated, a wider and more volatile constituency was mobilized that swamped the UDF's own structures set up to channel the protests.[58] Local activism regarding economic grievances was transformed into broader protest by repression and further economic downturn. As the townships became "ungovernable," mass mobilization pushed beyond even the opposition's own organizational capacity to "govern" or fully control.

By 1985, local protests had been whipped by popular fury into violent revolt. In August 1985, the month in which Prime Minister P. W. Botha fatuously announced that South Africa had "crossed the Rubicon" of reform, more than 160 people were killed in unrest, and by the end of that year between 650 and 879 people had died, including 371 killed by police.[59] Although the police were responsible for approximately half of the death toll, this period of violence was distinguished from the 1976 uprising by the large number of deaths attributed to conflict between black activists and perceived collaborators. A season of retribution was at hand, reminiscent of the attacks on local tax collectors in prerevolutionary France or the tarring and feathering of British loyalists in the American colonies. Press and South African government reports persisted in describing these conflicts as "black on black" violence, suggesting an element of irrational chaos that raised whites' racial fears and obscured the political nature of the conflict.[60] For angry blacks in the townships, assaults on collaborators represented a first wave of direct confrontation with representatives of the apartheid system.

It was not surprising that the main target of mass militancy were representatives of authority closest at hand, the black "councillors" and policemen who lived in the townships while working to uphold the apartheid state's local governance structures. By March 1985, the homes of 255 town councillors and policemen had been bombed, resulting in more such destruction than in all of 1976. Over one hundred of these officials had been personally attacked, resulting in eighteen deaths, and over three thousand vehicles had been damaged, as compared with fewer than five hundred damaged in 1976 and 1977.[61]

These incidents set the stage for counterattacks by police, which only fed the cycle of violence. On March 21, 1985—symbolically on the twenty-fifth anniversary of the Sharpeville massacre of sixty-nine protestors—the police opened fire on a crowd of mourners in the Langa township of Uitenhage, killing twenty. Less than thirty-six hours later, one of the few local councillors who had resisted community pressure to resign was brutally killed by a crowd. This was one of the first uses of immolation with a rubber-tire "necklace," by means of which between 350 and 625 died during the next year and a half.[62] The effects of this campaign of violence were evident by the end of 1985, by which time the continued killings and bombings of houses had resulted in massive resignations from town councils, leaving only three out of thirty-four of them still functioning.[63] The cost of this method of bringing down apartheid structures could be seen not only in the number of deaths and bombings but also in the extent to which such mass fury compromised the moral high ground occupied by nonviolent movements. Earlier idealism had clearly been deserted for practical advantage, symbolized by the carnage of smoldering corpses rather than discarded ideas.

Many in the townships were shocked by the most brutal aspects of unrest, including the apparent arbitrariness with which many necklacing victims were identified as collaborators. Nonetheless, the heightened militancy was widely supported. As in 1976 when parents had joined the uprising only after seeing the heroism of their own children, in the mid-1980s the initial fear and disgust of many township dwellers were often followed by respect and desire to join the movement. The militancy of a few youths led to even more violence, particularly after many youths had been detained, killed, or both. This transition is exemplified by the mother of Sicelo Dlomo, a young activist killed in 1988 by the police:

> Under the state of emergency in 1986. . . . [Sicelo] was taken to Krugersdorp Prison. That was the beginning of a change in me. I asked myself if I was doing enough, not only for Sicelo, but also for my people. I saw that he was right in all that he was doing and told myself that I would always stand by him. . . . I saw that I had been living with my eyes closed. It was my son who opened my eyes to the real world.
>
> My advice to all the mothers and families who have lost their loved ones like me is that they must try and understand their children. They must not tell them to stop going to meetings, but they must go with them to these meetings and stand with them, side by side. That is what Sicelo taught me.[64]

State repression later succeeded in dampening some of the more overtly militant expressions of opposition, but repression also had the unintended and more immediate effect of strengthening certain aspects of the Charterist movement. Anger over repression confirmed the resolve of many township residents to continue or to expand the boycotts, a form of opposition difficult to repress because attendance at work or school and patronage of white retailers could not be easily coerced.[65] The repression, which had left no sector of the black community immune from police attacks or detentions, helped unify support for a popular response to state attacks. Organizational cooperation among diverse constituents became essential to mere survival.[66]

The most important response to repression was the greater national focus of opposition activity. Whereas activism in the early 1980s had been directed to local demands, repression made it clear that material concessions were no longer available and that grievances could only and finally be resolved by challenging national state structures. Although the protests remained locally organized, by 1986 the demands associated with such protests no longer were confined to local issues but now called for the unbanning of the ANC, the release of Nelson Mandela, and an end to all apartheid legislation.[67] As described at the time by Zwelakhe Sisulu, by 1986 "the masses linked up local issues with the question of political power. A set of national demands emerged which transcended specific issues or regional differences."[68] Much as local material grievances had been channeled into a national political movement under the ANC in the early 1950s, economic decline and repression helped transform the narrow focus of activism in the early 1980s into the national antiapartheid movement led by the UDF for much of the remainder of the decade.[69]

The state's open use of force not only helped consolidate the national movement, but it also validated many of the basic precepts of Charterism around which that movement had been conceived. The Charterists had long called for the unity of all those opposed to the common enemy of apartheid and promoted a more active form of opposition than that implied by Black Consciousness. In a sense, having been designed and adopted in response to the state's suppression of the 1976 uprising, only under repression could Charterism show its strength, thereby turning adversity to its advantage. Under the harsh conditions of the mid-1980s, the practical benefits of united action became most apparent, offering not only protection in numbers but also means through which the momentum of protest could be maintained. The BC movement's focus on ideas and dependence on a relatively small elite of leaders had enabled the state to crush the 1976 uprising by force, against which ideas provided no protection. In contrast, the decentralized basis of the Charterist movement enabled activists to continue to organize a response consistent with the aim of the movement even after many national and local leaders had been detained.

Whereas BC had focused on ideas that became less relevant when conditions changed, Charterism's focus on a strategic response to material conditions became all the more compelling when the initial conditions under which the movement had developed were altered by economic downturn and repression. Open unrest and repression, having justified the basis of the movement, also heightened the opposition's sense of optimism. Many felt that the increasing turbulence was proof of the regime's impending collapse and accordingly redoubled their efforts at mass mobilization to achieve final victory.

Economic downtown and repression led to further mass mobilization, but they also required the opposition to adjust its activities and organization in the Charterist movement. In the heat of the moment, relatively spontaneous protest and violence had exceeded the capacity of affiliated organizations to control mass participation. Unlike the BC leaders who had welcomed such spontaneity in 1976, those Charterist leaders who remained at liberty were concerned that such angry outbursts would be crushed just as quickly as they had appeared unless local organizations exerted discipline to coordinate the unrest.[70] During the second state of emergency begun in 1986, activists rededicated themselves to providing such discipline and coordination, in the hope of consolidating wider mass participation under Charterist organizational structures.

One of the most prominent subjects of renewed efforts at national coordination were those activities by local parent groups seeking to control the local school boycotts. In December 1985, these parties came together to form the National Education Crisis Committee (NECC), which immediately set out to support the students' political demands and to encourage the students to return to their schools, where continued activism could be more easily coordinated and controlled.[71] The NECC recognized the faults of existing apartheid education, but it was also aware of the difficulty of quickly or fully replacing state schools with independent alternatives, as indicated by the ANC's failure to organize private schools during the student boycotts in the mid-1950s.[72] Instead, the NECC proposed that it effectively take control of the existing schools, using state resources to provide a more relevant form of "people's education" that would replace the rigid curriculum that had so alienated the students.

The details of the NECC's plans were never spelled out, and its basic conception remained naively inconsistent with demonstrable state intransigence on educational reform. But the vision of people's education did capture the students' imagination and gained credibility for the NECC, including an endorsement from the ANC.[73] This credibility enabled the NECC to moderate the student militancy, to coordinate local student protest, and to convince the students to return to school. The ideas may have been typically fuzzy, but the strategic advantages were real. State authorities engaged in a series of relatively fruitless negotiations with the

NECC and avoided impeding the committee's efforts at instilling discipline, thus allowing a more orderly student organization to develop. The NECC's evident success at moderating both student militancy and state repression demonstrated the continuing practical benefits of Charterist strategy.

The state of emergency also impelled activists to consolidate further the local structures that could continue to organize protests without the guidance of the now-imprisoned national and local individual leaders. The internal Charterists and their exiled ANC allies recognized that their call for "ungovernability" had heightened mass militancy but also reduced their own capacity to control their followers and to avoid repression. To remedy these shortcomings and enlarge the movement, local structures were called on again to coordinate the protests. As advocated in a significant speech by Zwelakhe Sisulu to the NECC in 1986, ungovernability was to be moderated by the development of alternative governance structures that could exercise "people's power" in the short term and provide the basis for more formal democratic governance in the long term.[74] UDF activists were not so naive as to believe that the state would cede local power to such popular structures, but they did believe that state power could be offset, if not replaced, in the "liberated zones" of townships that the local authorities had been unable to control. By further engaging local popular control, the Charterists sought to achieve a form of "dual power," which anticipated the final victory. Their remarkable success in implementing this design is a tribute to the continued growth of popular support for the UDF, which by 1987 was able to claim over two million members of affiliated and allied organizations.

The basic building blocks of people's power were the street and area committees formed in most of the large townships in the mid-1980s. The more that the state restricted the UDF on the national level—banning publicity campaigns or mass meetings and in October 1986 prohibiting foreign funding of the Front—the more that the opposition concentrated its activities on these local structures. By 1987, surveys found 43 percent of Sowetans reporting the existence of such committees in their streets.[75] These grass-roots structures in Soweto and other townships were able to withstand police attempts to crush them and the ongoing rent boycotts they orchestrated, as their low-profile activities and meetings were difficult to identify or disrupt. Such groups of local residents were also better situated than was the national leadership to discipline the young "comrades," whose coercive militancy had gotten out of control and alienated some older allies.[76] "People's courts" were established by these committees to hear grievances and punish local residents who took advantage of the current turmoil to steal from their neighbors or to engage in other forms of antisocial behavior. These efforts won wide popular support among an urban population eager to preserve some degree of social order. Even local police authorities, prevented from fulfilling their usual duties by unrest and army patrols, were known to refer cases informally to these alternative courts, thereby revealing the disarray among security personnel.[77]

Both the unrest in 1976 and the mass militancy in the mid-1980s appeared during periods of economic decline and heightened state repression, but the form of popular protest during these two periods differed. In each case, the opposition's ideology and strategy in previous years were evident in the tactics employed in the unfolding protests. During the 1970s the BC movement had been more interested in developing racial assertiveness than in organizing a broad antiapartheid coalition. In 1976, youths, angered by their declining prospects and inspired by Black Consciousness, demonstrated their anger in largely unorganized unrest. Worker stayaways were an afterthought; rent or consumer boycotts were only rarely organized or given priority.[78]

During the early 1980s, by contrast, local structures were created to pursue formally organized protests, aimed more at achieving material concessions than at changing ideas or values. When economic conditions worsened after 1983, the established popular structures and strategies were transformed into vehicles for more militant but still highly organized protests. Stayaways and boycotts were the first order of business. More spontaneous expressions of anger were kept in check by the people and their leaders. Marches other than funerals were avoided, depriving the police of an easy opportunity to identify or shoot activists. During the first eight months of protests after August 1984, fewer than 400 people were killed, as compared with 575 deaths during the first eight months of more isolated unrest after June 1976.[79] Although the carnage during both these periods was tragic, the decrease in the initial number of casualties in the mid-1980s suggests that by this gruesome measure, the Charterist-led protests were more effective. And however repugnant, "necklacing" in the mid-1980s did deprive the state of the informers and local black officials who might otherwise have helped undermine the opposition's organization.

This historical comparison suggests a consistent underlying pattern of how ideas and material relations have interacted to shape recent South African internal opposition. Both the Black Consciousness and the Charterist movements formulated their basic approaches and built their organizational structures during periods of relative economic growth and, more significantly, during diminished repression. Unrest surfaced in more militant forms under both the BC and the UDF banners during periods of worsening economic conditions and heightened repression. These parallel transitions imply that the timing of oppositional consolidation and militancy is strongly associated with shifts in material conditions.

Such a structural analysis cannot by itself account for the important differences of ideology and strategy pursued during the 1970s and 1980s. Ideas and intentions of political activists were also highly consequential for the content, if not the timing, of opposition efforts. We have already established that the ideology of Black Consciousness was evident in opposition activities before and during the outbreak of unrest in 1976. In turn, the Charterists' greater concern for strategic organization influenced the form of popular activity before and during the outbreak of mass militancy in 1984. Activism in the 1980s centered on specific targets and demands, was connected to local structures, and often led to direct negotiations, all of which the BC movement had purposely avoided. These differences in approach were themselves shaped by historical developments, but how each of these movements interpreted and responded to the shifting material conditions also determined the resulting opposition activities.

As much as ideas and material conditions have interacted in similar patterns to influence recent South African opposition, the particular historical developments of social movements have not simply been repeated. In the aftermath of the 1984–1986 unrest, the Charterist movement was particularly anxious to ensure that the history of BC's loss of popularity after 1977 would not be repeated for the UDF in the late 1980s. To preempt any such possibility, the

Charterists proceeded to ensure their leading role in the opposition, seeking to impose their control even more widely. But as a result of these efforts, the inherent weaknesses of the Charterist approach became clearer in the final years of the decade.

## Charterist Predominance and Rising Disillusionment

The revolt in the mid-1980s heightened the conflict in South Africa, promoting a euphoric belief among many UDF leaders and their followers that the minority regime was on the verge of collapse. Mass mobilization by the coalition of Front affiliates had successfully challenged state control of the townships, creating a crisis for the central state authority. Many of the more militant Charterists anticipating an imminent transfer of power were disinclined to share the fruits of their efforts with those smaller opposition groups that had resisted all entreaties to unify under the UDF banner. AZAPO members resented their increasing exclusion from purportedly united opposition activities and so engaged in a series of violent clashes with local UDF adherents. Leaders of the Front disclaimed responsibility for this internecine conflict while encouraging intolerance of competing groups that more militant young followers expressed in the violent idiom of the time. Four years after its inception, the Front abandoned earlier efforts to accommodate non-Charterist factions and formally adopted the Freedom Charter, bringing about symbolic unity in preparation for the final victory. Then, when the minority regime did not collapse, the Charterist movement lost momentum, and popular disillusionment turned against the same leaders who had been hailed as future rulers.

Militant Charterists' efforts at consolidation in late 1986 and 1987 were motivated by the belief that liberation would soon be won, despite the attempts of more circumspect leaders, including Zwelakhe Sisulu, to dampen expectations of an impending defeat of the regime. These expectations of victory may seem incredible in retrospect, but at the time unrest had reached exceptional levels of militancy, and the state seemed more uncertain than ever before. According to Kgotso Chikane, a young Soweto activist, "We have won the political struggle, there is only the military left," and even that last hurdle was minimized in the excitement of the moment, despite the continued strength of the state's military machine.[80] The inability of the authorities to control the townships or to restrain mass militancy was widely interpreted as a harbinger of the collapse of the apartheid regime as a whole. The ANC in exile joined in spreading this view in order to encourage further unrest and to push the state toward a negotiated transfer of power.[81] This message was quickly absorbed into the popular culture of the townships, where youth sang, "Do not believe them when they say it is far, it is coming today."[82] Warnings against the dangers of false optimism or more realistic assessments of the state's remaining strength fell on deaf ears.[83]

After so many years of struggle, eager not to be caught unprepared for the denouement, the younger Charterists began to prepare for the final act. Overconfidence had replaced the self-doubt of the previous decade, with unforeseen and dangerous consequences. Concerns about future reconciliation and preparations for power were abandoned in the excited expectation of impending victory. In place of activities with only long-term payoff, short-term efforts to solidify or enforce control of the opposition took precedence. The central strategy of Charterism, to unite all opponents of apartheid in a loose coalition, was overridden by the perceived need to assert a single, coherent opposition line. AZAPO adherents who did not subscribe to this line were dismissed by many Charterists for having resisted the mass mobilization of the UDF, thereby justifying their exclusion from reaping the impending rewards of those efforts. Calls for unity increasingly referred only to those who accepted the leadership of the UDF and its exiled ANC allies, rather than to a truly inclusive and ideologically diverse coalition.

The rush to consolidate support and to enforce unity under the Charterist banner was first evident in local excesses, which national leaders refused to condone but were unable or unwilling to prevent. The momentum of an intolerant revolutionary mood had developed beyond their control. State repression had generated widespread anger and had hampered many of the organizational channels through which the leaders might otherwise have been able to discipline their followers. The resulting lack of controls had first been evident in the occasional use of coercion by young "comrades" in the townships to enforce the various boycotts. Such coercion, including the ultimate sanction of necklacing, which had first been visited on accused agents of the state, was increasingly used against ideological opponents. The police and other state authorities, eager to distract mass violence away from whites and into the black community, actively encouraged such intolerance, division, and internecine violence. And many of the younger activists obliged them, turning the methods of oppression so ably demonstrated in recent years by the state onto their fellow victims of oppression.

Rising popular militancy and repression would not have resulted in open conflict between UDF and AZAPO adherents had there not been a long history of tension between these groups and their leaders. Until 1984, relations between the UDF and AZAPO had remained cordial despite exchanges of rhetorical abuse and occasional scuffles at mass meetings. By 1985, however, with unrest on the rise and the prize of political power seeming to more militant youth to be within reach, tensions between these two groups had deepened. As pointed out by Saki Macozoma, who was to become a spokesman for the ANC after its unbanning in 1990, "Leaders on both sides have made irresponsible statements at tense times and expressed their desire to snuff out their opposition."[84] Saths Cooper of AZAPO observed that "the conflict was more over hegemony than ideology; the fight to be sole representative. Each side was afraid that mutual recognition threatened their existence."[85] The leaders of both groups were vulnerable to such logic, for they had a direct interest in seeing their competitors fail, so as to avoid sharing the limelight, resources, or official positions in a broader coalition. The UDF's leaders were particularly inclined toward the dominance of one group over the other, as they stood a much greater chance than did those in AZAPO of emerging victorious from any contest for control of the opposition.

While the rising popularity of the Charterist movement exacerbated the tension between the UDF and AZAPO, the falling fortunes of the latter also were contributing to the conflict. AZAPO had retained some pockets of support, as suggested by the more than forty thousand mourners at the funeral in April 1986 of a BC leader, but AZAPO's national following and programs had largely dwindled.[86] Polls of urban blacks in 1985 and 1986 found that a significantly smaller percentage supported BC or Africanism, as compared with the wide popularity of Charterism.[87] Rather than addressing their own weaknesses, the AZAPO leaders blamed the relative popularity of the Charterists on biased media coverage and the resources controlled by the UDF. As Roland White of the UDF described the situation in 1985, "BC had always been small, but now they were facing extinction in the face of the total politicization around the UDF in the townships. The issue was one of political, organizational and personal survival."[88] Threatened in this way, AZAPO adherents became impulsively defensive.

Conflict between the UDF and AZAPO broke out at its worst where the survival of AZAPO members and organization was most uncertain. The eastern Cape around Port Elizabeth had long been a stronghold of Charterism and, with its small communities, single-language group, and particularly depressed economy, was a center of popular mobilization in the mid-1980s. Heightened tensions in the eastern Cape placed AZAPO at a significant disadvantage and led its adherents to employ desperate measures. To protect themselves from attack, dozens congregated in the large house of Rev. Mzwandile Maqina, who used the opportunity to raise his own standing in the organization. As their sense of encirclement grew, the AZAPO adherents under Maqina's informal leadership became more violent. For instance, veteran journalist Mono Badela, a Charterist, described being "abducted" and taken to Maqina's house, where "the whole regional executive of AZAPO" threatened him with necklacing if he did not convince the UDF "to stop harassing AZAPO."[89] Badela claims that other UDF activists, including Mathew Goniwe, were killed in this house. When large crowds of angered UDF supporters marched on Maqina's house, "the South African police and Defence Force protected him. . . . There were two [armored troop carriers] there at all times."[90] AZAPO's national executive hesitated to condemn Maqina while their followers benefited from his protection.[91] By the time a solution to the impasse was negotiated and Maqina was expelled from AZAPO, the remaining popular support for the BC group had been further eroded by its association with Maqina and his police protectors.

Conflict between the UDF and AZAPO in 1985 and 1986 was evident as well outside the eastern Cape. In January 1985, tensions flared when AZAPO protested the UDF-approved visit to South Africa by U.S. Senator Edward Kennedy, described by AZAPO as a liberal emissary of Western capitalist imperialism, much as his brother Robert's visit had been condemned by the PAC two decades earlier. According to Saths Cooper, such ideological objections were less pressing than was the affront that "AZAPO was not consulted on arrangements and timing. . . . They threw down the gauntlet."[92] Charterists argued that these protests against Kennedy demonstrated AZAPO's unreasonably militant position. Concurrent with this conflict over the Kennedy visit, speakers from both the UDF and AZAPO were attacked at black universities in the Transvaal, and by June 1986 forty-five houses belonging to leaders of each group had been bombed and more than a dozen people killed.[93] During 1985, AZAPO members living in Alexandra, outside Johannesburg, were forced to flee from UDF attacks and so resettled in the AZAPO-controlled areas of Soweto. The death toll of these conflicts is unknown, but a total of 260 has been estimated.[94] In December 1986, conflicts between Charterist and BC student groups in Soweto became so frenzied that the grandmother of one activist was killed in her bed as revenge for the death of another activist.[95]

The persistence and virulence of these conflicts between the Charterists and BC stalwarts in AZAPO were in part the result of direct state intervention. On this, both camps agreed, even though each accused the other of having been the greater beneficiary of state support.[96] Dwindling popular support of AZAPO in UDF-dominated townships contributed to AZAPO's particular dependence on official protection, such as that provided to the Reverend Maqina by the police and army. By bolstering the weaker side in this way, the state was able to maintain active conflict, loosening the UDF's local organization and diverting the attention of activists on both sides away from their common enemy.[97] Where little if any conflict existed between the UDF and AZAPO, state security officials worked surreptitiously to encourage antagonism. In Soweto, fake UDF pamphlets were distributed, calling for the destruction of AZAPO; bombs were allegedly placed by the police in the homes of leaders of the two movements; and AZAPO members were publicly accused of killing UDF activists.[98] Charterists already predisposed against AZAPO and eager to reinforce their sole legitimacy as the state's major opponents responded to these developments by vilifying AZAPO as a reactionary "fringe group" of "lost political bandits" who were collaborators "on the payroll" of the state and "enemies in the eyes of the people."[99] Such rhetorical vehemence attested to the state's success at widening this division in the opposition and at turning the Charterists' anger disproportionately onto AZAPO, which by itself represented little threat to the UDF's predominance.

A fragile peace between the UDF and AZAPO was finally restored, as much by the effort of the leaders as by the exhaustion of the participants. The first meetings to resolve the differences had either been interrupted by the police or attended by only one side.[100] But by January 1987, the leaders of the two groups had acknowledged their common interest in resisting further state repression and had agreed to end their violent conflict and to blame any further attacks on vigilantes.[101] This resolution, however, did not heal all of the wounds inflicted by the UDF and AZAPO on each other, with suspicion remaining long after the fighting had ceased, much as the state no doubt had hoped. Subsequent calls for nonpartisan unity were thus tempered by the memory of this internecine conflict.

The same exhaustion that had dampened the conflict between the UDF and AZAPO also eventually caught up with the UDF's local democratic structures. Civic associations and related groups had come to the fore in 1985 and 1986, after the national leadership had been detained and open forms of publicity curtailed. By 1987, police sweeps and massive detentions had broken the back of the local structures, shifting the impetus back to what remained of national leadership. Even the street committees were "smashed" by unrelenting repression, with the exception of those committees in Soweto, where local activists could still find refuge in the labyrinth of South Africa's largest township.[102] Although they continued to meet, the street committees in Soweto were also eventually weakened, as indicated by the rise of local criminal activity which had earlier been contained by the street committees and their related "people's courts."[103]

Repression eventually made it impossible for opposition strategy to continue to be based on local initiatives in a loosely coordinated front. The publicity and mass meetings on which the Front had depended to unify local efforts were interrupted by censorship and bannings. Affiliates of the UDF, fearful of being isolated, became increasingly eager for explicit instructions on how to respond to the new situation. Democratic procedures, such as the recording of minutes for vital meetings, were abandoned, and new structures, such as the South African Youth Congress secretly launched in 1987, were formed without wide public discussion.[104] As a result, control of the movement became more centralized under the remaining national leadership, which had little alternative but to take the initiative and act increasingly unilaterally. As the former UDF national treasurer Cassim Saloojee admitted, "The state of emergency created organizational problems. It makes democratic consultation more difficult. In its formation, the UDF was highly democratic . . . democracy was almost a retarding factor. . . . [Now,] democracy in the mass movement will be difficult, but not impossible."[105] Just as Lenin had argued that a revolutionary organization could not be fully democratic during repression, so the leaders of the UDF moved toward a top-down structure.

As repression forced compromises of various democratic controls and a greater centralization of power, open discussion within the movement was further curtailed. Previously, such discussions had focused on strategy rather than ideology, as the Front had been designed to include a diversity of ideological positions in order to permit broad alliances. But antagonism toward AZAPO had solidified the Front's ideological position, while repression had precluded wide-ranging consultation on strategy. The Charterists increasingly saw tolerance of internal dissent over either ideology or strategy as a luxury that they could no longer afford. Many of the UDF's followers, happy simply to follow established policies without discussion, were not concerned by this transition. Others objected to using "the emergency as an excuse to behave undemocratically," fearing that a greater reliance on centralized control would leave the movement vulnerable to internal dissension or to dislocation caused by the detention of a few leaders.[106] However, repression left the Front no alternative to functioning more hierarchically if it were to continue to function at all.

In August 1987 the four-year-old United Democratic Front officially adopted the Freedom Charter, symbolizing the centralization of the movement under its national leadership and the reduced concern for accommodating alternative views. This move was designed to assert positively and exclusively the predominance of

Charterist ideology. According to the usually more moderate veteran Soweto leader Dr. Motlana, "At this stage we cannot tolerate competing ideologies. . . . We cannot waste our time confusing people. . . . We must learn from Algeria in the 1950s, where everyone was smashed into one movement."[107] Many in the Front believed that such unity had already been achieved and so were encouraged in this belief by the diminished popular support for AZAPO and the wide media attention given to the UDF. Adoption of the Charter as a "comprehensive political program" indicated the UDF leadership's confidence that "the Front, through its correct line, has become the only viable political home for those in the legal opposition movement who stand for genuine change."[108] Apparently the UDF leadership had come to share the intolerance of alternative views exhibited earlier by its more militant followers.

The UDF leadership saw the adoption of the Freedom Charter as a signal that they represented the sole legitimate form of internal opposition, a view expressed in a number of less dramatic actions. Many Charterists agreed with Zwelakhe Sisulu that "the masses believe in hegemony, unlike the intellectuals, clinging to their own power and ideas," and that the UDF could now claim such hegemony.[109] The Charterists increasingly referred to themselves as the sole "progressive movement" and later as the "mass democratic movement," using such labels to dismiss alternative groups in a manner reminiscent of the Bolsheviks' denigration of their competitors for power as Mensheviks (translated as the minority). To reinforce their predominance within the opposition and their control over affiliates, in 1987 the UDF leadership claimed the right to regulate all available funding previously donated directly to local groups.[110] At the University of the Western Cape, students associated with Black Consciousness were denied official status and resources. Within the ranks of the UDF, mandated adherence to the Freedom Charter explicated by its house journal, *Isizwe*, was used to quash any regional differences and "factionalism" that remained.[111] The inconsistency between such intolerance and the inclusive tone of the Freedom Charter was largely ignored.

At the same time that the UDF leadership was asserting its control over the opposition, its movement was losing momentum. Local affiliates had been significantly weakened by repression, leaving the Front's national leadership with more centralized control but less capacity to ensure that their policies were enacted. Any efforts to resuscitate protests were quickly cut down by further detentions. The funding that had been so crucial to the Front's development was also becoming more scarce. In late 1986, the UDF was declared an "affected" organization that was no longer legally entitled to receive overseas funding, and by May 1987 its annual revenues had fallen from R2 million to approximately one tenth of that amount.[112] Before the impact of these difficulties had been widely perceived by the rank and file, the Front's leadership had acted, in part defensively, to consolidate its centralized control and to reinforce ideological conformity. These measures did not prove sufficient, however, to contain the damage of lost momentum and resources to a movement that had been based more on the mobilization of mass action and resources than on loyalty to particular leaders or ideas.

As the difficulties of continued mobilization became more widely felt, the exaggerated euphoria of 1986 was largely replaced by an exaggerated defeatism little more than a year later. In the wake of unrest and repression, the popular mood had lost its confidence, shaken even further in February 1988 when the state effectively banned the UDF and various of its larger affiliates. Much as the UDF had been credited for bringing an impending victory over the state, it was now faulted for the failure to gain that elusive goal. Popular disillusionment was widely expressed; for instance, the executive committee of the organized squatters at Thokoza concluded in 1988, that "we will never see change in our lifetime. The UDF tried and failed. The Front is still trying but nothing is coming right."[113] Even among the leadership, there was a growing feeling that this pessimism both marked and contributed to the Front's defeat. For example, as Soweto activist Sebolelo Mohajane stated, "The government has won. People are now keeping to themselves. . . . They are tired, just moving on like zombies. Repression has worked. It is very depressing. . . . 1985–1986 were the worst years in black history, but still there was no revolution. The state's tactics are winning. . . . There is a gap left."[114] Even the psychological gains credited to the BC movement of the 1970s were questioned in light of this new pessimism, with Saths Cooper wondering aloud if "the inferiority myth has been taken in and still exists."[115]

As optimism was replaced by popular disillusionment, the UDF's high-profile leadership, who had claimed responsibility for the leading opposition movement, became an obvious target for criticism. The Charterist leadership had consistently avoided more radical rhetoric, because it tended to be older, more conservative, and more wary of repression than were some of its more militant followers and also because this was part of its strategy of being as inclusive as possible. The leaders had assumed that its more radical constituency would remain loyal to the Front for lack of a viable alternative and that only by adopting a more moderate line could the Front incorporate the petty bourgeoisie, rural masses, and white liberals who would otherwise have shied away from joining the movement. As long as this strategy had contributed to the growth of the movement, many had supported it.

Once the opposition had lost its momentum, however, the leadership's resistance to radicalism was associated with the lack of radical results. Unlike its BC predecessors who had embraced black assertiveness, the Charterist leaders had tried "to hold back political mobilization while organizations were built to guide and direct the oppositional movements."[116] The leaders believed that such moderation was essential to the movement's preservation, although they were prevented from making this argument to their followers because of censorship and bannings. The rank and file were left with the impression that the leadership had supported a diminution of mass militancy just when it seemed on the verge of causing the regime to collapse. As has been the case in social movements elsewhere, the moderating influence of leadership was blamed for subverting further mass mobilization.[117]

Frustration with the Charterist leadership was concentrated among the youth, following in the tradition of those young students who had pushed for greater militancy in 1976. According to Fikile Bam, the UDF-aligned youth had always been "pushing for chaos. Even the elders of the UDF were concerned [that militancy] may lead to a backlash."[118] As the movement lost momentum, these young people felt betrayed by the restraint imposed on them. According to one young activist in Tembisa, "The leaders' call for nonviolence doesn't represent the people. It puts [the leaders] in a vulnerable position."[119] Many older activists had come to respect the more militant youth for their contribution to effective local mobilization. As a result, the youths' criticism of the leadership for having rejected a final push for victory was more widely acclaimed than might otherwise have been the case.

The growing popular resentment of the leaders' efforts at restraint was also directed against the liberal white allies with whom the leadership had worked more closely than had the rank and file. These white liberals had been particularly vocal in supporting the leadership's call for moderation. In 1987, many of the white affiliates had joined the top UDF leadership in calling for the masses to avoid further repression by pulling back from highly politicized campaigns. Almost all the white affiliates also came out strongly in favor of maintaining alliances with businesses, despite the rise of union agitation against those employers. A white affiliate in Johannesburg even contended that white fears and resistance to "one man, one vote" should be accommodated in order to maintain such alliances.[120]

Despite these controversial positions, the UDF leadership and the ANC in exile continued to argue strongly for the need to keep and even broaden alliances with whites and to allay white fears by guaranteeing "minority rights" in a postapartheid South Africa.[121] But more militant activists increasingly questioned the compromises necessary to maintain alliances with whites, reasoning that the benefits of such alliances had diminished with the need for resources provided by whites, as the state no longer permitted mass publicity and other expensive campaigns. Much as discontent over white involvement had led more militant Africanists to abandon the ANC and form the PAC in the late 1950s, the resurgence of such discontent contributed to a limited rise of spontaneous Africanist sentiment in the late 1980s, as we shall see in the next chapter.

In addition to criticizing leadership policies and alliances, UDF members voiced their personal resentment of the privileges enjoyed by their leaders. Working closely with whites and international donors, these leaders had become involved with numerous international conferences and funding agency boards, reinforcing the popular perceptions of an elite living in a rarified and increasingly inaccessible world. Although the resources gained through such contacts had been essential to the movement's growth, many leaders had also been able to travel widely, to send their own children to private schools not subject to boycotts, and to build lavish homes, including Winnie Mandela's construction of one of the largest houses in Soweto. Indeed, her contribution of R62,000 in twenty-rand notes to an "Unban the ANC" advertisement in 1987 suggested a lack of formal control over the leaders' collection and use of resources.[122] Once the state had restricted the wider distribution of such resources, popular resentment of the residual privileges enjoyed by the leadership grew rapidly. Many felt that the leadership had raised their own standards of living and reputations without suffering from the widespread deprivation that had generated international interest and donations in the first place. For instance, Bishop Tutu's righteous threat in July 1985 to leave South Africa if the necklacing did not stop was widely resented as an effort to use his reputation against the people who had made him a world hero.[123] But such criticism of the leadership did not completely overshadow the acknowledgment of their efforts and sacrifices, such as Tutu's popular and highly successful campaign for economic sanctions or Winnie Mandela's banishment from Soweto and long years without her imprisoned husband. Nonetheless, this criticism did reflect the growing resentment of some of the perks and prerogatives gained along the way.

The leaders who had symbolized the movement were the most obvious target for criticism when the movement's fortunes turned. People had come to rely on these leaders to represent their interests and vocalize their grievances, complementing the pressure exerted through local activism. Over time, these leaders inevitably became more distant from the people they represented, in accordance with "the iron law of oligarchy" common to many social movements and political parties.[124] As mass mobilization became more difficult, frustration grew among a populace that had been encouraged by the Charterists to concentrate more on action and material conditions than on rhetorical ideas. Once repression had crushed local activism, popular and media attention turned to those few leaders who were still free to speak out. However, those leaders could not maintain the momentum of the movement through rhetoric alone and so became the most obvious target for popular disillusionment. Little resentment was directed against the ANC in exile, however, which had remained distant enough from internal adherents to avoid being blamed for the movement's misfortunes. Of course, the state authorities were also criticized, although blaming them for the movement's shortcomings was popularly perceived as unproductive, as disruption and repression were taken for granted as part of setting in which the opposition functioned.

Although resentment of the leaders was an inevitable outcome of disillusionment in a hierarchical movement, the peculiarities of Charterism exacerbated this problem. The BC organizations, having remained relatively elitist, had never built enough of a formally incorporated mass base to be confronted by the difficulty of maintaining a close link between leaders and followers. The Charterist movement, on the other hand, had moved quickly to gather disparate affiliates under the umbrella of the UDF, using its resources and publicity to foster broad alliances and to create "unity in action." There had been little effort, however, to solidify this unity through discussion or agreement on principles that might have provided for greater cohesion between leaders and followers. The Front had been constructed on the assumption that "what is important is not the ninety-nine percent of the questions on which they are disagreed. What is important is the one percent on which they are agreed to act together."[125] In addition, formal channels or structures through which affiliates could hold national leaders accountable had not been established. Indeed, the Front had been popularly associated with prominent individuals who had not been formally elected, including Bishop Tutu and Allan Boesak, referred to by their critics as the "film star clergy." When repression curtailed the mass action around which the affiliates had united, popular attention was directed to the controversial statements and actions of those leading churchmen and others who remained relatively unrestricted, including Bishop Tutu's renunciation of "atheistic Marxism" and his call for a cessation of the ANC's popular armed attacks. Winnie Mandela also made controversial remarks encouraging the use of necklacing and was associated with the criminal activities of her bodyguards.[126] None of these actions or views had been formally sanctioned or fell within the category of issues around which the Front was united.

The basic precepts and organizational structure of Charterism that had been so effective in the mid-1980s made the movement vulnerable later in the decade. Unity under the banner of the UDF had been based on the common interest in mass mobilization and the redress of material and political grievances, with ideological differences intentionally ignored. As long as these strategic goals were realized—as they had been to an unprecedented extent—more divisive issues could be avoided. But once repression had curtailed mobilization, these unresolved differences surfaced with a vengeance. The loose structure of the national coalition had heightened dependence on prophetic leadership, which had been forced by repression to act and adopt unitary positions as though it were a vanguard party.[127] But their following had not been prepared to cede control of the movement to these leaders, and it had not engaged in sufficient discussion to guide their leaders or to reach a consensus. Leaders and followers grew more and more distant from each other, and resentment followed. Had the movement not been initially successful in mobilizing a wide following, or had that mobilization not been disrupted by repression, perhaps these difficulties would not have emerged. However, the focus on action over ideas was fundamental to the Charterist approach, leaving it open to division once the conditions under which it had grown had changed. By not insisting on ideological coherence, the movement had been able to attract a variety of followers, whose differences remained unresolved, however, and resurfaced once the momentum of collective action faltered.

The Charterist movement's vulnerability to internal division was apparently understood by the state, which sought to take advantage of this weakness by tailoring its repression accordingly. The Charterist movement was well equipped to withstand considerable repression, with the local organizations able to maintain momentum and discipline longer than had been the case in the 1970s. The state responded with large-scale detentions, which gradually broke down such grass-roots activism. Not content with this outcome, which could last only as long as people remained in detention, the state used a variety of counterinsurgency operations designed to create dissension within the Charterist movement and to open fissures in the amorphous alliance. The media's coverage of the unrest was censored, whereas reports of the privileges of leaders, conflict between the UDF and AZAPO, and the alternative approaches of the more conservative Zulu-based Inkatha movement, with its strongholds in Natal and Transvaal hostels, or progovernment church groups, were permitted and even encouraged. Fake pamphlets were distributed and vigilantes were employed to aggravate the opposition's internal conflict. Reports of UDF or ANC violence were carefully controlled by the authorities in the hope of alienating more conservative constituencies from the Charterist alliance. Indian and colored politicians participating in the tricameral parliament were given resources with which to campaign in their communities, while anti-Indian sentiment within the UDF was publicized in order to encourage ethnic discord.

Such counterinsurgency techniques had been less necessary and more rarely used in the 1970s, when the BC movement, weak on organization, was more easily crushed by sheer force. The broad national alliance of the UDF, more vulnerable to division, was hit both from above, with direct repression, and from below, with campaigns designed to deepen the disagreement among its diverse constituents. The movement's soft underbelly of ideological and social diversity, previously obscured by the hard shell of united action, was exposed through the wily efforts of the predatory state.

At the same time that it was sowing division by means of counterinsurgency, the state also began again to grant material concessions as a means of restoring order through peaceful cooptation. Selective townships that had recently been the sites of unrest were targeted for "beautifying" schemes designed to "win hearts and minds." In 1987, over R200 million were spent on improvements in Soweto; another R1.4 billion were distributed to township projects around the country; and over R7 million were spent on an advertising campaign encouraging blacks to pay again for rent and services. A year later, reports estimated total expenditures of R3.2 billion on improvements in thirty-four locations, quietly funded through increased taxation and privatization of public assets in order to avoid raising the ire of white voters.[128] These projects were designed to "exploit the people's need for survival at a time of growing unemployment and recruit them through financial incentives and promises of a better life."[129] By providing such concrete improvements, the state set out to meet the material interests to which the Charterists themselves had appealed and thereby to pull support away from the movement.

Not only did the state adopt Charterist-like strategies in an effort to divide and dilute support for the opposition, but it also mimicked the movement's own rhetoric in a vain effort to enhance the state's popular appeal. State President P. W. Botha claimed to have "gone too far to serve people, broaden democracy, remove hurtful and discriminating legislation and social practices, [and] provide for the needs of all on a scale found nowhere else on the continent."[130] Pretoria described these policies, for the first time, as the start of a process out of which would be born a single unified nation. Even the Freedom Charter itself was praised by government officials, including Defense Minister Magnus Malan, who called it "an exceptionally fine document. . . . Anybody who has not yet read it should do so."[131] The state's campaign to win hearts and minds, popularly known as "WHAM," thus sought to supplant the Charterists' own efforts to win popular allegiance through both economic incentives and rhetorical accommodations.

At the same time that it was adopting the Charterists' own strategies and rhetoric, the state tried to discourage protests by offering alternative channels of popular activity, thus creating even more division among the UDF leaders and within communities. In 1987 some of the Front's leaders in Natal began to talk publicly about the possibility of participating in local elections, for instance, by putting forward local candidates who would defeat unpopular councillors and then refuse to take office. UDF copresident Archie Gumede raised this possibility in public, only to be quickly pressured to renounce the idea, in a rare public disagreement among the Charterist leadership.[132] Although others agreed with Gumede that boycotting elections might no longer be the most effective strategy, they were concerned that the rank and file would be confused by a tactical participation in elections previously denigrated as a form of collaboration. And even though the state authorities may have been disappointed by the Front's decision to maintain its boycott policy, they were certainly gratified by divisions within the UDF over this issue.

These maneuvers by the state plus the divisions in the opposition created pressure in the Charterist movement to reassess its ideology and strategy. As in 1977, this process of reassessment was advanced by mass detentions that placed activists together in group cells where they could discuss alternative approaches. Similar discussions were held in various organizations and township locations. The outcome of these deliberations remained uncertain. According to the UDF-aligned lawyer Priscilla Jana, the reassessment in 1987 and 1988 was expected to "lead either to more emphasis on consciousness or to deeper involvement. Either people will opt out of overt political involvement and steer clear, or they will have greater zest."[133] The state was doing all it could to encourage former activists to abandon their struggle and to accept state reforms and participation in elections, with mixed success. Most Charterists remained committed to noncollaboration, though there was considerable disagreement over the nature of the continued opposition.

Even those activists who insisted on retaining the basic precepts of Charterism were forced to admit that the strategies of opposition pursued under this framework had reached an impasse. Mass mobilization had been crushed, and the national leaders associated with local protests were being prosecuted in the Delmas treason trial and in other court proceedings, suggesting that the UDF's broad alliances would not prevent the state from exercising repression. Nor were such alliances still justified by the resources they provided, as the state had prohibited the Front from fund-raising and had forbidden many of those activities for which resources were required. Rent boycotts had led to evictions and to fines of more than R250 million; school boycotts had upset parents hoping for economic advancement through their children; and consumer boycotts had made shopping difficult while profiting township merchants.[134] Plans to take over the schools or to change the curriculum had been rejected by the authorities. Some activists concluded that the only strategy that remained effective were the ANC's armed attacks, which had risen from 4 in 1976 to 234 in 1987.[135] Most remained convinced that the well-armed state could not be defeated militarily through such limited sabotage and that an alternative approach therefore needed to be developed.

Many in the Charterist movement came to believe that renewed and more effective efforts at opposition required a greater degree of ideological unity or cohesion than had thus far been achieved. They argued that the Charterist movement's primary concern for "unity in action" and purposeful avoidance of ideological discussion or education had left a legacy of disunity that was bound to emerge once mobilization had faltered. This view was expressed even by the rank and file; for instance, the squatters in Thokoza complained that "there can't be any change as long as [we] are fighting with each other. . . . People can't help us because we are not united."[136] To resolve this problem, many felt that the Charterism's central conception of national identity, subordinating ideological cohesion in favor of strategic unity, had to be amended or reconsidered. The painful lessons of recent experience had indicated that an exclusive focus on national identity, though effective at mobilizing protests that had succeeded in upsetting the regime, had also created vulnerabilities to internally generated and externally encouraged discord.

The difficulties plaguing the movement in 1987 and 1988 led activists to consider alternatives to the traditional Charterist focus on a loose national coalition. Concerns about the shortcomings of targeting racial identity, which had become evident in appraisals of the BC movement after 1976 and had been reinforced by conflict with AZAPO, made a return to this approach unpopular. Class analysis, which had been discussed earlier and used rhetorically, had not previously been a principal focus of opposition ideology and strategy, having instead remained secondary to race or nation. Activists were aware that this denigration of class analysis had contributed to the ongoing reluctance of organized workers to become fully engaged in either the Black Consciousness or the Charterist movement, at least through 1987. Yet all during this time, the labor unions had grown along with the burgeoning industrial base of the country, heightening both class divisions and more importantly class consciousness in the black community. This development captured the imagination of many Charterists, who perceived that a greater concentration on class identity could unite established unions and community organizations around their common economic interests and provide for greater ideological cohesion based on class consciousness.

The greater appeal of class identity attracted many Charterists as a means of tightening the opposition's organizational and ideological unity. Such an approach was also consistent with the increasing radicalization of many activists seeking to gather popular resistance for a final push to state power, in which the ANC and SACP were expected to play a leading role. Guided by such expectations, the attention of the movement during the last two years of the decade shifted from a national antiapartheid campaign to a combined antiapartheid and anticapitalist struggle. After many years of talking about how to incorporate class analysis, the "two strands of the South African movement for liberation—the national (for the people to rule their own country) and the worker's struggle"—finally came together.[137] With this development came a turn toward leadership by the workers and a stronger commitment to union-style organizational structures, aimed at preventing leaders and followers from becoming as disjointed as they had been under the Charterist banner. The trade unions, which had largely evaded state repression and its damaging impact, played a central role in directing this development.

The move toward a greater focus on class organization and consciousness built directly on what the opposition had already achieved and learned. Black Consciousness had succeeded in revitalizing mass mobilization, which the Charterists had channeled into more overt political activism. Both of these movements could be improved, however, by combining BC's focus on consciousness with Charterism's focus on activism and by resisting the idealism of the former and the lack of cohesion of the latter. A strong working-class movement had already formed in the trade unions, capable of organizing mass action informed by class consciousness and motivated by common economic interests, which had attracted both BC and Charterist adherents. Of course, this movement suffered from its own shortcomings as it challenged an increasingly sophisticated, if somewhat more divided, state. But the strengths of the working-class movement, under the leadership of the trade unions, proved to be considerable, finally bringing the South African opposition within sight of its ultimate goal of achieving state power. Amid all the recent discord, the struggle was entering its long-awaited "end game."

# 6

# *Toward a Black Working-Class Movement and the Watershed of 1989–1990*

To this point, our study has concentrated on internal opposition movements characterized by their self-defined focus on racial or national identity. In the 1970s, the Black Consciousness movement set out to revive black resistance by asserting a positive self-image based on race, culminating in the explosive uprising of 1976. During the 1980s, the Charterists tried to redirect popular resistance into more active, inclusive, and carefully organized efforts at mobilizing local protests, culminating in the widespread unrest of the mid-1980s. As much as the Charterists were able to build on the significant achievements of BC, the approach of these two movements remained distinct, with each suffering from its own vulnerabilities to state attack. BC's principal concern with spreading its ideology did little to prepare the movement to withstand repressive force. The Charterists' subordination of ideological concerns to the strategic necessity of mobilizing the nation did little to resolve differences within the movement that the state used to encourage discord. By 1988, neither movement had been able to combine ideological and organizational coherence, and neither had succeeded in ending white domination.

Particularly after the state effectively banned the UDF, AZAPO, and related popular organizations in 1988, the focus of opposition activity shifted to the less severely restricted churches and, more significantly, to the labor unions. Although these unions had been influenced by BC, the Charterist movement, and earlier labor organizations, they had remained formally self-governing during more than a decade of growth and were distinguished by their greater focus on class analysis and on advancing the economic interests of workers. By the late 1980s, the unions had established a strong organizational base of more than a million members, had demonstrated their capacity for mobilizing mass action, and had developed formal democratic structures through which leaders could be held accountable to the rank and file. Educational programs, debates, and participation in union governance had also reinforced class consciousness among the membership, expressed as increasingly radical demands for the end of racial discrimination, political domination, and economic exploitation. Despite the increasing diversion from regular union activities into national politics, the efforts of the unions at forging a well-organized and ideologically coherent form of resistance constitute a notable advance in the development of an effective opposition, building on the achievements of others. Even though these unions have been somewhat constrained by the narrow economic interests of their members, they have significantly added to the pressures exerted on the state to enter into serious negotiations regarding alternative political and economic structures.

## The Emergence of the Modern Black Union Movement

The history of large-scale trade unionism among black South Africans began in 1919 with the formation of the Industrial and Commercial Workers' Union of Africa (ICU) among dock workers in Cape Town. This union successfully organized a work stoppage by forty thousand African mineworkers in 1920 and within a few years had attracted over one hundred thousand members into a largely rural-based social movement. Despite these gains, the ICU continued to be weakened by feuding among its leadership even after the expulsion of Communist party members, corruption, a lack of financial resources, and difficulties in forming democratic structures among a membership which was scattered throughout small workplaces and farms rather than concentrated in the still small industrial sector.[1] By the 1930s, the ICU had all but collapsed (though it enjoyed a brief resurgence in the 1940s), and the organizationally distinct Joint Committee on Trade Unions had been formed. Much of this committee's efforts were directed at working through the wage boards of the Department of Labour, which offered occasional accommodations but, in return, required considerable limitations on the workers' activism. But the committee effectively collapsed in 1940 when its chief organizer, Max Gordon, was jailed.[2] Later unionists looked back on these experiences and concluded that their success depended on building strong shop-floor structures that reduced dependence on leadership, thereby gaining resources and avoiding both excessive cooperation with the state and state repression.

Many white workers joined the war effort in the 1940s, providing the newly formed Council of Non-European Trade Unions (CNETU) with a considerable negotiating advantage because of the increased reliance on black labor. Under the able leadership of J. B. Marks, a longtime member of the Communist party, more than one hundred fifty thousand members were attracted by the gains that CNETU negotiated. This dramatic growth and success led to a strike by seventy thousand African mineworkers in 1946, which was defeated after a violent attack by the police. CNETU never recovered from this setback, aggravated by its communist-influenced leaders' reluctance to disrupt South Africa's war effort against Hitler after Germany's invasion of the Soviet Union.[3] Later unionists interpreted this experience as confirming the disadvantages of relying on leaders with their own political agenda and of a premature confrontation with the state.

In 1955, remnants of CNETU and other unions remaining outside the more conservative Trade Union Council of South Africa came together to form the South African Congress of Trade Unions, SACTU. This union congress built strong factory committees and was the first to call successfully for community support in the form of a consumer boycott. The economic recession and activities of the ANC at this time pulled SACTU away from a narrow economic agenda toward greater political involvement. Immediately following its formation, SACTU had joined the ANC's Congress Alliance and largely subordinated itself to ANC control. This association led to considerable state repression, particularly after the ANC embarked on sabotage in December 1961 in the wake of the Sharpeville massacre, and eventually SACTU joined the ANC in exile.[4] Conservative analysts, such as Edward Feit, have argued that SACTU's association with the ANC was an inappropriate and destructive distraction from the basic economic agenda of trade unionism.[5] Others have countered that SACTU had little alternative and that this earlier federation "grew most rapidly in those regions where its relationship with the national movement was closest."[6] This debate was resumed in the late 1980s by unionists who disagreed over how closely the largest union federation should be associated with the UDF and the ANC.

More recent efforts at black unionization have been made in the context of the tremendous growth of South Africa's industry since the late 1960s. We have already noted how particular spurts in this growth contributed to the consolidation of opposition movements, for instance, by bringing together the core constituency of the BC movement in the universities during the late 1960s and by encouraging local mobilization for material benefits in the late 1970s. As had been the case in the 1920s and 1940s, economic growth was also conducive to organizing workers in unions, for during periods of expansion wage and related concessions were more likely to be granted. Long-term economic modernization since the 1960s further encouraged unionization, with both developing steadily over the decades since, whereas the more explicitly political movements, BC and the UDF, exploded on the scene before the state responded with repression. Of course, the achievements of BC and the UDF also inspired workers to organize themselves, though the former played little if any role in organizing the 1973 strikes in Durban.

Unionization in the 1970s and 1980s cannot be explained without further noting the economic developments during this period. Since the 1960s, private economic assets in South Africa have been increasingly concentrated under the control of fewer but larger oligopolies, increasingly devoted to manufacturing. Already in 1972, 10 percent of private manufacturing, construction, wholesale, retail, and transportation firms controlled 75 percent of the relevant markets. By 1981, eight corporate groups controlled over 60 percent of all nonstate assets in the country, and by 1986 over 80 percent of the shares traded on the Johannesburg Stock Exchange were controlled by four conglomerates.[7] By 1981, the largest mining and manufacturing cartel in the country, the Anglo-American Corporation, controlled assets worth more than the combined gross domestic product of the nine countries closest to South Africa.[8]

The rapid pace of industrial concentration and development in South Africa since the 1960s has increased the economic leverage of blacks, as both workers and consumers. With not enough white workers to fill all of the newly created jobs, both the state and private businesses were forced by the demands of advanced industrial practice to create a stable, trained black work force, even in the more mechanized mining sector. This pressure remained relatively constant, resulting in a steady rise in the number of black workers with enough skills to be highly valued and with unprecedented potential bargaining power. The number of Africans working in manufacturing increased from 308,332 in 1960 to 780,914 in 1980, representing a rise in the proportion of economically active Africans working in manufacturing from 7.9 to 14 percent.[9] In addition, the South African economy became even more dependent on black consumption as an important component of internal markets.[10]

Liberal analysts have argued that these developments created tension between business interests and the state's maintenance of general apartheid restrictions on black advancement, although this contention has been refuted by more radical observers.[11] There is a more narrow agreement that after the groundbreaking wildcat strikes in Durban in 1973, businesses were eager to avoid similar disruptions in production and so urged the legalization of black unions with which they could negotiate. In 1979, the government's Wiehahn Commission recommended wide-ranging reforms in labor regulations, leading to the official recognition of black unions, which the state hoped would help discipline industrial workers. As we shall see, the state's expectations that the unions would encourage the development of a complacent "labor aristocracy" proved to be misguided.

In addition to creating pressure for more formalized labor relations, industrial development also led to a marked rise in urbanization and in the concentration of labor, enhancing opportunities for workers to discuss common concerns and to organize. From 1960 to 1985, the percentage of Africans living in urban areas increased from 31.8 to 39.6 percent, not including the millions living illegally in the townships and squatter camps. Workers were also brought together in larger factories, with the total number of workers in the manufacturing sector rising by 124 percent between 1960 and 1982 and the average size of the work force in each "establishment" increasing from 58.5 to 82.4 persons.[12] This burgeoning urbanization and industrialization made all forms of popular organization easier, and so it is not surprising that during this period, opposition movements became more mass based. The unions also were affected by this social transformation, with the first attempts at worker organization quickly replicated. One worker explained how his workplace was unionized: "No organizer came to us, but they came to neighboring factories. We became aware and wanted to join as well."[13] This process was repeated throughout the country from the late 1970s onward.

The further development of the union movement was influenced by a combination of economic and political factors, too closely intertwined in South Africa to be easily distinguished. Both the demand for skilled labor and collective action by unionized workers contributed to a relative rise in black wages. The overall ratio of wages paid to whites and blacks fell from 5.8:1 in 1970, to 4.3:1 in 1979, while the number of black "man days" lost in industrial disputes rose sporadically from 13,381 in 1972 to 390,314 in 1983.[14] Much as the Charterists had consolidated their support by gaining localized material concessions, the unions were able to attract a larger following by demonstrating their capacity to organize strikes and win higher wages. Overlapping membership between unions and local or political groups, rising popular activism, and state repression all contributed to the rising militancy in the unions.

The external influences of the economy and the state cannot by themselves explain the growth of the unions or of class consciousness among the rank and file. Objective conditions have been interpreted by union leaders and followers, who themselves helped shape the history of the union movement, for example, through the development of particular organizational structures, resources, and educational programs. Although many unionists have come out of the BC and Charterists movements, prominent among those who helped found the current unions were increasingly radicalized white intellectuals who had been excluded from BC in the 1970s. Lacking alternative avenues of involvement, these whites had turned their attention to setting up regional "industrial aid" service organizations around the time of the first major strikes in Durban in 1973.

At the same time that the BC movement was encouraging the development of racial identity and establishing its own unions, these white service organizations helped workers develop a class consciousness and organize unions independently of the BC movement. For instance, members of the Wages Commission of NUSAS—the white student organization from which the first BC group had broken away—established the Industrial Aid Society in Johannesburg. This society, together with the General Factory Workers' Benefit Fund in Durban, helped form what became the Federation of South African Trade Unions (FOSATU). The Urban Training Project, founded by two whites in 1971, assisted in the formation of what became the Council of Unions of South Africa (CUSA).[15]

The BC movement, the Soweto uprising, and the early maneuverings toward a Charterist revival captured the spotlight of public attention in the 1970s, but throughout this period the emergent unions and their white-led service organizations persevered. In 1979, this persistence paid off with the formal establishment of FOSATU, bringing together approximately forty-five thousand members of three affiliated unions.[16] Whites were included as members, officials, and service professionals, with the federation formally committing itself to a policy of nonracialism just when many community groups were abandoning the racially exclusive BC movement. Indeed, three of the five officials directly responsible for forming FOSATU were white, including Alec Erwin, who had earlier been involved with NUSAS and lectured at the University of Natal.

FOSATU was most clearly distinguished by its insistence on building unions from a strong base of member participation and on pursuing its members' economic interests as workers. This direction was in sharp contrast with the BC movement's wavering efforts to establish unions from the top down, as a means of spreading its message of racial assertiveness. Even FOSATU's educational programs were designed to teach democratic organizational procedures rather than to alter values according to a preset ideology. Radical rhetoric was eschewed in favor of developing institutional processes and economic gains, a strategy later employed by the UDF, with compromises such as legal "registration" hesitantly accepted as necessary for building a strong worker organization.[17] According to Alec Erwin, FOSATU's first general secretary:

> As an initial attempt to build unions, [we believed that] FOSATU could survive only if it was based on the shop floor. [In this way we] could resist repression and allow for organization. . . . [We set out to organize] factories as a base of strength. If not [factory based, we would be] just posturing. We were resistant to doing what seemed futile. Our worker stewards felt that success could be achieved if we avoided [unnecessarily] dangerous activities which would divert resources and provoke state action against [our] embryonic movement.[18]

Jay Naidoo, the general secretary of COSATU—a federation that later incorporated FOSATU and other unions—labeled this initial FOSATU position as essentially "antipolitical."[19] Although white union officials no doubt felt alienated from the then predominant BC movement, it would be more accurate to describe them as insisting on being independent of any political affiliation that would have diluted the federation's practical efforts at working-class organization. The implications of this commitment proved to be highly political.

As FOSATU grew, with a membership exceeding one hundred thousand within three years of its founding, it was pressured to enunciate its political stance more clearly. Workers were becoming increasingly involved at home with the local groups that later formed the UDF, and they were eager for their federation to become more active in the same realm. Initially, such pressures were resisted by the more cautious leaders fearful of too close an association with popular organizations that, they argued, had led to the exile of the ANC-aligned SACTU unions in the 1960s. In addition, they were concerned that their federation's focus on class issues and insistence on shop-floor democracy did not fit well with the UDF's multiclass constituency and looser organizational structures.[20]

At FOSATU's 1982 congress, the then general secretary Joe Foster gave a landmark address clarifying the federation's political position. He stated that a "populist" alliance of various classes was necessary but that the ANC, as the leader of such an alliance, was erring too much on the side of opportunism and accommodation of capitalists and others outside the working class. As a result, South Africa needed a more explicitly working-class movement that would enable the "workers to play a major political role as workers."[21] Even though FOSATU alone was too small to constitute such a movement by itself, it would seek to avoid becoming consumed by overly narrow concerns and to help develop a larger working-class movement that would unite all unions under a strong central authority. FOSATU's democratic structures could be a model of how to organize such a workers' movement, which would have to be less inclusive than the ANC's Congress Alliance, less elitist than BC, and more tightly controlled by the rank and file than the UDF would be. Foster concluded, with remarkable prescience, that "united front unity, with or without a loose federation, can destroy the hope of greater unity by creating unresolved differences and no acceptable way of resolving these. Disciplined unity . . . requires common political purpose, binding policy on affiliates and close working links based on specific organizational structures."[22] The only possible basis for such unity, in Foster's view, was the leadership of the working class.

Foster's speech attracted considerable attention and was widely criticized by those in the reemerging Charterist camp who favored just the sort of broad alliance Foster disparaged as "populist" and vulnerable to division. His call for an exclusively working-class movement was condemned both as a form of narrow "workerism," a term used against equally extreme accusations of Charterist "populism," and for ignoring the South African Communist party (SACP) as an existing class-based component of the Charterist movement. Foster's criticism of the ANC hit a raw nerve, to which Alec Erwin responded:

> The speech was intended for discussion at the Congress and had been collectively drafted. We never saw the [ANC] exiles as in opposition to us, [but we also did] not see them as an alternative. We were against vanguardism as a party, since we prefer a movement. The SACP itself was not addressed, partly for security and because they are a party and not a movement.
>
> We were arguing for a class orientation in politics. We need mass action but we also need a leading component. Now we need mass organization, beyond just mobilization.[23]

Despite these controversies, Foster's speech did signal FOSATU's recognition that it could not avoid "involvement in general political issues versus just shop floor issues. We said you can't separate the two; fear of being hijacked by the populists [threatened] to weaken and divide the union."[24]

It was not long before the FOSATU leadership's reluctance to become more deeply involved in issues not solely the concern of workers, and to working more closely with the growing Charterist movement, was overcome by events. For instance, the unionists were increasingly subject to state repression, to which FOSATU and other unions were compelled to respond. The 1982 death in detention of unionist Neil Aggett contributed to the realization by Aggett's previously unaffiliated African Food and Canning Workers' Union that they could not remain above the political fray. This union, together with the General Workers Union, joined FOSATU in the wake of Aggett's death, strengthening the federation and adding to the pressure for its greater involvement in the popular struggle against apartheid repression.[25] By 1984, when the UDF was leading the opposition to the parliamentary proposals, FOSATU joined in calling for a boycott of elections.[26] Later that year, when various FOSATU officials were detained for participating in the Vaal stayaways, the Federation was urged to play "a more key role in politics, without abandoning FOSATU's principles."[27] The militancy and class rhetoric of many UDF activists in the following years further eroded the unionists' suspicions about the Charterist movement.[28] Although FOSATU and other unions continued to refuse to affiliate formally with the Front, the distinction between union organizing and popular opposition became less clear as the stayaways and other forms of cooperation expanded.

FOSATU, with its primary focus on class issues and its hesitant relationship with the Charterists, was not the only union federation to emerge out of the service organizations established by whites in the 1970s. The other major federation was the Council of Unions of South Africa (CUSA), claiming forty-nine thousand members of its affiliated unions in 1982, half the number of FOSATU in the same year.[29] Unlike FOSATU, the policies and rhetoric of CUSA combined a focus on class with race in calling for an exclusively "black working-class leadership," thereby suggesting an ideological affinity with BC that was openly embraced by many of its individual leaders and members. CUSA was also more open to overt political alliances, proclaiming its willingness to "participate in the activities of all genuine liberation organizations," including the UDF and the

National Forum.[30] In terms of its own activities, CUSA was on balance more concerned with the traditionally BC strategy of encouraging assertiveness among its members than with developing binding organizational controls, such as the structures of "shop-floor democracy" that FOSATU emphasized.[31] A CUSA affiliate that showed a greater concern for "bread and butter" issues was the newly formed National Union of Mineworkers, which grew quickly, later abandoning its insistence on black leadership and breaking away from CUSA.[32]

At the same time that the FOSATU and CUSA federations were growing in numbers and militancy, other unions remained outside these federations and became even more explicitly involved in community issues. For instance, the South African Allied Workers' Union and the General and Allied Workers Union were also gaining in strength, though they were still formally independent.[33] In addition, the South African Boilermaker's Society gained considerable notoriety for welcoming both white and black members.[34]

All of this growth and activity fueled discussions and formal negotiations regarding the possibility of merging into a single union federation as a means of strengthening the unions' economic and political bargaining position. The formation of the UDF in 1983 added to the pressure for unity, by providing both a forum for debate among unionists who were also members of the Front's various affiliates and an example of cooperation among diverse groups. In 1984, the UDF succeeded in gaining union support for a massive protest against the heightened repression, in which more than eight hundred thousand workers stayed off their jobs in protest. According to Chris Dlamini, then president of FOSATU, "The unity talks begun in 1981 were further speeded up after the stay-aways" and the unrest in 1983–1984, when all unions were pressed "to fall in line" in support of mass opposition.[35] The slow and steady efforts to build worker-controlled unions from the bottom up were increasingly swept up in the pressure for united action against the state.

Despite such pressures for greater involvement with the popular struggle, not all unionists were enthusiastic about uniting under a single federation. In part, such resistance was based on the incompatible organizational structure of different unions and the self-interests of their officials. Many of the unaffiliated unions had a general membership, which had made it easier for them to organize workers from various industries.[36] Because unity could be achieved only with unions that did not compete for members across different industries, a single federation implied the breaking up of the general unions and the merging of overlapping unions in CUSA and FOSATU, with a corresponding loss of leadership positions. Officials often camouflaged their personal concern about losing their jobs with abstract ideological debates and ad hominem attacks, with FOSATU accusing CUSA of using race to protect incompetent black officials, and CUSA accusing FOSATU of using nonracialism to protect white intellectual leaders. The pressures from the rank and file to unite against their employers and the state directly conflicted with such internally generated resistance based on ideological disputes reinforced by self-interest.

Given the rising popularity of the Charterist movement in the 1980s, it was clear that the effort to unify the labor movement would remain incomplete unless the non-Charterist unions agreed to subordinate their views. But CUSA's leaders refused to cut their ties with BC and in August 1985 ended their attempts to form a united federation, although their motivation in doing so was hotly debated. Both the former president and the general secretary of CUSA insisted that they withdrew from the unity talks only after they were purposely "not invited" to key meetings and after their requests for a postponement to allow further consultation with members were denied. They also objected to the willingness of other unionists to cede worker control of a united federation to the ANC.[37] Chris Dlamini, president of FOSATU at the time, counters that "CUSA pulled out due to fear of losing positions. . . . They used ideological differences as [an excuse], but most of their members don't have a BC ideology. Their workers were not kept informed."[38] Officials in FOSATU certainly also feared losing their positions in the event of a merger, though their larger membership made it less likely they would lose out to CUSA leaders in any combined election. Such concerns about control and ideology were of less concern to the rank and file eager for unity, and so CUSA officials would have found it advantageous to blame the failure of the unity talks on their being excluded by the Charterists.

Withdrawal from the unity talks created tensions within CUSA and led to the departure from that federation of the largest union in the country, the National Union of Mineworkers (NUM). According to NUM's general secretary, Cyril Ramaphosa, this break was the result of the growing disagreement with CUSA's insistence on black leadership, seen as inconsistent with its rhetorical focus on class issues.[39] Because NUM at the time had few if any white members or officials, it is unlikely that this ideological concern alone can explain its decision to leave CUSA. Instead, NUM was drawn to the group moving toward unity because of the practical advantages of being in a larger federation that could better assist the mineworkers in confronting their monopoly employers. In addition, Ramaphosa and other NUM leaders were disinclined to alienate themselves and their union from the more popular Charterist camp, which was strongly represented among the unions still eager to unite. His critics have accused Ramaphosa of having pushed NUM to abandon CUSA in order to win favor with the ANC, which, they argue, Ramaphosa calculated was likely "to come to power shortly."[40] CUSA loyalists saw opportunism where NUM saw expediency. Although CUSA felt betrayed, Ramaphosa and his union's shift toward Charterism was consistent with the well-established popular trend and unusual only in its scale and for having come after many others had already made the move away from BC. The unions outside CUSA were, of course, delighted to have gained such a prize.

Once the mineworkers had left CUSA, the unity talks among the remaining unions were concluded, leading to the formation of the Congress of South African Trade Unions (COSATU), with NUM as its largest affiliate. At its inauguration in November 1985, during the first partial state of emergency, 1,870 delegates represented almost half a million signed-up members.[41] Within eighteen months, these members had been redistributed into new industry-specific affiliates, in most cases successfully overcoming earlier resistance to such mergers.[42] At this inauguration, a vice-president of NUM and member of the ANC in the 1960s, Elijah Barayi, was elected president of the Congress, and a former BC adherent, Jay Naidoo, was elected as general secretary. These and other national officials were given nonvoting membership on the Central Executive Committee composed of two delegates for each affiliate, plus additional delegates for the larger unions.

An elaborate hierarchy of regional and local committees was

constructed to connect the national leadership to the rank and file, represented most directly by an average of one shop steward for every twenty-nine union members.[43] According to Naidoo, the congress's structure was designed to maximize "worker control from the shop floor, with election of shop stewards to determine policies and practices. There is always a tension with the need to quickly respond, but [such responses by the leadership can be kept] within broad parameters, with occasional slips."[44] Despite such compromises, COSATU's structure ensured far greater accountability by the national leadership than had either the BC movement or the UDF.

The establishment and consolidation of organizational structures remained COSATU's principal activities, at least through 1987. As with the Charterists, significant foreign donations were used to pay for staff and publicity, with 76 percent of COSATU's total 1986 income of R2.4 million drawn from foreign "relief assistance."[45] Educational programs remained of secondary importance, funded in 1987 with R321,000, or less than one-half rand per member, which was well below the level required for the daunting tasks of reaching a rank and file then numbering seven hundred thousand or of implementing COSATU's own ambitious educational proposals.[46] Affiliates supplemented these centralized efforts with their own smaller educational programs, which, like the national programs, generally included lectures and group discussions of topics ranging from union structure and policy to political and class analysis. These programs often targeted shop stewards in the hope that they would spread what they had learned in their factories, although this strategy for dissemination was occasionally hampered by the tendency for employers to dismiss shop stewards during labor disputes.[47]

Educational programs were also waylaid by repression and limited by the long hours that workers spent on their jobs, which often left them too exhausted to study. As for repression, one unionist suggested that it was not a coincidence that the bombing of COSATU's headquarters in 1987 occurred one week after a new printing press vital to the educational programs had been installed there. Despite such setbacks and unavoidable shortcomings, COSATU's efforts at education indicated a significant concern with individual development. With all of its resources, the UDF had not organized any similar formal educational programs, in part because of the controversies among its diverse constituencies that would have arisen over their content.

Although COSATU had placed more emphasis on education and democratic structures than had the UDF, the "superfederation's" initial political stance resembled the UDF's early efforts to avoid divisive ideological associations. According to President Elijah Barayi, "At first we said rather than affiliating [with a particular political camp,] . . . we were prepared to work with all progressive organizations, and in 1985 we did not define progressive."[48] As late as 1987, the UDF acknowledged COSATU's efforts to avoid any "element of division."[49] Throughout this early period, COSATU continued to call for CUSA and the other unions that had withdrawn from the unity talks to join it. Officially, COSATU recognized that in order for its worker members "to begin to assert their leadership role," they would eventually "have to locate themselves" politically.[50] Even though the federation did include and hoped to attract unionists with a variety of views, they were united by their first commitment to advancing the economic and political interests of workers as a class. As a result, COSATU had less to fear from clarifying its political position than did the diverse UDF coalition.

During this period of intensive popular mobilization, the COSATU leaders could no more hide their preference for Charterism than could those individuals associated with the UDF who had contradicted the Front's initial formal claims of nonpartisanship. From its inception, the nonaffiliation of the CUSA unions and the ANC backgrounds of Barayi and other leaders signaled COSATU's strongly Charterist tendencies. Shortly after COSATU was established, General Secretary Naidoo held a widely reported meeting with ANC officials in Harare, further undermining the credibility of claims of neutrality. This meeting, not discussed in advance by COSATU structures, seemed to violate Naidoo's own rhetorical commitment to "act through the will and mandate of the people and be under the discipline of democratically controlled organization."[51] Despite complaints from some affiliates about violating the democratic process, the COSATU leadership had not misread their members' suport for the ANC. By early March 1986 a formal meeting had cemented the implicit alliance between COSATU and the exiled group.[52]

This accord did not imply wholesale adoption by the union group of the ANC's strategies, for COSATU remained distinguished by its remarkable combination of emphases on building both organization and consciousness. The ANC itself had struggled toward such a fusion of strategies in the 1940s, but had come to favor organizational unity over ideological cohesion in the intervening years. The union federation clearly wanted the popular prestige that came with ties to the ANC, but COSATU's large internal constituency gave it considerable leverage to differ with the exiled movement's ideological vagueness. ANC-inspired Charterists in the UDF had avoided talking about ideas that would have alienated potential allies. This strategy had at first proved effective in attracting a broad spectrum of supporters but had left differences unresolved. Instead, the unionists were eager to embrace and disseminate ideas about class that defined and united their movement. At the same time, they had learned from the BC experience that too great a reliance on ideas alone would attract only an elite of followers.

COSATU set out to develop a middle course between the Scylla of idealism and Charybdis of incoherence, organizing around the material interests of their members while spreading a coherent political vision based on class identity. This combined approach was evident in COSATU's official resolution:

> Take the lead in organizing and mobilizing not only in our factories but in our townships. Bring the lessons of solid organizing to our people. . . . Raise the issues of social, political and economic transformation now and not leave it to some future unspecified date. Build workers to gain confidence in themselves and in their ability to lead our struggle. . . . Form disciplined alliances. . . . Through our activity and education programmes to develop an increasingly coherent political perspective.[53]

Consistent with this concern for both organization and consciousness, the unionists were also looking to the interaction of their economic and political goals. The experience of confronting both employers and the state in constructing unions had led them to appreciate how economic exploitation and political domination were linked and had to be confronted together. They understood that an exclusive focus on short-term economic interests could result in complacency once concessions were granted, unless the workers had broader goals. Postponing economic issues until after democracy had been achieved—as implied in the traditional SACP conception of a two-staged struggle—ran the risk of leaving capitalism intact. The unionists acknowledged that alliances could help in meeting these challenges, but only as long as they did not require compromising the workers' fundamental interests.[54] A new form of opposition, shaped by class identity and correcting the excesses of earlier concepts of racial or national identity, was beginning to take shape, in theory if not fully in practice.

Despite its formal independence and focus on class issues, COSATU was heavily influenced by the rising popularity of the internal Charterist movement and related developments. The union federation was drawn closer to the UDF through their cooperation on stayaways and through police harassment, including the detention of its officials and members, many of whom were also active in UDF affiliates. As a result of conflict with AZAPO, both the UDF and COSATU became less concerned about alienating potential supporters from among the thinning and increasingly isolated ranks of BC loyalists. Although COSATU had earlier declared itself ready to work with any progressive organization, according to President Elijah Barayi, "In 1986 we defined what we meant by progressive. The civics were fighting in the locations. We could now form alliances with the civics, youth and the UDF."[55] In the heat of the moment, pressed by state repression and buoyed by militant victories, the fine points of ideological debate were put aside, and diversity was substituted for unity under the Charterist banner.

Just as the pressures to adopt the Freedom Charter came to a head for the UDF in 1987, in that same year COSATU was urged by the Charterists to make a similar pledge of allegiance. The UDF considered it essential to have a formal alliance with the federation, both to collect forces for a transfer of power and to resist the growing state repression. COSATU accommodated the Front by adopting the Freedom Charter at its second national congress in July 1987. At the same time, COSATU pointed out that the Charter provided only a set of "minimum democratic demands" that would not diminish their commitment to look beyond the first stage of national liberation to economic transformation based on working-class interests.[56] Even though the Charter does not include an explicit commitment to socialism, it is intentionally vague enough to appear consistent with this goal openly advocated by the unions. COSATU interpreted the Charter accordingly, adopting it as a useful tool for mobilization while claiming not to be restricted to pursuing only those demands it set forth.

For all of the effort to reconcile its adoption of the Charter with its commitment to socialism, COSATU could not easily avoid the tension between its goals as a working-class movement and the cross-class nature of the Charterist alliance. This tension was evident at the 1987 COSATU congress, which was urged by the UDF and even by SACTU and the Communist party in exile to avoid any premature calls for socialism.[57] COSATU unionists tried to resolve this apparent conflict by explaining that the Charterists were not opposed to the principle of socialism but wanted it downplayed only for the tactical purposes of avoiding state repression and focusing attention on the more immediate "tasks at hand."[58] Although the UDF and its allies could not force COSATU to abandon its commitment to socialism, its adoption of the Charter did signal COSATU's formal allegiance to the popular movement and its willingness to give greater priority to immediate practical concerns than to specific working-class issues and unity.

The end of COSATU's formal nonpartisanship clarified the ideological differences between COSATU and those unions that had chosen to remain outside it. The majority of those, led by CUSA and the smaller AZACTU group of BC unions, had merged to form an alternative "superfederation," the National Council of Trade Unions (NACTU), established in October 1986 with a notable display of Pan-Africanist symbols.[59] Initially claiming a rank and file of a quarter-million, after its first year NACTU had grown to include approximately 420,000 members. Its organizational design was essentially the same as that of COSATU, although NACTU affiliates were widely reported to be more fully controlled by their officials and to have less fully developed shop-floor structures. In 1987, NACTU's overall income of just under R3 million was substantially less than that of COSATU, though its smaller size and proportionately greater reliance on external grants provided a comparable level of funding per member.[60]

NACTU appeared to give somewhat greater emphasis to its educational programs than did COSATU, reflecting in part its affinity with the BC movement's traditional focus on developing consciousness more than organization. Phiroshaw Camay, the former general secretary of CUSA who was elected to the same position in NACTU, claimed that his federation was spending more than R1 million on educational programs, a proportion almost twice the 19 percent allocated out of COSATU's overall budget.[61] Ninety percent of NACTU's educational resources were used to fund programs organized by the Urban Training Project, the same service group that had helped establish CUSA. In comparing the content of these programs with those of COSATU, Camay observed: "Our analysis and presentation would rely less on Marx. . . . We would deal more with reality than theory . . . or mental gymnastics," for instance, by providing seminars on public finance.[62] Camay may have exaggerated these differences, and his remarks certainly ignore the significant educational programs of many COSATU affiliates, most notably those of the National Union of Metalworkers of South Africa. A more detailed comparison of the educational programs of these two federations would require a more complete study than is currently available.

NACTU's political position has combined elements based on class and racial identity. As a coalition of unions dedicated to pursuing the economic interests of its members, NACTU has refused to become "affiliated to any political movement, though we are put in the BC box."[63] Official meetings were held with both the ANC and the PAC in exile, and NACTU recognized both the Freedom Charter and the National Forum's Azanian Manifesto as legitimate expressions of popular demands, although it did not officially adopt either. NACTU remained committed to an exclusively "black working-class leadership" and had no white officials, suggesting its greater focus on race than was evident in COSATU. Many of NACTU's officials remained loyal to AZAPO or the PAC, and the relative weakness of its affiliates' shop-floor structures left those leaders less restricted in expressing their own views. Leading members of NACTU's executive were widely quoted criticizing the Charter as divisive and as describing South Africa as essentially divided "in two camps—the black and the white camp."[64]

Despite years of unity talks and a considerable overlap in ideology, by the late 1980s the South African union movement was indeed divided into two camps. Formed on the basis of the workers' economic interests, both COSATU and NACTU incorporated elements of an emerging class identity and analysis in their efforts to pressure employers through strikes or related actions, and in their educational programs. But NACTU, with its historical links to the BC movement and the PAC, combined class analysis with policies aimed at reinforcing racial identity, and COSATU, with its links to the Charterists, combined class analysis with efforts to help mobilize a national antiapartheid coalition. The union movement had clearly not been immune from the historical divide between the two exiled opposition groups, with the ANC enjoying greater sympathies within COSATU and the PAC being more influential within NACTU. Nor had the unions avoided the legacy of the ideological split of the internal opposition between NACTU's relatively greater concern about race and consciousness and COSATU's greater concentration on nonracial national unity and organized action.

As much as the union movement inherited the divide between national and racial identity, such a division reflected a deeply held conviction more often among union leaders than among the rank and file in COSATU and NACTU. Union leaders in both federations agreed that "for ordinary workers, bread and butter issues will be the first concern" and that ideological differences were less intense among the rank and file than among the leadership.[65] Many officials came into their unions with predetermined loyalties, though others felt pressures from sources other than their membership to join one ideological camp or the other. According to one former union leader:

> Ideological issues were not raised by workers but by intellectuals. The workers don't care about ideology as long as the union is powerful. Ideology is mainly a leadership thing. We were prestigious [as an effective union] and people wanted us in their ranks. . . . We needed to ally to one camp once we became high profile. We had to decide which meetings to go to. At first we went to both, but eventually we had to choose from what platform we would speak.[66]

Although initial union membership often did not reflect rank and file ideological loyalties, these loyalties did develop later according to how the unions were formed and operated. COSATU and NACTU leaders agreed that workers anxious for assistance in gaining higher wages and benefits most often joined whichever union offered or provided such a material service, with more abstract ideas of relatively little concern at first. As NACTU's president James Mndaweni pointed out, "Ideology for members is developed once joined. Workers are organized by COSATU or NACTU [depending] on who comes first. It is rare that a person has a clear ideology and chooses accordingly."[67] We saw in Chapter 4 that local civic organizations and squatter communities affiliated with the UDF in order to gain resources and learned about the Freedom Charter only later. The union member's loyalties for COSATU or NACTU were similarly based on pragmatic considerations, with ideology debated only later. As the former chairman of COSATU's Johannesburg local executive explained: "Workers have been conditioned. . . . Affiliates tend to protect workers, even from information, and organizers have a great influence."[68]

As the ideology of union leaders was passed down to the rank and file, the division between the two leading federations deepened. Members tended to be loyal to those leaders with whom they associated the material benefits of unionization and on whom they depended for information and interpretation of events. These leaders used their influence to spread their ideology, reinforcing the rift between the two federations. But this rift had not been as pronounced during the period following the 1973 strikes when many union leaders purposely avoided political issues and concentrated instead on building organizational structure and negotiating strength. The split did become more evident in the late 1980s, when the unions were separated into two federations and after unrest and repression heightened general interest in using the unions as a political base for continued opposition.

## A Search for Class Consensus

As the unions in the late 1980s came to play a more prominent role in the opposition, they were forced to assess more carefully their relationships with the working class as a whole and with the established ideological tendencies within the movement. Union efforts to represent the interests of unaffiliated workers, the restricted popular organizations, and the exiled groups all raised difficult questions about the proper role, independence, and democratic processes of organized labor. These issues were widely debated in COSATU, reflecting the huge size of the new federation and the diversity of views of those who had been brought together within it. By 1987, COSATU faced a significant challenge in keeping its affiliates united. Only the unionists' common concern for their members' economic interests and class identity enabled COSATU to avoid the sorts of divisions that had threatened the United Democratic Front. These shared concerns also kept COSATU and NACTU from engaging in open conflict. Before the end of the decade, the unions' continued development as a relatively coherent and effective working-class movement helped set the stage for a dramatic turn in the South African struggle for liberation.

By 1987, COSATU and NACTU each had a strong organizational base, with even those unionists from the FOSATU tradition of independent unionization ready to engage in a more active and less rhetorical challenge to the state. Much of the pressure for such an engagement came from the unions' rank and file, who had been increasingly drawn into the community-based protests of the period. These workers understood that their union activity could not be pursued apart from township unrest and the broader political struggle to which organized labor action made a significant contribution. Already in 1986, stayaways by black workers to support community protests accounted for three quarters of the 1.3 million "man days" lost in industrial disputes, with only a quarter motivated by more traditional wage and benefit disputes.[69] This level of political engagement reflected not only the consolidation of union structures and the overlap of membership in unions and community groups but also the current state of the South African economy. Between 1981 and 1986, the average annual per-capita GDP had fallen dramatically, by 2.1 percent, further encouraging a shift of union activism from unavailable material gains to popular protest.[70]

As much as the developments inside the unions, unrest, and economic recession all contributed to the rise in union participation in popular protest, it was the actions of the state that finally pushed the unions into the forefront of the opposition. State repression made it ever more apparent to most unionists that they did not have the luxury of remaining narrowly focused on their economic interests. The proportion of detainees identified as workers or unionists rose from 4 percent in 1986 to 24 percent in 1987, the same year that COSATU's Johannesburg headquarters were destroyed by a bomb allegedly planted by agents of the state or by right-wing vigilantes.[71] Just as the 1982 death in detention of Neil Aggett had sparked a greater political involvement by FOSATU, the bomb blast in 1987 was evidence of the growing confrontation between COSATU and the state. The pivotal moment came in February 1988, when the state effectively banned the UDF, NECC, AZAPO, and thirteen other groups from political activity while imposing less severe restrictions on COSATU. According to veteran unionist Emma Mashinini, "By banning the political organizations, the government forced ideology into other organizations," mainly the unions.[72] Dammed from its worn course, the river of opposition flowed into the space left open to it.

The unions' rising political prominence and involvement in popular stayaways implied a shift from the advancement of the members' material benefits, for which most unions had originally been organized, to the interests of the working class as a whole. South Africa's superimposition of economic exploitation with racial discrimination and political domination had tied the interests of unionized workers to a much broader constituency. Union membership in the mid-1980s had grown to over 1 million, out of 4.6 million blacks with nonagricultural jobs.[73] By 1988, unionists began to perceive themselves as having an agenda largely consistent with the interests of all seven million "economically active" blacks and, by extension, with the twenty-five million black South Africans that by most definitions could be considered part of the working class. Unionists became increasingly aware that despite their organizational strength, "industrial workers are a tiny section of the working class. They can't draw up a political program on their own and chart a path for the introduction of socialism. This has to be done by the masses."[74] Exactly how the interests of this broader constituency could be formulated or advanced by the unions without undermining established organizational procedures and goals became the topic for considerable debate, particularly in COSATU.

Early efforts by COSATU to press for the extension of economic benefits beyond formal union membership were relatively uncontroversial, for they were generally consistent with the specific interests of the rank and file. For instance, in 1987 COSATU launched a

"Living Wage Campaign," demanding not only adequate wages for union members but also full employment.[75] The federation also agreed to establish a National Unemployed Workers' Coordinating Committee (NUWCC) to provide training and support for cooperatives and from which the unions demanded that future employees be drawn. In 1987, this project received over half a million rands from COSATU.[76] These efforts signaled an extension of working-class consciousness and solidarity, but they also suited the interests of the union membership. By offering such support, the unions sought to benefit those outside its ranks and also to strengthen their own bargaining position by offering an alternative to the unemployed who might otherwise have worked for the state as vigilantes or scabs who could be used to break strikes. COSATU unionists' major objections to these programs were the lack of formal democratic structures in the NUWCC and this organization's high administrative expenses.[77] Later efforts guided by similar objectives, such as COSATU and NACTU's joint call for spreading employment by imposing a ban on overtime work, required greater sacrifice by union members eager for overtime pay. This overtime ban was not strictly enforced.[78]

Union efforts to support the unemployed generated considerably less controversy than did efforts to associate the union movement with a political program that represented the working class beyond union membership. The unions were aware that they could not pretend to represent this greater constituency on their own and that continued repression made it impossible to canvass democratically the millions of unorganized South Africans. To the large number in COSATU who already believed that the Charterist movement represented the aspirations of the majority of the country, linking the federation to this movement seemed to be the most direct way of ensuring that the unions embraced a broader view of the struggle. But for others in COSATU, adoption of the Freedom Charter in 1987 was interpreted more as a partisan alignment than as an association with the working class as a whole. Critics objected that this alignment would not ensure unity but, rather, would exacerbate divisions in the working class, for instance, by making cooperation with NACTU less likely. They expressed dismay at "how COSATU reconciles its commitment to a united working class movement, but in practice, engages with only one political grouping, dominant as it may be."[79] Adoption of the Charter as a unifying document ironically forced to the surface such serious divisions in the federation.

Objections within COSATU to adopting the Charter initially focused on the process by which it had been endorsed by the federation's leading affiliates. NUM, for example, had adopted the Charter at a congress in March 1987 only after top union officials had expressed support for the document and before a major educational program on the Charter began.[80] According to NUM president James Motlatsi, "The Charter was adopted unanimously," although others have claimed that several of NUM's regions had opposed its adoption.[81] The disaffection of those regions may have added to the discontent among miners who lost their jobs during a difficult 1987 strike, which resulted in significant tensions in NUM that year. COSATU's second largest affiliate, the National Union of Metalworkers of South Africa (NUMSA), somewhat grudgingly adopted the Charter as "a good foundation stone [from] which to start building our working class program."[82] Even COSATU's Johannesburg Branch Executive noted that "an ideology must be a program of a particular class" and that the Freedom Charter, as a "program of the people," was "not an ideology."[83]

Discontent over how affiliates had adopted the Charter was reinforced by the manner in which the document was adopted by COSATU as a whole. Eight of the federation's smaller affiliates had not yet adopted the Charter before the entire federation acted to do so in July 1987, suggesting that the federation had been less than fully democratic in its rush to fall into the Charterist line.[84] NUM's general secretary had openly committed his union to "push [the Charter] through to the mother body," and according to Alec Erwin, "NUM bulldozed" its adoption.[85] Cassim Saloojee of the UDF pointed out that NUM was simply doing the bidding of the UDF, in that "COSATU was forced to accept the Charter by the broad political movement," which believed that "the movement is of many classes" and that the Charter is appropriately "not socialist."[86] This interpretation implies that COSATU's adoption of the Charter was intended to dilute more than to consolidate working-class unity. Whereas many of its affiliates sought further discussion on this issue, COSATU's leadership acted quickly to head off any such debate, insisting that the federation's adoption of the Charter was final and binding.

Adoption of the Charter acted as a lightning rod for a more fundamental ideological disagreement in COSATU. On the one side was NUM, coming out of the CUSA tradition of strong leaders less constrained by democratic structures, with a more explicit political position and embracing the inclusive Charterist alliance rather than BC. According to this view, the organized workers in the unions could play a leading role in the opposition but could not speak for the broad working class or remain outside the UDF's multiclass coalition.[87]

Adopting an interpretation of vanguardism consistent with the Charterist emphasis on mass organization, NUM officials argued that the mineworkers and all other unions should effectively subordinate themselves to the popular movement and to the Communist party as the leading representative of the working class.[88] According to COSATU President Barayi, a former NUM official, "The SACP is the political vanguard party and has wide support. We accept their policy and advice. . . . We are independent and autonomous, but we are not prepared to do anything to offend the vanguard."[89] Because the SACP had formed an alliance with the ANC, the mineworkers' officials contended that the unions would most effectively support the working class by aligning themselves with the ANC's internal supporters in the UDF. The unions should also accept a two-staged theory of revolution, which postponed transformation to socialism until after democratic rights had been won, a policy long propounded by the SACP. According to Cyril Ramaphosa, by 1991 an ANC official, "There have to be two stages. . . . What prevents transformation first is having to deal with the eradication of apartheid through massive mobilization . . . using instruments such as the Freedom Charter, to mobilize, to encourage people to continue struggling for immediate demands."[90]

On the other side of this argument were many of the veterans of the FOSATU tradition, particularly well represented by the leaders of the metalworkers' union, NUMSA, then the second largest affiliate. This group favored a more independent worker-oriented line, which was denounced by others as a form of "workerism" or "economism." According to this view, union policies should be determined by shop-floor democratic structures and not subordinated to any external group, particularly one dominated by nonworkers. This faction had a much more selective view of alliances, which should only be entered into "with anti-capitalist organizations, with unambiguous goals, accountable to their membership and the working class. Anything short of this will subordinate us to other classes."[91]

Many in NUMSA believed that although the unions could not claim to represent the entire working class, they could provide leadership in a class struggle as the most advanced "core of the organized working class."[92] The Charter was suspect for its lack of explicit class analysis and acceptable only as a set of minimum demands. These demands should be supplemented by a separate "workers' charter," drawn up by the workers alone, that would not avoid an explicit commitment to economic transformation. Early drafts of such a supplementary document guaranteed worker control over production and distribution, communal landownership, and the right to strike, all more explicitly than did the Freedom Charter.[93] This group sought to enshrine such ideals in order to avoid their being compromised by strategic necessity.

Despite denials of any disagreement by COSATU's Charterist-dominated national officials, the debate led by the two largest affiliates reverberated throughout the federation.[94] As acknowledged by Herbert Mkhize, a COSATU unionist loyal to the UDF–ANC alliance, "The Freedom Charter may have been prematurely adopted; it has caused rifts."[95] Continued debates over adoption of the Freedom Charter had become symbolic of the more fundamental disagreement over the proper relationship between organized workers and groups claiming to represent the broader working class. For example, one COSATU affiliate of the unemployed in Cape Town that insisted on independence from the Charterists was accused by another of putting the interests of "the workers over the working class."[96] Even within NUM, there were rumors of divisions between the majority supporting greater adherence to Charterist policy and another group favoring greater independence, with the latter group more heavily represented among the third of NUM's membership drawn from migrant Lesotho miners. As COSATU's Johannesburg Branch chairman Duma Nkosi concluded, the problems of division were "in general terms, everywhere."[97]

The ideological disputes in the COSATU unions were reinforced by contests for control among competing groups of officials, much as officials had earlier used ideology to justify their self-interested support or resistance to merging into the federation. Such a combination of ideology and self-interest only aggravated the well-publicized dispute in the Commercial Catering and Allied Workers Union (CCAWUSA), the fourth-largest affiliate in COSATU. Representing retail shop workers, the membership of CCAWUSA was one of the most urban and well educated of all the unions. Seventy percent of the union were women, including Emma Mashinini, its founder and its general secretary from 1975 to 1986.

Begun with the encouragement of white shop workers hoping to raise the cost of the black labor with which they were being replaced, CCAWUSA was open first only to Africans and had affiliated with CUSA before becoming independent. CCAWUSA broke ranks with CUSA to join the unity talks that led to the formation of COSATU. These developments resulted in a policy of nonracialism and a fitful merger with other retail unions, swamping the union's structures which had been designed for a smaller membership. By 1986, "CCAWUSA had a heterogeneous leadership, more so than in other unions, . . . [because] the union had been put ahead of politics. When the political level was raised, they were caught with divided loyalties."[98] As CCAWUSA grew, the fight for control of such a prize became more intense. According to Mashinini, "worker control" was lost to officials "clamoring for glory more than achievement."[99]

On one side of the dispute in CCAWUSA were anti-Charterist officials, some with links to the PAC or independent socialist groups who controlled the union's largest branch in Johannesburg. These officials used an unusually strong education program to build the loyalty of their members and to spread their ideas. For instance, they were particularly critical of the COSATU leadership's unilateral decision in 1986 to cooperate with the UDF. They also criticized the ANC's cordial discussions with the head of Anglo-American in 1987, at the same time that ten thousand CCAWUSA members were striking against one of Anglo's retail chains.[100] Led by veteran organizer Vivian Mtwa and by Kaizer Thibedi in Johannesburg, this anti-Charterist faction denounced the UDF and COSATU's national leadership for pandering to nonworking class allies, for being "less serious about worker control" or socialism, and for imposing allegiance to the "ambiguous" Charter at the risk of dividing the unions and inviting state repression.[101] Although these views were similar to the arguments of many in NUMSA, because CCAWUSA had not been in FOSATU there were few personal or historical links between the two groups. In order to avoid antagonizing COSATU's Charterist leadership, NUMSA officials generally refused to take sides in this dispute.

Even without external support from potential allies in NUMSA, the anti-Charterist wing of CCAWUSA was strong enough to resist pressures to conform. The continued existence of two factions in the union generated considerable conflict. The Charterists in CCAWUSA, led by Papi Kganare and Herbert Mkhize, criticized their adversaries as radical purists who "prefer talk to action," ignored the necessity of cross-class alliances, and were overly influenced by Black Consciousness and NACTU.[102] The anti-Charterists replied that they had never recommended excluding whites and that they represented the majority of union members, whereas their adversaries relied on the support of COSATU's Charterist leadership, which had argued that "CCAWUSA must be forced to abide by the majority of COSATU."[103] Anti-Charterists such as Kaizer Thibedi objected to efforts to crush their dissent, criticizing COSATU officers for interfering and declining to "apologize to anyone for exercising our democratic rights. . . . We refused to be hijacked and became more strong in our position."[104] By 1987, this dispute was hindering many of the union's regular activities, as even physical force was being used to take control of union offices and death threats were exchanged.[105] For instance, the anti-Charterists were warned to stop "spreading your ideological misconceptions to cause disunity within COSATU. . . . If you do not comply with these demands, be sure that you will be dealt with by our military command."[106]

The animosity that the CCAWUSA dispute created cannot be explained simply on ideological grounds without taking into account the particular interests and influence of the union leaders. CCAWUSA officials on both sides of the dispute were at least as influential as officials in other unions had been in spreading their views through loyal shop stewards and educational programs. By spreading their views, each set of leaders had reinforced its control over groups of workers who could then be counted on to support those leaders in their fight for control of the union as a whole. The rank and file certainly had less at stake in the ideological disputes and conflict over control of the union than did those officials whose jobs were on the line. However, the continued election of the disputing leaders suggests that the membership did support their respective officials and their positions in the internal conflict.

As much as the membership of CCAWUSA was drawn into the conflict among their officials, the main concern of the rank and file remained more pragmatic than ideological, providing a continued impetus for resolving the dispute. The leadership and their followers in both factions of CCAWUSA recognized that "if we concentrate on political issues and not bread and butter, unions will collapse."[107] By 1989, the two factions were again working together and were able to win average wage gains of 20 percent.[108] Because remaining as a single union in COSATU provided a stronger position from which to bargain with employers, even the anti-Charterist faction had a direct interest in avoiding a split and in continuing to pressure for change within the federation. In late 1989, under the supervision of representatives from NUM and NUMSA, the two factions agreed to work together under a new structure that ensured united action in the workplace and continued discussion of differences.[109] Both the idea and the practical necessity of worker unity had proved more compelling than had insistence on ideological purity or on maintaining a divided structure and multiple officials.

CCAWUSA was not the only union to recognize that a primary concern with advancing working-class interests required the resolution of ideological differences. By 1987 and in subsequent years, the rank and file of many unions were insisting on unity, urging their officials in both COSATU and NACTU to put aside their differences and to cooperate in negotiations with employers.[110] In part, this development was the result of continued state repression, which had hobbled the UDF and left the unions in the forefront of popular mobilization. Under these conditions, many unionists agreed with CCAWUSA's Kaizer Thibedi that although "the working class is politically split . . . we have no choice but to defend ourselves. The only method of defense historically is the formation of a united front of working class organizations."[111]

Repression certainly encouraged unity, but the more fundamental explanation of the unions' greater cooperation was that their differences were simply outweighed by their common interests and ideas as organizations of workers. Although most of the unions had a secondary focus on Charterism, racial identity, or "workerism," they all shared a primary focus on class. Their different ideologies and loyalties had stood in the way of unity within a single federation, but all the unions had essentially used similar methods to organize in the workplace and to use collective action to gain formal recognition and improved working conditions, wages, and benefits. Largely as a result of these efforts, the ratio between the average wages of white and African workers had fallen by more than 35 percent, from 5.1:1 in 1973, to 3.3:1 fourteen years later.[112] It was this success at obtaining such economic concessions from employers that defined and strengthened the unions, attracting more than a million members. Even in regard to more overtly political issues, the unions had followed parallel strategies of mass stayaways to exert indirect pressure on the apartheid state, and they all had accepted some degree of self-sacrifice in calling for international sanctions against doing business with South Africa.[113] Although the unions' disagreements often received disproportionate attention, their essential class commonality remained, making cooperation possible. By the late 1980s, recognition of shared purposes had begun to eclipse past differences, with their mutual basis as working-class organizations thereby asserting itself.

Both the leading federations recognized the emerging consensus on the need for greater union cooperation across the ideological divide. President Barayi, citing the "need for compromises for unity from both sides," committed COSATU to exploratory discussions with NACTU.[114] Banners at earlier COSATU meetings hailing the Freedom Charter and socialism were exchanged at a special COSATU Congress in May 1988 for banners proclaiming "health and welfare," in an apparent effort to replace ideological rhetoric with a pragmatic message more conducive to cooperation.[115] These conciliatory efforts were matched by NACTU, which set out to distance itself from AZAPO, for instance, with the replacement of its general secretary, who later joined the ANC, and his first assistant, a BC loyalist who became the president of AZAPO. Based on such developments, NACTU President James Mndaweni proudly described his federation as being "at the forefront of pushing unity."[116] To advance these moves toward cooperation, COSATU and NACTU agreed that neither adoption nor repudiation of the Charter need be a prerequisite for their united action.[117] Even though the two federations remained formally divided, their antagonism had clearly diminished, as they both recognized that "history and workers will not judge us kindly if we allow the hopes of democracy and freedom from exploitation to be dashed on the rocks of our division."[118]

By 1989, these efforts toward greater cooperation by COSATU and NACTU had begun to inspire similar efforts by the more overtly political organizations. In order to coordinate their protests against the Labour Relations Amendment Act, which imposed new restrictions on unions, the two federations and those unions that had remained independent met in a series of "worker summits." COSATU's Barayi hailed these meetings as "a powerful statement that our differences are nothing compared to our commitment to the principle of working class unity."[119] The UDF, circumventing its restrictions by acting under the new name of the Mass Democratic Movement, pursued a similar agenda of cooperation in calling for an inclusive Conference for a Democratic Future, held in December. Only at the last minute did representatives from NACTU, the PAC's internal wing, and some from AZAPO withdraw from the meeting to protest the presence of parties from the "dummy" homeland parliaments.[120] But even though the Conference for a Democratic Future failed to unite all opposition groups, it did signal a renewed commitment to work toward such unity, inspired in large part by the example of union cooperation.

These developments suggest that by the last years of the 1980s, the unions had emerged as an influential, politically engaged, and strong working-class movement. Although these unions were neither fully independent of influences from established political tendencies nor formally united in a single federation, they had distinguished themselves by their primary focus on class issues, providing a common ground for cooperation that had largely offset the remaining divisions. The unions' focus on class also impelled a dual concern for developing both democratic organizational structures, through which mass action was mobilized, and a coherent class-based ideology, generated through the experience of collective action and reinforced in educational programs. Of course, the unions had not perfected their development of worker organization and consciousness, remaining to varying degrees divided, oligarchic, and economistic. But in seeking to improve on Black Consciousness's greater emphasis on ideas than on organization, and the Charterists' priority given to strategic unity over ideological coherence, the unions attempted to combine the strengths of both these movements. This effort was evident not only in the unions themselves but also in the popular organizations influenced by the unions.

In terms of organization, the unions provided an important example of the necessity of connecting officials and followers through formal structures that ensured mass participation and leadership accountability. The BC movement had assumed that agreement on ideas would unite their movement, even though this reliance on ideas had failed to attract a broad membership that would have required more attention to organization in order to ensure its continued coherence. Charterist leaders had largely taken such coherence for granted, building local and national structures linked more by shared resources and the influence of charismatic leaders than by formal structures. The unions had instead tried to build democratic procedures through which elected leaders were held accountable and were given specific mandates by shop-floor structures. These efforts were justified on theoretical grounds by the recognition that for any mass movement, "the leadership and policy is the form, is what people see, but the content is the membership. The two must interact dialectically."[121] Pragmatic concerns also drove such efforts to link leaders and followers more closely, so as to avoid any divisions that might damage organization and create vulnerabilities of which the state could take advantage.

Union structures designed to increase mass participation have also inspired recent efforts to apply similar organizational procedures to more overtly political groups. According to the UDF's Cassim Saloojee, "The experience of the last few years makes it impossible for a few to impose a solution. . . . There is a new deep consciousness of the need to consult. Democracy is now part of the culture of resistance. . . . Leaders don't just follow, but there is more interaction."[122] This recognition of the importance of democratic structures further impelled the UDF's and the ANC's efforts to revitalize local organizations after they were unbanned in 1990. In the wake of reforms in the Soviet Union and the unbannings in South Africa, even the SACP renounced its earlier endorsements of Stalinism and acknowledged that its claims to represent the working class would have to be validated through democratic processes giving local structures greater involvement in setting party policies.[123] BC loyalists, similarly admitted that "unions push democracy and carry the concept back to the community," where AZAPO attempted to consolidate local support.[124] The PAC, even before its unbanning with the ANC, also attempted to establish a formal organizational base of local groups more closely linked to national leaders.[125]

Unionists recognized that substantial educational programs would be required if their membership were to exercise greater democratic control through local structures in an informed manner. In order to build up their membership, the UDF's Albertina Sisulu argued that many unions had first used "too much organization and too little education. They rushed, due to their enthusiasm."[126] As a result, union members had often felt ill equipped to participate in union governance, often sitting silently through formally required meetings while allowing their officials to take the lead. In later years, after the unions had become more consolidated, many unionists agreed with COSATU's Barayi that "we must go back to the ground floor and educate people."[127] Only by recommitting themselves to further educational "spade work" previously "neglected," did union leaders such as Cyril Ramophosa believe that the ongoing disagreements could be resolved and that working-class consciousness could be raised to the point that the workers would participate in setting the direction of their unions and of the opposition as a whole.[128]

The unions were not alone in recognizing the need for further popular education, to complement efforts toward greater and more informed mass participation. The Charterists observed that during the rush to form the UDF, "there had been too little political education and self-criticism. . . . The weakness now is too little political understanding."[129] After the UDF's activities were restricted in 1988, the Front put somewhat greater emphasis on correcting its previous shortcomings, although its continued focus on mobilization and the decline in available resources precluded the launching of any formal educational programs. During this period, the ANC also acted to inform the populace in more detail of its specific policies, principally by circulating a new set of "constitutional guidelines" based on the Freedom Charter.[130] After its unbanning, the ANC increased its focus on developing mass consciousness, for instance, by naming a new education director in its structures. The ANC also used this opportunity for media coverage to spread its message, although the diversity of views represented in the ANC also became more evident, such as the simultaneous calls for militancy and reconciliation which probably confused many people.[131] The PAC and AZAPO similarly used media publicity to inform a wider audience of their respective policies, whose relative coherence reflected both groups' long-standing emphasis on ideas over strategic advantage.

The union movement's influential example of a combined focus on organization and the dissemination of ideas was reflected in its efforts to mobilize workers and develop their class consciousness. All these activities were based on class analysis, the explication of which helped union members better enunciate the connection between their economic and political grievances. For example, workers came increasingly to appreciate that reforms allowing blacks to enter shops from the same door as whites were merely cosmetic as long as blacks did not have the money to buy what they needed. The occasional employment of blacks in supervisory positions was disparaged on similar grounds for leaving the majority of black workers no better off. Education programs helped union members explore the connection between the state and their employers, who paid taxes, relied on the police to break up strikes, and continued to reap profits while appeasing workers with mild protestations against apartheid. These discussions reinforced the belief among most unionists that their deprivation, chronic unemployment, and domination all were inherent in capitalism, which should be replaced with socialism.

Despite their enthusiasm for the concept, exactly what is meant by socialism has remained relatively vague for unionists and others, as it has in other countries. Many South Africans simply equated socialism with the solution to all their difficulties, or as the negation of capitalism with which they had come to associate their grievances. Using rhetorical references and chants about socialism to encourage worker militancy, the unions made little effort to refine the concept, often linking socialism with freedom or with worker control of factories, despite the recognition of some union leaders that you "can't have socialism in a factory alone. You have to change the state apparatus. Factories are the training ground for workers, but [worker democracy is] not the same as achieving socialism."[132] In part, this vagueness reflected the incomplete development of class consciousness, with the workers somewhat torn between wanting the fruits of their labor in a market economy and supporting the disruption and replacement of such an economy that had failed to provide them with sufficient material benefits. Only in the aftermath of the dismantling of communist regimes in Eastern Europe have the specifics of a socialist economy begun to be more fully discussed; for instance, NUMSA unionists have argued that social ownership of production need not imply a command economy.[133]

The remaining ambiguity about the precise nature of socialism and the turn away from it in Eastern Europe have not diminished the popularity of this ideal in South Africa or the degree to which union rhetoric about socialism has influenced the more overtly political movements. Polls of black South Africans have consistently shown a strong preference for socialism over capitalism, with the popular desire for economic transformation increasingly added to demands for the dismantling of apartheid.[134] Elements of the Charterist movement have embraced this popular commitment to socialism, intentionally reinterpreting the Freedom Charter as consistent with this more radical economic goal and with the leadership of the unions as representatives of the working class as a whole. Responding to the rising class consciousness among union members and others, Charterist groups have also moved away from their avoidance of an explicit commitment to socialism in contending that "the route to socialism has begun in and is not postponed to after the national democratic stage of the revolution."[135] Africanist and Black Consciousness groups had similarly advocated socialism and dismissed any distinction among stages of the struggle to end apartheid and capitalism. Adherents of all of these groups had tried to put into practice this concern about class issues, both by supporting various unions and by opening small-scale production and distribution cooperatives intended to provide employment and alternative models of economic organization.

In addition to helping bring economic issues to the forefront of opposition concerns, union activism also raised the issue of women's rights, though on this front the unions found a considerably less receptive audience. Unions with a high proportion of women members, such as CCAWUSA, insisted that "the issue of women's oppression must not be seen as a matter to be taken up only after we have achieved our new society. Exploitation and oppression on the basis of class, color and gender are all linked and must be fought together."[136] This insistence that gender issues not be relegated to a remote second stage of struggle was unfortunately less influential than was the similar insistence on addressing economic concerns. Popular movements have continued to reflect widespread sexism defended as part of what men have described as an ascriptive African "tradition," justifying the underrepresentation of women in most organizations and the denigration of gender issues as distractions from the struggle against race, class, or national oppression.[137] In instances in which women have taken the lead in mobilizing their local communities, they often have been later replaced by men.[138] In the last three decades, no mobilization around women's issues has commanded as much active response as did the women's marches of the 1950s. In respect to gender issues, the move to incorporate various relevant issues into opposition activities has remained largely incomplete.

Despite their failing to give gender relations greater prominence, the unions have recently offered an influential example of cooperation among diverse opponents of the South African regime. They have demonstrated the need to combine democratic forms of organization with educational programs and discussion of ideas, in order to mobilize and inform mass participation. Their focus on class identity and use of strikes to pressure employers or the state have raised economic issues and the goal of socialism to the top of the opposition's agenda. In large part, the unions' influence in these areas has been bolstered by their own ability to organize a growing membership among an urbanized black work force enlarged by South Africa's industrial development. Their influence was also an unintended consequence of state repression against the UDF and related organizations, which had pushed the unions to the forefront of opposition activism. Finally, the unions benefited from the lessons learned by their members and leaders from previous experiences with mass mobilization. As a result of all these factors, the unions were able to refine significantly, albeit imperfectly, their strategies and ideology. Despite state repression and economic recession, the unions were able to maintain the momentum of opposition.

## A Breakthrough Toward Negotiations

By late 1989, a variety of slowly emerging developments inside and outside the country had come to a head together, leading to a set of state actions that dramatically transformed the South African conflict. The state's efforts to crush its opponents had failed, with popular mobilization not only having persevered but also showing signs of increasing organizational and ideological vitality. Even though the opposition movement had not been strong enough to overthrow the minority regime militarily, it had succeeded in exacerbating an economic crisis and dividing the regime's supporters. A military stalemate in Angola had demonstrated the South African state's vulnerability, and the devolution of the cold war had begun to redraw international alliances, diminishing both Soviet support for the ANC and Western interests in maintaining the white rule. None of these developments alone would have been sufficient to undermine the continued viability of the Pretoria regime. Even the confluence of popular resistance, economic dislocation, potential military vulnerability, and international pressures did not lead to the complete collapse of the state, although a more fundamental combination of such factors did contribute to the demise of the prerevolutionary regimes in France, Russia, and China. These mutually reinforcing developments did significantly weaken the resolve of the South African state and set in motion a process that may yet have a revolutionary outcome.

The unions played a major role in bringing the South African conflict to its latest stage. They managed to maintain the momentum of popular mobilization, undermining the state's confidence in its ability to quell protests and heightening the fears of foreign businesses that were less and less willing to invest in such an unstable environment. Although the unions represented a relatively small proportion of all workers compared with those in more industrialized countries, this was more than compensated by their militancy and leverage over vital industries in which they had organized massive strikes that had cost local businesses considerable lost production and reduced the state's tax revenues.[139] Countrywide stayaways demonstrated the unions' capacity to launch a general strike that could cripple an economy that had become dependent on black labor. As the most notable example, in June 1988 more than three million participated in a stayaway to protest the proposed Labour Relations Act intended to thwart further union activity.[140] The threat of further working-class action was reinforced by the unionists' overwhelming advocacy of international economic sanctions, which polls suggested were supported even by a large percentage of adult blacks who recognized that some might lose their jobs as a result of less foreign trade and investment.[141] This willingness to sacrifice short-term economic interests for long-term benefits demonstrated the extent to which a militant class consciousness had permeated the country's work force.

Class consciousness encouraged by unionization was reinforced by greater deprivation during almost a decade of economic decline. A vicious cycle of rising militancy, popular unrest, and strikes scared away foreign investors and increased public pressure in other countries for sanctions. As a result, the South African economy continued to suffer from a chronic decline even after the Western economies had recovered from the recession of the early 1980s, thus reducing the amount of resources available to the state for mollifying its black populace, aggravating continued unrest, and further dislocating the economy. Average annual capital inflows to South Africa of $2 billion during the first three years of the decade were replaced by similar outflows between 1985 and 1989, at the same time that approximately $40 billion was lost as a result of trade sanctions.[142] These reversals had a strong impact on the South African economy, which had long been especially dependent on foreign trade and capital due to the underdevelopment of its internal markets.[143] Already in 1986, private-sector investment had fallen behind asset depreciation, while inflation rose to 16 percent, as compared with 3 percent in the United States.[144] By 1989, government officials acknowledged the economic crisis, made worse by the already-heavy financial burdens of maintaining duplicate apartheid structures and a large military and police force. Privatization of public industries to replace tax revenues gave the state only temporary relief from the continued economic decline.

Economic dislocation provoking further unrest created other difficulties for the state. The prospect of continued recession undermined the resolve of many white South Africans to support further repression while encouraging fanatical conservatism among others attracted by the neofascist rhetoric of groups such as the Afrikaner Resistance Movement (AWB), formed in 1973 by former policeman Eugene TerreBlanche. As divisions grew within the state's white constituency, public discord appeared for the first time among colored police and prison warders, of whom over five thousand reportedly disobeyed orders and formed their own union.[145] The security forces were further rocked by public revelations of their involvement in secret assassinations of activists and by rumors that the state was losing control of its conservative white policemen. For the army, psychologically draining duty in the townships took a heavy toll, including attempted suicides and by 1985 a failure of approximately 30 percent of those called up to report for duty.[146] The military stalemate and withdrawal from Angola undermined the state's earlier bravado about the ineffectiveness of the arms boycott and so further weakened its morale.[147] By May 1990, hints of division appeared even in the top leadership of the defense forces over participation in a joint conference with ANC military commanders.[148]

In addition to these internal fissures, the state was also affected by a realignment of international forces. Support for the South African regime had long been waning in the United States and other former allies, where voters had been outraged by Pretoria's continuing repression. Declining superpower tensions and Soviet foreign involvement had further reduced any incentive for the United States to support the white regime as a regional bulwark against a Soviet threat. Under the younger and more flexible leadership of F. W. de Klerk, the South African government responded to these pressures with talk of reform. But this change in policy direction only widened the split between the ruling National party and its right-wing opposition led by Andries Treurnicht's Conservative party, which by 1988 had won 22 of the 177 seats in the whites' house of parliament. .Although this development presented no immediate threat of a Conservative Party majority and indeed freed the government to push harder for a resolution of the conflict, it also increased the risk that the ruling party would lose control of right-wing components of its white constituency and police force.

Ironically, the Pretoria regime's efforts toward resolution met with a more positive response among the leadership of the ANC than among many whites. The exiled leadership of the congress was eager to consolidate its gains of recent years with the initiation of formal negotiations. Declining support from the Soviet Union—lowering the ANC's strength in conducting an armed struggle—added to pressure on the congress to reach an agreement with the government that would allow the exiled group to return home and to rebuild its internal structures. The De Klerk government was similarly anxious to reach an agreement with the ANC that would permit a resumption of foreign investment and economic growth. Delaying this process not only risked aggravating the unrest but also increased the likelihood that the ANC's more moderate older leadership would be replaced by more militant younger officials with whom agreement would be more difficult. The government was particularly eager to begin negotiations with then seventy-two-year-old Nelson Mandela, who had become an international figure without having been seen in public for almost thirty years. Rather than keeping Mandela in prison, where his death would likely have touched off even greater unrest, De Klerk opted for freeing him and entering into negotiations in the hope that Mandela would use his considerable prestige to control his more militant followers.

Taking all of these factors together, it is easy in retrospect to see how both material and ideological pressures were pushing the state toward some dramatic action, although the exact form of that action remained difficult to predict at the time. The state had to contend with and interpret popular unrest, economic strain, international realignment, division among whites, and assessments of the likely actions of various black opposition groups. Other South African leaders might have chosen a different response, but F. W. de Klerk decided on unprecedented reform. As in other historical examples, once this reform process was set in motion, neither the minority regime nor its opponents would be able to control its outcome. But the state did remain strong enough to continue to determine much of what followed.

In October 1989, the South African government was ready to test the waters of reconciliation by releasing seven of its most prominent prisoners, including the ANC's Walter Sisulu. Encouraged by the orderly popular response to these releases, four months later State

President de Klerk formally unbanned the ANC, PAC, and SACP while lifting restrictions on the UDF and other internal groups. On the warm, sunny afternoon of February 12, 1990, in a moment of poignancy televised throughout South Africa and much of the world, Nelson Mandela walked out of twenty-seven years of imprisonment as a martyr reborn. Three hundred years after the arrival of white settlers, the South African struggle for democracy entered its home stretch, the exact nature and timing of future change remaining uncertain.

The ANC immediately set out to revitalize its internal structures and to urge the return of all exiles, the freeing of the remaining political prisoners, the lifting of the state of emergency, and the repeal of apartheid regulations established since 1948, all as preconditions to negotiations. Relying first on COSATU for administrative support, the ANC under the internal leadership of Walter Sisulu began the difficult tasks of reconstituting its local, regional, and national organization and delicately redistributing official positions among internal leaders and former exiles and prisoners. At a historic meeting in early May at the official residence of the South African state president, Groote Schuur, the former site of Cecil Rhodes's mansion, the government and the ANC committed themselves to a process of negotiations. To strengthen the ANC's bargaining position in these talks, Mandela led a vigorous campaign to maintain international pressure on the South African regime. Welcomed in the United States, Europe, and Africa by ecstatic crowds and politicians wanting to be associated with such a popular hero, Mandela pressed for assurances that sanctions would not be lifted until after the process toward democracy had become irrevocable. Despite these efforts, by late 1990 the European community showed signs of preparing to reward the De Klerk government for its reforms by easing sanctions, despite the ANC's call for their continuation at a contentious conference in Johannesburg in December.

The ANC was not alone in using the period leading up to formal negotiations to try to strengthen its position. The PAC also sought to consolidate its internal support, solidified in the late 1980s by its informal association with NACTU, an increase in armed attacks attributed to Africanists, and a limited resurgence in the popular appeal of the PAC as an alternative to the faltering UDF.[149] These gains were partially offset by continued divisions in the PAC leadership and by the group's relative lack of a strong symbolic appeal and organization, as compared with those of the ANC. At the same time, AZAPO also enjoyed some resurgence of popular support, with up to eight thousand attending its April 1990 annual congress, but this resurgence was marred by occasional conflict with both the ANC and PAC.[150] In general, both the PAC and AZAPO opposed negotiations with the government over any issues short of a transfer of power, hoping to position themselves as the leaders of a rise in popular militancy that they expected would follow if the talks between the ANC and the state became deadlocked.[151] ANC militants responded by embracing aspects of traditionally BC rhetoric.

Despite occasional formal and informal meetings among representatives of the ANC, the PAC, and AZAPO, the latter two groups remained unwilling to join the ANC in preliminary discussions with De Klerk.[152] The prospects for reconciliation between the ANC and PAC were set back further with the death in October 1990 of PAC president Zeph Mothopeng, who had retained unofficial friendly relations with ANC veterans dating back to the 1940s and to their long imprisonment together on Robben Island. Nevertheless, by April 1991, the ANC and PAC had announced their agreement to form a joint "patriotic front,"[153]

The reopening of space for popular political organization also encouraged a resurgence of independent socialist organizations and efforts by unionists to ensure that the workers' interests would be considered in the formal negotiations. In April, the Cape Action League and its allies established the Workers Organization for Socialist Action headed by veteran activist Neville Alexander. Operating separately from this new group, unionists in COSATU insisted that they be represented at formal negotiations and that the Charterist movement adopt a workers' charter.[154] In this way, COSATU attempted to persuade the ANC to put more emphasis on economic issues rather than postpone these for consideration only after majority rule had been achieved. This pressure for addressing workers' interests reflected the rising influence in the federation of NUMSA. By midyear, several of the metalworkers most prominent leaders had publicly proclaimed their membership in the SACP, which they had formerly criticized for postponing socialism to a second stage of struggle and which they now hoped to link more closely with the economic agenda of unionized workers.

To complicate matters, the ANC's efforts to win popular support and push for formal negotiations were hindered by rising violence in Natal between the Charterists and supporters of Chief M. G. Buthelezi's ethnically based Inkatha movement. During the rise of the Charterist movement in the 1980s, Inkatha had lost much popular support among its traditional Zulu constituency, particularly in urban areas.[155] Inkatha's effort to launch its own trade union federation, UWUSA, had also been largely unimpressive. To raise its lagging position, Inkatha began to fall back on intimidation, such as forced recruitment. Inkatha's coercion and patronage continued to be encouraged and indirectly funded by the South African government annual subvention of up to $700 million to the Kwa-Zulu homeland government, which had refused independence and was also headed by Chief Buthelezi. By 1987, fearful of being eclipsed by the Charterist movement, Inkatha began to stage attacks on UDF supporters, with the tacit and occasionally material support of police and army units in the region. During the next three years, the Natal region was racked by mounting violence, the majority of which was initiated by Inkatha, leaving more than three thousand dead, most of whom were Charterist supporters and innocent bystanders.[156] That such conflict in Natal pitted Zulu against Zulu suggested less an ethnic conflict than a conflict between allies and opponents of the white regime. By 1990, these conflicts exploded into the Transvaal, where migrant Zulu workers, isolated in single-sex hostels and reportedly armed by right-wing vigilantes, attacked UDF supporters and bystanders, much as they had launched an attack from Soweto's Mzimhlope hostel in Soweto in 1976. Over one thousand persons were killed in such incidents by the end of the year, with another two thousand killed in other incidents of unrest.[157]

This conflict between the Charterists and Inkatha reflected both historical developments and the pressure of unfolding events. The state had long supplied Inkatha with resources and support in order to offset the ANC and thus could not easily tame its client once the process toward negotiations had begun. At that point, white conservatives eager to disrupt negotiations had implicitly, and for some individuals directly, joined forces with Inkatha, which shared their belief in ascribed ethnic divisions and power sharing in a divided South Africa, advocated capitalism as preferable to socialism, and condemned the armed struggle of the ANC.[158] Meanwhile, the ANC, having long denounced Inkatha, worked with its Charterist allies to further subvert Inkatha's support in Natal. Though this conflict did fan previously latent ethnic tensions, apparent popular support for Inkatha remained relatively limited. With its existence and prominent participation in a new dispensation thus threatened, Inkatha supporters had turned to the use of force. This development resembled AZAPO's use of force to assert and protect itself in the mid-1980s, though of course Inkatha differed in its rejection of the principles of countrywide, noncollaborationist opposition common to AZAPO and the Charterists. Inkatha retained considerable resources and allegiance, which it seemed increasingly willing to use to block any resolution in which it was not a major actor, even at the risk of spreading a civil war.

Spurred on by the threat of further disruptions and violence, the ANC and the De Klerk government proceeded with their discussions, laying the groundwork for formal negotiations. Citing the example of the trade unions, whose "meteoric rise symbolizes the centrality of the working class in our struggle," the ANC declared that such talks did not preclude continued mass mobilization or armed struggle that might strengthen their bargaining position, much as strikes reinforced the unions' bargaining position.[159] Accordingly, the number of ANC guerrilla attacks rose from a monthly average of eighteen in 1989 to twenty-seven in the early months of 1990, before the ANC formally ceased such operations in August 1990 as a demonstration of its commitment to negotiations.[160] The ANC also demanded that it be given the right to report back to its constituents on the process of negotiations, as unions had required in their own negotiations with employers, in order to avoid losing support among its constituents wary of any accommodations being made "behind the backs of the people."[161] The state, for its part, tried to maintain the momentum toward negotiations while weakening its major opponents' position by failing to curtail the violence between the ANC and Inkatha, by arresting key SACP leaders accused of planning mass insurrection, and by delay. The state's prosecution of Winnie Mandela for incidents in the late 1980s further added to the ANC's tribulation and certainly distracted Mr. Mandela.

By mid-1990, South Africa remained poised on the threshold of a new era, though the precise nature of future developments remained uncertain. The ANC and the government had reached a stalemate, which both unsuccessfully attempted to resolve through various counter maneuvers, including the ANC's temporary withdrawal from formal negotiations. The unions tried to influence the agenda for future negotiations while continuing muted debates on their political alliances. More radical black groups dismissed the possibility of any peaceful settlement and enjoyed some resurgence of support among militants dismayed by the ANC's accommodations to the state. Conservative black groups, most notably Inkatha, used violence to enforce their right to a seat at the negotiating table, threatening to work more closely with right-wing whites to block this process if their demands were not met.

As these groups jockeyed for position, the people suffering from continued economic decline again turned to militancy, with unrest leaving more than 250 dead in regions outside Natal during the first three months of 1991.[162] Even more extensive violence remained a real possibility after raised expectations of an imminent transfer of power were disappointed by deadlocked negotiations. Although some in the opposition argued that "the regime has its back against the wall," the state certainly retained sufficient military capability to meet further unrest with a massive show of force.[163] The possibility also remained of vigilante attacks by conservative white extremists on Mandela, De Klerk, or others. South Africa thus stood on the edge of change that could be ushered in through negotiations, violence, or, most likely, some continuing combination of both. This precipitous situation has created anxiety, excitement, and eagerness for a resolution, but even a temporary hiatus in the rapid flow of events has remained elusive.

# 7

# *Lineages and Prospects of the South African Opposition*

The relation between ideas and material structures in determining social relations has continually fascinated philosophers, historians, social scientists, and political actors. Pondering the issue as a young man, Karl Marx argued that ideas do not exist independently of the material relations that shape them. But despite his primary emphasis on material relations, Marx could not deny that ideas also shape material relations. The circle of causality between ideas and material relations seemed impossible to escape, contradicting the Western tradition of a clear distinction between them. In a flash of brilliance, Marx abandoned his attempts to reduce historical explanation to a single cause. Using Hegel's dialectic to refute his teacher's idealism, Marx concluded that "material force must be overthrown by material force. But theory, too, will become material force as soon as it seizes the masses."[1] Although some aspects of Marx's political theory have been refuted, his conception of the dialectical relationship between ideas and material structure has remained powerful.

In this study, I have tried to clarify the integral relation between analytically distinct ideas and material structure in shaping the South African opposition movement, without imposing a single-cause view of historical events. Two sets of questions have guided my inquiry. First, what are the central ideas around which opposition has organized and how have these ideas been "seized by the masses" as ideology and influenced their actions? Second, how have state policies, economic conditions, international pressures, and the interpretations of these determined the ideology and actions of the regime's opponents? In the final sections of this chapter, I shall discuss the implications of my findings for South Africa's prospects and for the underlying theoretical debates.

## Ideology Shaping Collective Action

Ideology, as it is lived through, is more than just a set of abstract ideas. It is a way of experiencing reality, a form of "practical consciousness,"[2] based on a combination of culture and individual and historical processes. Ideology is encapsulated in images of collective identity, such as race, nation, or class, that imply different potential constituencies, goals, and strategic affinities. Elites manipulate such images for political advantage but are constrained in this process by the need to project ideas that will resonate with the masses under particular historical circumstances. In this section, we shall review the implications of relatively distinct ideological formulations for recent South African opposition, and in the following section, we shall explore the circumstances that gave rise to each.

During the last three decades, the South African opposition has shifted among focuses on racial, national, and class identity, using variations of ideas expressed by the ANC, the PAC, unionists, and others during earlier years. Combinations of ideologies were adopted and reshaped in various sequences before 1960, as they may continue to be in the future. Accordingly, we should not see the transitions discussed here as implying a necessary progression, for the starting and end points of this analysis are determined by the historical period under review. Nor do central concepts of identity remain static, for the subjective meanings of race, nation, and class have interacted and evolved continuously according to prevailing conditions. Ascriptive definitions of identity, used by the state to justify discrimination, domination, and exploitation, have been consistently rejected by the regime's opponents. But activists have not concentrated exclusively and consistently on only one of these concepts of identity. Individuals have changed and combined their ideas about which form of identity was most salient; such reconsiderations coincide in collective agreements of varying stability. These shifts of ideology have occurred amidst considerable uncertainties and disagreements; they have clearly not followed a linear process of neatly compartmentalized stages, despite the order implied by retrospective analysis.

That the opponents of the South African regime have assiduously shifted, debated, and revised their concepts of identity reveals their serious concern with such ideas, despite the complexity of the process. Activists have well understood that each ideological variation attracts different followers, who engage in specific actions with varying effects. This does not mean that activists can fully calculate the impact of their adoption of different ideologies and strategies, but they do adopt ideas cognizant that these ideas encourage certain actions. The impact of ideas is evident in the history of recent opposition.

Through most of the 1970s, South Africa's internal opposition leadership united around the ideology of Black Consciousness, for reasons more fully explored in the next section of this chapter. After the harsh repression of the early 1960s and the relative quiescence for the remainder of that decade, activists turned to race as an immediately relevant form of social identity, which could again invigorate the opposition. Being black was defined as a matter of malleable consciousness based on the experience of discrimination; the BC movement sought to unite those who rejected the idea of their own inferiority and who refused to remain subservient. The intellectual appeal of this approach drew students and other black elites, with the exclusion of sympathetic whites justified as necessary to building blacks' confidence in their ability to act for themselves. By the mid-1970s the rhetoric, if not the fine points, of this ideology took root in the townships, where emotions replaced abstractions and mass militancy became an explosive reality. A generation of opposition leaders had learned an important lesson in the power of ideas to fuel social transformation.

The focus on change through ideas about race can be seen in the conception of BC as a set of personal beliefs more than as a concrete strategy for challenging the physical aspects of established power. As one longtime member of the movement explained, "BC has always been a movement, not an organization."[3] The movement's goal of ending subservience to domination overshadowed the necessary complement of extending formal organization beyond the relatively small elite membership of affiliated groups. BC looked forward to a nonracial democracy, when the movement's racial exclusiveness would no longer be relevant, with little consideration of the more concrete intermediate steps needed to reach this inspiring but elusive goal. The group's activities initially were directed mostly at spreading its message of racial assertiveness rather than at orchestrating mass mobilization. Student organizations, the Black People's Convention, and community and union projects all remained relatively small; they rejected the use of material incentives to attract a broader following as a distraction from their central ideas. The relatively spontaneous nature of the Soweto uprising in 1976 demonstrated that both the movement's ideological priorities and its relative inattention to organization had been "seized by the masses."

Limitations aside, BC's renewed invigoration of internal resistance was remarkable, coming at a time when little other opposition existed and when many former activists had been cowed by repression. BC emerged from the generation that reached adolescence during the repressive 1960s. Their ideology of opposition developed before the practical skills of mass organization could be honed more finely from experience. Idealistic enthusiasm overcame fear, essential at that point to the development of the opposition.

By the late 1970s, a reassessment of BC contributed to a shift toward Charterism, seen as more consistent with an effort to address directly material grievances and to pose an organized challenge to state repression. Not all BC adherents embraced this strategy, for responses to repression inevitably varied amidst debates and efforts to encourage different organizational and ideological loyalties. But many of the student leaders had become disillusioned with the idealism of BC and joined forces with an older generation, still loyal to the symbols of the ANC, whose hopes were rekindled by their children. The resurgence of guerrilla activities by the ANC in exile further encouraged this consolidation of the transition away from BC.

The Charterists conceived of their movement in national terms, eschewing BC's abstract ideas about race and its exclusion of whites. The Charterists defined the nation to include all South Africans who did or could be convinced to oppose apartheid, united by direct experience of oppression, pervasive images, and symbols, in what Weber generalized as a "specific sentiment of solidarity."[4] Rather than aim toward changing ideas about being black, the Charterists tried to mobilize active resistance. Strategy replaced ideology as the main concern. At first the Charterists sought to bring people together into local protests based on hopes of material gains made possible by state reform and economic recovery. Later, publicity and resources enabled them to channel local groups and the more militant youths into a coalition under a national leadership. The exact terms on which these groups came together were never fully defined, making it possible to unite diverse interests that could act more effectively together than apart. The practical appeal of this approach drove the rapid development of the UDF, uniting local affiliates less concerned with ideological purity than with strategic advantage. By the mid-1980s most of South Africa's townships were engaging in boycotts, stayaways, and other well-organized and coordinated protests that reflected Charterist priorities.

The strengths of Charterism, however, were also its weaknesses. The movement relied on substantive reforms, external funding, and publicity to build unity. It could not easily adjust when the economy deteriorated further; the "real material concessions . . . required to demonstrate the benefits of collective action" slowed; and reources were cut off by the state, creating popular frustration often attributed to problems of the movement iself.[5] The Charterists were never able to consolidate fully national democratic structures to link disparate local groups. In their zeal to achieve maximum national unity, they spent little time establishing principles that could more firmly unify their core constituency, as distinct from temporarily strategic allies. The Charterists apparently put the lessons of BC too far behind them, neglecting the cultivation of unifying ideas despite the unresolved differences within their coalition. By 1987, state repression took advantage of these vulnerabilities, sowing division as the momentum of apparent national unity waned.

The Charterist movement of the 1980s attempted to build on the achievements of the BC movement but also to distinguish itself from that movement's idealism. BC organizations had remained relatively small, concentrated among students and other elites attracted by the movement's ideas and exclusion of whites. The Charterists tried, on the other hand, to incorporate formally the wider constituency that BC had excluded or inspired but not organized. They used local organization and resources to gain more practically motivated adherents and to mobilize a national coalition that was considerably more inclusive and physically confrontational than BC was. Identity formation through the development of malleable ideas was replaced as the opposition's principal goal, by mobilizing resources and collective action to confront more directly the institutions of domination. As was pointed out in Chapter 1, the opposition shifted from seeking change through a fluid transformation of ideas to linear strategic action.

Despite their significant differences, both BC and the Charterists were to a large extent led by the black middle class and aspirants to it who subordinated economic transformation to ending racial discrimination and national domination. The black unions, on the other hand, were necessarily built from working-class membership through more formal democratic structures established in places of employment. This constituency had been influenced by BC and the Charterists but was identified by its own short-term economic interests and its emerging consciousness of the long-term interests of the whole working class. Exactly how the unions should balance these interests and associate with other organizations was continuously debated. These issues were explored through education programs, which helped unify the union movement around the workers' commitment to socialism. As discussed in the previous chapter, the extent to which union members embraced ideas about class identity and pursued strategies implicit therein was revealed in their use of strikes, not only to pressure for wage gains, but also to support community protests. Class solidarity was evident in the unionists' willingness to accept economic sacrifice to support the unemployed and endorse international sanctions.

These ideas and practices of class identity spread to the community organizations in which many unionists were also active. Socialist rhetoric became more pervasive, as did union-inspired democratic procedures requiring shop-floor consultation and mandates for leadership. By the late 1980s, many outside the unions had become convinced that they could significantly weaken the state through economic pressure, including general strikes and sanctions.

These activities significantly contributed to the conditions necessary to push the state toward legalizing the ANC and other exiled groups in 1990 and toward initiating negotiations. But the influence of union activism also added to the pressure on the ANC itself to link more tightly its leadership and followers through formal structures and to embrace more explicitly the economic interests of the working class.

Varying ideas about race, nation, and class identity have been embraced "by the masses" as ideology and have shaped the "material force" of popular action. Groups based more on each of these identities had different concepts and experiences of how their ideologies would translate into action. The BC movement, guided by its central concept of race as a mental construct, set out to revitalize the opposition with its ideas, rather than to organize mass action. The Charterists' concept of national unity based on common opposition to state control was consistent with their emphasis on popular mobilization, rejecting potentially divisive efforts to shape consciousness while insisting on the sole authenticity of their movement as the center of all opposition. The unions' concept of class identity based on material interests and worker consciousness impelled them to organize and educate for collective action. Each of these approaches had inherent shortcomings: BC remained relatively elitist, the Charterists diffuse, and the unions economistic. But that each was effective suggests in retrospect that ideology can translate into mass action through more than one process. These shifts in approach demonstrate the power of varying combinations of identity formation to raise consciousness, and of resource mobilization to gird organization.

But not all ideas have translated into mass action. Ideas of gender identity and equality have not widely influenced the opposition movement, in large part because of the extent to which gender roles have been ingrained. In addition, many of the men who have controlled organizations do not view gender as salient to the fight against oppression. Women who have suffered from sexual oppression continue to urge greater representation in these organizations, with limited success thus far.

More encouraging has been the popular disinterest in organizing according to African ethnic identity. Unlike racial, national, class, or even gender identity, ethnicity cannot form the basis for uniting most South Africans; it can only divide the country into warring factions. Nonetheless, ethnic identities have been manipulated by the state and others for political advantage, though such identities have been widely discredited by the state's efforts to encourage tribalism as a means of dividing its opponents. Except for Chief Gatsha Buthelezi's Inkatha movement and remaining language differences, economic development and urban migration have substantially diluted African ethnic identities. South African history suggests considerable fluidity in these ethnic identities, and for many years there was very little ethnic tension among Africans in the townships or opposition organizations.[6] There has, however, been occasional strife between Africans and Indians in Natal,[7] and resentment of the coloreds in the Cape. Though Buthelezi's use of state-funded patronage to manipulate Zulu loyalties and the state's creation of separate tribal homelands have generated sustained conflict, the majority of South Africans have refused to identify themselves and their struggle in primarily ethnic terms. But such tensions remain and are likely to be manipulated and further aggravated by competition for power. Inkatha, in particular, will continue to disrupt the negotiating process, but as state support for Inkatha wanes in the face of public revelations, its capacity for disruption will probably diminish over time.

Gender and ethnicity have not thus far shaped countrywide collective action, but ideology based on varying emphases and combinations of race, nation, and class have clearly done so. Why the influence of these different ideas about identity has varied remains to be explained more fully. Simply acknowledging that ideas matter dilutes any attribution of the development of South Africa's internal opposition to material pressures. An exaggerated attribution to the influence of ideas must be similarly avoided. Shifts in the force of distinct ideologies—such as the recently varying influence of BC's idealism, Charterism's organizational strategies, and the unions' class focus—cannot be explained without reference to both their ideas and material conditions. Not only has the opposition shifted its internal emphases among combinations of ideas and structure, these shifts also flow from external interactions of ideas with material reality. Ideas feed material forces, but these forces also feed ideas. To complete this circle, we must now delineate the origins of variations in ideology.

## The Determinants of Ideological Transitions

The constant relation of ideas and material structure makes it impossible to resolve theoretical debates about social causation in favor of either. However, we can distinguish influences on collective action in a particular case, analyzing their sequence and interactions. Such an approach avoids reducing any explanation to a single cause, rejecting the attractions of theoretical simplicity in favor of historical specificity. Accordingly, in this study I have highlighted the factors that have determined recent shifts of ideology within the South African opposition. To summarize them requires distinguishing the impact of economic conditions, state policies, international influences, and developments internal to the opposition. All of these factors blend to shape opposition ideology and action, but I here maintain the analytic distinctions both to help order this analysis of the past and to help inform the subsequent discussion of the future.

I begin this analysis by exploring the apparent effect of recent economic conditions on opposition actions, particularly the impact of short-term economic trends and longer-term economic transformation. We shall see how economic conditions themselves have been affected by state policies and popular unrest or quiescence. Although the economic impact also depends on these other material conditions and on interpretations of them, we can still identify and analyze apparent patterns of response to structural economic determinants.

The history of recent South African opposition suggests that economic advancement has fed the desire for material gains more than it has stimulated politically radical demands. Material gain is likely only in times of economic growth, and so it is precisely then that demands for further gains are most frequently made. During these periods, economic growth has also provided the state with the resources to consolidate its policies, as suggested by the imposition of apartheid during the economic boom of the 1950s and 1960s, and to try to restrain or mollify instead of repress its opponents. But growth, accompanied by relaxation in the use of state force, also gives opposition groups more resources. Such conditions in the early 1970s and, to a lesser degree, in the early 1980s, offered opposition groups the opportunity to consolidate their organizations and to recruit additional supporters.

In times of relative prosperity, recent South African opposition movements have tended to press for reforms that do not risk blocking further economic gains. Between 1969 and 1974, South Africa continued to enjoy a period of unprecedented growth. Though the impact of this growth was diluted by population increases, economic expansion did affect popular experience and raised the demand for skilled labor to be provided through an increase in black university enrollment. During this period, the BC movement focused on removing racial barriers from the paths of this relatively privileged elite of black students and emerging middle class, in part to set an example of black self-reliance. From 1977 to the early 1980s, when the economy briefly recovered from recession, activists helped establish community groups and service projects in order to resolve local and material grievances. Similarly, in the 1970s, skilled workers in South Africa joined unions to gain a greater share of the economic benefits of industrialization, avoiding more direct confrontation with the state. As unionist Kaiser Thibedi observed, this pattern suggests the "danger of economic privilege leading to less political participation."[8] It would perhaps be more accurate to conclude that such circumstances do not dampen participation as much as they influence the form it takes.

This pattern of black South African responses to economic growth implies a strong degree of mass pragmatism. Political allegiances depend, in part, on the perception of which group can best obtain resources now or will most likely be a profitable association later on. For example, the UDF's effective use of service organizations and funding to build loyalty suggests that "analysis by the masses is based on bread and butter issues, not on intellectual analysis."[9] This pragmatism may be particularly strong in a society of such extreme deprivation and, by state design, offering little education to prepare people to follow more theoretical motivations.

Although black South Africans have taken advantage of economic growth and resources, economic downturns have often produced more widespread emotional responses. South Africa contains millions of marginally urbanized and impoverished people who are relatively integrated into the modern industrial economy, through either their own earnings or their dependence on the wages of others. But for many years, state policies, including restrictions on where blacks may live or work, have exacerbated their plight.

With no cushion for hard times, South Africa's urban poor have been highly vulnerable to economic shifts reflected most directly in higher prices for corn "mealies" and other food on which they spend much of their income. Their anger over increased hardship has exploded during economic downturns in South Africa. As discussed in previous chapters, the unrest in 1976–1977 and 1984–1987 came in the wake of major recessions.[10] The 1976 uprising began during a period of rising unemployment, and the protests in the Transvaal against the drastic rent increases triggered the unrest in 1984. Deprivation and economic shifts alone do not explain such militancy, but they did intensify the processes that created this volatile population.

Responses to the economy have not only followed short-term trends but have also varied according to socioeconomic position. The small black middle class, protective of its advantages, has responded less radically to recessions. The limited economic gains of migrants, the working class, and the poor in urban areas are more vulnerable to reversals, and in South Africa these groups have become more volatile during economic decline, when their willingness to follow the black middle class's less militant leadership has decreased. For those deprived groups, as a worker in Soweto explained, "Mealie meal is politics here. We have no other politics."[11] A longtime activist concluded that during relative prosperity, "There are no issues, people are led by the middle class. But if there is general dissatisfaction, then leaders are forced to follow the masses."[12] Although economic shifts may influence the middle and working classes in terms of who leads their efforts at opposition, such shifts only marginally affect the truly destitute, including the rural poor who continue to grow or barter barely enough to survive. That economic changes had varying effects on different social and geographic groups also suggests the significance of other factors, such as the extent of political organization, which are discussed later in this section.

Economic influences on opposition activity also include longer-term structural changes. Industrial growth during the three decades after World War II fundamentally altered South African society and the opportunities for opposition action. Attracted by greater employment opportunities, including a sharp rise in the number of jobs in the manufacturing sector, approximately 57 percent of blacks, amounting to over 15 million, now live in urban areas.[13] The historical trends of urbanization and the growing concentration of labor in large factories have spread mass communication and popular organization among blacks, contributing to the rising level of participation in urban-based opposition. In addition, increased reliance on skilled black labor has strengthened that group's bargaining power and wages; such gains have attracted larger numbers to the unions, which then have consolidated into large federations. Such power and organization have enabled workers to confront more effectively the monopoly business interests that now dominate the South African economy and, more recently, to challenge the state.

Since the mid-1970s, the South African economy has increasingly suffered from the structural constraints of an apartheid system that is maldistributive, inefficient, and costly to administer and enforce. From the mid-1980s, population growth, unrest, and the resulting capital flight and sanctions have further squeezed the economy. South Africa's average per-capita GDP between 1981 and 1986 fell by 2.1 percent, in a period when the same measure of the United States economy grew by 2 percent.[14] In the next four years the South African economy continued to decline, further diverging from the pattern of other Western economies which, until the early 1980s, it had tended to follow. This economic decline has encouraged a shift in the unions' focus from unavailable material gains to political protest and has contributed to a significant expansion of mobilization, conflict, and militancy beyond the ranks of the unions, consistent with the pattern just discussed.

Both daily economic conditions and long-term economic trends appear to be affecting the opposition's immediate goals and mass activity. At the same time, economic trends cannot account for the ideological parameters or goals, let alone the opposition's specific strategies. These variables also respond to the policies of the state, which at first glance appears to have the advantage of selecting the terrain of the struggle against it. Of course, the state is neither unitary nor unchanging in its policies, for instance, with its security apparatus having effectively advocated more repression until these officials had lost some of their influence on the retirement of state president P. W. Botha, a former minister of defense. The opposition has not reacted passively to shifts in state policy but has probed the weak spots in the state's actions. For instance, the opposition has inverted the state's efforts to reinforce racial, national, and class divisions to its own advantage. Racial discrimination has brought assertions of black unity; minority domination has led to national mobilization; and economic exploitation has stimulated working-class organization. The state has then had to respond to these challenges, albeit restricted by economic conditions and its political constituencies.

In the 1960s and early 1970s, the state's grand apartheid design of separate homelands for blacks, together with forced "removals and influx control," aimed at reinforcing racial and ethnic divisions. Black students, who had not yet joined the work force or who had not directly suffered economic exploitation, were brought together in unprecedented numbers in racially segregated and inferior schools and universities. The BC movement, which grew up among these students, rejected these ethnic divisions and inverted the state's aim of imposed racial identity, in part by including coloreds and Indians with Africans. Black Consciousness asserted the power of the majority to determine its own destiny, contesting racial discrimination and state efforts to project blacks as inferior to whites and subordinate to Afrikaner control and culture. Not surprisingly, the BC-inspired Soweto uprising of 1976 began when students rejected the state's imposition of Afrikaans as a medium of instruction.

In the early 1980s, the state adopted a somewhat more reformist line, hoping to buttress continued national domination by the limited inclusion of other minority groups. A new tricameral parliament was designed to involve coloreds and Indians in the continued exclusion of the African majority, for whom the state created centrally controlled structures of local "self-governance." The National Forum and shortly thereafter the UDF formed to coordinate the widespread resistance to these policies, with the state's initiatives giving a national and nonracial underpinning to previously locally based organizations. When the state turned to more fundamental reform in 1989, initiating negotiations with the ANC, the Charterists sought advantage in those negotiations to expedite a transfer of power.

In 1979, the state legalized the emerging black labor unions, in the hope of creating a more disciplined and complacent "labor aristocracy." The unions have used this opening to build up their organizations. Unionized workers increasingly challenged both the established political order and the economic exploitation that affects their class. The unions thereby sought to widen the cracks in state rule that had developed partly as the result of the economic constraints imposed by apartheid.

These developments suggest the extent to which the South African state's varying oppression has determined the struggle by its opponents, who have continually responded by trying to find vulnerabilities. Leaders of the ANC and the PAC have agreed in principle that "the state can't directly dictate the terms of opposition but it can make a set of alternatives more attractive at a time."[15] The opposition has tried to strengthen itself in response to these policies of domination: to benefit from the process by which "the character of the state conditions not only the terms of domination and submission, but also the ideologies and political behavior that challenge . . . it."[16]

Although the state apparently influences its opposition, the regime is not free to shape its opponents as it might wish. Just as aspects of opposition ideology have responded to state policy, so have state policies formed in response to earlier opposition. Certainly the state's banning of the ANC and PAC in 1960 was a direct response to their increased activism, leading up to the Sharpeville massacre by the police. As opposition has expanded in the years since, the state has been forced to respond even more directly to its opponents. For instance, the state's 1983 proposal of a tricameral parliament was, in part, an effort to win back the Indian and colored communities that BC had claimed. The legalization of black unions in 1979 recognized the extent of unionization already achieved, which the state hoped to regulate.

The state's responses to opposition are not always defensive. The regime also tailors its repression to the particular vulnerabilities of the opposition movements. For example, BC's focus on reshaping racial identity and its intentional de-emphasis of organizational structures encouraged the relatively impulsive unrest of 1976. The state was able to crush this uprising by force; it did not ban BC organizations until a year later. In 1984 through 1987, unrest was more carefully orchestrated but also more dependent on political space for organization and on media publicity to guide it. In response, the state became more sophisticated, initially using detentions, bannings, censorship, and misinformation to disrupt and divide the UDF coalition, rather than resorting only to lethal force. The state also encouraged its local clients and competing opposition groups (i.e., AZAPO) to combat UDF affiliates and followers. Most notably it allegedly encouraged or, at least, permitted the use of violence by Chief Gatsha Buthelezi's Zulu-based Inkatha movement in Natal. By 1988, state security officials were explicitly advocating that the "governing power" must adapt to "the revolutionary strategy and principles and [apply] them in reverse."[17]

Just as it must respond to opposition forces, the state also must respond to the same economic conditions that constrain its opponents. For example, the state has dispensed reforms and redressed material grievances to quell the opposition only when it could obtain the resources that such reforms required. Therefore, with inadequate funds during periods of recession and economically aggravated mass militancy, the state reverted to control through repression, relying more on its well-financed military and less on optional social programs. Though it is difficult to assign causal primacy, recession, militancy, and repression have tended to coincide, except in recent years, when the state curtailed its repression in order to encourage the negotiations that it hoped would restore investor confidence. The general economic dependency of state policy might seem odder than that recent exception given the relative autonomy from private capital of the South African state, with public-sector expenditures in 1985 accounting for 37.8 percent of the GDP and approximately 57 percent of all fixed capital owned by the state.[18] But autonomy from private capital is not the same as independence from all economic pressures, which no state can achieve. Instead, the scale of the South African public sector has left state policy all the more subject to downturns in the business cycle, to resulting decreases in its tax revenue, and to economic dislocations, including the flight of international capital, reduced trade, and sanctions. Fear that such sanctions would continue or increase helped bring the state to initiate negotiations in 1990.

For all its relative ability to resist pressure from private capital, the South African state has still had to bend to the mandate of its electoral base. The state's own long-standing apartheid propaganda has reinforced whites' resistance to any material sacrifice aimed at appeasing blacks. This has created a structural resistance to any significant reforms. Pretoria has been particularly submissive to its own white bureaucrats and the employees of state-owned firms, both to maintain state control and to satisfy that constituency, which makes up over 34 percent of the economically active, eligible voters.[19] These functionaries, in particular, resist any effort to share power with blacks, as they are the white South Africans who would be most directly affected by a transfer of political power and patronage. The state has gained autonomy from private business interests but has lost it to this pampered constituency. F. W. de Klerk's government must therefore remain concerned by the potential wrath of the white constituency, many of whom do not believe that they gave the state president a mandate for the sweeping changes initiated in 1990.

State efforts to mollify black opposition have been limited by the economy and political rigidities and also by failures to anticipate the full results of its own policies. When the state has attempted to persuade the black populace to go in a certain direction, it has only been able to do so clumsily, for instance, by using clandestine techniques transparently camouflaged. And whatever the state has advocated, its opponents have generally rejected simply for its association with continued oppression. Economic, racial, or ethnic privileges and "group rights" aimed at protecting minorities all have been sullied by state advocacy as well as by their actual effects. Rejection of these techniques of oppression are evident not only in the opposition's rhetoric but also in its recent efforts to build popular organizations that meet social needs and are nonracial, ethnically diverse, and democratic.

State advocacy has backfired, and as de Tocqueville warned, reforms and delays in crushing dissent have also unintentionally added to the peril of the minority regime.[20] The South African state did little to stop the formation of the BC movement, which it misinterpreted as consistent with apartheid's racial distinctions, enabling BC to consolidate and to further erode subservience. We have already seen how the state's 1983 constitutional reforms provided space for the UDF and other groups, which then organized challenges to the state on various fronts. In the hope that resolving material grievances would buy support for the government, the state declined to stop affiliates of the UDF from organizing communities, and it permitted unions to organize black workers, at least until it became obvious that the resulting organizations were using material gains to motivate further political activity. The state's failure to curtail the discussion of class analysis led to an increasing radicalization of the unions and a shift of popular attention away from the relatively petty reforms of apartheid toward the more fundamental brutalities of poverty. The state's current policy of permitting the ANC, the PAC, and other groups to reconstitute their internal structures is sure to strengthen those movements as they consider negotiations with the state and also call for mass protests. As the space for airing grievances has been filled, it has led to new forms of activism.

The South African state's use of force deserves special attention in our consideration of the factors that shape the opposition. In the short term, repression has not only discouraged mass action it has also chilled discussion among opposition leaders and groups, thus exacerbating the conflicts through which the authorities seek to keep opponents divided. As the state has curtailed debate and participation, the opposition camps have exhibited a greater insistence on conformity, on occasion enforced by hooliganism, as well as internecine conflict and demoralization. For example, violent conflict between the UDF and the BC adherents in AZAPO exploded in the eastern Cape at the height of the repressive state of emergency in 1985.

In the longer term, however, repression has revealed weaknesses in current opposition activity, thereby directing and encouraging reconsideration that has, on occasion, refined that activity. For instance, repression after 1976 encouraged emphasis on organizing more active local opposition than that pursued by the BC movement. Repression in the mid-1980s encouraged greater efforts to keep leaders accountable to the masses than the UDF had done. In such instances, prolonged repression has had the unintended benefit of turning the activists' attention to evident weaknesses in their approach and forcing adjustment.

One of the most direct ways in which prolonged repression has sparked reconsideration is that it has forcibly brought together activists for discussion. During the active phases of opposition, after the initial planning and before evaluation in the aftermath, such discussion often is put aside. Ironically, group prison cells have regularly given leaders an opportunity to again evaluate their achievements and talk over their differences, undisturbed by immediate pressures. This has particularly been true for prisoners sent to Robben Island. Such prison meetings do not necessarily produce agreement, but they do often lead to greater respect across ideological divides. Below the leadership, imprisonment and detentions have also given the rank and file similar chances to talk among themselves and with their leaders. Those not imprisoned have also taken advantage of repression's curtailment of mass activity to try to reconcile differences or adjust strategies.

In the gap between immediate disruption and long-term adjustment, repression has often driven greater numbers to the opposition, making it harder for the state to impose the sort of submission it achieved in the 1960s. Police violence and detentions, in their most extreme form, have caused such grief as to unify and politicize many more, adding to the number of South Africans who see the status quo as directly threatening their survival. More measured but constant repression through draconian laws, such as those that imposed severe penalties for pass offenses, have further unified apartheid's victims in opposing the existing political order. Legislation mandating black homelands and massive forced migration have politicized millions more and helped spread opposition from the urban centers, where it had been concentrated, to rural areas. In addition, state efforts to use education to train and discipline black youth meant that students could organize themselves in schools, from which they have staged unrest. Limitations and disruptions of black education have also ensured that the undereducated poor include many talented activists who might otherwise have been mollified by personal advancement. As former unionist Eddie Zwane concluded, no doubt somewhat optimistically, "The harder [the state] tries, the better they make things for us. They organize for us."[21]

The unintended benefits of state actions for the opposition are also evident in the extent to which repression popularized its targets, unifying diverse groups while dividing regime supporters. For instance, the state's crushing of the BC movement after 1976 actually increased popular support for that movement in the years before the emergence of the Charterists. Similarly, in 1988 a leading student organization argued that the "UDF being banned shows it was not a failure" and that repression of COSATU was a signal of its "correctness in political approach."[22] At the same time that repression temporarily strengthened loyalty to such groups, it encouraged them to cooperate more closely in challenging their common enemy. For instance, in the wake of the bannings of the UDF and other organizations in 1988, these groups and the two leading union federations launched a series of meetings to decide on united action. During this same period, repression also offended some former supporters of the regime, deepening conflicts among white politicians and dissent within the state's police force, which further weakened and isolated the regime. None of these positive effects diminishes the repugnancy of apartheid repression, but they do suggest that state brutality can work against itself, as reforms have, thereby reducing the state's effective options for reinforcing its rule.

The state has been weakened by its own practices and economic pressures, and it has also suffered from international developments that have bolstered the opposition movements' ideological loyalties and encouraged other transitions. For instance, evidence of Pretoria's occasional military or diplomatic ineffectiveness has raised activists' expectations and directed loyalty to whatever group then seems most likely to obtain power. The BC movement rallied supporters to protest in support of Mozambique's independence in 1975. Successful incursions by the ANC in the late 1970s and early 1980s gained popular support for that exiled group and its internal allies. Similarly, the state's inability to crush the PAC in exile remained a source of encouragement for internal Africanists. In addition, international antiapartheid activities and support for sanctions provided a source of hope for many internal activists, particularly during periods of heightened repression.

On the other hand, Pretoria's regional successes have encouraged shifts in the opposition's strategy. For example, the 1984 Nkomati Accord between South Africa and Mozambique, which deprived the ANC of its closest external bases, discouraged internal reliance on armed attacks supplied from the outside, thereby moving the impetus for opposition more clearly to internal unrest, which resumed that year. Continued economic and military pressure by South Africa on its neighbors have led many of the frontline states to press the ANC to negotiate a settlement that would bring regional peace. In addition, the combination of international economic pressures adopted in response to internal unrest, a fading Soviet threat, and the reduced strategic interests of the West in supporting the regime have pushed the state toward the negotiating table and improved the ANC's bargaining position. At the same time, the collapse of the command economies in Eastern Europe has also begun to generate debate within the opposition.

This brief look at the influences of economic conditions, state policies, and international factors indicates the extent to which material forces have shaped South Africa's internal opposition. For instance, economic growth through the early 1970s brought together the students who formed BC in an effort to overcome the submissiveness enforced by the state in the 1960s. State policies shifting according to varying pressures were also influential on the opposition. Repression in 1976 demonstrated the need for a broader, more active opposition. Local organizations galvanized by state reforms in the early 1980s came together in the UDF to protest the tricameral parliamentary proposals. Industrialization and urbanization also contributed to the growth of the unions, which provided a model of democratic processes and a vehicle for the increasing influence of the working class. More recent repression has further politicized and united these unions, and economic decline in the 1980s has encouraged a dramatic increase in the extent and mobilization of the masses. Pressured by these developments and by the international community, the state unbanned the ANC and other organizations, in this way commencing a process of negotiations to which the opposition has responded, as discussed in the next section of this chapter.

In retrospect, this development of the opposition may appear almost mechanical in its progression, although the reality has been far from linear. True, opponents of the regime have had to respond to changing external conditions over which they had little control, but they have consciously chosen those responses through a complex, subjective process. Economic growth has spurred consolidation of divergent ideologies and strategies, and recessions have aggravated either spontaneous or more organized unrest. Repression has stimulated both division and unity; it has revived mass protest while also forcing realignments. These varying responses and differences in local activities have reflected a significant diversity of opinion and levels of organization inside the opposition. For instance, even before the 1976 uprising, activists in the BC movement had disagreed over the need to move beyond ideas about race to class identity and mass organization. During the late 1980s, the UDF debated the proper role of leadership and the question of alliances. The union movement similarly struggled over how much to subordinate their focus on class and economic issues to the political agenda of the multiclass ANC. Each of these opposition debates contributed to the formulation and growth of new approaches. To explain this process we must look beyond material influences; we must examine these internal processes and tensions, the focal point through which external factors have been interpreted and have evoked patterned responses.

My analysis here shifts from the material conditions to the more subjective aspects of individual and historical development. We cannot fully account for transitions in opposition ideology and strategy if we ignore the thoughts, discourse, and agency of those who perceived a need for, argued for, and implemented these new approaches. As much as activists have attempted to respond to new conditions, these efforts have depended on individual biography, interpretations, and different personal experiences. For some, established loyalties, ideology, or interest in preserving personal status has meant an unwillingness to change. This possibility helps explain, for example, the continued dedication to Black Consciousness among those who remained in AZAPO. But for the majority, new conditions have encouraged new interpretations and changes in affiliation. In the last three decades, many of those first politicized by BC later worked for the UDF and the union movement, reflecting their own self-interest, experiences, changes of ideas, or the influence of family and friends.

Activist elites and the rank and file have played somewhat different roles in this process of interpreting, debating, and implementing responses to change. The formulation or dissemination of the fine points of ideology is generally concentrated among intellectuals and leaders who can be distinguished from the populace accordingly.[23] This distinction can be applied to analysis of recent South African opposition. For instance, in the disillusionment after high points of militancy against repression, those who have become most quickly involved in appraisal and consolidation for the next phase of opposition have used this process to consolidate their leadership positions. Theoretical discussions and reading often are part of such elite reappraisal. The BC's evocation of Frantz Fanon, the unionists' references to Karl Marx, their familiarity with historical precedents of earlier ANC, PAC, and union experiences all demonstrate this. International trends and experiences, as interpreted by elites distinguished by their ability to travel and to make foreign contacts, have also become influential. In their travels, established leaders have had opportunities to meet with officials of exiled groups, such as the ANC, and have used such contact to consolidate their positions. The difficulties of dissemination under oppression and the elites' own ambiguity may slow this process, but still the elites' influence in shifting opposition ideology and strategy has been substantial.

The ideas and rhetoric that these elites developed became reified among the masses and shaped the regular practices, or "repertoires," of the opposition's organized action. As the first section of this chapter described, shifting the primary focus from race, to nation, and to class justified the varying emphases on raising consciousness, organizing protests, or some combination of these. Examples of how these ideas devolved from cultivation among elites to organized mass action include the BC-inspired emotional outburst of 1976 and the Charterists' use of boycotts and protests in the 1980s, for which there was little precedent in the 1970s. Material influences cannot fully explain these outcomes, however. It was elites responding to changing circumstances who first debated and shifted their attention to racial discrimination, national domination, or economic exploitation and to corresponding strategies, even though all of those elements of oppression continued to coexist materially. Varying groups of followers responded to new conditions according to the paradigm projected by the elites; for instance, the Soweto students became more consciously angered by evidence of racial discrimination than by the economic downturn that preceded the 1976 uprising. That popular rhetoric at the time focused on issues of racial and cultural oppression, such as the imposition of Afrikaans instruction, more than on economic deterioration, underlines the influence and popular responsiveness to elite formulations. In this way elites may guide mass mobilization, but only to the extent that their ideas resonate with the current disposition of the people.

In addition to the elites' influence through ideas, the rank and file have pursued practical needs that their leaders could neither ignore or override. The majority of people in South Africa seek an end to minority rule and have been inclined toward ideas and strategies that seem most likely to achieve this. Alliances across classes and races thus have been attractive, owing less to any abstract justification than to the practical advantages of alliances, for instance, with whites and Indians who can provide resources. As the practical need for such resources disappears, the masses have become more critical of compromises needed to retain such allies. The greater immediate priority given to ending apartheid than to economic redistribution reflects the popular appeal of achievable goals more than it demonstrates the influence of the SACP's abstract theories of a two-staged revolution. Increasingly, economic issues have been brought to the fore by the masses more out of necessity and negative experiences with capitalism than as the result of abstract notions of socialism. People have often become frustrated with the divisive and distracting debates among elites and so have pressed for the practical advantages of united action, for instance, through the cooperation of COSATU and NACTU. Elites have responded to such pressures from below, reformulating ideology and strategy to fit the interests of a constituency that since the 1960s has grown from student organizations, to an alliance of youth and community groups, and to a coalition led at the end of the 1980s by unionized workers.

The leaders' ability to influence the masses has also met the resilient constraint of mass symbolic loyalty, more often tied to practical concerns than contrary to them. Many in South Africa have a long-standing attachment to symbols such as the Freedom Charter, to the ANC's history and leaders, or, less commonly, to the PAC. Such loyalties are often inherited through family ties and lifetime associations, picked up from friends, and reinforced by organizations, press reports, or a ground swell of popularity from which many do not want to be left out. Loyalty to a particular opposition group can result from the practical desire to avoid ostracism or physical attacks against those labeled as dissenters.

Given the difficulty of convincing leaders to unite without a national means of democratic control, such loyalties to unifying symbols and conformist pressures help explain why the opposition has not become more splintered by its leaders' disputes.

The ability of leaders to influence followers should not be exaggerated, and neither should the constraints that popular loyalties impose on shifts by the opposition. Unresolved doubts, new experiences not yet integrated, fear, and ambivalence always remain. For instance, racial identity and the rank and file's anger toward whites has coexisted with personal attachments, respect, envy, and fear of whites. As a result, the popular commitment to the principle of nonracialism has not been absolute, nor does it remain inviolable. Opponents have embraced alliances with business for the resources they provide, even though they may resent the same businesses for profiting from apartheid. Capitalism is still suspect, although many people also want the benefits that capitalism can provide and have only a vague notion of what a socialist alternative would look like. Union members have wavered between advancing their own interests within established economic relations and accepting sacrifices in order to challenge those relations. Ethnicity has been largely diluted by urbanization, subordinated to common grievances, and discredited by state manipulation, but has reemerged during periods of social dislocation. Opposition leaders have sought to resolve such issues through various forms of mass education.

Popular commitments have often remained ambiguous, and the development of mass political consciousness has also remained incomplete or localized, despite the tendency of activists to take such development for granted. Certainly the BC movement and opposition activities before and since have helped blacks break "out of the mental enslavement which in the past, could have persuaded them that they were in any way inferior."[24] But fear is constant despite such advances, particularly in the countryside. For instance, one rural mother confessed that "if I could, I would swallow my son every night and be pregnant, rather than have him on the run, sleeping in the mountains."[25] Authority occasionally still scares militants: In 1988, a lone white police officer was able to convince a young man to surrender his AK-47 during an attempted homeland coup.[26] Activists and observers often assume the opposition to be national in scope, and yet anomalous actions—such as the 1980 Cape Town school boycott that anticipated the economic downturn and nationwide activism of 1984—are common. Persistent regional differences are also evident, as informed by the particular traditions that migrants have brought with them from rural areas and as the result of influences or varying local levels of organization and exhaustion. Such variation was evident, for instance, in the outbreak of unrest in 1984 in the Vaal townships before it emerged in Soweto. People want their organizations to be democratic but are still to varying degrees inexperienced, uninformed, or impatient regarding democratic procedures. Workers claiming loyalty to the Charterists in one breath have in the next confessed their unfamiliarity with the content of the Freedom Charter.

Despite these shortcomings, a consensus regarding certain ideals has emerged out of the overarching experience of multifaceted oppression and increasingly extensive mobilization. Although those who favor and those who reject letting whites join the struggle continue to debate, few blacks object to the ultimate goal of achieving a South Africa in which there are no racial divisions, about which they are no doubt reassured by black predominance under majority rule. There is a similar consensus regarding the principles of democracy and the need for countering the economic maldistribution created by capitalism, despite differences over organizational procedure and economic interests. Unionists have proved willing to accept some short-term sacrifices in order to pursue these goals, such as by advocating sanctions despite the risk of job losses. These ideals, which leaders and their followers share, have evolved from their direct experience of discrimination, domination, and exploitation and from their interpretations of how these realities can be inverted by a revolutionary process. Of course, historically, such aspirations have often emerged from direct hardship; many of the basic ideals of "society," "freedom," and economic justice came from similar historical processes elsewhere, attesting to the human capacity to imagine alternatives to material reality.[27]

Such shared ideas and agreement on repertoires of strategy were created in South Africa from a complex interplay of material pressures and elite and mass influences. Indeed, economic change and state policy has affected the opposition only through its interpretation of these factors. Both leaders and followers have incorporated the lessons of experience, imperfectly seeking to refine and strengthen the opposition by means of improved strategies and united action. Much of this process has been concentrated and initiated in urban townships, where the opportunities for education, discussion, and analysis are greatest. There people have directly experienced the cruel lessons of premature uprisings, insufficient organization, and disunity, although they have differed on how to understand and respond to these lessons. The repetition of these lessons and the persistence of strategies previously abandoned have led to disagreements contributing to wide swings between expectations of imminent victory and equally exaggerated pessimism. But the resulting internecine conflicts have raised valuable issues and contributed to progressive development at least as much as they have been divisive.

Overall, the opposition's organizational achievements and growth to date suggest that much of its reasoning on how to redirect popular activism has been sound. But the learning process has been neither infallible nor linear and has not progressed according to some abstract notion of disembodied rationality. The failure to achieve liberation has been a powerful teacher, from which South Africans have drawn different conclusions. The lessons of struggle, drawn from ideas and experience, success and failure, unity and diversity, have been learned in a conscious process of energetic debate and changed minds. These lessons cannot be explained as the outcome of a mechanical response to structural conditions. Nor can the impact of these lessons on shifting opposition strategies of varying effectiveness be denied. The agency and ability of the regime's opponents must be given analytic weight equal to that of the will and capacity of the state to continue to rule, as weaknesses in the regime can only lead to a transfer of power when the opposition has developed to take advantage of these state vulnerabilities. The breakdown of authority and the consolidation of the opposition are integrally related and equally necessary as conditions for the historical development toward liberation.

## Implications for the Future

An overview of recent transitions in South African opposition reveals that explanations of such shifts do not fit any single category. Interacting structure and ideas have determined such outcomes in regular, if not always predictable, patterns. Ideological goals have partly reflected the current focus of state policy: Overt discrimination provoked racial assertiveness; reforms of political dispensation were confronted by national mobilization; and limited material concessions encouraged worker organization. Opponents of the regime have pursued such goals less confrontationally during periods of economic growth and more militantly during economic downturns. Such economic trends have also influenced state policy, which relies more on repression during recession, though neither state policy or opposition tactics can be explained by economic affects alone. The opposition's responses to both the economy and the state have been guided by the conscious efforts of leaders, international influences, long-standing loyalties, and popular beliefs, all of which have been reflected in identifiable strategies.

These factors will continue to shape the opposition to South Africa's established order. However, the complexity of past patterns of opposition development makes it difficult to project these patterns into the future. The landscape of literature on the South African conflict is littered with unfulfilled predictions, which this analysis can only marginally improve. Previous analyses that exclusively examined the state were flawed by their simplifying assumption that opposition activities were either constant or irrelevant to the outcome of the conflict. But the necessary addition of analysis of the opposition increases the difficulty of prediction. Varying interpretations and other aspects of self-determination only augment our appreciation of the subjective element in those factors that affect the opposition and determine the outcome of its efforts.

Recent events have altered some of the preconditions on which our analysis of past patterns rests, making a projection of that analysis into the future even harder. Historical developments have simply overwhelmed the previous logic of key actors in the South African conflict, including the state and the ANC.

Periods of economic downturn have, in the past, reduced the state's capacity to appease its opponents, resulting in its greater dependence on repression. Despite the continuing economic dislocation caused by unrest, investors' fears, and formal sanctions, State President de Klerk has not abandoned his current reformist approach, hoping to win international acceptance by de-racializing

South Africa's social order. In part, this disjuncture can be explained by Pretoria's fears that, despite such reforms, instability will continue and that investors are unlikely to return, as they have in the past. With no forseeable economic recovery ahead, even if formal sanctions are lifted, the state will be threatened with even greater economic dislocation and unrest if it loses the existing opportunities for reconciliation. Under pressure, President de Klerk's government has committed itself to negotiate a new political dispensation before the next scheduled election.

The ANC has faced similarly unprecedented pressures to accept Pretoria's overtures for resolution. The Soviet Union now appears unwilling or unable to continue funding the ANC's military and has advocated a negotiated settlement, as have neighboring states. But these developments have also undermined Pretoria's assumption that fear of a Soviet advantage in the region would ensure continued support from the West, which was already questionable. In addition, the ANC may have been persuaded by fear that its internal popularity—based in part on symbolic loyalty to Mandela and to other imprisoned leaders—would suffer if there were no resolution during the lifetime of this older generation. The older, more moderate ANC leadership was encouraged by De Klerk to believe that an accommodation among elites, resulting in majoritarian rule with various checks, was possible. All of these factors combined to give both the ANC and the state the sense that they had to reach a historical compromise "now or never." Such a denouement alone reduces the applicability of past patterns of political action.

But as much as recent historical developments may have interrupted patterns of past activity by the state and its opponents, specific aspects of those patterns may still hold and help reveal future possibilities. Having long fostered popular demands for a nonracial, unitary, economically redistributive democracy, neither the ANC nor its allies can now abandon those basic principles without risking the confusion or the alienation of their followers. Yet these principles cannot be easily reconciled with De Klerk's insistence on discussing a "sharing of power" rather than an explicit "transfer of power" or state demands for guarantees of existing property rights, its rejection of a proportionately representative constituent assembly, and its continued commitment to "group rights" as a means of protecting white interests. This suggests a lack of common ground for negotiations. At the same time, economic dislocation continues to provoke both a rising crime rate and mass militancy, which threatens to explode beyond levels generally conducive to negotiations, despite the ANC's official suspension of its guerrilla campaign.[28] A growing world recession will likely exacerbate these difficulties, generating zero-sum choices of distribution more than opportunities to meet competing demands and further reducing the South African state's ability to redress material grievances that remain unmet by legal reforms. For instance, the lifting of basic apartheid restrictions in February 1991 allows blacks to buy land but provides no resources for them to exercise such rights.

If these conditions lead to heightened mass militancy, the resulting conflict will likely be particularly sharp. The clash of conflicting interests is increased through the spread of union-style organization and class consciousness, linking national political issues to material demands that the state cannot meet. Conflict may also be exacerbated by right-wing white vigilanteeism, ethnic divisiveness spread by Inkatha with continued state support, mass exasperation with the ANC's efforts to accommodate whites, or the state's intransigence fanning a revival of militant Africanism sufficient to disrupt formal negotiations. The historical development of individual consciousness reflected in the same activists' progressing from BC to Charterism or to the unions cannot be assumed to have reached a static ideological or strategic position, for this historical process will continue, and diversity remains. Though mass politicization elsewhere in Africa was often defused by nationalist demands for unity after "independence," the length and depth of the South African struggle makes it less likely that evolving popular demands will be easily suppressed in the long term, even after agreement is reached on a new inclusive political dispensation.

Mass participation and deprivation, combined with the raising of expectations by public discussions of a negotiated settlement, is already creating an increasingly volatile situation in South Africa. If the De Klerk government is weakened or negotiations falter further, the opposition may face a division between the ANC leadership—continuing to seek a resolution—and its less patient younger followers. The ANC remains weakened by long years of repression and exile, insufficient funding, unresolved differences within its coalition, and underdeveloped internal democratic structures. As a result the ANC may have difficulty uniting developed and disparate elements of civil society, controlling the people, gaining popular acceptance for any settlement negotiated by a partnership of ANC and state elites, or avoiding further compromises.

The ANC's suspension of its armed struggle and reorganization of underground structures into legal entities, together with international pressure to end sanctions, had by early 1991 weakened three of the congress's "four pillars of struggle," leaving mass mobilization as its only remaining form of pressure on the state. As a result, more militant followers, disgruntled by these accommodations, increasingly gravitated to the SACP without also joining the ANC, raising the possibility of future tension within the long-standing ANC–SACP alliance. Should the ANC agree to guarantees of existing property rights in return for political concessions by the state, even many of its less militant followers may later object to such an abandonment of their fundamental economic aspirations. Such potential disillusionment and tension in the Charterist camp would strengthen the PAC and other radicals who are currently positioning themselves for such an eventuality. Under Nelson Mandela's active leadership, the ANC and its allies must therefore prepare for the possibility of further violent conflict with its political competitors and with the state. Their immediate struggle is to channel mass militancy at a level that will strengthen their bargaining position but not preclude a dramatic resolution.

The future of the South African opposition and of the conflict in which it has engaged remain impossible to predict. History diverts from its expected course, as global events in the late 1980s and early 1990s repeatedly demonstrated. But the prospects for significant change in South Africa in the near future are now certain. The state has been weakened in its resolve and capacity, even though its power remains. Increasingly extensive oppositon has strengthened mass consciousness and organization, although it still has not been able to defeat the regime. The conflict cannot be resolved through the unilateral action of either side. Nor can either side impose its will on the other. In the interregnum, all variety of possibilities remain, except for the possibility of stability. Minority rule is being reformulated amidst discussions of an interim coalition government pursued through a continuing combination of negotiation and violence. Of course, the struggle will not end with these developments, for the form of unfolding liberation will continue to be debated as the various groups vie for power and privilege. As the unifying focus of opposition to legal apartheid shifts more explicitly to a struggle for power, conflict over unmet economic demands pursued by the organized working class and militant youth, as well as ethnic conflict, may emerge with greater force.

## The Centaur

> You must know, then, that there are two methods of fighting, the one by law, the other by force: the first method is that of men, the second of beasts; but as the first method is often insufficient, one must have recourse to the second. It is therefore necessary for a prince to know well how to use both the beast and the man. This was covertly taught to rulers by ancient writers, who relate how Achilles and many others of those ancient princes were given to Chiron the centaur to be brought up and educated under his discipline. The parable of this semi-animal, semi-human teacher is meant to indicate that a prince must know how to use both natures, and that the one without the other is not durable. (Niccolo Machiavelli, *The Prince*, p. 92)

Machiavelli's evocation of the centaur applies not only to the ruling prince but also to would-be princes, who must combine force and consent to defeat the state's physical and mental domination.[29] The man and the beast act as one, guided by both ideas and material needs. Both the state and its opponents reflect the combined nature of the centaur, as they battle with each other for power. An opposition must use persuasion to build popular consciousness and support, appealing to human idealism; it must use organization to win the material benefits that appeal to man's baser materialistic nature. Both are necessary; either alone is insufficient to win or to hold power. Freedom to imagine an alternative society must come together with necessity, meeting real needs through change. For freedom without necessity leads to romantic idealism, and necessity without freedom leads to tyranny.[30] The two guises of the centaur may appear incompatible, but they instead constitute a necessary and unifying tension, the genius and the genesis of revolution.

A revolutionary transformation of socioeconomic and political structures may begin with the creation and spread of new ideas that challenge the established order, for without a revolution of ideas no alternative social order can be imagined or constructed. Psychological and cultural liberation helps inspire and direct popular mobilization and the organization of opposition. But an exaggerated focus on ideas harbors danger. Idealism may overlook the needs of the destitute, a reality that leaves hollow the most visionary of republics. Intellectuals and analysts, for whom ideas are a way of life, may overestimate the power of ideas alone to create change, without the necessary complement of organized action. Once a set of alternative ideas has been proposed and "seized by the masses," there is the risk that these ideas will become static, held in place by those leaders and thinkers who invest in them. The ideas that underlie any struggle must be constantly open to revision according to new experiences and circumstances.

To confront the established order effectively, an opposition must act through organization to direct both its force and its persuasion. Without such deeds, its words can have no effect and may not even be allowed to be spoken. To win space for the discussion of ideas, at some point analysis must be put in abeyance and acted upon, with the action itself further shaping consciousness. But necessary action—if not tempered by the freedom of reconsideration—may become dogmatic and often may provoke renewed idealism in response.

It is not surprising that actors tend to overplay their focus on ideas and on action, for both draw their converts deeper into their spell. Once engaged in a certain mode, it becomes difficult to deviate from the path implied by inertia. As a result, an opposition movement tends to make a fetish of that form of activity in which it is currently engaged. But the secret of political effectiveness is to avoid becoming spellbound by a single mode of operation or direction, that is, to remain flexible. Although conscious flexibility is difficult to maintain, circumstances provide a reminder of what has been left out. If the centaur forgets one side of its nature, the beast's hunger or the man's principled aspiration will reassert itself and necessitate an adjustment.

The South African opposition has long struggled to find such a flexible approach, to learn the lesson that the centaur, Chiron, taught the ancient princes. What appears to have been a set of transitions among competing opposition movements can instead be understood as such a learning process, with all of the fits, missteps, tensions over remaining differences, and frustrations that this implies. Division and failure have led to recurrent consideration and renewed effort. BC's focus on ideas confronted its limits in the face of physical repression, and adjustment was made in the direction of greater organization. The Charterist focus on organizational unity confronted its limits in the face of state-reinforced ideological divisions, and adjustment inspired by class analysis has begun in the direction of greater attention to ideological cohesion. The shifts in focus between these two facets of the South African opposition have led to a greater appreciation of the need to combine them. The "engine of revolution" requires both "the steam and the piston box" of ideas and organization.[31] The South African opposition continues to evolve, realizing that to succeed it must both organize and inspire its constituents to break and tame the state. As acknowledged by one longtime activist, "Freedom will only come when we have matured enough to seize it," with such maturation the incremental result of learning from experience.[32]

The opposition's progress toward maturity has always included significant tension. But the debates over ideology and strategy that have been held again and again in the South African opposition have not merely devolved into factional disintegration or paralysis. Instead, I believe that these debates have also served to ensure the sorts of readjustments necessary for continuing effectiveness. Major debates engage the people, forcing "every member to take a position, to come to terms and to understand," rather than to rely simply on leadership, which tends to become invested in that set of views with which it is popularly identified.[33] And once a wider populace becomes engaged in such debates, the mass's pragmatic interest in unity often adds pressure for a resolution. Debate raises the popular consciousness, acting as an informal mechanism of popular education and possibly of enhanced democratic control over itself. Debate also enriches the ensuing ideologic and strategic positions.[34] As Lenin recognized, at least in theory if not always in his party practices, the oppressed "must in the long run be educated by political controversy to a deeper understanding of [their] position and tasks."[35]

Intraopposition conflict reveals the lack of a formal democratic process, but it also becomes a substitute forum for debate. Of course, it is not an ideal mechanism for resolving differences. As Saths Cooper admitted, "We've never seen democracy in practice, therefore it is hard for us to visualize democratic discussion without paranoia, discrimination and bullying."[36] Debates are still limited by intolerance. Smaller factions tend to attack more prevalent movements as monopolistic. Leaders of larger groups may become intolerant of dissent, particularly when the dissenters gain adherents as part of a transition. Such intolerance is fed by the desire for power, by frustration over remaining powerless, and by the experience of living under an oppressive regime. But for all of these excesses, the debate generated by such factional conflicts is the only such mechanism for resolution available under repression.

That debates and conflicts within the opposition can lead to an improved understanding of the situation and to greater effectiveness is indicated by the progress that the opposition has been made to date. This process always includes missteps and the indulgence of excesses. The Whiggish notion of inevitable historical progress remains a fantasy. An indirect process is the only way to move forward against oppression, and each reassessment, if not its results, shows that the actors do "feel the lash of Santayana's words" to learn from historical success and failure.[37] The shifts of focus between Black Consciousness, Charterism, and the unions, for instance, have formed part of a mutually enriching continuum, feeding into and correcting each one's tendency to concentrate mostly on race, nation, or class identity and their concordant strategies. After so many years of squabbles, the complete victory of one camp over another is unlikely, making practical if not ideological accommodation among them all the more necessary. Increasing mass participation has raised pressure for the opposition to cooperate, though it has not immediately subverted its differences, for popular consciousness itself is refined by debate. Ironically, debate is the only way to achieve lasting unity.

Much of the unity that has already been reached exists on the level of broad principle on which "pragmatism and recognition of human dignity" are often reconciled.[38] For instance, arguments in favor of postponing concern for economic justice until after national liberation have been challenged, particularly with the rising prominence of the labor unions and their economic concerns. Socialism is no longer referred to in a whisper; people now understand that it cannot be realized if it is kept a secret. Such consistency is defended as a practical necessity, for "history has proved time and again that in any struggle for a new society, if any form of oppression [is] left to be dealt with at a later date, then [it] is never dealt with and continues into the new society."[39] More and more activists are seeing socialism as consistent with nonracialism. Pragmatic compromises and alliances with whites can provide resources and thereby strengthen the working class in its struggle for major social and economic transformation, though the specific criteria needed to guide such decisions are still being debated.

Ideological disagreements persist, but differences are most evident on the level of strategy, where changing circumstances continue to elicit various responses. Economic growth and state concessions have been met with mass pragmatism, whereas economic decline and repression have led to militancy. This pattern will likely both continue and change, entailing controversy along the way. The state appears willing to make concessions, for as long as the state's constituency and the economy permit. The ANC will seek its own advantage in this situation for as long as it can, and it will struggle to control its followers, but not always with complete success. If the state resorts to further repression, frustrated expectations and continued deprivation will feed mass militancy, underground action, and further economic dislocation. While such developments may hasten a transition of power, unfortunately they would also make governance under majority rule more difficult. This dilemma hangs over the future of South Africa.

In my view, much of the more immediate remaining debate over strategy within the South African opposition centers on this long-term relation between the means and the ends of the struggle. On the one side is the belief that the means and ends must be consistent even if they slow the struggle, for otherwise more expedient means will cause undesired ends. As many Charterists argue, at least rhetorically, "We must live as democrats and non-racially now . . . to plant the seeds for the future."[40] By extension, issues of economic redistribution must be discussed at present if they are likely to be implemented in future. On the other side are those who contend that the ends justify any means; that without more expedient means, the primary goal of liberation will not be reached; and that the resulting frustration will bring consequences graver than any means used to gain liberation. As one activist has argued, "There are no better or worse means. Means are debatable and the criterion for the means is only if they help to win. . . . We may have a less democratic means to introduce a democratic end, or even have democracy to bolster non-democracy."[41] Freedom and necessity are in tension: The desire for any means to achieve liberation limits the freedom that others seek to embody certain ideals in the struggle for that liberation. Agreement on final goals has been clouded by differences over the strategic issues; such disagreements are often confused as ideological.

But even these two apparently contradictory views of the relation between means and ends can be reconciled in pragmatic, if not theoretical, terms. Even many of those committed to keeping democratic and nonracial ends and means consistent have had to compromise. They have often had to organize groups by means of separate residential areas or by interests, and they have had to recognize the need for strong leadership. At the same time, however, the values of nonracialism and democracy, according to Beyers Naude, "are important to people," even if they "delay revolution."[42] These principles have countered expediency and have promoted the coordination of different groups and the accountability of leadership, even if further democracy remains to be achieved. Excesses in either direction will continue to be corrected by conflict and debate. South Africa's future leaders will continue to compromise ideals but will also be challenged by those ideals to correct excesses, in a process that is as unavoidable in history as it is troubling.

The relation of means to ends is muddied not only by practical necessity but also by the fading distinction between the two. There is no final end of the struggle for democracy and justice in South Africa, for that struggle will surely continue even after the white minority's rule ends. Full democracy will not be the immediate outcome, as suggested through historical analogy by the original restrictions on the franchise and on "seditious" speech in the United States and by imperfections even in mature democracies. In South Africa, organizations will remain imperfectly participatory or effective, and personal consciousness will continue to develop, never reaching what one poet has described as the "last reactionary corner of the mind."[43] The central lesson of this struggle is that liberation is a continuous process without end. The dual powers of the centaur will always depend on each other and will always be in tension, with unpredictable results. The South African opposition continues to learn this lesson even as it lives the dialectic between pragmatic organization and idealistic principle.

# APPENDIX A

## *The Freedom Charter*

**Adopted at the Congress of the People on June 26, 1955.**

**Preamble:**

We, the people of South Africa, declare for all our country and the world to know:

That South Africa belongs to all who live in it, black and white, and that no government can justly claim authority unless it is based on the will of the people;

That our people have been robbed of their birthright to land, liberty and peace by a form of government founded on injustice and inequality;

That our country will never be prosperous or free until all our people live in brotherhood, enjoying equal rights and opportunities;

That only a democratic state, based on the will of the people, can secure to all their birthright without distinction of colour, race, sex or belief;

And therefore we, the people of South Africa, black and white, together equals, countrymen and brothers, adopt this Freedom Charter. And we pledge ourselves to strive together, sparing nothing of our strength and courage, until the democratic changes set out here have been won.

**The people shall govern!**

Every man and woman shall have the right to vote for and stand as a candidate for all bodies which make laws.

All the people shall be entitled to take part in the administration of the country.

The rights of the people shall be the same regardless of race, colour or sex.

All bodies of minority rule, advisory boards, councils and authorities shall be replaced by democratic organs of self-government.

**All national groups shall have equal rights!**

There shall be equal status in the bodies of the state, in the courts and in the schools for all national groups and races.

All national groups shall be protected by law against insults to their race and national pride.

All people shall have equal rights to use their own language and to develop their own culture and customs.

The preaching and practice of national, race or colour discrimination and contempt shall be a punishable crime.

All apartheid laws and practices shall be set aside.

**The people shall share in the country's wealth!**

The national wealth of our country, the heritage of all South Africans, shall be restored to the people.

The mineral wealth beneath the soil, the banks and monopoly industry, shall be transferred to the ownership of the people as a whole.

All other industries and trades shall be controlled to assist the well-being of the people.

All people shall have equal rights to trade where they choose, to manufacture and to enter all trades, crafts and professions.

**The land shall be shared among those who work it!**

Restriction of land ownership on a racial basis shall be ended, and all the land redivided among those who work it, to banish famine and land hunger.

The state shall help the peasants with implements, seeds, tractors and dams to save the soil and assist the tillers.

Freedom of movement shall be guaranteed to all who work on the land.

All shall have the right to occupy land wherever they choose.

People shall not be robbed of their cattle, and forced labour and farm prisons shall be abolished.

**All shall be equal before the law!**

No-one shall be imprisoned, deported or restricted without fair trial.

No-one shall be condemned by order of any government official.

The courts shall be representative of all the people.

Imprisonment shall only be for serious crimes against the people and shall aim at re-education, not vengeance.

The police force and army shall be open to all on an equal basis and shall be the helpers and protectors of the people.

All laws which discriminate on the grounds of race, colour or belief shall be repealed.

**All shall enjoy human rights!**

The law shall guarantee to all their right to speak, to organise, to meet together, to preach, to worship and to educate their children.

The privacy of the house from police raids shall be protected by law.

All shall be free to travel without restriction from countryside to town, from province to province, and from South Africa abroad.

Pass laws, permits and all other laws restricting these freedoms shall be abolished.

**There shall be work and security!**

All who work shall be free to form trade unions, to elect their officers and to make wage agreements with their employers.

The state shall recognise the right and duty of all to work and to draw full unemployment benefits.

Men and women of all races shall receive equal pay for equal work.

There shall be a 40-hour working week, a national minimum wage, paid annual leave and sick leave for all workers, and maternity leave on full pay for all working mothers.

Miners, domestic workers, farm workers and civil servants shall have the same rights as all others who work.

Child labour, compound labour, the tot system and contract labour shall be abolished.

**The doors of learning and culture shall be opened!**

The government shall discover, develop and encourage national talent for the enhancement of our cultural life.

All the cultural treasures of mankind shall be open to all, by free exchange of books, ideas and contacts with other lands.

The aim of education shall be to teach the youth to love their people and their culture, to honour human brotherhood, liberty and peace.

Education shall be free, compulsory, universal and equal for all children.

Higher education and technical training shall be opened to all by means of state allowances and scholarships awarded on the basis of merit.

Adult illiteracy shall be ended by a mass state education plan.

Teachers shall have the rights of all other citizens.

The colour bar in cultural life, in sport and in education shall be abolished.

**There shall be houses, education and comfort!**

All people shall have the right to live where they choose, to be decently housed, and to bring up their families in comfort and security.

Unused housing space shall be made available to the people.

Rent and prices shall be lowered, food shall be plentiful and no-one shall go hungry.

A preventative health scheme shall be run by the state.

Free medical care and hospital treatment shall be provided for all, with special care for mothers and young children.

Slums shall be demolished and new suburbs built where all shall have transport, roads, lighting, playing fields, creches and social centres.

The aged, orphans, the disabled and the sick shall be cared for by the state.

Rest, leisure and recreation shall be the right of all.

Fenced locations and ghettoes shall be abolished and laws which break up families shall be repealed.

**There shall be peace and friendship!**

South Africa shall be a fully independent state which respects the rights and sovereignty of all nations.

South Africa shall strive to maintain world peace and the settlement of all international disputes by negotiation, not war.

Peace and friendship among our people shall be secured by upholding the equal rights, opportunities and status of all.

The people of Basotholand, Bechuanaland and Swaziland shall be free to decide for themselves their own future.

The rights of all the people of Africa to independence and self-government shall be recognised, and shall be the basis of close cooperation.

**Let all who love their people and their country now say, as we say here: "These freedoms we will fight for, side by side, throughout our lives, until we have won our liberty."**

# APPENDIX B

## *Azanian Manifesto*

*Our struggle for national liberation is directed against the historically evolved system of racism and capitalism which* holds the people of Azania in bondage for the benefit of the small minority of the population, i.e. the capitalists and their allies, the white workers and the reactionary sections of the middle classes. The struggle against apartheid, therefore, is no more than the point of departure for our liberatory efforts.

*The Black working class inspired by revolutionary consciousness is the driving force of our struggle* for national self-determination in a unitary Azania. They alone can end the system as it stands today because they alone have nothing at all to lose. *They have a world to gain in a democratic, anti-racist and socialist Azania, where the interests of the workers shall be paramount through worker control of the means of production, distribution and exchange.* In the socialist republic of Azania the land and all that belongs to it shall be wholly owned and controlled by the Azanian people. The usage of the land and all that accrues to it shall be aimed at ending all exploitation.

It is the historic task of the Black working class and its organizations to mobilise the oppressed and exploited people in order to put an end to the system of oppression and exploitation by the white ruling class.

## Our Principles

Successful conduct of the national liberation struggle depends on the firm basis of principle whereby we will ensure that the liberation struggle will not be turned against our people by treacherous and opportunistic "leaders" and liberal influences. The most important of these principles are:

- *Anti-racism, anti-imperialism and anti-sexism.*
- *Anti-collaboration with the ruling class and all its allies and political instruments.*
- *Independent working class organization, free from bourgeois influences.*

## Our Rights

In accordance with these principles the following rights shall be entrenched in Azania:

- *The right to work.*
- *State provision of free and compulsory education for all. Education shall be geared towards liberating the Azanian people from all oppression, exploitation and ignorance.*
- *State provision of adequate and decent housing for all.*
- *State provision of free health, legal, recreational and other community services that will respond positively to the needs of the people.*

## Our Pledges

In order to bring into effect these rights of the Azanian people, we pledge ourselves to struggle tirelessly for:

- *The abolition of all laws, institutions and attitudes that discriminate against our people on the basis of colour, sex, religion, language or class.*

- *The re-integration of the bantustan human dumping grounds into a unitary Azania.*
- *The formation of trade unions that will heighten revolutionary worker consciousness.*
- *The development of one national culture inspired by socialist values.*

# NOTES

## Chapter 1

1. A plaque at the site of Harrison's claim, originally the Langlaagte Farm of G. C. Oosthuizen located on the outskirts of modern Johannesburg, notes that a letter was sent to Paul Kruger, president of the Transvaal, on June 9, 1886, to announce the discovery of gold. Since then, over ninety mines have produced 40,000 tons of gold (worth $390 per ounce at 1990 prices), 138,484 tons of uranium oxide, and 4,843 tons of silver.

2. For an overview of this period, see Davenport, *South Africa*; Roux, *Time Longer Than Rope*; and Thompson, *A History of South Africa.*

3. A 1978 study showed that South Africa's gini coefficient, a measure of income inequality, was the highest of any of the countries for which data were available. See Wilson and Ramphele, *Uprooting Poverty*, p. 18.

4. See, for example, Greenberg, *Race and State in Capitalist Development*; Wolpe, *Race, Class and the Apartheid State*; Legasick, *Class and Nationalism in South African Protest*; and Johnstone, *Race, Class and Gold.*

5. See, for example, Saul and Gelb, *The Crisis in South Africa.*

6. For example, see Lipton, *Capitalism and Apartheid.*

7. Ruth First, "After Soweto: A Response," *Review of the African Political Economy*, 7 (September-December 1976), p. 97.

8. See Hirschman, *Exit Voice and Loyalty*, esp. pp. 122–23.

9. Brewer, *After Soweto*, p. 51, and for a more general discussion of Inkatha, see pp. 338–406. See also Adam and Moodley, *South Africa Without Apartheid*, p. 89.

10. See Therborn, *The Ideology of Power and the Power of Ideology.* For a further discussion of race, nation, and class as central ideological concepts in South Africa, see Lebamang Sebidi, "The Dynamics of the Black Struggle in South Africa: A Critical Analysis," Lecture 6, New Horizons Project, Roodeport, September 1984.

11. Karl Marx, "The Eighteenth Brumaire of Louis Bonaparte," in McLellan, ed., *Karl Marx: Selected Writings*, pp. 317–18.

12. For a discussion of the importance of such superimposition of social

categories, see Dahrendorf, *Class and Class Conflict in Industrial Society*, chap. 6; Enloe, *Ethnic Conflict and Political Development*; and Kornhauser, *The Politics of Mass Society.*

13. Quoting Lybon Mabasa, "The AZAPO Conference," *Work in Progress* 30 (February 1984), p. 10.

14. It was for this reason that Adolf Hitler argued that racism could be useful in domination, regardless of any scientific basis for the concept. See Montagu, *Man's Most Dangerous Myth*, p. 50.

15. Patterson, *Slavery and Social Death.*

16. The scientific invalidity of race is discussed in No Sizwe, *One Azania, One Nation.*

17. Situational theories of race are developed and defended in Rex, *Race Relations in Sociological Theory*; Young, *The Politics of Cultural Pluralism*; Horowitz, *Ethnic Groups in Conflict*; and Kuper, *Race, Class and Power.*

18. Biko, *I Write What I Like*, p. 68.

19. Interview with author, February 1988.

20. South African Students Organization, "Policy Manifesto," 1970, p. 1.

21. Barney Pityana, "Power and Change in South Africa," in Welsh and van der Mewre, eds., *Student Perspectives in South Africa*, p. 189.

22. Polanyi, *The Great Transformation*, p. 169.

23. See Jean L. Cohen, "Strategy or Identity: New Theoretical Paradigms and Contemporary Social Movements," *Social Research* 52 (Winter 1985), p. 663.

24. See Gusfield, "Social Movements and Social Change: Perspectives of Linearity and Fluidity," *Research in Social Movements, Conflict and Change* 4 (1981), pp. 317–39.

25. Gramsci, *Selections from the Prison Notebooks*, p. 238.

26. See Thompson, *The Political Mythology of Apartheid.*

27. H. Davis, *Toward a Marxist Theory of Nationalism*, p. 71.

28. Quoting Pallo Jordan of the ANC National Executive, in Diepen, ed., *The National Question in South Africa*, p. 10.

29. Quoting "Terror" Lekota, UDF publicity secretary, from correspondence with the author, April 1988.

30. Gerhart, *Black Power*, p. 16.

31. Anderson, *Imagined Communities.* For further discussion of the ascriptive conception of Afrikaner nationalism, as contrasted with the ANC's and the UDF's more voluntaristic conception, see Adam and Moodley, *South Africa Without Apartheid*, p. 28.

32. Emergent Afrikaner nationalism faced a similar dilemma in forging unity among diverse regional interests. See Adam and Moodley, *South Africa Without Apartheid*, p. 46.

33. See Cohen, "Strategy or Identity"; and McCarthy and Zald, "Resource Mobilization and Social Movements."

34. Gusfield, "Social Movements and Social Change."

35. Gramsci, *Selections from the Prison Notebooks*, p. 238.

36. See Foszia Fischer, "Class Consciousness Among Colonized Workers in South Africa," in Schlemmer and Webster, eds., *Change, Reform, and Economic Growth in South Africa*, pp. 198–201.

37. Max Weber, "Class, Status, Party," in Gerth and Mills, eds., *From Max Weber*, p. 184.

38. Parkin, *Marxism and Class Theory*, p. 139.

39. Lukács, *History and Class Consciousness*, p. 164.

40. E. P. Thompson, *The Making of the English Working Class*, p. 832.

41. See, for instance, Karl Marx, "Preface to a Critique of Political Economy," in McLellan, ed., *Selected Writings*, pp. 388–91.

42. Karl Marx, "The German Ideology," in ibid., p. 164.

43. Ibid., p. 160.

44. Nolutshungu, *Changing South Africa*, p. 41.

45. Skocpol, *States and Social Revolutions*; see also Moore, *Social Origins of Dictatorship and Democracy.*

46. See Skocpol, *States and Social Revolutions*, p. 95, in which she argues that the 1905 crisis was defused by the Russian czar's judicious withdrawal from Manchuria. She makes no comment on the disunity of the opposition at the time, which Lenin implies was at least partially to blame for the opposition's failure to take advantage of this crisis. See Wolfe, *Three Who Made a Revolution*, p. 341.

47. Max Weber, *The Protestant Ethic and the Spirit of Capitalism*, pp. 90–91.

48. See, for instance, Johnson, *Revolutionary Change.*

49. Tocqueville, *The Old Regime and the French Revolution*, p. 177. The role of intellectuals in precipitating the French Revolution is also highlighted in Brinton, *The Anatomy of Revolution*, p. 43.

50. For a discussion of this debate in Russia, see Haimson, *The Russian Marxists and the Origins of Bolshevism.*

51. See Schama, *Citizens: A Chronicle of the French Revolution*, pp. 639–44.

52. Haimson, *The Russian Marxists*, pp. 127–35.

53. Lenin, *State and Revolution*, p. 97; "What Is to Be Done?" and "Left Wing Communism—An Infantile Disorder," in Tucker, ed., *The Lenin Anthology*, pp. 101, 556.

54. Quoted in Hammond, *Lenin on Trade Unions and Revolution*, pp. 33, 27.

55. Gramsci, *Selections from the Prison Notebooks*, p. 181.

56. Ibid., pp. 169–70.

57. Karl Marx, "Thesis on Feuerbach," in McLellan, ed., *Selected Writings*, p. 156. For an interpretation of Marx that emphasizes his idealism, see Avinieri, *The Social and Political Thought of Karl Marx.*

58. Weber, *The Protestant Ethic and the Spirit of Capitalism*, p. 183. For an interpretation of Weber that emphasizes his materialism, see Parkin, *Max Weber*, esp. p. 58.

59. Lenin, "Two Tactics of Social Democracy in the Democratic Revolution," in Tucker, ed., *The Lenin Anthology*, pp. 121–22.

60. Gramsci, *Selections from the Prison Notebooks*, p. 185. The pitfalls for any social movement that dilutes inspiration by relying too heavily on organization are discussed in Piven and Cloward, *Poor Peoples' Movements.* The importance of organizing material resources to inspire opposition is discussed in Goldrich, "Political Organization and Politicization of the Poblador," pp. 176–202.

61. Adam and Moodley, *South Africa Without Apartheid*, p. 7.

62. Rosa Luxemburg's distinction between a revolutionary rupture and a more fundamental revolutionary challenge is applied to South Africa in Brewer, *After Soweto*, p. 99.

63. Hunt, *Politics, Culture, and Class in the French Revolution*, p. 13.

64. Ibid., p. 10.

65. Quoting Trotsky, in Deutscher, *The Prophet Armed*, p. 193.

## Chapter 2

1. Quoting from the Congress of South African Trade Unions, *Notes on Political Organizations*, internal document, p. 2. For a full description of this period, see Lodge, *Black Politics*, chap. 1; Karis and Carter, *From Protest to Challenge*; and Wilson and Thompson, eds., *The Oxford History of South Africa.*

2. Lodge, *Black Politics*, p. 6.

3. Ibid., p. 9.

4. Gerhart, *Black Power*, pp. 91–92.

5. Lodge, *Black Politics*, p. 21; Gerhart, *Black Power*, p. 55.

6. See "Business Cycles in South Africa During the Post-War Period, 1946 to 1968," *Bulletin of the South African Reserve Bank*, September 1970, pp. 21–46.

7. The history of the Charter is contained in Suttner and Cronin, *Thirty Years of the Freedom Charter.* A more critical interpretation can be found in the Pan Africanist Congress's publication *The Rise of Azania*; and in the Azanian Labour Monitoring Group, "The Freedom Charter and Trade

Unions in South Africa," (photocopy), July 1987. The lack of debate at the Congress of the People is acknowledged by Lodge in *Black Politics*, p. 72.

8. COSATU Johannesburg Local Branch Executive, interview with author, June 1988.

9. Fatton, *Black Consciousness in South Africa*, p. 17.

10. Mandela, *No Easy Walk to Freedom*, pp. 178–79.

11. Gerhart, *Black Power*, p. 223.

12. For further background, see Gerhart, *Black Power*, esp. chaps. 5 and 6; and Lodge, *Black Politics*, esp. p. 85.

13. From Anton Lembede's 1946 "seven cardinal principles," reprinted in Hirson, *Year of Fire, Year of Ash*, p. 315.

14. Lodge, *Black Politics*, p. 202.

15. Gerhart, *Black Power*, p. 301.

16. Cassim Saloojee, interview with author, February 1988.

17. Ronnie Kasil, "Peoples' War, Revolution and Insurrection," *Sechaba* (April 1986), p. 3; and "Present Tasks of the Azanian Revolution," *Ikwezi* 13 (October 1979), p. 30.

18. *Mayibuye* 3:3 (February 28, 1969), p. 10; Lodge, *Black Politics*, p. 244, and for a comparison of Poqo and MK, see p. 231.

19. See Carl Keyter, "Lecture 11: The PAC, New Horizons Project."

20. See, for example, Nkondo, ed., *Turfloop Testimony*.

21. Biko, *I Write What I Like*, p. 67.

22. Robert Davies, "Nationalization, Socialization and the Freedom Charter," University of York Conference Paper (September 29 to October 2, 1986), pp. 7–10.

23. Republic of South Africa, Central Statistical Services, *South African Statistics, 1988*, Table 7.5. See also Davies, "Nationalization, Socialization and the Freedom Charter," pp. 4–9; Braverman, "The African Working Class: Recent Changes and New Perspectives," *African Communist* 59 (1974), p. 52.

24. Simkins and Hindson, "The Division of Labour in South Africa," pp. 7–9.

25. Lodge, *Black Politics*, p. 11.

26. As early as 1964, a survey suggested that 64 percent of urban blacks claimed to feel no tribal loyalty. Hanf et al., *South Africa: The Prospects for Peaceful Change*, p. 340. See also Vail, *The Creation of Tribalism*.

27. Hirson, *Year of Fire, Year of Ash*, pp. 63, 94–99; South African Institute of Race Relations, *Topical Briefing*, May 7, 1984.

28. Brooks and Brickhill, *Whirlwind Before the Storm*, esp. chap. 2.

29. Despite dramatically different circumstances, a comparison of discriminatory education in South Africa and prerevolutionary Russia is suggestive. Compare, for example, statements by South African Prime

Minister Verwoerd about the importance of not educating blacks for better jobs when "there is no place for [them] . . . above the level of certain forms of labor," with the statement of Russian Czar Alexander's education minister, Delyanov, that "the children of coachmen, servants, cooks, laundresses, small shopkeepers and suchlike should not be encouraged to rise above the sphere in which they were born." Lodge, *Black Politics*, p. 116; Wolfe, *Three Who Made a Revolution*, p. 68.

30. For instance, the University of the North (Turfloop) in the early 1970s was a meeting ground for many future leaders, including Lybon Mabasa and Ishmael Mkhabela, now of AZAPO, Cyril Ramaphosa, founding general secretary of the National Union of Mineworkers, and Frank Chikane, general secretary of the South African Council of Churches in the late 1980s.

31. Hirson, *Year of Fire, Year of Ash*, p. 41, quoting a secret Broederbond document of 1943.

32. Jay Naidoo, interview with author, March 1988.

33. Hirson, *Year of Fire, Year of Ash*, p. 284.

34. One such anecdote of how the formal curriculum was subverted by students' interpretations is reported in "Student Rioters Inspired by French Revolution," *Rand Daily Mail*, November 6, 1976.

35. A list of those books seized with the arrest of Black Consciousness leaders in 1975—attesting to a breadth of interest not easily contained—includes works by Frantz Fanon, Leon Trotsky, Che Guevara, James Baldwin, Plato, Leopold Senghor, Machiavelli, Paulo Freire, Baron and Sweezy, Samir Amin, and Julius Nyerere.

36. Kgelema Mothlahte, interview with author, April 1988.

37. See H. Davis, *Toward a Marxist Theory of Nationalism*, chap. 8.

38. Gerhart, *Black Power*, p. 275. See also Fanon, *The Wretched of the Earth* and *Toward the African Revolution*; and Brewer, *After Soweto*, p. 221.

39. As discussed by Dr. Mamphela Ramphele, interview with author, August 1986. See also Heribert Adam, "The Rise of Black Consciousness," *Race* 15:2 (October 1973), p. 154; and Cabral, *Revolution in Guinea*.

40. Interviews with author, July 1986 and February 1988. See also Gerhart, *Black Power*, p. 275.

41. Biko, *I Write What I Like*, p. 31. See also Boesak, *Black and Reformed*, esp. pp. 1–21.

42. Interview with author, March 1988.

43. The pervasiveness of apartheid is described in Biko, *I Write What I Like*, p. 27. The bond forged by this experience is denigrated as abstractly political—in my view incorrectly—in Adam and Moodley, *South Africa Without Apartheid*, p. 49.

44. Biko, *I Write What I Like*, p. 68.

45. Interview with author, March 1988.

46. Interview with author, February 1988.

47. Biko, *I Write What I Like*, p. 105.

48. See, for example, "The Repugnant Elements of White Culture," submitted as evidence in the "SASO Nine" trial (May 1974); and Biko, *I Write What I Like*, p. 23.

49. Interview with author, March 1988.

50. The exclusion of whites from BC was described as a "tactical matter" in Ben Khoapa, "The New Black," *Azania News* 10:1–3 (January-March 1975), p. 8.

51. Quoting Ben Khoapa in Fatton, *Black Consciousness*, p. 77.

52. Interview with author, February 1988.

53. See Biko, *I Write What I Like*, p. 63.

54. Ibid., p. 25. See also Henry Isaacs, "The Emergence and Impact of the Black Conscious Movement," *Ikwezi* 2:4 (December 1976), p. 11.

55. Biko, *I Write What I Like*, pp. 90–91; SASPU, *National Student*, 1 (1977). Interview with Bishop Manas Buthelezi, *Rand Daily Mail*, April 7, 1976.

56. Isaacs, "Message from the Vice President," in "SASO on the Attack," Durban, 1973, p. 2.

57. See Nengwekhulu, "Community Action and Development," p. 3., SASO internal document, from the Karis–Gerhart Collection.

58. See Fatton, *Black Consciousness*, p. 99.

59. Boesak, *Black and Reformed*, p. 55; Brewer, *After Soweto*, p. 227.

60. For examples of public pronouncements of nonviolence by BC adherents, see Nolutshungu, *Changing South Africa*, p. 172; and interview with Saths Cooper, *Rand Daily Mail*, April 29, 1976.

61. "SASO Nine Found Guilty," *Rand Daily Mail*, December 16, 1976.

62. Interview with author, August 1988.

63. Biko, *I Write What I Like*, p. 90.

64. Interview with author, April 1988.

65. See Biko, *I Write What I Like*, pp. 50, 89; Nolutshungu, *Changing South Africa*, p. 158; and Hirson, *Year of Fire, Year of Ash*, p. 300.

66. Black Peoples' Convention, "Mafeking Manifesto," May 1976.

67. Jay Naidoo, former BC adherent and now general secretary of COSATU, interview with author, March 1988.

68. Adam, "The Rise of Black Consciousness," esp. p. 156.

69. Interview with author, April 1988.

70. As discussed by Aubrey Mokoena, interview with author, February 1988.

71. See Garvey, "A History of Liberation Organizations in South Africa," *Azania Worker*, 4:1 (February 1987), p. 9.

72. Patrick Laurence, "Would Biko Have Joined the Non-Racial Movement Today?" *The Star*, September 12, 1987.

73. Gerhart, *Black Power*, pp. 257, 284.

74. As discussed by Philip Dlamini, interview with author, February 1988. Sobukwe's criticism of BC is reported in Andrew Silk, "Robert Sobukwe of the PAC," *Africa Report* (May-June 1975), p. 19.

75. Interview with author, March 1988.

76. See Patrick Laurence, "Beneath the Faded Pictures, the Ghost of Sobukwe Rises," *Weekly Mail*, September 19, 1986.

77. Hanf et al., *South Africa: The Prospects of Peaceful Change*, p. 250.

78. Interview with author, April 1988.

79. See "South African Students' Organization Historical Background," 1970, Karis–Gerhart Collections; Biko, *I Write What I Like*, p. 10; and Hirson, *Year of Fire, Year of Ash*, pp. 70–71.

80. See the University Christian Movement General Secretary's Report, "How It Really Happened" (n.d.). Among those who became friends initially through the Student Christian Movement and later joined BC were future AZAPO leaders Griffiths Zabala, Ishmael Mkhabela, and Lybon Mabasa, as well as Cyril Ramaphosa, founding general secretary of the National Union of Mineworkers. As described by Griffiths Zabala and Tom Manthata in interviews with author, March 1988.

81. For a full discussion of the founding of SASO, see Gerhart, *Black Power*, chap. 8; and Fatton, *Black Consciousness*.

82. SASO, "Policy Manifesto," 1970.

83. Ibid.

84. SASO, "Leadership Training Programme," 1972, p. 5.

85. Interview with author, August 1986.

86. Hirson, *Year of Fire, Year of Ash*, pp. 73, 86.

87. Ibid., p. 312. Tiro's rhetoric resembled that of the black American abolitionist Frederick Douglass and of the founder of the PAC, Robert Sobukwe.

88. Fanyana Mazibuko, interview with author, April 1988.

89. Buthelezi, ed., "The Black People's Convention," p. 5.

90. Lodge, *Black Politics*, p. 323; Hirson, *Year of Fire, Year of Ash*, p. 107.

91. "The Black People's Convention," in Sipho Buthelezi, ed. "South Africa: Historical Background and Basic Documents," 1979, Karis-Gerhart Collection, p. 7.

92. As discussed by Tom Manthata, interview with author, March 1988; Mamphela Ramphele, interview with author, August 1986.

93. Interview with author, February 1989.

94. Brewer, *After Soweto*, p. 226.

95. Interview with author, April 1988.

96. Hirson, *Year of Fire, Year of Ash*, p. 200.

97. As discussed with Mamphela Ramphele, interview with author, August 1986; Peter Jones, interview with author, May 1988; Ben Khoapa, interview with author, February 1989. See also Republic of South Africa, *Report of the Eloff Commission*; Hirson, *Year of Fire, Year of Ash*, p. 160.

98. Interview with author, February 1989.

99. Nolutshungu, *Changing South Africa*, pp. 203, n.16.

100. Peter Jones, interview with author, May 1988. Jones succeeded Khoapa in 1977 as the executive director of BCP.

101. See Pandelani Nefolovhodwe, "Roots of BC Trade Unionism," *Work in Progress* 33 (1984), pp. 21–23.

102. Samson Ndou, founding official of BAWU, interview with author, April 1988.

103. Biko, *I Write What I Like*, pp. 50, 71; Hirson, *Year of Fire, Year of Ash*, p. 293.

104. Congress of South African Trade Unions, *Notes on Political Organizations*, chapter on Black Consciousness, p. 5.

105. S. Davis, *Apartheid's Rebels*, p. 26; Y. M. Dadoo, "South Africa—A Time of Challenge," *African Communist* 56 (1974), p. 43; Hirson, *Year of Fire, Year of Ash*, pp. 129, 156; Republic of South Africa, Central Statistical Service, *South African Statistics, 1988*, Table 7.31.

106. Pandelani Nefolovhodwe, interview with author, March 1988.

107. Brewer, *After Soweto*, p. 76; Hirson, *Year of Fire, Year of Ash*, pp. 127–30.

108. Friedman, *Building Tomorrow Today*, pp. 44, 61. By 1978, the BAWU's efforts at organizing workers were further hampered by political infighting between the ANC and PAC sympathizers among its leadership. See *Africa Confidential*, April 28, 1978, p. 8.

109. Alec Erwin, interview with author, March 1988; Friedman, *Building Tomorrow Today*, p. 47.

110. Institute for Industrial Education, *The Durban Strikes, 1973*, p. 94. See also Hirson, *Year of Fire, Year of Ash*, pp. 133–43; and Lodge, *Black Politics*, pp. 326–28.

111. See the quotations from Muntu Myeza, "Workers Are Being Forced to Accept the Charter," *City Press*, July 26, 1987; Gerhart, *Black Power*, pp. 297–98.

112. Interview with author, May 1988.

113. Hirson, *Year of Fire, Year of Ash*, p. 107.

114. Smangaliso Mkhatshwa, "Putting the Black Renaissance Convention into Correct Perspective," *Reality* 7:2 (May 1975), pp. 7–9.

115. See Steven Gelb, "Making Sense of the Crisis," *Transformation* 5

(1987), pp. 33–50; Brooks and Brickhill, *Whirlwind Before the Storm*, pp. 201–2; Hirson, *Year of Fire, Year of Ash*, pp. 123–25.

116. See Brooks and Brickhill, *Whirlwind Before the Storm*, pp. 201–2; and Kane-Berman, *Soweto*, p. 50.

117. Kane-Berman, *Soweto*, p. 51; Brooks and Brickhill, *Whirlwind Before the Storm*, p. 204.

118. "Blacks Are Losing Hope, Poll Finds," *The Star*, June 12, 1975.

119. Brooks and Brickhill, *Whirlwind Before the Storm*, p. 178; Kane-Berman, *Soweto*, pp. 48–83.

120. Hirson, *Year of Fire, Year of Ash*, p. 4.

121. Brooks and Brickhill, *Whirlwind Before the Storm*, p. 41.

122. See "No High Schools Will Be Built Here," *The Star*, June 9, 1975; Kane-Berman, *Soweto*, p. 110.

123. See, for example, "Black Anger Starts Young," *Sunday Times*, June 13, 1976; "Our Children Blame Us," *Rand Daily Mail*, June 21, 1976.

124. Kane-Berman, *Soweto*, pp. 80–83.

125. See, for example, Duncan Innes and Dan O'Meara, "Class Formation and Ideology: The Transkei Region," *Review of African Political Economy* 7 (September-December 1976), esp. pp. 71–82.

126. Kane-Berman, *Soweto*, p. 14.

127. Biko, *I Write What I Like*, pp. 75–76.

128. Wilmot James, "Nolutshungu's South Africa," *Social Dynamics*, 12:1 (1986), p. 45.

129. Institute for Black Research, *Soweto*, p. 8. Support for violence was also higher for respondents 46 years of age and older.

130. Hanf et al., *South Africa*, p. 326.

131. Interview with author, February 1989.

132. Lodge, *Black Politics*, p. 326.

133. The "wage gap" between white and African workers in 1972 and 1976 increased from R377 to R594 in mining, from R297 to R420 in manufacturing, and from R312 to R414 in construction. See Brooks and Brickhill, *Whirlwind Before the Storm*, pp. 202–4.

134. Letter from Bishop Tutu to Prime Minister Vorster, May 8, 1976.

135. Interview with author, February 1989.

136. Cassim Saloojee, interview with author, February 1988.

137. Eric Dlangamandla, interview with author, May 1988; see also Hirson, *Year of Fire, Year of Ash*, p. 191.

138. Biko, *I Write What I Like*, p. 134.

139. Brooks and Brickhill, *Whirlwind Before the Storm*, p. 76; see also Lodge, *Black Politics*, p. 325.

140. Manas Buthelezi, interview with author, February 1988.

141. Anonymous, interview with author, March 1988.

142. Bongi Mkhabela, former general secretary of SASM, interview with author, March 1988; Brooks and Brickhill, *Whirlwind Before the Storm*, p. 7.

143. Interview with author, May 1988.

144. Interview with author, April 1988.

145. See S. Davis, *Apartheid's Rebels*, pp. 28–29.

146. Fatton, *Black Consciousness*, p. 100; see also Tebello Motopanyane, "How June 16 Demo Was Planned," *Sechaba*, September 1977, pp. 49–59.

147. Kane-Berman, *Soweto*, p. 146; Hirson, *Year of Fire, Year of Ash*, p. 245.

148. See "The National Question," *Sechaba*, November 1980, p. 7; Moeti, "Ten Years of Soweto Uprising," *Sechaba*, June 1986, p. 2.

149. I am here disagreeing with Hirson, *Year of Fire, Year of Ash*, esp. p. 104; and S. Davis, *Apartheid's Rebels*, pp. 26–31.

150. Brewer, *After Soweto*, p. 79.

151. Brooks and Brickhill, *Whirlwind Before the Storm*, p. 250.

152. Kane-Berman, *Soweto*, p. 113.

153. Interview with author, May 1988.

154. Brooks and Brickhill, *Whirlwind Before the Storm*, pp. 63, 256–60. An official government commission conservatively estimated that 575 were killed during the uprising. See also Lodge, *Black Politics*, p. 330.

155. Biko, *I Write What I Like*, pp. 146–47.

156. Hanf et al., *South Africa*, p. 322; Hirson, *Year of Fire, Year of Ash*, p. 278.

157. Nengwekhulu, "The Meaning of Black Consciousness in the Struggle for Liberation in South Africa," United Nations Centre Against Apartheid, New York, 16 July 1976, p. 8; Brooks and Brickhill, *Whirlwind Before the Storm*, p. 132.

158. Cassim Saloojee, interview with author, February 1988.

159. Quoted in "Biko Lives," *Revolutionary Worker*, September 8, 1986, p. 3.

160. Hirson, *Year of Fire, Year of Ash*, p. 234.

161. Interview with author, May 1988.

162. Martin Ramokjadi, interview with author, April 1988.

163. Fatton, *Black Consciousness*, p. 129.

## Chapter 3

1. Frank Chikane, interview with author, April 1988. Among the new ideas discussed in the SASO were the writings of Richard Turner, author of

*The Eye of the Needle*, a friend of Biko, and a strong advocate for socialism.

2. Diliza Mji, interview with author, March 1988.

3. Interview with author, February 1988. For further discussion of the tensions between SASO and BPC and their implications, see Mokoeana, "Black Consciousness in Perspective," *City Press*, April 20, 1984, p. 2; and the rebuttal by Muntu Myeza, "Losers Can't Define the Struggle . . . We've Got the Baton Now," *City Press*, April 27, 1984.

4. Lodge, *Black Politics*, p. 37.

5. Diliza Mji, interview with author, March 1988.

6. *SASO News Bulletin* 1.1 (June 1977), pp. 2–3.

7. Ibid., p. 3.

8. Interview with author, March 1988.

9. Interview with author, March 1988.

10. Bishop Manas Buthelezi, interview with author, February 1988.

11. Nengwekhulu, "Speech to the Assembly of the IUEF," November 22, 1976, Geneva, p. 1.

12. Biko, *I Write What I Like*, p. 151.

13. Ibid., p. 148.

14. "Factors Determining Liberation in S.A.: The Socio-Economic Aspect," *SASO News Bulletin* 1.1 (June 1977), p. 8.

15. See, for example, *Ikwezi* 6 (August 1977), p. 12.

16. Orkin, "Of Sacrifice and Struggle," p. 454.

17. Biko, *I Write What I Like*, p. 148.

18. Interview with author, May 1988.

19. Interview with author, May 1988.

20. Ben Khoapa, interview with author, February 1989.

21. Interview with author, May 1988.

22. Peter Jones, interview with author, May 1988.

23. Peter Jones, interview with author, May 1988.

24. Correspondence with author, April 1988.

25. Lodge, *Black Politics*, p. 310.

26. Orkin, "Of Sacrifice and Struggle," p. 414.

27. Interview with author, April 1988.

28. Interview with author, April 1988.

29. *Azapo Education Policy* (xerox, n.d.), p. 14.

30. See Wauchope, "The Role of the Workers," September 1979, p. 4.

31. Father Smangaliso Mkhatshwa, interview with author, April 1988.

32. See "Zwelakhe Sisulu," *Leadership SA*, October 1986, esp. pp. 86–88; Maphai, "Resistance in South Africa: AZAPO and the National Forum," 1986; and Keyter, "The Azanian Peoples Organization," New Horizons Project, July 1984.

33. Interview with author, April 1988.

34. Z. Sisulu, "Nkondo Spells It Out," *Sunday Post*, October 7, 1979, p. 5.

35. Ibid.

36. Brewer, *After Soweto*, p. 269.

37. See A. Akhalwaya, "Nkondo Out," *Rand Daily Mail*, January 15, 1980.

38. Interview with author, March 1988.

39. Interview with author, March 1988.

40. S. Davis, *Apartheid's Rebels*, p. 57; Kane-Berman, *Soweto*, pp. 144–45.

41. Interview with author, March 1988. "Panel beaters" refers to township residents who make a living banging dented car bodies back into shape. Mogane uses the analogy to describe the process of ideological education or indoctrination.

42. "Yesterday's Men: The PAC and ANC," *The World*, June 12, 1977.

43. Anonymous.

44. Alfred Nzo, "ANC Calls for Unity," *Sechaba*, October 1979, p. 18.

45. S. Davis, *Apartheid's Rebels*, pp. 57, 28.

46. Lodge, *Black Politics*, p. 340.

47. Slovo, "People's War," *Sechaba*, April 1983, p. 10.

48. See Joe Ngwenya, "A Further Contribution on the National Question," *African Communist* 67 (1976), pp. 48–59; R. S. Nyameko and G. Singh, "The Role of Black Consciousness in the South African Revolution," *African Communist* 68 (1977), pp. 34–47.

49. Alfred Nzo, "ANC Calls for Unity," *Sechaba*, October 1979, p. 16. See also Toussaint, "Fallen Among the Liberals: An Ideology of Black Consciousness Examined," *African Communist* 77 (1979), pp. 18–30; and Brewer, *After Soweto*, p. 255.

50. Interview with author, May 1988.

51. "South Africa: The Black Exiles," *Africa Confidential*, February 28, 1979, pp. 1–2.

52. By 1980, polls suggested that the ANC had replaced BC as the most popular opposition group among black South Africans. See Orkin, "Of Sacrifice and Struggle," p. 454.

53. Interview with author, March 1988.

54. Interview with author, March 1988.

55. Interview with author, June 1988.

56. See Gerhart, *Black Power*, pp. 107, 116; Lodge, *Black Politics*, p. 27.

57. Bunman, "From Hell Hole to Blessing," p. 127. See also Naidoo and Sachs, *Robben Island*.

58. See Thami Mkhwanazi, "My Years on Robben Island," *Weekly*

*Mail*, August 21, 1987; "No Man Was an Island on Robben Island," *The Star*, April 15, 1988, p. 11.

59. Interview with author, February 1988.

60. Interview with author, April 1988.

61. Interview with author, August 1986.

62. Interview with author, June 1988.

63. Interview with author, March 1988. See also Dan Sechaba Montsitsi, "Lessons from 1976," in National Union of South African Students, ed. *Beyond Reform*, p. 39.

64. Gerhart, *Black Power*, p. 190.

65. Joe Ngwenya, "A Further Contribution . . . ," *African Communist* 67 (1976), p. 56.

66. Azchar Bhaum, interview with author, April 1988. See also Fatton, *Black Consciousness*, p. 129.

67. Correspondence with author, April 1988.

68. Orkin, "Of Sacrifice and Struggle," pp. 404–5. See also Brewer, *After Soweto*, p. 7.

69. Vincent Mogane, interview with author, March 1988.

70. Cooper, "Address," 1983 AZAPO Congress, p. 4.

71. Quoted in Fatton, *Black Consciousness*, p. 138.

## Chapter 4

1. Republic of South Africa, Central Statistical Service, *South African Statistics, 1988*, Table 21.9. See also David Kaplan, "The Current Upswing in the South African Economy and the International Capitalist Crisis," *Work in Progress* 16 (February 1981), p. 5; and Gelb, "Making Sense of the Crisis," p. 42.

2. S. Davis, *Apartheid's Rebels*, p. 98.

3. *The Star*, February 20, 1984, p. 8.

4. Kaplan, "The Current Upswing," p. 5.

5. Republic of South Africa, Central Statistical Service, *South African Statistics, 1988*, Table 5.39.

6. "Student Committee Against the New Constitution," August 4, 1983 (photocopy).

7. Republic of South Africa, Central Statistical Service, *South African Statistics, 1988*, Table 1.7.

8. Kenneth W. Grundy, *The Militarization of South African Politics*, pp. 19–20. See also S. Davis, *Apartheid's Rebels*, p. 180; and Frankel, *Pretoria's Praetorians*.

9. Wolfe, *Three Who Made a Revolution*, p. 120.

10. Popo Molefe, "Responses to State Strategy," in National Union of South African Students, ed., *Beyond Reform*, pp. 28–29. See also Cassim Saloojee, "The Role of the Extra-Parliamentary Opposition in the Democratization of South Africa: A UDF Perspective" (Speech, 1988).

11. See Cole, *Crossroads*, esp. pp. 60–68.

12. Tom Manthata, interview with author, March 1988.

13. Interview with author, April 1988. See also Tom Lodge, "Freedom in Our Lifetime," *Reality*, November 1986, pp. 6–10.

14. "United Front" (anonymous, n.d.), p. 9.

15. Bundy, "Street Sociology and Pavement Politics." See also Shaun Johnson, "The Soldiers of Luthuli," in Johnson, *South Africa*, pp. 74–152.

16. Mark Swilling, interview with author, April 1988. See also Molteno, *1980: Students Struggle for Their Schools.*

17. See Neville Alexander, "Ten Years of Educational Crisis: The Resonance of 1976" (manuscript); SASPU, *State of the Nation*, May 1985, p. 9.

18. See Committee of 81, *Manifesto to the People of Azania*, May 14, 1980, p. 4.

19. See Matiwana and Walters, *The Struggle for Democracy*; "Making Apartheid Unworkable: The People's Mass Resistance," *Sechaba*, November 1984, pp. 5–13.

20. Interview with author, February 1988.

21. A. Akhaluaya, "AZAPO on Race, Class—and White Liberals," *Rand Daily Mail*, January 28, 1981.

22. Adam and Moodley, *South Africa Without Apartheid*, p. 71.

23. Interview with author, March 1988.

24. "TIC Revived: The Case Against," *Work in Progress* 26 (1983), p. 18.

25. Popo Molefe, in National Union of South African Students, eds., *Beyond Reform*, p. 29.

26. See Alexander, *Sow the Wind*; No Sizwe (pseudonym for Alexander), *One Azania, One Nation.*

27. The National Forum Committee included, among others, Bishop Tutu, then at the SACC, Dr. Allan Boesak, a prominent Cape Town minister, R. A. M. Saloojee of the Natal Indian Congress, and Dr. Motlana from the Soweto Committee of Ten, all of whom came to be identified with the UDF. They were joined by Phiroshaw Camay, general secretary of the CUSA union federation; Emma Mashinini, founder of the CCAWUSA union described in Chapter 6; and Saths Cooper, Lybon Mabasa, Kehla Mthembu, and Ishmael Mkhabela, from AZAPO. Bishop Manas Buthelezi, Dr. Alexander, Rev. Lebamang John Sebidi, and Tom Manthata of the Soweto Committee of Ten also were members.

28. Vincent Mogane, interview with author, March 1988; Molefe Tsele, interview with author, August 1986.

29. See AZAPO, "Black Consciousness and the Class Struggle," *Frank Talk* 1:1 (February/March 1984), pp. 12–13.

30. See A. Callinicos, "Working Class Politics in South Africa," *International Socialism* 31, esp. pp. 23, 49; Trotsky, *On Black Nationalism*, pp. 84–86; Yunuz Carrim, "Interview: Hassim on APDUSA," *Work in Progress* 31 (May 1984), pp. 14–18.

31. See "AZAPO Affirms All-Black Fight," *The Star*, October 31, 1983; Rarc Msomi, "Multi-Racialism, Non-Racialism and Anti-Racialism" (speech, photocopy), September 3, 1983.

32. Sefako Nyaka, interview with author, March 1988; Saths Cooper, interview with author, August 1988. See Phil Mtimkulu, "AZAPO Leader Spells Out Role Envisaged for Whites," *The Star*, March 28, 1984. UDF copresident Archie Gumede hailed Cooper's election as the president of AZAPO as a signal of a diminished emphasis on a narrow view on race, as reported in *The Star*, December 27, 1985.

33. A. Callinicos, "Working Class Politics in South Africa," *International Socialism* 31, p. 27. See also AZAPO, "Report of the 4th Congress" (1984), p. 6.

34. Interview with author, April 1988.

35. See Adam and Moodley, *South Africa Without Apartheid*, p. 99.

36. Lybon Mabasa, "In Search of National Unity," (speech, photocopy), June 11, 1983.

37. Pandelani Nefolovhodwe, interview with author, March 1988. See also A. Sivanandran, "Race, Caste and Class in South Africa," *Frank Talk* 1:5 (November 1989).

38. Interview with author, May 1988.

39. Mzala, "The Freedom Charter and its Relevance Today," in African National Congress, *Selected Writings*, p. 82.

40. Ibid., p. 96.

41. Correspondence with author, April 1988.

42. See the remarks by Steve Tshwete in Suttner and Cronin, *Thirty Years of the Freedom Charter*, p. 217.

43. Diepen, *The National Question in South Africa*, pp. 10, 118.

44. Mabasa, "Presidential Address," AZAPO Fourth Congress (1984), p. 6.

45. Gerhart, *Black Power*, p. 78.

46. AZAPO, Durban Branch, "Annexure A: Black Consciousness as a Driving Force," (n.d., photocopy), p. 2.

47. See, for example, Gerhart, *Black Power*, p. 103.

48. Correspondence with author (written during the "Delmas Treason Trial," Pretoria Supreme Court), April 1988.

49. Nat Ramokgopa, interview with author, April 1988. The term *non-*

*racialism* was probably invented by the Webbs and George Bernard Shaw in England in the 1920s, according to Neville Alexander, interview with author, May 1988. The PAC claims that its president, Robert Sobukwe, introduced the term in South Africa to differentiate the PAC's goal from the ANC's multiracialism, though Sobukwe rejected nonracialism as a preliberation strategy. See *Azania Struggle*, April 1983, p. 2.

50. Correspondence with author, April 1988.

51. See Suttner and Cronin, *Thirty Years of the Freedom Charter*, p. 252; Barrell, "The UDF and National Forum: Their Emergence, Composition and Trends," in South African Research Service, eds., *South Africa Review II*, p. 10.

52. Interview with author, June 1988. For the historical precedent, see Lodge, *Black Politics*, p. 41.

53. Smangaliso Mkhatshwa, interview with author, April 1988.

54. Press conference, Lusaka, June 25, 1985, published as part of African National Congress, "Documents of the Second National Consultative Conference," p. 43.

55. Boesak, *Black and Reformed*, p. 32.

56. Thabo Mbeki, "The Fatton Thesis: A Rejoinder," *Canadian Journal of African Studies* 18:3 (1984), pp. 609–10. In 1985, ANC officials met in Zambia with the chairman of the Anglo-American Corporation and other industrialists, as described by Bloom, "Notes of the Meeting at Mfuwe Game Lodge," September 13, 1985 (photocopy).

57. Mbeki, "The Fatton Thesis," p. 610.

58. See Peter Hudson, "The Freedom Charter and the Theory of National Democratic Revolution," *Transformation* 1 (1986), pp. 6–34.

59. Interview with author, June 1988.

60. Zwelakhe Sisulu, interview with author, August 1986.

61. Nyawuza, "The National Question and Ethnicity," *African Communist* 98 (1984), p. 27.

62. Zwelakhe Sisulu, interview with author, August 1986.

63. Mamphela Ramphele, interview with author, August 1986.

64. Suttner and Cronin, *Thirty Years of the Freedom Charter*, p. 213.

65. "Terror" Lekota, as quoted in Murray, *South Africa*, p. 229.

66. Gerhart, *Black Power*, p. 118.

67. Allan Boesak, as quoted by Allistar Sparks, *The Washington Post*, February 8, 1983.

68. *SASPU National*, 4:3, (September 1983).

69. Jean de la Harpe and Andrew Manson, "The UDF and the Development of Resistance in South Africa," *Africa Perspective* 23 (1983), p. 66.

70. Chikane, "Launch of the UDF" (South African police transcript, Karis-Gerhart Collection), August 20, 1983, p. 3.

71. Interview with author, February 1988.

72. Albertina Sisulu, interview with author, June 1988. See "Lekota on the UDF," *Work in Progress* 30 (1984), pp. 4–8; *SASPU National* 4:3 (September 1983), p. 3.

73. Popo Molefe, "Resisting the Constitution," *Financial Mail*, November 25, 1983.

74. Allan Boesak, "Launch of the UDF," p. 48.

75. See *SASPU National* 4:3 (September 1983), p. 14.

76. Curtis Nkondo, "Opening Address," in National Union of South African Students, eds., *Beyond Reform*, p. 7.

77. Georg Sewpersadh, "Launch of the UDF," p. 32.

78. Helen Joseph, "Launch of the UDF," p. 22.

79. Aubrey Mokoena, "Launch of the UDF," p. 39.

80. Stephen Davis, *Apartheid's Rebels*, p. 101; Foster, "The Workers' Struggle: Where FOSATO Stands," *South African Labour Bulletin* 7:8 (1982), p. 76.

81. "NEC Report," African National Congress, *Documents of the Second National Consultative Conference of the ANC*, June 16–23, 1985, p. 15.

82. Sampson Ndou, "Launch of the UDF," p. 20. For another example of socialist rhetoric in the UDF, see the comments of the unionist Thozamile Gqweta, "North Coast UDF Meeting: Verulan Civic Hall" (South African police transcript, Karis-Gerhart Collection), 1984, p. 63.

83. Allistar Sparks, *Washington Post*, February 8, 1983.

84. "North Coast UDF Meeting," transcript, pp. 5, 8.

85. Archie Gumede, "Launch of the UDF," p. 15.

86. Interview with author, June 1988.

87. Tom Lodge, "The United Democratic Front: Leadership and Ideology," in Brewer, ed., *Can South Africa Survive?* p. 206.

88. Interview with author, March 1988.

89. The UDF "patrons" included Nelson Mandela and others from the ANC, church leader Father Smangaliso Mkhatshwa, and Dr. Allan Boesak. The patrons also included veteran white activists Beyers Naude, Helen Joseph, and Amy Thornton, a white who had done secretarial work for Mandela during his period in hiding in the early 1960s and who in 1990 chaired the white "Cape Democrats," a UDF affiliate.

90. Lodge, "The United Democratic Front," in Brewer, ed., *Can South Africa Survive?*, p. 207; Swilling, "The United Democratic Front," p. 27.

91. Lodge, "The United Democratic Front," p. 213.

92. Interview with author, May 1988. See also Alexander, *Sow the Wind*, p. 9.

93. Interview with author, May 1988.

94. Interview with author, July 1986. See also Mabasa, "Address," AZAPO Fourth Congress, 1984.

95. Interview with author, February 1988.

96. "UDF Education Committee," April 27–29, 1986, Daleside, p. 7. The Western Cape Hostel Workers Association is one example of a UDF affiliate created by the UDF itself.

97. Archie Gumede, "Launch of the UDF," p. 15.

98. See David Lewis, "The General Workers' Union and the UDF," *Work in Progress* 29 (October 1983), pp. 11–18.

99. "Lekota on the UDF," *Work in Progress* 30 (1984), p. 4.

100. Interview with author, June 1988.

101. Cassim Saloojee, interview with author, February 1988; Azhar Cachalia, interview with author, June 1988.

102. Ambassador Birgitta Karlstom-Dorph (member of the Swedish legation to South Africa, 1982 to 1988), interview with author, May 1988; Nat Ramokgopa, interview with author, April 1988.

103. For historical background on the finances of the SACC, see Republic of South Africa, *Report of the Eloff Commission.*

104. Interview with author, February 1988.

105. Interview with author, February 1988.

106. Graham van Wyck and Jeremy Daphne, interview with author, May 1988.

107. See Congress of South African Trade Unions, "Notes on Political Organizations," chapter on UDF; Lodge, "The United Democratic Front," in Brewer, ed., *Can South Africa Survive?*, pp. 206–30.

108. See Mark Swilling, "The United Democratic Front and Township Revolt," *Work in Progress* 49 (September 1987), p. 28.

109. See Lodge, *Black Politics*, p. 43; Lodge, "Freedom in Our Lifetime," pp. 6–10.

110. Murray, *South Africa*, p. 218.

111. Interview with author, April 1988.

112. Interview with author, April 1988.

113. Saki Macozoma, interview with author, June 1988.

## Chapter 5

1. Steven Gelb, "Making Sense of the Crisis," *Transformation* 5 (1987), p. 42.

2. Republic of South Africa, Central Statistical Service, *South African Statistics, 1988*, Table 21.5.

3. PLANACT, "The Soweto Rent Boycott," p. 21.

4. Murray, *South Africa*, pp. 354, 361; *Financial Mail*, June 12, 1985; R. S. Nyameko, "A Giant Is Born," *African Communist* 105 (1986), p. 28; Neville Alexander, "Ten Years of Education Crisis: The Resonance of 1976," speech, 1986, p. 3.

5. PLANACT, "The Soweto Rent Boycott," p. 22.

6. Ibid., pp. 32–33.

7. Ibid., p. 22; *SA Barometer* 2:15 (August 12, 1988), p. 238; *SA Barometer* 3:1 (January 27, 1989), p. 8.

8. PLANACT, "The Soweto Rent Boycott," p. 22; "Maize Crop Could Fail Once Again," *Rand Daily Mail*, January 26, 1984; "30% Rise in Price of Maize Likely," *Rand Daily Mail*, January 10, 1985; "Food Bills Soar by Up to 21% in Twelve Months," *Rand Daily Mail*, March 6, 1985.

9. *Drum*, January 1985, p. 25; "Food Bills Soar by Up to 21% in 12 Months," *Rand Daily Mail*, March 6, 1985; Republic of South Africa, Central Statistical Service, *South African Statistics, 1988*, Table 7.6.

10. See George Rude, "The Outbreak of the French Revolution," in Habakkuk and Postan, eds., *The New Cambridge Modern History*, vol. 8, esp. pp. 654–56, 677.

11. "Facts and Figures," in "The Emergency Convocation of Churches in South Africa," May 30–31, 1988 (internal document).

12. Adam and Moodley, *South Africa Without Apartheid*, p. 25; *SA Barometer* 1:4 (April 24, 1987), p. 58; "Civil Service Has Swelled by 50% Under Botha," *Rand Daily Mail*, April 26, 1984; South African Institute of Race Relations, *Survey of Race Relations in South Africa*, 1983, pp. 99–100.

13. Peter Sullivan, "SPP's Removal Figures," *The Star*, May 16, 1984, p. 11.

14. Republic of South Africa, Central Statistical Service, *South African Statistics*, 1988, Table 5.4.

15. See, for example, Gurr, *Why Men Rebel.*

16. Orkin, *Disinvestment*, p. 34.

17. Lawrence Schlemmer, "Political Unrest and African Rights," *Political Monitor: Indicator SA* 2:3 (October 1984), p. 1.

18. PLANACT, "The Soweto Rent Boycott," p. 25.

19. Mark Swilling, "The United Democratic Front and Township Revolt," *Work in Progress* 49 (September 1987).

20. Ibid., p. 32; PLANACT, "The Soweto Rent Boycott," p. 25.

21. Interview with author, March 1988.

22. See Devan Pillay, "The Port Elizabeth Stayaway: Community Organization and Unions Conflict," *Work in Progress* 37 (1985), pp. 4–13.

23. For historical parallels, see, for example, Gerhart, *Black Power*, p. 89; and Lodge, *Black Politics*, p. 166.

24. See Melissa DeVilliers, "The Port Alfred Experience," *Between the Lines*, Student Union for Christian Action 5:2 (1988), pp. 10–11.

25. See K. Helliker, A. Roux, and R. White, "Asithengi: Recent Consumer Boycotts," South African Research Service, eds., *South African Review* 4 (1987), pp. 33–52.

26. Lodge, *Black Politics*, p. 158.

27. Ibid., pp. 160, 179, 181.

28. PLANACT, "The Soweto Rent Boycott," p. 25. See also White, "A Tide Has Risen," *South African Labour Bulletin* 11:5 (April/May 1986), pp. 69–99.

29. Jeremy Seeking, "Workers and the Politics of Consumer Boycotts" (manuscript, n.d.).

30. Interview with author, April 1988.

31. Among the defendants in the Delmas treason trial were "Terror" Lekota, Popo Molefe, and Moss Chikane of the UDF, Tom Manthata of the SACC, as well as the Reverend Geoff Molesane and others more closely associated with AZAPO.

32. Mark Swilling, "Local-Level Negotiations: Case Studies and Implications" (unpublished), as quoted in Mufson, *Fighting Years*.

33. Lodge, *Black Politics*, p. 52.

34. Anonymous, interview with author, May 1988.

35. Interview with author, May 1988.

36. See Orkin, *Disinvestment*, p. 51.

37. Interview with author, March 1988.

38. Interview with author, April 1988.

39. "ANC Call to the Nation: The Future Is Within Our Grasp!" (pamphlet), April 25, 1985. See also Oliver R. Tambo, "Render South Africa Ungovernable" (pamphlet), January 1985; Oliver R. Tambo, "Address to the Nation," Radio Freedom, July 22, 1985; "Prepare the Conditions for the Seizure of Power by the People" (undated pamphlet).

40. Benson, *Nelson Mandela*, p. 237. See also Mandela's interview with Lord Bethell, reprinted in the *Sunday Mail*, January 27, 1985.

41. Gavin Evans, "Over 200 ANC Attacks in 1987," *Weekly Mail*, March 11, 1988, p. 11. See also Repression Monitoring Group, *Weekly Fact Sheet*, March 26–31, 1986; Lodge, "The African National Congress After the Kabwe Conference," in South African Research Service, eds., *South African Review* 4 (1987), p. 7.

42. See, for example, Schlemmer, "Aspects of Political Consciousness Among African Workers," *Political Monitor* 2:3 (October 1984), pp. 5–6; Orkin, *Disinvestment*, p. 35.

43. S. Davis, *Apartheid's Rebels*, p. 118; "PAC Bids High," *Weekly Mail*, May 11, 1990, p. 13.

44. See Alexander, *Sow the Wind*, pp. 98–125.

45. Thami Mkhwanazi, interview with author, April 1988.

46. See "Interview with Joe Modise," *ANC Struggle Update*, 3 (1985); Joe Slovo, "People's War," *Sechaba*, November 1984, pp. 17–18; Lodge, "The Second Consultative Conference of the ANC," *South Africa International* (October 1985), pp. 80–97; PAC, "Plenary Session of the Central Committee," August 9–20, 1986.

47. Mufson, "The War for South Africa," *Washington Post*, December 14, 1986, p. H1.

48. Tambo, "Tambo Speech: We Are A Force," *Sechaba*, October 1984, p. 13.

49. Repression Monitoring Group, *Weekly Fact Sheet*, April 21–26, 1986; Webster, "Repression and the State of Emergency," in South African Research Service, eds., *South Africa Review* 4 (1987), p. 141; and S. Davis, *Apartheid's Rebels*, p. 94.

50. Baker, "Dismantling South Africa's Secret Government" *Washington Post*, December 16, 1989.

51. "South Africa (4): The UDF," *Africa Confidential*, January 28, 1987, p. 5.

52. See *The Star*, January 14, 1987.

53. "Secretarial Report," United Democratic Front, "National Working Committee Conference," May 29–30, 1987, p. 5.

54. Commonwealth Group of Eminent Persons, *Mission to South Africa*, pp. 117–25.

55. Investor Responsibility Research Center, "U.S. Banks and South Africa," Analysis L (1989) Washington D.C. See also Sampson, *Black and Gold*, pp. 38–59.

56. Interview with author, June 1988.

57. See Ronnie Kasrils, "People's War, Revolution and Insurrection," *Sechaba*, April 1986, pp. 2–10; ANC, "Building People's Power: 1976–1986"; (pamphlet); and *Weekly Mail*, February 20, 1987.

58. See Mark Swilling, "The United Democratic Front," p. 29.

59. Repression Monitoring Group, *Weekly Fact Sheet*, April 21–26, 1986; *The Star*, September 9, 1985; *The Star*, March 1, 1986.

60. See Haysom, *Mabangalala*, p. 1.

61. George Hower, "Cycles of Civil Unrest 76/84," *Political Monitor* 3:1 (Winter 1985), p. 12.

62. *The Star*, January 14, 1987.

63. Hower, "Cycles of Civil Unrest 76/84," p. 12.

64. "A Mother's Memories," *Learn and Teach* 1 (1988), 8.

65. K. Helliker et al., "Asithengi," South African Research Service, eds., *South Africa Review* 4 (1987), p. 34.

66. See "Tasks of the Democratic Movement in the State of Emergency,"*Isizwe* 1:1 (November 1985), p. 16; Anonymous, "Toward a National Program of Action," (pamphlet, 1988); UDF Militants, "Build a United Front," (pamphlet), May 1985.

67. See, for example, *The Sowetan*, March 3, 1986.

68. Zwelakhe Sisulu, "Keynote Address," National Education Crisis Committee, Second National Consultative Congress, March 29, 1986, p. 9.

69. See Lodge, *Black Politics*, pp. 52, 165. For a discussion of an analogous transition from local material grievances to national political demands in the years leading up to the Russian Revolution, see Deutscher, *Soviet Trade Unions*, p. 13; and Wolfe, *Three Who Made a Revolution*, p. 158.

70. See, for example, United Democratic Front, "National General Council," April 5, 1985, esp. pp. 6–19.

71. See Johan Muller, "People's Education and the NECC," South African Research Service, eds., *South Africa Review* 4 (1987), pp. 18–32.

72. Lodge, *Black Politics*, p. 125.

73. See Oliver Tambo, "Attack! Advance! Give the Enemy no Quarter" (pamphlet, January 8, 1986).

74. See Sisulu, "Keynote Address," pp. 14–19; and ANC, "Call to the People: From Ungovernability to People's Power" (pamphlet, May 20, 1986).

75. PLANACT, "The Soweto Rent Boycott," p. 25.

76. Swilling, "The United Democratic Front," p. 31.

77. See Tom Lodge, "The UDF Leadership and Ideology," in Brewer, ed., *Can South Africa Survive?* pp. 220–26; and Raymond Suttner, "Popular Justice in South Africa Today," Sociology Seminar, School of Law, University of the Witwatersrand, May 5, 1986.

78. See Hirson, *Year of Fire, Year of Ash*, pp. 164–66, 284–85.

79. George Hower, "Cycles of Civil Unrest 76/84," *Political Monitor* 3:1 (Winter 1985), p. 11.

80. Interview with author, June 1988.

81. See, for example, ANC, "Call to the Nation: The Future is Within our Grasp," (pamphlet, April 25, 1985); Alex Mashinini, "Dual Power and the Creation of People's Committees," *Sechaba*, April 1986, pp. 25–30; and Cassius Mandla, "The Moment of Revolution is Now or Never in Our Lifetime," *Sechaba*, November 1985, pp. 23–30.

82. Shaun Johnson, "The Soldiers of Luthuli," in Johnson, ed., *South Africa*, p. 121.

83. See Sisulu, "Keynote Address," Second National Consultative Conference; and Peter Jones, "Struggle for a Socialist Azania," *The Marxist Review* (January 1987), p. 20.

84. Interview with author, June 1988.

85. Interview with author, August 1986.

86. *The Star*, April 21, 1986.

87. See Orkin, *Disinvestment*, pp. 35, 39; and Institute for Black Research, "Political and Economic Choices of Disenfranchised South Africans," 1986, p. 9.

88. Interview with author, April 1988.

89. Interview with author, April 1988.

90. Interview with author, April 1988. See also Mzwandile Maqina, interview with Tom Lodge, January 28, 1987 (transcript provided by Lodge); and Haysom, *Mabangalala*, pp. 132–33.

91. Lybon Mabasa, interview with author, April 1988; Peter Jones, interview with author, May 1988; Philip Dlamini, interview with author, February 1988.

92. Interview with author, August 1986. See also Vanesco Mafora, "Kennedy, the Media and AZAPO," *Frank Talk* 1:6 (February–March 1985), pp. 10–16.

93. See "AZAPO Members Attacked Again," *The Sowetan*, April 23, 1985; "Turf SRC Refutes Claims," *The Sowetan*, April 24, 1985; "Attacks on AZAPO, AZASM Men Flayed," *The Sowetan*, May 2, 1985; "UDF, AZAPO Battle It Out," *The Sowetan*, May 6, 1985; "8 UDF Houses Petrol Bombed," *The Sowetan*, May 8, 1985; Sefako Nyaka, "Soweto Leaders Disturbed at UDF vs. AZAPO Clashes," *Weekly Mail*, May 30, 1986; and N. Mathlane, "Deadly Duel of the Wararas and the Zim Zims," *Frontline*, February 1987, pp. 24–26.

94. Martin Ramokjadi, interview with author, April 1988; Maphai, "Resistance in South Africa," p. 8.

95. Vivienne Walt, "If We See You in School, Tell Us What Size Tyre You Wear," *Weekly Mail*, December 12, 1986.

96. "UDF vs. AZAPO: Ending the Feud," *Financial Mail*, May 17, 1985.

97. See Tshwete, "I Will Not Be Bought," *Sechaba*, April 1986, pp. 4–5.

98. See "Bishop Tutu Fails to Heal Rift," *The Sowetan*, May 7, 1985; "Cops Suspect AZAPO," *The Sowetan*, July 8, 1985; "Pamphlets Condemned," *The Sowetan*, April 29, 1986; and "UDF Denies Publishing Call to Eliminate AZAPO," *The Citizen*, December 5, 1986.

99. ANC, "Power to the People" (pamphlet, 1988); "The UDF in Its Fourth Anniversary," *New Nation*, August 20, 1987, p. 6; group interview with Johannesburg Local Executive of COSATU, June 1988; *UDF Update*, 2:2, June 1986.

100. Bishop Manas Buthelezi, interview with author, February 1988; "Unity Plea," *The Sowetan*, May 20, 1985.

101. Repression Monitoring Group, "Weekly Fact Sheet," August 25–31, 1986; "COSATU, UDF and AZAP in Peace Bid," *The Star*, January 26, 1987.

102. Nat Ramakgopa, interview with author, April 1988; Jay Naidoo, General Secretary COSATU, "Memorandum to All General Secretaries," March 24, 1988, p. 4; Anonymous, "Towards a National Programme of Action," (pamphlet, 1988).

103. See, for example, *The Star*, October 3, 1989, p. 2.

104. See United Democratic Front, "National Working Committee Conference," May 29–30, 1987, pp. 1–4; David Niddrie, "Emergency Forces New Forms of Organization," *Work in Progress* 47 (April 1987), pp. 3–7; "Youth Politics: Learning to Live in the Shadows," *Work in Progress* 53 (April–May 1988), pp. 11–14. For a critique of this use of clandestine techniques, see Meer, "Time We Stopped This Name-Calling," *Weekly Mail*, October 13, 1989, p. 15.

105. Interview with author, February 1988.

106. Observatory and Claremont UDF Area Committees, *Upfront* 7, August 1987. See also United Democratic Front, "National Working Committee Conference," esp. pp. 1–11; UDF, "Discussion Paper," July 1985, esp. p. 45; "On Discipline," *Isizwe*, 1:1 (November 1985), pp. 23–30.

107. Interview with author, August 1986. For a discussion of the Algerian example, see Horne, *A Savage War of Peace*.

108. UDF, "National Working Committee Conference," p. 9.

109. Interview with author, August 1986.

110. UDF, "National Working Committee Conference," p. 49.

111. Ibid., p. 29.

112. "UDF in Court Challenge to Curb in Funds," *The Star*, May 7, 1987.

113. Interview with author, April 1988.

114. Interview with author, January 1988.

115. Interview with author, August 1988.

116. Swilling, "The United Democratic Front," p. 33.

117. See Piven and Cloward, *Poor People's Movements*, as discussed in Chapter 1.

118. Interview with author, July 1986. See Johnson, "The Soldiers of Luthuli," in Johnson, ed., *South Africa*, p. 122.

119. Eric Dlangamandla, interview with author, May 1988.

120. Johannesburg Democratic Action Group, "Winning White Support for Democracy," *Work in Progress* 53 (April–May 1988), p. 32.

121. See UDF, "Mesage to All South Africans on the Whites Only Election," (pamphlet, March 19, 1987); Tom Lodge, "The Second Consultative Conference of the ANC," *South Africa International* 16:2 (October

1985), p. 85; Anthony Heard, "A Conversation with Oliver Tambo of the ANC," *The Cape Times*, November 4, 1985, p. 9; Sheila Rule, "South African Rebel Leader Calls for Widening of Armed Attacks," *New York Times*, January 9, 1987, p. A2.

122. Kitt Katzin, "Munnik Told of Winnie's Cash for Ads," *The Star*, March 22, 1987.

123. See "Leaders Back Tutu," *The Star*, February 24, 1986; *The Sowetan*, July 25, 1985.

124. See Michels, *Political Parties.*

125. Mac Maharaj, "UDF: An Historical Development," *Sechaba*, March 1984, p. 17.

126. C. Le Grange, "Tutu Asks ANC to Consider Ending Violence," *The Star*, March 23, 1987; "ANC Says Winnie's Words Were Unfortunate," *The Star*, September 30, 1987; letter from Archbishop Desmond Tutu to State President P. W. Botha, April 8, 1988; *New York Times*, February 17, 1989, p. A10.

127. See Richard de Villiers, "Front or Political Party," *Work in Progress* 40 (February 1986), pp. 14–17.

128. "The UDF on Its Fourth Anniversary," *New Nation*, August 20, 1987, p. 6; Hilary Joffe, *Weekly Mail*, May 27, 1988, p. 21; Mark Swilling, "WHAMing the Radicals," *Weekly Mail*, May 20, 1988, p. 15; and Jay Naidoo, "Memorandum to General Secretaries," COSATU, March 24, 1988, p. 5.

129. SASPU, *State of the Nation* 5:1 (April 1987), p. 2.

130. P. W. Botha, letter to Frank Chikane of the SACC, March 24, 1988, reprinted in South African Council of Churches, "The Emergency Convocation of Churches in South Africa," May 30–31, 1988.

131. Barry Streek, "Government Starting to See Freedom Charter in New Light," *Cape Times*, October 23, 1987. In the same article, a senior Nationalist party member of parliament claimed that the government had already granted many of the Charter's demands, implying that the government itself was Charterist.

132. Gumede's suggestion of the possibility of participating in local elections was reported in "UDF Hints at Active Role in Next Election," *The Star*, July 3, 1987, and was refuted in "Gumede's Suggestion Under Fire," *The Star*, July 8, 1987; and by Murphy Morobe, UDF publicity secretary, in "UDF Won't Take Part in Elections," *The Citizen*, July 9, 1987.

133. Interview with author, March 1988.

134. "The UDF on Its Fourth Anniversary," *New Nation*, August 20, 1987, p. 6; Mufson, "The Fall of the Front," *The New Republic*, February 20, 1987, pp. 17–19.

135. Patrick Laurence, "Slide into Terror," *The Star*, June 11, 1988, p. 11.
136. Interview with author, March 1988.
137. "UDF Discussion Paper," *UDF Update* 1:1 (July 1985), p. 4. See also Simons, "Our Freedom Charter," *Sechaba*, June 1985, p. 8.

## Chapter 6

1. Friedman, *Building Tomorrow Today*, pp. 11–16; Lodge, *Black Politics*, pp. 5–8, 57–58. See also Bradford, *A Taste of Freedom: The ICU in Rural South Africa.*
2. Friedman, *Building Tomorrow Today*, pp. 17–22.
3. Ibid., pp. 22–26.
4. Ibid., pp. 26–33; Lodge, *Black Politics*, pp. 188–99.
5. Feit, *Workers Without Weapons.*
6. See Rob Lambert, "Trade Unions, Nationalism and the Socialist Project in South Africa," South African Research Service, eds., *South Africa Review* 4 (1987), p. 236; Luckhardt and Wall, *Organize or Starve.*
7. Davies, "Nationalization, Socialization and the Freedom Charter," University of York Conference Paper, September 29–October 2, 1986, pp. 7–10.
8. Murray, *South Africa*, p. 130.
9. Republic of South Africa, Central Statistical Service, *South African Statistics*, 1988, Table 7.5. For further background on the rise of manufacturing output and concentration, see Chapter 2.
10. See Brewer, *After Soweto*, p. 21.
11. See Lipton, *Capitalism and Apartheid*; Saul and Gelb, *The Crisis in South Africa.*
12. Republic of South Africa, Central Statistical Service, *South African Statistics, 1988*, Table 12.6.
13. Anonymous, interview with author, May 1988.
14. "South Africa: The Union Factor," *Africa Confidential*, July 7, 1982, p. 2; Republic of South Africa, Central Statistical Service, *South African Statistics, 1988*, Table 7.31. See also Adam and Moodley, *South Africa Without Apartheid*, p. 171.
15. See Johann Maree, "Democracy and Oligarchy in Trade Unions," *Social Dynamics* 8:1 (1982), esp. pp. 45–51; Friedman, *Building Tomorrow Today*, chap. 2.
16. See Friedman, *Building Tomorrow Today*, pp. 180–87.
17. Brewer, *After Soweto*, p. 203.
18. Interview with author, March 1988.
19. Interview with author, March 1988.

20. For a discussion of concerns about the UDF corresponding to those of FOSATU, see David Lewis, "The General Workers' Union and the UDF," *Work in Progress* 29 (October 1983), pp. 11–18. This article was not an official statement by FOSATU.

21. Joe Foster, "The Workers' Struggle: Where Does FOSATU Stand?" *South African Labour Bulletin* 7:8 (1982), p. 78.

22. Ibid., p. 85.

23. Alec Erwin, interview with author, March 1988.

24. Chris Dlamini, president of FOSATU in 1982, interview with author, April 1988.

25. Friedman, *Building Tomorrow Today*, pp. 277–99; "South Africa: Black Union Power," *Africa Confidential*, November 16, 1983, pp. 2–3.

26. "Don't Vote," *FOSATU News* 31 (August 1984).

27. Alec Erwin, interview with author, March 1988.

28. See Rob Lambert, "Trade Unions," South African Research Service, eds., *South Africa Review* 4 (1987), p. 6; "COSATU Speaks," *SASPU Focus* 5:1 (May 1, 1986), p. 6.

29. Davies et al., *The Struggle for South Africa*, vol. 2, pp. 333, 345.

30. "CUSA National Executive Council," *South African Labour Bulletin* 11:5 (April–May 1986), p. 8. See also *CUSA News* 1:5 (June 1983).

31. See, for instance, *CUSA News* 1:1 (February 1983), p. 1.

32. See Ramaphosa, "Why Black Trade Unionism," reprinted by AZAPO, 1984.

33. See Sisa Njikelana, "Unions and the UDF," *Work in Progress* 32 (July 1984), pp. 30–33; Murray, *South Africa*, chap. 3; "South Africa: Black Union Power," *Africa Confidential*, November 16, 1983, pp. 1–4; and Davies et al., *The Struggle for South Africa*, vol. 2, chap. 7.

34. See Ike Van der Walt, "Boilermakers Breaking New Ground," *Work in Progress* 34 (October 1984), pp. 7–11.

35. Interview with author, April 1988.

36. See "Debating Alliance Politics," *Work in Progress* 34 (October 1984), pp. 12–15; Ingrid Obery, "Trade Union Talks: Long Road to Unity," *Work in Progress* 37 (June 1985), pp. 22–26.

37. James Mndaweni, former president of CUSA, interview with author, March 1988; Phiroshaw Camay, former general secretary of CUSA, interview with author, April 1988.

38. Interview with author, April 1988.

39. Interview with author, June 1988.

40. James Mndaweni, interview with author, March 1988.

41. See "COSATU Launch," *South African Labour Bulletin* 11:3 (January 1986), p. 43; see R. S. Nyameko, "A Giant Is Born," *African Communist* 105 (1986), pp. 25–35.

42. For a description of how the merger process led to the creation of COSATU's second largest affiliate, see Ingrid Obery, "A New Road to Socialism," *Work in Progress* 48 (July 1987), pp. 8–12.

43. R. S. Nyameko, "A Giant Is Born," *African Communist* 25 (1986), p. 29.

44. Interview with author, March 1988.

45. COSATU, "Financial Statements for the Thirteen Months Ending 31 December 1986," p. 5.

46. COSATU, "National Budget," 1987; COSATU, "Recommendations of COSATU Education Conference," October 23–25, 1987; Khetsi Lehoko, COSATU Education Secretary, interview with author, March 1988.

47. Kgelema Mothlahte, NUM education coordinator, interview with author, March 1988.

48. Interview with author, May 1988.

49. United Democratic Front, "UDF National Working Committee Conference," May 29–30, 1987, p. 18.

50. Jay Naidoo, "The Role of the Working Class in Our Struggle for Liberation," Address to the World Council of Churches and the South African Council of Churches, December 4–6, 1985, pp. 3–4.

51. Ibid., p. 7. See "Unions Raise Storm over COSATU Politics," *The Sowetan*, December 13, 1985.

52. See "Document: ANC–SACTU–COSATU Talks," *South African Labour Bulletin* 11:5 (April/May 1986), pp. 29–31.

53. Naidoo, "Document: The Significance of COSATU," *South African Labour Bulletin* 11:5 (April/May 1986), pp. 38–39.

54. See Alec Erwin, "The Question of Unity in Struggle," *South African Labour Bulletin* 11:1 (September 1985), pp. 51–70; Cronin, "The Question of Unity—A Reply," *South African Labour Bulletin* 11:3 (January 1986), pp. 29–42.

55. Interview with author, May 1988.

56. See COSATU, "Second National Congress Report," July 1987, p. 8; Yunus Carrim, "COSATU: Toward Disciplined Alliances," *Work in Progress* 49 (September 1987), pp. 11–18.

57. See "COSATU Second National Congress," *South African Labour Bulletin* 12:6–7 (August/September 1987), p. 3; Carrim, "COSATU: Toward Disciplined Alliances," *South African Labour Bulletin* 49, p. 12; Glenn Moss, "National Liberation and Socialism," *Work in Progress* 50 (November 1987), p. 15.

58. Cyril Ramaphosa, interview with author, June 1988; Papi Kganare, interview with author, March 1988.

59. See "Black Union Federation Is Born," *Business Day*, October 6, 1986.

60. Phiroshaw Camay, then general secretary of NACTU, interview with author, April 1988.

61. Phiroshaw Camay, interview with author, April 1988.

62. Phiroshaw Camay, interview with author, April 1988.

63. Phiroshaw Camay, interview with author, April 1988. Also see NACTU, "Policy of the Federation," 1987.

64. Themba Molefe, "Blacks Must Lead, Says NACTU," *The Sowetan*, June 17, 1988, p. 4. See also Mathatha Tsedu, "1000 Told Charter Is Divisive," *The Sowetan*, December 12, 1987; "Blacks Dominate the Struggle," *The Star*, June 10, 1987.

65. Calvin Mahalene, president of the Chemical Workers' Industrial Union, a COSATU affiliate, interview with author, April 1988.

66. Gatsby Mazrui, former official of the Black Municipal Workers' Union, interview with author, March 1988.

67. Interview with author, March 1988.

68. Duma Nkosi, interview with author, April 1988.

69. Greg Ruiters and David Niddrie, "Curbing Union Power," *Work in Progress* 52 (March 1988), p. 17; Republic of South Africa, Central Statistical Service, *South African Statistics, 1988*, Table 7.31.

70. Republic of South Africa, Central Statistical Service, *South African Labour Statistics, 1988*, p. 485.

71. "Worker Detentions Soar," *New Nation*, February 17, 1988.

72. Interview with author, March 1988.

73. Press, "SACTU and Trade Union Unity," *Sechaba*, May 1984, p. 28; Republic of South Africa, Central Statistical Service, *South African Statistics, 1988*, Table 7.5.

74. Cyril Ramaphosa, interview with author, June 1988. For earlier discussions of this point, see "COSATU Launch," *South African Labour Bulletin* 11:3 (January 1986), p. 44; Naidoo, "The Role of the Working Class," Speech to World Council of Churches/South African Council of Churches, December 4–6, 1985, p. 6.

75. See SASPU, "COSATU Demands a Living Wage," *State of the Nation* 5:1 (April 1987), p. 11.

76. See "Create Jobs for All," *SASPU Focus*, 5:1 (May 1, 1986), p. 18; Jay Naidoo, "Developments Since COSATU's Formation," *South African Labour Bulletin* 12:8 (October 1987), p. 17; and COSATU, "National Budget," 1987.

77. See "Issues Raised on the Discussion Paper: The Way Forward," CCAWUSA Johannesburg Branch, September 12–13, 1986, p. 2.

78. See "Overtime Ban to Be Intensified," *New Nation*, October 13, 1989, p. 17; "Overtime Ban May Be Slipping," *The Star*, November 14, 1989, p. 5.

79. Keith Browne, "COSATU and Independent Working Class Politics," *South African Labour Bulletin* 12:2 (January/February 1987), p. 61.

80. "Cyril Ramaphosa on the NUM Congress," *South African Labour Bulletin* 12:3 (May/June 1987), pp. 46–47.

81. Interview with author, May 1988; "1987—The Year Mineworkers Take Control," *South African Labour Bulletin* 12:2 (March/April 1987), pp. 47–49; Azanian Labour Monitoring Group, "The Freedom Charter and Trade Unions in South Africa," 1988 (photocopy) pp. 7–9; Myeza, "Workers Are Being Forced to Accept Freedom Charter," *City Press*, July 26, 1987.

82. "NUMSA Political Resolution," *South African Labour Bulletin* 12:5 (July 1987), p. 12.

83. Interview with author, June 1988.

84. See *NUM News*, August 1987, p. 4.

85. Alec Erwin, Interview with author, March 1988; "Cyril Ramaphosa on the NUM Congress," *South African Labour Bulletin* 12:3 (May/June 1987), p. 49.

86. Interview with author, February 1988.

87. For further discussion of this position, see Sisa Njikelana, "Unions and the UDF," *Work in Progress* 32 (July 1984), pp. 30–33; Jay Naidoo, "The Significance of COSATU," *South African Labour Bulletin* 5 (April/May 1986), pp. 33–39; "COSATU Speaks," *SASPU Focus* 5:1 (May 1, 1986), p. 5; Jeremy Cronin, "The Question of Unity—A Response," *South African Labour Bulletin* 11:3 (January 1986), pp. 29–37.

88. See Hammond, *Lenin on Trade Unions and Revolution*, esp. p. 42. For an alternative interpretation of Leninism, defending the independence of trade unions, see Dunayevskaya, *Marxism and Freedom*.

89. Interview with author, May 1988.

90. Interview with author, June 1988.

91. Quoting a NUMSA representative, May Day commemoration, 1988. See also Alec Erwin, "The Question of Unity in Struggle," *South African Labour Bulletin* 11:1 (September 1985), p. 61–62.

92. Moses Mayekiso, general secretary of NUMSA, interview with author, November 1989.

93. "Points Toward a Workers' Charter," July 1987 (anonymous).

94. See "Jay Naidoo on COSATU," *South African Labour Bulletin* 12:5 (July 1987), p. 63.

95. Herbert Mkhize, former vice-president of CCAWUSA, interview with author, May 1988.

96. Meeting of the Unemployed Workers' Movement, Cape Town, May 1988. The other COSATU affiliate working with the unemployed in Cape Town at the time was the Unemployed Workers' Union.

97. Interview with author, April 1988.

98. Pule Pule, interview with author, March 1988.

99. Interview with author, March 1988. For further background, see Marcel Golding, "CCAWUSA: Ten Years," *South African Labour Bulletin* 11:1 (September 1985), pp. 27–28.

100. See CCAWUSA, "Report Back on COSATU Central Executive Committee Meeting," May 19–21, 1986, p. 2; "Strike at OK Bazaars," *South African Labor Bulletin* 12:3 (January/February 1987), pp. 5–11; "Anti-Apartheid Bosses Are Not Our Friends," *Work in Progress* 46 (February 1987), pp. 3–6.

101. Vivian Mtwa, interview with author, April 1988. See also "Angry Words Mark Union Rift," *The Sowetan*, March 7, 1988, p. 2; "CCAWUSA Conference," *South African Labour Bulletin* 12:5 (July 1987), pp. 17–25; David Niddrie, "The Bumpy Road to Working Class Unity," *Work in Progress* 52 (March 1988), pp. 34–38; CCAWUSA, "Seminar Report," September 12–13, 1986; CCAWUSA, "Policy Seminar Report" October 18–19, 1986; Miller Moela, "Speech," *CCAWUSA Bulletin* 1 (January–June 1987), p. 5.

102. Papi Kganare, interview with author, March 1988. The position of the charterist faction of CCAWUSA was presented in "What Is the Problem in CCAWUSA?" (internal document).

103. Chris Dlamini, vice-president of COSATU, interview with author, April 1988.

104. Kaiser Thibedi, CCAWUSA Johannesburg Branch secretary, speech to annual general meeting, March 1988.

105. Len Maseko, "Breakaway Union Seizes Offices," *The Sowetan*, November 5, 1987.

106. R. P. C., "Power to the People."

107. Kaiser Thibedi, interview with author, March 1988.

108. "Still in Search of Unity," *Work in Progress* 60 (August/September 1989), p. 5.

109. "Factions Unite to Form New Union," *New Nation*, November 17, 1989, p. 19. The re-united CCAWUSA was renamed SACCAWU.

110. See "Locals Link Unions," *Work in Progress* 49 (September 1987), pp. 23–25.

111. Kaiser Thibedi, CCAWUSA Johannesburg branch secretary, speech to annual general meeting, March 1988.

112. Republic of South Africa, Central Statistical Service, *South African Statistics, 1988*, Table 7.7. These figures do not include workers in the mining sector, for which average wages are not provided after 1984.

113. See Hilary Joffe, "The Policy of South Africa's Trade Unions Toward Sanctions and Disinvestment," in Orkin, ed., *Sanctions Against Apartheid*, pp. 57–67.

114. Interview with author, May 1988; Steven Friedman, "COSATU's Choice," *Weekly Mail*, May 27, 1988, p. 14. See also Eddie Koch, "COSATU Unlocks Its Doors to Rivals—But Keeps the Latch On," *Weekly Mail*, May 20, 1988, p. 7.

115. Cas St. Leger, "Jobs Become the Issue as COSATU Drops Its Traditional Chants," *Sunday Times*, May 22, 1988, p. 2.

116. Interview with author, March 1988.

117. See Eddie Koch, "Old Foes Circle Warily as Talk Turns to Unity," *Weekly Mail*, May 13, 1988, p. 9.

118. COSATU Central Executive Committee, "The Way Forward—Establishing Tasks and Priorities," August 15–16, 1987, p. 3.

119. "Worker Summit," *Azanian Labour Journal* 2:1 (January/March 1989), p. 10. See also Eddie Koch, "The Crucial First Steps Toward Labour Unity," *Weekly Mail*, September 1, 1989, p. 9.

120. See "Conference for a Democratic Future," *New Nation*, November 16, 1989, pp. 6–7; and Christopher S. Wren, "Foes of Apartheid Hold Unity Talks," *New York Times*, December 10, 1989, sec. 1, p. 4.

121. Kgelema Mothlahte, NUM education coordinator, interview with author, March 1988.

122. Interview with author, February 1988.

123. See Gavin Evans and Thandeka Gqubule, "Goodbye, Joe Stalin," *Weekly Mail*, August 25, 1989, p. 13. Stalin had earlier been hailed as "a great state and party leader," in Mafosi Shombela, "Our Armed Offensive," *Sechaba*, March 1986, p. 14.

124. Ishmael Mkhabela, interview with author, April 1988.

125. Cassandra Moodley, "Africanists to Form Joint Group," *Weekly Mail*, November 10, 1989, p. 1; Cassandra Moodley, "PAC Welcomes Launch of New Africanist Group," *Weekly Mail*, November 17, 1989, p. 12.

126. Albertina Sisulu, interview with author, June 1988.

127. Interview with author, May 1988.

128. Cyril Ramaphosa, interview with author, June 1988.

129. Joe Seremane, interview with author, April 1988.

130. See David Niddrie, "Building on the Freedom Charter," *Work in Progress* 53 (April/May 1988), pp. 3–6.

131. For an example of somewhat contradictory views presented by ANC representatives, see Carmel Rickard, "Lekota Pleads for Peace"; and Tshokolo Molakeng, "ANC Man Warns the AWB: We Will Face You with Guns," *Weekly Mail*, July 27, 1990, p. 2.

132. Cyril Ramaphosa, interview with author, June 1988. A banner at the NUM Congress in August 1987 read "Socialism Means Freedom."

133. Eddie Koch, "COSATU's Planners Take Advantage of Democracy," *Weekly Mail*, March 9, 1990, p. 6.

134. See, for instance, Orkin, *Disinvestment*, pp. 52, 73.

135. South African Youth Congress, "Everyone and Everything for the Liberation Struggle . . . ," COSATU Second National Congress, 1987; See also *New Era* 2:2 (June 1987); "Interest in Socialism Growing," *South*, May 4, 1988, p. 14; and Lodge, "Freedom in our Lifetime," *Reality*, November 1986, pp. 6–10.

136. "Understanding and Fighting Women's Oppression," *CCAWUSA News*, November 1989, p. 8.

137. See Ramphele, "The Dynamics of Gender Politics in the Hostels of Cape Town," *Journal of Southern African Studies* 15:3 (April 1989), pp. 393–414; Cassandra Moodley, "A Woman's Place is in the Struggle for Equality," *Weekly Mail*, March 16, 1990, p. 7.

138. See, for example, Cole, *Crossroads*, pp. 60–68.

139. See Brewer, *After Soweto*, p. 165.

140. Eddie Webster, "The Rise of Social-Movement Unionism: The Two Faces of the Black Trade Union Movement in South Africa," in Frankel et al., eds., *State Resistance, and Change*, pp. 186–87; Centre for Policy Studies, *Policy Perspectives 1989*, p. 207.

141. *The Star*, December 1, 1986.

142. William Claiborne, "South Africa's Quiet Revolution," *Washington Post National Weekly Edition*, January 22, 1990, p. 24; "South African Sanctions Bill R100bn—Top Banker," *Argus*, November 3, 1989, p. 3; and Ovenden and Cole, *Apartheid and International Finance*, pp. 165–72.

143. U.S. Government Accounting Office, "South Africa: Trends in Trade, Lending and Investment," April 1988, pp. 14–16, 24–26.

144. Richard Moorsman, "Foreign Trade and Sanctions," in Orkin, ed., *Sanctions Against Apartheid*, p. 259; Ovenden and Cole, *Apartheid and International Finance*, p. 64.

145. "Rockman Gets the Sack," *Weekly Mail*, March 23, 1990, pp. 1–2.

146. S. Davis, *Apartheid's Rebels*, p. 186.

147. Robert Davies, "After Cuito Cuanavale," in Orkin, ed., *Sanctions Against Apartheid*, pp. 198–206.

148. See Gavin Evans, "Magnus Makes Every Effort to Stop the Conference," *Weekly Mail*, June 1, 1990, p. 10.

149. See Tony Stirling, "PAC Revives Terrorist Wing," *Citizen*, June 1, 1988, p. 5; Tom Lodge, "Is the Spirit of Robert Sobukwe Rising?" *Weekly Mail*, August 5, 1988, p. 5; Ken Owen, "Listen to a New Voice from the Townships," *Business Day*, October 31, 1988; and "What the Concept Is All About," *Sowetan*, October 11, 1989, p. 8.

150. See "The Third Force Gathers Momentum," *SA Dialogue* 2:5 (May 1990), p. 6; Cassandra Moodley, "Several Killed in UDF vs. AZAPO Violence," *Weekly Mail*, March 23, 1990, p. 7; Cassandra Moodley, "Can

No-Talks PAC Put the Squeeze on ANC?" *Weekly Mail*, April 5, 1990, p. 10.

151. See *The Star*, October 3, 1989, p. 11; Christopher Wren, "Rival Congress Wants No Talks with Pretoria," *New York Times*, March 4, 1990, sec. 1, p. 14; "Mandela Rebuffed by a Rival Group," *New York Times*, March 7, 1990, p. A7; and Gavin Evans, "PAC Rids High," *Weekly Mail*, May 11, 1990, p. 13.

152. Cassandra Moodley, "Government Could Force a New Patriotic Front," *Weekly Mail*, May 25, 1990, p. 6; "New Unity Mood in Black Politics," *Weekly Mail*, June 8, 1990, p. 1.

153. Andrew Meldrum, "A 33-year-old Feud comes to an End," *Weekly Mail*, April 19, 1991, p. 5.

154. See "Charting Workers' Rights," *New Nation*, September 29, 1989, p. 6; and Eddie Koch, "Unions Want Their Own Seat at the Groote Schuur Table," *Weekly Mail*, May 11, 1990, p. 9.

155. See Orkin, *Disinvestment*, pp. 35–45; and Brewer, *After Soweto*, pp. 338–406.

156. See John Aitchison, "Numbering the Dead," pp. 10–17; Wally Mbhele and Eddie Koch, "On the Trail of the Third Force," *Weekly Mail*, May 10, 1991, pp. 4–5; Wally Mbhele, "This Time Police Must Explain: Where Were They?" *Weekly Mail*, May 17, 1991, p. 1; "Notes and Comments," *The New Yorker*, May 27, 1991, pp. 27–28.

157. Phillip van Niekerk and Wally Mbhele, "Peace in the Balance as the Season of Violence Returns," *Weekly Mail*, March 28, 1991, p. 1.

158. Mark Gevisser, "IFP Seeks Elusive White Magic," *Weekly Mail*, May 10, 1991, p. 13.

159. Walter Sisulu, "Let's Shape the Future Together," *South*, November 2, 1989, p. 14; Mass Democratic Movement, "Resource Documents on Negotiations," September 1989, p. 17.

160. Gavin Evans, "Number of Armed Attacks Reaches Peak," *Weekly Mail*, May 4, 1990, p. 11.

161. "Negotiations as a Weapon," *New Nation*, October 20, 1989, p. 9.

162. Thandeka Gqubule, "Nowhere in the World Is Political Violence Worse," *Weekly Mail*, April 27, 1990, p. 3.

163. Institute for Contextual Theology, "Negotiations, Defiance and the Church," 1988, p. 4.

## Chapter 7

1. Karl Marx, "Toward a Critique of Hegel's Philosophy of Right," in McLellan, ed., *Selected Writings*, p. 69.

2. Karl Marx, "The German Ideology," in McLellan, ed., *Selected Writings*, p. 167.

3. Geoff Molesane, interview with author, March 1988.

4. Max Weber, "The Nation," in Gerth and Mills, eds., *From Max Weber*, p. 172.

5. Mark Swilling, "City Politics Come of Age," in Schrire, ed., *Critical Choices for South Africa*, p. 424.

6. See Vail, ed., *The Creation of Tribalism*; and Thompson, *A History of South Africa*.

7. See Adam and Moodley, *South Africa Without Apartheid*, pp. 84–85.

8. Interview with author, March 1988.

9. Geoff Molesane, interview with author, March 1988.

10. See "The Coincidence of Recession and Socio-Economic Protest," in the Centre for Policy Studies, *Policy Perspectives 1989*, p. 164; and Brewer, *After Soweto*, p. 15. For a more general discussion of such patterns, see Ted Robert Gurr, *Why Men Rebel*; and Tilly, *From Mobilization to Revolt*.

11. Anonymous interview with author, April 1988.

12. Tom Manthata, interview with author, March 1988.

13. "Verwoerd's Grand Homeland Plan Is Consigned to History," *SA Dialogue* 2:6 (June 1990), p. 12.

14. Republic of South Africa, Central Statistical Service, *South African Labour Statistics, 1988*, p. 485.

15. Peter Jones, interview with author, May 1988. See also "Prepare the Conditions for the Seizure of Power by the People," ANC pamphlet, n.d.; and PAC, "Principles of a United Front in People's War" (pamphlet), p. 23.

16. Nolutshungu, *Changing South Africa*, p. 147.

17. Mark Swilling, "WHAMming the Radicals," *Weekly Mail*, May 20, 1988, p. 15.

18. R. P. Gouws, "The Growth of the Public Sector and Use of Privatization Proceeds in South Africa," Rand Merchant Bank, Johannesburg, 1989, p. 2. See also Adam and Moodley, *South Africa Without Apartheid*, p. 6; and Peter Lewis, *Economics of Apartheid*, p. 155.

19. Republic of South Africa, *South African Statistics 1988*, Table 1.16.

20. de Tocqueville, *The Old Regime and the French Revolution*, p. 177.

21. Interview with author, May 1988.

22. South African Youth Congress, "Everyone and Everything . . . ," COSATU Second National Congress, 1987, p. 3.

23. See Karl Mannheim, *Ideology and Utopia*; and Samuel H. Barnes, "Ideology and the Organization of Conflict," *Journal of Politics* 28 (August 1966), pp. 513–30.

24. "Excerpts from Mandela and De Klerk Remarks as Talks Open," *New York Times*, May 3, 1990, p. A6.

25. Anonymous, interview with author, May 1988.

26. *Sunday Times*, February 14, 1988, p. 1.

27. See, for instance, Polanyi, *The Great Transformation*, esp. p. 238; Patterson, *Slavery and Social Death*, p. 340; and Lukács, *History and Class Consciousness*.

28. See Alan Cowell, "African National Congress Suspends its Guerilla War," *New York Times*, August 7, 1990, p. A2; Philippa Garson, "Fear and Loathing Behind High Walls," *Weekly Mail*, December 7, 1990, p. 8.

29. See Gramsci, *Selections from the Prison Notebooks*, pp. 169–170, n. 70, 71.

30. See Arendt, *On Revolution*, pp. 54–61.

31. Quoting Leon Trotsky, in DeNardo, *Power in Numbers*, p. 24.

32. Neville Alexander, interview with author, November 1989.

33. Graham Van Wyck and Jeremy Daphne, interview with author, May 1988.

34. See, for instance, "The National Question," *Sechaba*, November 1980, p. 7; Mzala, *Latest Opportunism and the Theory of the South African Revolution*, p. 41.

35. Quoted in Wolfe, *Three Who Made a Revolution*, p. 357. See also Francis Meli, "Nationalism and Internationalism in South African Liberation," *African Communist*, 57 (1974), p. 49.

36. Interview with author, August 1988.

37. Alexander, *Sow the Wind*, p. 77.

38. Beyers Naude, interview with author, April 1988.

39. "Understanding and Fighting Women's Oppression," *CCAWUSA News*, November 1989, p. 8.

40. Joe Seremane, interview with author, April 1988. See also Morobe, "Towards a People's Democracy," *South Africa International* 18:1 (July 1987), p. 30; and Mbeki, "The Historical Injustice," in African National Congress, *Selected Writings*, p. 36.

41. Ishmael Mkhabela, interview with author, April 1988.

42. Interview with author, April 1988.

43. Dora Maria Pellez, unpublished poetry.

# SELECTED BIBLIOGRAPHY

This bibliography includes all books referred to in the text and footnotes, as well as some of the significant journal articles and other works of specific or general relevance cited. Full citations for material not included in the bibliography are provided in the notes. A list of newspapers, journals, and serial publications of political organizations from which articles have been cited is also provided. Primary documents cited in the notes but not included in this bibliography were gathered from the collections of Professors Tom Karis, Gail Gerhart, and Tom Lodge; the University of the Witwatersrand and the University of Cape Town Libraries; the Congress of South African Trade Unions; the National Council of Trade Unions; the Azanian Peoples' Organization; the Commercial, Catering, and Allied Workers Union of South Africa; and the SACHED Trust.

## Newspapers and Magazines


*Argus*
*Business Day*
*Cape Times*
*Citizen*
*City Press*
*Drum*
*Financial Mail*
*Frontline*
*New Nation*
*New York Times*
*Rand Daily Mail*
*SASPU Focus*
*SASPU National Student*
*SASPU State of the Nation*
*South*
*The Sowetan*
*The Star*
*Sunday Mail*
*Sunday Post*
*Sunday Times*
*Washington Post*
*Weekly Mail*
*The World*


## Journals and Serials


*Africa Confidential*
*Africa Perspective*
*Africa Report*
*American Journal of Sociology*

*Bulletin of the South African Reserve Bank*
*Canadian Journal of African Studies*
*Comparative Political Studies*
*Comparative Politics*
*Indicator SA*
*Journal of Modern African Studies*
*Journal of Southern African Studies*
*Leadership SA*
*The Marxist Review*
*New Horizons Project*
*Political Monitor*
*Race*
*Reality*
*Review of African Political Economy*
*Revolutionary Worker*
*SA Barometer*
*SA Dialogue*
*Social Dynamics*
*Social Research*
*South Africa International*
*South African Labour Bulletin*
*Transformation*
*Work in Progress*
*World Politics*

## Regular Publications by Political and Labor Organizations

*African Communist* (SACP)
*ANC Struggle Update* (ANC)
*Azanian Combat* (PAC)
*Azania News* (PAC)
*Azania Struggle* (PAC)
*CCAWUSA NEWS*
*FOSATU NEWS*
*Frank Talk* (AZAPO)
*Ikwezi* (PAC)
*Isizwe* (UDF)
*Mayibuye* (ANC)
*NUM News*
*SASO Bulletin* (BC)
*Sechaba* (ANC)
*United Democratic Front Update* (UDF)
*Upfront* (UDF)

## Books, Selected Articles, and Other Works

Adam, Heribert (1971). *Modernizing Racial Domination: The Dynamics of South African Politics*. Berkeley and Los Angeles: University of California Press.

——— (1973). "The Rise of Black Consciousness in South Africa." *Race* (October) 15: 149–66.

———, and Hermann Giliomee (1979). *Ethnic Power Mobilized: Can South Africa Change?* New Haven, Conn.: Yale University Press.

———, and Kogila Moodley (1986). *South Africa Without Apartheid: Dismantling Racial Domination*. Berkeley and Los Angeles: University of California Press.

Adamson, Walter L. (1980). *Hegemony and Revolution: A Study of Antonio Gramsci's Political and Cultural Theory.* Berkeley and Los Angeles: University of California Press.

African National Congress (1969). "Strategy and Tactics of the African National Congress." Morogoro, Tanzania.

——— (1985). *Documents of the Second National Consultative Conference, June 16–23.* London: African National Congress.

——— (1985). *Selected Writings on the Freedom Charter: A Sechaba Commemorative Publication.* London: African National Congress.

Aitchison, John (1988). "Numbering the Dead: Patterns in the Midlands Violence." Pietermaritzburg: Centre for Adult Education, University of Natal.

Alexander, Neville (1985). *Sow the Wind.* Johannesburg: Skotaville.

Amin, Samir (1980). *Class and Nation: Historically and in the Current Crisis.* New York: Monthly Review Press.

Anderson, Benedict (1983). *Imagined Communities: Reflections on the Origins and Spread of Nationalism.* London: Verso.

Anderson, Perry (1977). "The Antimonies of Antonio Gramsci." *New Left Review* 100: 5–78.

Arendt, Hannah (1963). *On Revolution.* Middlesex: Penguin.

Astrow, Andre (1983). *Zimbabwe: A Revolution That Lost Its Way.* London: Zed.

Avineri, Shlomo (1968). *The Social and Political Thought of Karl Marx.* Cambridge: Cambridge University Press.

Barnes, Samuel H. (1966). "Ideology and the Organization of Conflict: One Theory of the Relationship Between Political Thought and Behavior." *Journal of Politics* 28 (August): 513–30.

Benson, Mary (1986). *Nelson Mandela: The Man and the Movement.* New York: Norton.

Bernstein, Edward (1961). *Evolutionary Socialism.* New York: Schocken.

Bienen, Henry (1968). *Violence and Social Change.* Chicago: University of Chicago Press.

Biko, Steve (1986). *I Write What I Like*, ed. Aelred Stubbs. New York: Harper & Row.

Boesak, Allan (1984). *Black and Reformed: Apartheid, Liberation and the Calvinist Tradition.* Johannesburg: Skotaville.

Bradford, Helen (1987). *A Taste of Freedom: The ICU in Rural South Africa.* New Haven, Conn.: Yale University Press.

Brewer, John D. (1986). *After Soweto: An Unfinished Journey.* Oxford: Clarendon Press.

——— (1989). *Can South Africa Survive: Five Minutes to Midnight.* New York: St. Martin's Press.

Brinton, Crane (1965). *The Anatomy of Revolution*. New York: Random House.

Brooks, Alan, and Jeremy Brickhill (1980). *Whirlwind Before the Storm*. London: International Defence and Aid Fund for Southern Africa.

Bundy, Colin (1979). *The Rise and Fall of the South African Peasantry*. Berkeley and Los Angeles: University of California Press.

——— (1987). "Around Which Corner? Revolutionary Prospects and Contemporary South Africa." Institute of Commonwealth Studies, postgraduate seminar, October 16.

——— (1987). "Street Sociology and Pavement Politics: Some Aspects of Student/Youth Consciousness During the 1985 Schools Crisis in Greater Cape Town." Manuscript.

Bunman, Lisa (1987)."From Hell Hole to Blessing in Disguise: A Study of Politics on Robben Island, 1963–1987." M.A. Thesis, University of the Witwatersrand, Johannesburg.

Burroway, Michael (1982). "State and Social Revolution in South Africa." *Kapitalistate* 9: 93–122.

Cabral, Amilcar (1969). *Revolution in Guinea: An African People's Struggle*. New York: Monthly Review Press.

Callaghy, Thomas M., ed. (1983). *South Africa in Southern Africa: The Intensifying Vortex of Violence*. New York: Praeger.

Callinicos, Alex (1988). *South Africa Between Reform and Revolution*. London: Bookmarks.

Callinicos, Alex, and John Rogers (1977). *Southern Africa After Soweto*. London: Pluto Press.

Carmichael, Stokely, and Charles V. Hamilton (1967). *Black Power: The Politics of Liberation in America*. New York: Random House.

Carnoy, Martin (1984). *The State and Political Theory*. Princeton, N.J.: Princeton University Press.

Carr, E. H. (1950). *Studies in Revolution*. New York: Barnes & Noble.

Cell, John W. (1982). *The Highest Stage of White Supremacy*. Cambridge: Cambridge University Press.

Centre for Policy Studies (1989). *Policy Perspectives 1989: South Africa at the End of the Eighties*. Johannesburg: University of the Witwatersrand.

Cobbett, Wiliam, and Robin Cohen, eds. (1988). *Popular Struggles in South Africa*. Trenton, N.J.: Africa World Press.

Cohen, Jean L. (1985). "Strategy or Identity: New Theoretical Paradigms and Contemporary Social Movements." *Social Research* 52 (Winter): 663–716.

Cole, Josette (1987). *Crossroads: The Politics of Reform and Repression, 1976–1986*. Johannesburg: Ravan Press.

Commonwealth Committee of Foreign Ministers on Southern Africa (1989). *South Africa: The Sanctions Report*. Harmondsworth: Penguin Books.

Commonwealth Group of Eminent Persons (1986). *Mission to South Africa: The Commonwealth Report*. Middlesex: Penguin.

Communist Party of South Africa (n.d.). *The Road to South African Freedom*. London: Inkululeko.

Congress of South African Trade Unions (1986). *Notes on Political Organizations* (photocopy). Johannesburg: COSATU.

Dahrendorf, Ralf (1959). *Class and Class Conflict in Industrial Society*. Stanford, Calif.: Stanford University Press.

Davenport, T. R. H. (1977). *South Africa: A Modern History*. London: Macmillan.

Davidson, Basil, Joe Slovo, and A. R. Wilkinson (1976). *Southern Africa: The New Politics of Revolution*. Middlesex: Penguin.

Davies, Robert H., Dan O'Meara, and Sipho Dlamini (1984). *The Struggle for South Africa*. London: Zed.

Davis, Horace B. (1978). *Toward a Marxist Theory of Nationalism*. New York: Monthly Review Press.

Davis, Stephen M. (1987). *Apartheid's Rebels: Inside South Africa's Hidden War*. New Haven, Conn.: Yale University Press.

DeNardo, James (1985). *Power in Numbers: The Political Strategy of Protest and Rebellion*. Princeton, N.J.: Princeton University Press.

Deutscher, Isaac (1950). *Soviet Trade Unions*. Oxford: Oxford University Press.

——— (1954). *The Prophet Armed: Trotsky, 1879–1921*. New York: Vintage Books.

——— (1959). *The Prophet Unarmed: Trotsky, 1921–1929*. Oxford: Oxford University Press.

Diepen, Maria van, ed. (1988). *The National Question in South Africa*. London: Zed.

Dunayevskaya, Raya (1975). *Marxism and Freedom: From 1776 to Today*. London: Pluto Press.

Durkheim, Emile (1933). *The Division of Labor in Society*. New York: Free Press.

Eckstein, Harry, ed. (1966). *Internal War: Problems and Approaches*. New York: Free Press.

Enloe, Cynthia (1973). *Ethnic Conflict and Political Development*. Boston: Little, Brown.

Evans, Peter, Dietrich Rueschmeyer, and Theda Skocpol (1985). *Bringing the State Back In*. Cambridge: Cambridge University Press.

Fanon, Frantz (1967). *Black Skin, White Mass*. New York: Grove Press.

——— (1967). *Toward the African Revolution.* New York: Grove Press.

——— (1968). *The Wretched of the Earth.* New York: Grove Press.

Fatton, Robert, Jr. (1984). "The African National Congress in South Africa: The Limitations of a Revolutionary Strategy." *Canadian Journal of African Studies* 18: 593–608.

——— (1986). *Black Consciousness in South Africa.* Albany: State University of New York Press.

Fay, Brian (1975). *Social Theory and Political Practice.* London: Allen & Unwin.

Feierman, Steve (1990). *Peasant Intellectuals: Anthropology and History in Tanzania.* Madison: University of Wisconsin Press.

Feit, Edward (1967). *African Opposition in South Africa.* Stanford, Calif.: Hoover Institution Press.

——— (1978). *Workers Without Weapons: SACTU and the Organization of African Workers.* New York: Doubleday/Anchor.

Frankel, Philip H. (1984). *Pretoria's Praetorians: Civil Military Relations in South Africa.* Cambridge: Cambridge University Press.

Frankel, Philip H., Noam Pines, and Mark Swilling, eds. (1988). *State, Resistance and Change in South Africa.* Kent: Croom Helm.

Fredrickson, George M. (1981). *White Supremacy: A Comparative Study in American and South African History.* Oxford: Oxford University Press.

Friedman, Steven (1987). *Building Tomorrow Today: African Workers in Trade Unions, 1970–1984.* Johannesburg: Ravan Press.

Geertz, Clifford, ed. (1963). *Old Societies and New States: The Quest for Modernity in Asia and Africa.* New York: Free Press.

Gelb, Steve (1987). "Making Sense of the Crisis." *Transformation* 5: 33–50.

Gerhart, Gail (1978). *Black Power in South Africa: The Evolution of an Ideology.* Berkeley and Los Angeles: University of California Press.

Glazer, Nathan, and Daniel Patrick Moynihan (1975). *Ethnicity: Theory and Experience.* Cambridge, Mass.: Harvard University Press.

Goldrich, Daniel (1970). "Political Organization and the Politicization of the Poblador." *Comparative Political Studies* 3 (July): 176–202.

Gramsci, Antonio (1971). *Selections from the Prison Notebooks*, ed. Quinton Hoare and G. H. Smith. New York: International Publishers.

Greenberg, Stanley B. (1980). *Race and State in Capitalist Development: Comparative Perspectives.* New Haven, Conn.: Yale University Press.

——— (1987). *Legitimating the Illegitimate: State, Markets and Resistance in South Africa.* Berkeley and Los Angeles: University of California Press.

Grundy, Kenneth (1986). *The Militarization of South African Politics.* Bloomington: Indiana University Press.

Gurr, Ted Robert (1970). *Why Men Rebel.* Princeton, N.J.: Princeton University Press.

Gusfield, Joseph (1981). "Social Movements and Social Change: Perspectives of Linearity and Fluidity." In Kriesberg, ed., *Research in Social Movements, Conflict and Change.* Vol. 4. Greenwich, Conn.: JAI Press.

Habakkuk, H. J., and M. Postan, eds. (1965). *The New Cambridge Modern History.* Vol. 8. Cambridge: Cambridge University Press.

Haimson, Leopold (1967). *The Russian Marxists and the Origins of Bolshevism.* Cambridge, Mass.: Harvard University Press.

Hammond, Thomas Taylor (1957). *Lenin on Trade Unions and Revolution, 1893–1917.* New York: Columbia University Press.

Hanf, Theodor, H. Weiland, and G. Vierdag (1981). *South Africa: The Prospects of Peaceful Change.* Bloomington: Indiana University Press.

Harrison, David (1981). *The White Tribe of Africa.* Berkeley and Los Angeles: University of California Press.

Haysom, Nicholas (1986). *Mabangalala: The Rise of Right-Wing Vigilantes in South Africa.* Johannesburg: University of Witwatersrand.

Hirschman, Albert O. (1970). *Exit, Voice and Loyalty.* Cambridge, Mass.: Harvard University Press.

Hirson, Baruch (1979). *Year of Fire, Year of Ash; The Soweto Revolt: Roots of a Revolution?* London: Zed.

Hobsbawm, Eric (1962). *The Age of Revolution, 1789–1848.* New York: Mentor Books.

Hobsbawm, Eric, and Terence Ranger, eds. (1983). *The Invention of Tradition.* Cambridge: Cambridge University Press.

Horne, Alistair (1977). *A Savage War of Peace: Algeria, 1954–1962.* Middlesex: Penguin.

Horowitz, Donald L. (1985). *Ethnic Groups in Conflict.* Berkeley and Los Angeles: University of California Press.

Horowitz, Ralph (1967). *The Political Economy of South Africa.* London: Weidenfeld and Nicolson.

Hunt, Lynn (1984). *Politics, Culture, and Class in the French Revolution.* Berkeley and Los Angeles: University of California Press.

Huntington, Samuel P. (1968). *Political Order in Changing Societies.* New Haven, Conn.: Yale University Press.

Institute for Black Research (1976). *Soweto: A People's Response.* Durban: Institute for Black Research.

Institute for Industrial Education (1976). *The Durban Strikes, 1973: Human Beings with Souls.* Johannesburg: Ravan Press.

Johnson, Chalmers (1966). *Revolutionary Change.* Boston: Little, Brown.

Johnson, Shaun, ed. (1989). *South Africa: No Turning Back.* Bloomington: Indiana University Press.

Johnson, R. W. (1977). *How Long Will South Africa Survive?* London: Macmillan.

Johnstone, Frederick (1976). *Class, Race and Gold.* London: Routledge & Kegan Paul.

Kane-Berman, John (1978). *Soweto: Black Revolt, White Reaction.* Johannesburg: Ravan Press.

Karis, Thomas G. (1983–1984). "Revolution in the Making: Black Politics in South Africa." *Foreign Affairs,* Winter, pp. 378–406.

Karis, Thomas, and Gwendolen Carter (1972, 1973, 1977). *From Protest to Challenge: A Documentary History of African Politics in South Africa 1882–1964.* 4 vols. Stanford, Calif.: Hoover Institution Press.

Kornhauser, William (1966). *The Politics of Mass Society.* New York: Free Press.

Kuper, Leo (1974). *Race, Class and Power: Ideology and Revolutionary Change in Plural Societies.* London: Duckworth.

Leatt, James, Theo Kneifel, and Klaus Nurnberger, eds. (1986). *Contending Ideologies in South Africa.* Cape Town: David Philip.

Legassick, Martin (1973). *Class and Nationalism in South African Protest: The South African Communist Party and the "Native Republic," 1928–1934.* Syracuse, N.Y.: Syracuse University Press.

Lelyveld, Joseph (1985). *Move Your Shadow.* New York: Times Books.

Lenin, V. I. (1932). *State and Revolution.* New York: International Publishers.

Lewis, Stephen R. (1990). *The Economics of Apartheid.* New York: Council on Foreign Relations.

Lipsky, Michael (1968). "Protest as a Political Resource." *American Political Science Review* 62 (December): 1144–58.

Lipton, Merle (1985). *Capitalism and Apartheid.* Gower: Aldershot.

Lodge, Tom (1983). *Black Politics in South Africa Since 1945.* Johannesburg: Ravan Press.

——— (1986). "Freedom in Our Lifetime: Popular Resistance Politics in the 1950s and 1980s." *Reality,* November, pp. 6–10.

Luckhardt, Ken, and Brenda Wall (1980). *Organize or Starve: The History of the South African Congress of Trade Unions.* London: Lawrence and Wishart.

Lukács, Georg (1971). *History and Class Consciousness.* Cambridge, Mass.: MIT Press.

Luxemburg, Rosa (1961). *The Russian Revolution and Leninism and Marxism.* Ann Arbor: University of Michigan Press.

——— (1976). *The National Question: Selected Writings.* New York: Monthly Review Press.

Machiavelli, Niccolo (1952). *The Prince.* New York: New American Library.

Malcolm X (1964). *The Autobiography of Malcolm X.* Middlesex: Penguin.

Mandela, Nelson (1965). *No Easy Walk to Freedom.* London: Heinemann.

Mannheim, Karl (1936). *Ideology and Utopia.* New York: Harcourt Brace & World.

Maphai, Vincent (1986). "Resistance in South Africa: Azapo and the National Forum." Manuscript.

Marcum, John (1982). *Education, Race and Social Change in South Africa.* Berkeley and Los Angeles: University of California Press.

Maree, Johann (1982). "Democracy and Oligarchy in Trade Unions." *Social Dynamics* 8: 41–52.

Martin, David, and Phyllis Johnson (1981). *The Struggle for Zimbabwe.* Johannesburg: Ravan Press.

Marx, Anthony W. (1989). "South African Black Trade Unions as an Emerging Working Class Movement." *Journal of Modern African Studies* 27 (September): 383–400.

——— (1991). "Race, Nation and Class-based Ideologies in Recent Opposition in South Africa." *Comparative Politics* 23 (April): 313–28.

——— (forthcoming). "The State, Economy and Self-Determination in South Africa: Explaining the Changing Configurations of Recent Internal Opposition." In *Political Science Quarterly.*

——— (forthcoming). "Contested Images and Implications of South African Nationhood." In Kay Warren, ed., *Confronting Violence: Cultural and Political Analyses of National Conflicts.*

Mass Democratic Movement (1989). "Resource Documents on Negotiations." Internal document, Johannesburg.

Matiwana, Mizana, and Shirley Walters (1986). *The Struggle for Democracy.* Bellville: University of the Western Cape.

Mbeki, Govan (1964). *South Africa: The Peasants' Revolt.* Middlesex: Penguin.

Mbeki, Thabo (1984). "The Fatton Thesis: A Rejoinder." *Canadian Journal of African Studies* 18: 609–12.

McCarthy, John D., and Mayer Zald (1977). "Resource Mobilization and Social Movements: A Partial Theory." *American Journal of Sociology* 82 (May): 1212–39.

McLellan, David, ed. (1977). *Karl Marx: Selected Writings.* Oxford: Oxford University Press.

Michels, Robert (1962). *Political Parties: A Sociological Study of the Oligarchic Tendencies of Modern Democracy.* New York: Free Press.

Migdal, Joel (1974). *Peasants, Politics, and Revolution: Pressures Toward Political and Social Change in the Third World.* Princeton, N.J.: Princeton University Press.

Molteno, Frank (1987). *1980: Students Struggle for Their Schools.* Cape Town: University of Cape Town Press.

Montagu, Ashley (1952). *Man's Most Dangerous Myth: The Fallacy of Race.* New York: Harper Bros.

Moore, Barrington, Jr. (1966). *Social Origins of Dictatorship and Democracy.* Boston: Beacon Press.

Motlhabi, Mokgethi (1988). *Challenge to Apartheid: Toward a Morally Defensible Strategy.* Grand Rapids, Mich.: Eerdmans.

Mufson, Steven (1990). *Fighting Years: Black Resistance and the Struggle for a New South Africa.* Boston: Beacon Press.

Murray, Martin (1987). *South Africa: Time of Agony, Time of Destiny.* London: Verso.

Mzala, Comrade (1983). *Latest Opportunism and the Theory of the South African Revolution.* London: African National Congress.

Naidoo, Indres, and Albie Sachs (1982). *Island in Chains: Ten Years on Robben Island.* Middlesex: Penguin.

National Union of South African Students, eds. (1983). *Beyond Reform: The Challenge of Change.* Cape Town: University of Cape Town.

Nattrass, J. (1981). *The South African Economy: Its Growth and Change.* Cape Town: Oxford University Press.

Nkondo, Gessler Moses, ed. (1976). *Turfloop Testimony: The Dilemma of a Black University in South Africa.* Johannesburg: Ravan Press.

Nolutshungu, Sam (1982). *Changing South Africa: Political Considerations.* Cape Town: David Philip.

No Sizwe (Neville Alexander) (1979). *One Nation, One Azania: The National Question in South Africa.* London: Zed.

O'Donnell, Guillermo, and Philippe Schmitter (1989). *Transitions from Authoritarian Rule: Tentative Conclusions.* Baltimore: Johns Hopkins University Press.

O'Meara, Dan (1983). *Volkscapitalisme.* Cambridge: Cambridge University Press.

Orkin, Mark, ed. (1986). *Disinvestment: The Struggle and the Future.* Johannesburg: Ravan Press.

——— (1989). "Of Sacrifice and Struggle: Ideology and Identity Among Black High School Students," Ph.D. diss., University of the Witwatersrand, Johannesburg.

——— (1989). *Sanctions Against Apartheid.* Cape Town: David Philip.

Ovenden, Keith, and Tony Cole (1989). *Apartheid and International Finance: A Program for Change.* Middlesex: Penguin.

Parkin, Frank (1979). *Marxism and Class Theory: A Bourgeois Critique.* New York: Columbia University Press.

——— (1982). *Max Weber.* Chichester: Ellis Horwood.

Patterson, Orlando (1982). *Slavery and Social Death.* Cambridge, Mass.: Harvard University Press.

Piven, Frances Fox, and Richard A. Cloward (1977). *Poor People's Movements: Why They Succeed, How They Fail.* New York: Vintage Books.

PLANACT (1989). "The Soweto Rent Boycott: A Report by PLANACT." Commissioned by the Soweto Delegation, Johannesburg.

Polanyi, Karl (1944). *The Great Transformation.* Boston: Beacon Press.

Price, Robert (1991). *South Africa: The Process of Political Transformation.* New York: Oxford University Press.

Price, Robert M., and Carl G. Rosberg, eds. (1980). *The Apartheid Regime: Political Power and Racial Domination.* Berkeley, Calif.: Institute of International Studies.

Republic of South Africa (1983). *Report of the Eloff Commission of Enquiry into the South African Council of Churches.* Pretoria: Government Printer.

———, Central Statistical Services (1989). *South African Labour Statistics, 1988.* Pretoria: Government Printer.

———, Central Statistical Services (1989). *South African Statistics, 1988.* Pretoria: Government Printer.

Rex, John (1970). *Race Relations in Sociological Theory.* London: Weidenfeld and Nicholson.

Roux, Edward P. (1966). *Time Longer Than Rope: A History of the Black Man's Struggle for Freedom in South Africa.* Madison: University of Wisconsin Press.

Rude, George (1959). *The Crowd in the French Revolution.* Oxford: Oxford University Press.

Russell, D. E. H. (1974). *Rebellion, Revolution and Armed Force: A Comparative Study of Fifteen Countries with Special Emphasis on Cuba and South Africa.* New York: Academic Press.

Rustow, Dankwart A. (1970). "Transitions to Democracy: Toward a Dynamic Model." *Comparative Politics* 2 (April): 337–63.

Sampson, Anthony (1987). *Black and Gold: Tycoons, Revolutionaries and Apartheid.* London: Coronet Books.

Saul, John S. (1979). *The State and Revolution in East Africa.* New York: Monthly Review Press.

Saul, John S., and Stephen Gelb (1986). *The Crisis in South Africa: Class Defense, Class Revolution.* New York: Monthly Review Press.

Schama, Simon (1989). *Citizens: A Chronicle of the French Revolution.* New York: Vintage Books.

Schlemmer, Lawrence, and Eddie Webster, eds. (1978). *Change, Reform, and Economic Growth in South Africa.* Johannesburg: Ravan Press.

Schrire, Robert A., ed. (1990). *Critical Choices for South Africa: An Agenda for the 1990s.* Cape Town: Oxford University Press.

Simkins, Charles, and Doug Hindson (1979). "The Division of Labour in South Africa, 1969–1977." *Social Dynamics* 5 (December): 6–12.

Simons, H. J., and R. E. Simons (1969). *Class and Colour in South Africa.* Middlesex: Penguin.

Sisulu, Zwelakhe (1986). "Keynote Address to the Second National Consultative Conference of the National Education Crisis Committee," March 29.

Sklar, Richard (1979). "The Nature of Class Domination in Africa." *Journal of Modern African Studies* 17: 531–52.

Skocpol, Theda (1979). *States and Social Revolutions: A Comparative Analysis of France, Russia and China.* Cambridge: Cambridge University Press.

Smith, Anthony D. (1971). *Theories of Nationalism.* London: Duckworth.

South African Institute of Race Relations (annual). *Survey of Race Relations in South Africa.* Johannesburg: South African Institute of Race Relations.

South African Research Service, eds. (1984, 1985, 1986, 1987, 1988). *South African Review.* Vol. 1–5. Johannesburg: Ravan Press.

Stone, Lawrence (1966). "Theories of Revolution." *World Politics* 18 (January): 159–76.

Study Commission on United States Policy Toward Southern Africa (1981). *South Africa: Time Running Out.* Berkeley and Los Angeles: University of California Press.

Suttner, Raymond, and Jeremy Cronin (1986). *Thirty Years of the Freedom Charter.* Johannesburg: Ravan Press.

Swilling, Mark (1987). "The United Democratic Front and Township Revolt." *Work in Progress* 49 (September): 26–33.

Therborn, Goran (1980). *The Ideology of Power and the Power of Ideology.* London: Verso.

Thompson, E. P. (1966). *The Making of the English Working Class.* New York: Random House.

Thompson, Leonard (1985). *The Political Mythology of Apartheid.* New Haven, Conn.: Yale University Press.

——— (1990). *A History of South Africa*. New Haven, Conn.: Yale University Press.

Thompson, Leonard, and Jeffrey Butler, eds. (1975). *Change in Contemporary South Africa*. Berkeley and Los Angeles: University of California Press.

Tilly, Charles (1975). "Revolutions and Collective Violence." In Fred Greenstien and Nelson Polsby, eds., *The Handbook of Political Science*. Vol. 3. Reading, Mass.: Addison-Wesley.

——— (1978). *From Mobilization to Revolt*. Reading, Mass.: Addison-Wesley.

——— (1985). "Models and Realities of Popular Collective Action." *Social Research* 52 (Winter): 717–48.

de Tocqueville, Alexis (1955). *The Old Regime and the French Revolution*. Garden City, N.Y.: Doubleday.

Trotsky, Leon (1967). *On Black Nationalism and Self-Determination*. New York: Pathfinder Press.

——— (1969). *The Permanent Revolution*. New York: Pathfinder Press.

Tucker, Robert C. (1969). *The Marxian Revolutionary Idea*. New York: Norton.

———, ed. (1975). *The Lenin Anthology*. New York: Norton.

———, ed. (1978). *The Marx–Engels Reader*. New York: Norton.

Turner, Richard (1972). *The Eye of the Needle*. Johannesburg: Spro-cas.

United Democratic Front (1985). "National General Council." Johannesburg: Khotso House.

——— (1987). "National Working Committee Conference," May 29–30. Johannesburg: Khotso House.

United States General Accounting Office (April 1988). "South Africa: Trends in Trade, Lending, and Investment." Washington, D.C.: United States Government Printing Office.

Vail, Leroy (1989). *The Creation of Tribalism in Southern Africa*. Berkeley and Los Angeles: University of California Press.

Van den Berghe, Pierre (1967). *South Africa: A Study in Conflict*. Berkeley and Los Angeles: University of California Press.

Walzer, Michael (1985). *Exodus and Revolution*. New York: Basic Books.

Weber, Max (1946). *From Max Weber: Essays in Sociology*, ed. H. H. Gerth and C. Wright Mills. New York: Oxford University Press.

——— (1958). *The Protestant Ethic and the Spirit of Capitalism*. New York: Scribner.

Welsh, David, and H. van der Mewre, eds. (1972). *Student Perspectives on South Africa*. Cape Town: David Philip.

Wilson, Francis, and Mamphela Ramphele (1989). *Uprooting Poverty: The South African Challenge*. New York: Norton.

Wilson, Monica, and Leonard Thompson, eds. (1969, 1971). *The Oxford History of South Africa*. 2 vols. Oxford: Clarendon Press.

Wilson, William Julius (1975). *Power, Racism and Privilege*. London: Macmillan.

Wolf, Eric (1969). *Peasant Wars in the Twentieth Century: Class Basis of Peasant Revolution*. New York: Harper & Row.

Wolfe, Bertram (1948). *Three Who Made a Revolution*. Boston: Beacon Press.

——— (1965). *Marxism: One Hundred Years in the Life of a Doctrine*. New York: Delta Press.

Wolin, Sheldon S. (1973). "The Politics of the Study of Revolution." *Comparative Politics* 5 (April): 343–58.

Wolpe, Harold (1988). *Race, Class and the Apartheid State*. London: Currey.

Young, Crawford (1976). *The Politics of Cultural Pluralism*. Madison: University of Wisconsin Press.

# Index

Printed in the United States
133507LV00003B/3/A

9 780195 073485